Flammable Societies

FLAMMABLE SOCIETIES

Studies on the Socio-economics of Oil and Gas

Edited by
John-Andrew McNeish and Owen Logan

PlutoPress
www.plutobooks.com

First published 2012 by Pluto Press
345 Archway Road, London N6 5AA

www.plutobooks.com

Distributed in the United States of America exclusively by
Palgrave Macmillan, a division of St Martin's Press LLC,
175 Fifth Avenue, New York, NY 10010

British Library Cataloguing in Publication Data
A catalogue record for this book is available from the British Library

ISBN   978 0 7453 3118 8   Hardback
ISBN   978 0 7453 3117 1   Paperback

Library of Congress Cataloging in Publication Data applied for

This book is printed on paper suitable for recycling and made from fully managed
and sustained forest sources. Logging, pulping and manufacturing processes are
expected to conform to the environmental standards of the country of origin.

10 9 8 7 6 5 4 3 2 1

Designed and produced for Pluto Press by Chase Publishing Services Ltd
Typeset from disk by Stanford DTP Services, Northampton, England
Simultaneously printed digitally by CPI Antony Rowe, Chippenham, UK and
Edwards Bros in the United States of America

Contents

PART 3   SUPPLY-SIDE GOVERNMENTALITY

List of Figures

Acknowledgements

Your names are too many to mention, but we recognise with thanks all of the assistance and support that have been given to this project by the Norwegian Research Council, institutional partners, colleagues, family and the communities in which we have worked and lived. Only one individual name must be mentioned. Hanne, without you the inspiration for this book would never have been found.

Introduction

From allegories inside the oil economy. The hunter as warrior, oil storage tank under construction, Port Harcourt, Nigeria. Photograph by Owen Logan.

1
Rethinking Responsibility and Governance in Resource Extraction

Owen Logan and John-Andrew McNeish

In December 2009 Farouk al-Kasim was invited to give a seminar in Bergen. As a result of life's vicissitudes, al-Kasim, an Iraqi petroleum geologist, had settled in Norway in 1968. He found employment first as consultant for the Ministry of Industry and then in the early 1970s helped create the Norwegian Petroleum Directorate (NPC), becoming its director of resource management. The NPC is often credited in policy circles as the key example of effective management of state and corporate interests in the petroleum business. As a result 'the Norwegian model' has become a byword for avoiding the negative effects of large-scale oil and gas production on a nation's domestic markets and social fabric – an impact controversially captured in the hypothesis of 'the resource curse'. Al-Kasim's role in assisting the formation of Norway's regulatory framework did not receive much attention until August 2009, when the London *Financial Times* published a profile article under the headline, 'The Iraqi who saved Norway from oil'.[1]

Al-Kasim's role in Norway's adaptation of the oil economy was of great interest to the audience at his seminar in Bergen. However, his experience and propositions about transparency and good governance did not go entirely unchallenged. Surely, it was asked by members of the audience, Norway's success story was not due to the influence of a single enlightened technocrat, and was Norway's governance of the petroleum economy really as transparent as al-Kasim implied? In answering these points al-Kasim humbly conceded that the development of NPC policy had always been conditioned by the possible reaction of the Norwegian Confederation of Trade Unions.

The Scandinavian labour movement has a rich ideological history and retains considerable strength in Norway, something not mentioned in the *Financial Times* profile, which alluded to the

3

national character of Norwegians, not their differences. When the radical complexity of civil society is acknowledged – and there does tend to be a great degree of historical forgetfulness about labour militancy in Scandinavia – the same factor also calls into question technocratic thought on transparency and good governance. While such virtues may be planned for, and drafted as rules and codes of conduct, a genuinely empowered labour movement is won, not managed into historical existence. Moreover, the forces arrayed against labour power can hardly be made transparent, at least in any technocratic sense, since the struggle for social justice is never conducted on a level playing field.

It is only quite recently that an adequate picture of Norway's oil economy has come to light. New film documentaries, books and media articles in Norway have re-examined the past, in an effort to answer the question why in the space of 100 years Norway has gone from being one of the poorest to one of the richest countries in the world per capita. A key voice amongst these revisions has been the historical sociologist Helge Ryggvik, who has forcefully argued that 'there is no single Norwegian oil experience'.[2] In concluding the English synopsis of earlier work, Ryggvik states that if there is a central lesson to be drawn from Norway, 'it must be the presence and significance of conflict between oil actors and society, and the importance of society's determination to secure its own power and position vis-à-vis the big companies'.[3]

As Ryggvik explains, the dominant social-democratic attitude in Norwegian State policy was informed by an earlier contest over hydropower concessions, in which the state had managed to gain both control and technological know-how. The domination of the oil business by archetypal global corporations, the need to develop an off-shore industry and the fact that oil was a finite resource had all presented far greater challenges to the formation of a national oil company and the pursuance of social democratic policy. Arguably, the most profound manifestation of the public interest was, however, the political commitment (formed in the face of contrary market pressures in the 1970s) to a moderate pace of extraction. Not only did the adoption of this model of sustainability prolong the life of the oil fields and increase the total recoverable reserves, it has also allowed the domestic political and state actors to gain the necessary experience and knowledge before production peaks.[4] Indeed without this sense of socio-economic timing, any commitment to defending 'the people's property' might well have missed the mark.

Yet, overall, the rate of production in Norway has not been especially moderate. From the 1980s neoliberal free-market policies put pressures on the social-democratic strategies at a number of levels. The emergence of a neo-corporate power elite, seen too in other oil-producing nations, added to the challenge of neoliberalism at global scale. In the Norwegian case this meant that Statoil quickly became regarded as a state within a state. Moreover, the tensions that have existed between private, state and public interests throughout the last 30 years tell us that the technocratic role of NPC, as a body overseeing the Norwegian public interest, was more complex, and certainly less glorious, than would appear from the above-mentioned *Financial Times* profile. The NPC has gone through significant internal crises and break-ups, which reflect the wider political struggles over the meaning of oil to Norway and Norwegians. Natural-resource wealth became the focus of contestation and a means to express and articulate different positions and values. We see also that it was the interplay of these positions and values which provided rationales not only for individual action, but for political and technical decisions.

POSITIONS AND VALUES

The works of Karl Marx (1818–83) and of the classical political economy of Adam Smith (1723–90) and David Ricardo (1772–1823) centre on the labour theory of value. Ultimately, this theory cannot be maintained without also theorising human exploitation, as Marx came to do. With the work of Jean-Baptiste Say (1767–1832) neoclassical economics was able to reject the labour theory of value and offer, in its place, relational theories of market equilibrium.[5] The contemporary notion of 'the petro-state' may need no introduction except as a reminder that it signals the problem of disequilibrium. Indeed, in many instances the reality of petroleum-centred national economies may be regarded as striking failures of the doctrine of international comparative advantage promulgated by Say. Critical theories of rent rooted in the earlier work of Ricardo, and which now extend to the idea of 'the rentier state', have been vigorously applied to this problem in the global south, most recently in Omeje (2008). From this perspective the neocolonial state apparatus may be characterised as a gatekeeper state; it provides rule of law for the extractive industries but does little more for its citizens than provide a dignified arena for the advancement of rentier capitalism and primitive exploitation. However, when critiques move away from the labour theory of value (which occupied Ricardo throughout his life) and prioritise the theory of rent, they appear to strike a limited bargain with the tenets of neoclassical economics. In this sense it may be argued that the application of rentier theory risks producing a self-fulfilling prophecy for the global south by wrenching the theory of rent from its counterpart, the labour theory of value, the latter being an integral concept that shaped development in the global north.

Many valuable insights have been gained from recent oral history research. In a life-story interview recalling the development of the oil industry in Norway, Paal Holme, a former human resources manager for Phillips Petroleum, tells how the American company was not prepared for contests with a workforce that was both knowledgeable and strongly organised.[6] At a theoretical level, it may well be argued that such a potentially threatening arrangement of class forces necessitates a technocracy like the NPC, and also mediates its power, not the other way around. Although the political fortunes and misfortunes of labour on opposite sides of the North Sea can do much to explain the divergent national and industrial experiences of the same geological resources, this was hardly evident from a historiographical point of view.

Nevertheless, these different trajectories, leading towards greater or lesser equality, or more even or uneven patterns of development, also reveal the cleavages within Marxist thought on political economy, especially when used to analyse African or Latin American nations. What came to be known as 'neo-Marxist' theory, emerging from dependency theorists such as Andre Gunder Frank (1966) and Walter Rodney (1972), among others, challenged the communist orthodoxy which more or less condemned societies that had not overcome feudalism – at least in theory – to await the onset of a bourgeois revolution on their territories. Before that stage was reached, so the orthodoxy went, there would be little hope of working-class power and social democracy. Although broadly supporting the neo-Marxist challenge to such reasoning, writers such as Björn Beckman in the 1980s[7] put the emphasis much more on the ongoing development of imperialism and *its* complex recon-figuration of class relations. Of course, such discussions are not resolved at the level of theory. Indeed, it is striking how after the collapse of communism in Eastern Europe, and with it the popular diminishment of Marxism, resource politics appeared much less as a strategic target of class analysis, and much more as a liberal organising discourse aimed at various undesirable governments.

Indeed, following the ideological shift to market economics in the 1980s, studies of the interplay of power and social class in the oil industry, such as Nore and Turner's (1980) *Oil and Class Struggle*, disappeared from mainstream analysis.

Alongside this liberal revival, the critique of colonialism was reformulated. Problematically for some, postmodern theory almost became synonymous with the arena of postcolonial studies that came to prominence in Western metropolitan universities in the 1980s and 1990s. Looking back, it would appear that academic ideas of 'resistance' increasingly came at the expense of what were apparently outdated problems of structure and agency. For example, Keith and Pile's (1997) anthology *Geographies of Resistance*, exploring an array of social experiences internationally, was quite typical in paying no attention to organised labour. The oddly limited scope of such studies has since been criticised for entailing a shift from 'Eurocentrism' to 'globalcentrism', the latter effectively 'dissolving the West into the market', a market which is in fact dominated by the operations of finance capital centred in the West. For the late Fernando Coronil (1944–2011), who made this critique, globalcentrism articulates the ongoing development of imperialism.[8]

The general downgrading of classical Marxist interest in labour and class politics could only boost liberal cultural mores and the ideology of consumer sovereignty. A profound effect of the spirit of ideological homogeneity, frequently associated with Fukuyama's (1992) book, *The End of History and the Last Man*, was blindness to history's potential for recidivism. In whatever direction history might move, it would now seem perfectly clear that it does not stand still. In keeping with the sense of a backward movement in history, social democratic gains in Norway are currently being eroded, although perhaps not to the same extent as those in Sweden and Denmark, because of the political and economic shelter provided by the creation of Norway's oil fund. Given that Norway has not, at least in any obvious way, suffered from the so-called resource curse, this book examines the general applicability of a discourse which has been taken up academically and popularly. What is striking about resource curse discourse is that it names a beast apparently capable of stalking any nation and practically every continent. However, as more studies have appeared, this phenomenon, increasingly identified with the global south, appears to be a case of mistaken identity encouraged by insufficient comparisons and hasty generalisations. Rather than seeing resource politics as a prism of historical temporality, the hypothesis of the resource curse tends to stereotype national politics and flatten out critical social and historical evaluation, as we discuss below. The effect is to forestall the multiple ways in which historical, social and economic struggles are articulated in the present. Indeed the dull light of liberalism today may remind one of Soviet reasoning about international development, in the sense that what comes to the fore is a peremptory goal (good governance in place of socialism) and simplified roadmaps to show how such historical prizes are to be attained.

Yet, clearly there is a great need, globally, for better governance in resource-rich lands, and there are many like Farouk al-Kasim willing to help install what they see as the necessary policies and administrative mechanisms. The significance of these instruments intended to support government transparency and corporate social responsibility is a question that goes to the heart of this book. From the outset the authors of this book felt that it was important to work in an international frame that included the social experience of the oil and gas industries in the northern and southern hemispheres. This has encouraged us to reflect beyond the technocratic aspects of resource politics which operate between north and south.

If proof is needed that the Norwegian model should not be historically sanitised and turned into a commodity for export along with the services of Statoil, then there is no better example than the fate of al-Kasim's efforts in his native Iraq. After the fall of Saddam Hussein, and in a very different political horse-trading environment to that of social democratic Norway, al-Kasim drafted the oil industry legislation for Iraq. He also disowned the legislative result. Statoil's record of working abroad has also shown the company in compromising positions and operating with less integrity than its verbal statements and formal commitments to corporate social responsibility would suggest. Despite Norway's widely praised commitments to environmental sustainability, one of the currently heated national political debates is focused on government plans to open Lofoten Vesterålen for oil exploration, with Statoil being a major actor. Lofoten is otherwise known as an area recognised for its natural beauty and its importance as the spawning ground for all North Atlantic cod. Whilst Norway is a country of wealth and peace, its ownership of a company and fund that is increasingly involved in questionable investments and dealings abroad,[9] and the provision of a harbour to numerous *mosquito* companies known for their operation in high-risk markets,[10] must raise questions about the continuing validity of a benign 'Norwegian model'. Indeed, it also gives grounds for pausing over the meaning and significance of the *resource curse* and its almost exclusive application to countries of the global south. Rather than adding to the critical discussion of imperialism, this focus on the south has tended to supplant it, whilst also overlooking the dynamics of oil and political transformation in countries such as Norway, or the United Kingdom, in the 1980s.

THE PROLIFERATION OF THE RESOURCE CURSE

Prior to the late 1980s, conventional wisdom concerning the relationship between natural-resource abundance and development regarded the former as advantageous for the latter.[11] In the 1960s, the prominent development theorist Walter Rostow (1960) argued that natural-resource endowments would enable developing countries to make the transition from underdevelopment to industrial 'take-off', just as they had done for countries such as Australia, the United States and Britain. However, since the late 1980s, a sizeable scholarly literature has emerged which suggests that natural-resource abundance (or at least an abundance of particular types of natural resources) increases the likelihood that countries will experience negative political and social-economic outcomes, including poor economic performance, low levels of democracy and civil war. This literature has become extremely influential on both policy and practice and the idea that natural resources are bad for development is now widely accepted by researchers and officials at the major international financial institutions[12] as well as by many NGOs.[13]

The resource curse thesis shifted critical discussions on poverty and development away from earlier explanations centred on the impacts of imperialism, dependency and the impacts of foreign intervention to an analysis largely concerned with the failures and inefficiencies of economic planning and state institutions in the global south. As result, the conventional wisdom in recent years has, arguably, become the exact opposite of what it was two decades ago. However, despite the weight of convention, the question that concerns a growing alternative scholarship is whether in recognising the interaction between the specificity of the social politics of resources, and the global operation of commodity markets, there is not now sufficient evidence to reconsider the direction of consensus once again. This is one of the key debates towards which this book is addressed.

The term *resource curse* is now commonly applied to describe how countries rich in natural resources are unable to use that wealth to boost their economies, and how, counter-intuitively (if one discounts imperialism), these countries have lower economic growth and development outcomes than countries without an abundance of natural resources.[14] In the post-cold-war period, during which economic stability became a key concern of international governance and investment, discussion of a resource curse also became a way for northern governments to account for the complicated state of affairs faced by resource-rich countries in the global south: intractable conflicts, resource wars, complex political emergencies, conflict trap, resource securitisation, petro-violence, petro-populism, blood diamonds.[15]

The consensus built between these different terminologies and perspectives was that an abundance of natural resources is frequently at the root of violent conflict. As a result there was a general acknowledgment of a *paradox of plenty*, i.e. that the majority of conflict-prone and war-ravaged states in the global south, including those recently emerging from violent conflict, are extractive economies that despite being endowed with strategic natural wealth cannot avert a decline into debilitating violence and war. Equally puzzling for many scholars was the observation that whilst these states contribute essential inputs to the global economy, they largely remain underdeveloped and politically unstable, with a sizeable majority of their citizens living on less than a dollar a day.

Early work on the economic performance of resource-abundant countries suggested that the causal mechanisms linking natural-resource abundance and economic performance were essentially economic in nature.[16] Some authors[17] have argued for example that the problem for resource-abundant countries was that international commodity markets were inherently unstable and that any instability within them could easily be transferred to domestic economies, in turn affecting the reliability of government revenues and foreign exchange supplies and dramatically increasing risks for private investors.[18] In the early 1980s, several commentators argued that resource-abundant countries were susceptible to so-called 'Dutch disease' – a condition in which a resource boom leads to the appreciation of the real exchange rate and in turn damages manufacturing and other tradable sectors.[19]

Subsequent studies of trends in international commodity prices have responded to these explanations with scepticism. It is suggested that while, in overall terms, international commodity prices have declined during the twentieth century, this has been due largely to declines in the prices of commodities that are exported exclusively by developed countries or more or less exclusively by relatively successful developing ones.[20] In contrast to a stress on the negative economic consequences of natural-resource discoveries, some authors now argue that the answer to the association with conflict lies more with the extent to which countries are abundant or dependent. Resource abundance or resource wealth means that there is a high production *per capita* of the resources in question, while resource dependence implies that the resources constitute a high proportion of the country's exports.[21]

Recent work on the economic effects of resources has also focused on a discussion on which types of resources, and particularly whether they are non-renewable or renewable, are most clearly connected to conflict. In particular, there is discussion of the 'lootability', or ease with which resources can be appropriated. The less capital-intensive the process of extracting a resource is, the more lootable it is. Moreover, in keeping with this logic, the further the resource is located from centres of state power, the higher market value it has per unit of weight. The lootability of natural resources, i.e. their physical properties and location, have also been considered by Ross (2004) as the basis for other common mechanisms of conflict, including foreign intervention and 'booty futures' (i.e. the sale by rebels of the future exploitation rights to speculators in exchange for financial support). However, as McGinty (2004) notes, use of the term 'lootability' implicitly assumes that the main motivation for violent conflict is economic, and does not recognise that the violence may be spurred by other reasons. In this regard strategic looting may be part of a wider politico-military project, while selective looting indicates that particular attention is paid to target selection. High-value resources that are easy to appropriate can also be associated with political order, as in Myanmar, or civil war, as in Sierra Leone. The outcome depends on the institutions of extraction in the country in question, and the extent to which these institutions enable rulers to control the revenue stream from the extracted resources.[22]

Work on the relationship between natural-resource abundance and economic performance has, over time, given greater attention than earlier writing to the role of political variables in mediating this relationship. On the one hand, economists have gradually incorporated ideas from political science into their work on the resource curse, particularly, although not exclusively, ideas from neoclassical political economy and the new institutionalism.[23] On the other hand, political scientists have entered debates on the resource curse, bringing with them analytical frameworks such as behaviouralism, public choice theory, institutionalism/ statism, and fiscal sociology, all of which give central attention to the role of political factors in shaping economic outcomes. These four particular perspectives have become particularly influential. Indeed, it is important to note that all of the key policy mechanisms developed by states (e.g. Extractive Industry Transparency Initiative, Natural Resource Charter, the Kimberley Process, Capital Flight Programmes) or non-governmental organisations (Transparency International, Publish What You Pay) to encourage and increase international resource governance in recent years have been premised on either one or a combination of these understandings.

Behaviouralist perspectives suggest that natural-resource abundance leads to various types of emotional or irrational behaviour on the part of political elites, in turn contributing to poor economic policymaking and institutional deterioration. In particular, it is argued, resource booms induce in political elites myopia, sloth, and/or over-exuberance.[24] For example, Mitra argues that resource booms produce a 'tendency to optimism', leading to excessive government spending.[25] Similarly, Krause has suggested that natural resources lead to 'wishful thinking' among policymakers in resource-rich countries. In contrast to such behaviouralist perspectives, rational-actor perspectives portray political actors as rational utility-maximising individuals.[26] Accordingly, they have suggested that the problem with natural-resource abundance is not that it leads to irrational behaviour on the part of political actors, but that it provides them with an opportunity to line their own pockets by engaging in rent-seeking. Ross (2001), for instance, argues that when governments receive windfalls from a resource boom, rational political elites will take the opportunity either to directly seize the rents created by resource booms or to gain control over the right to allocate them – a process he calls 'rent-seizing'. State-centred perspectives suggest that natural-resource abundance leads to poor economic performance, not by influencing the behaviour of political elites or social actors, but by influencing the state's capacity to promote economic development (Mahdavy 1970; Beblawi and Luciani 1987; Luciani 1987; Tanter 1990; Chaudhry 1994; Vandewalle 1998; Gunn 1993). Karl has also argued that dependence on oil revenues leads to the emergence of 'petro-states', that is, states that are geared towards the 'political distribution of rents' rather than the promotion of private investment, production and economic growth.[27] The emergence of petro-states, she suggests, is particularly likely where oil's domination of the economy coincides with the process of state formation.

Of these perspectives, the rational-actor perspective has been granted particular credibility by analysts and policymakers as a means of identifying the causal mechanisms linking natural-resource abundance and the onset of civil war. Indeed, these theoretical approaches have had significant impact on both peace-building literature and policy in recent years. In contrast to other perspectives in which grievances (stemming from inequalities of wealth, limited political rights, or ethnic and religious divisions) may play a key role, the rational-actor perspective emphasises the economic incentives and opportunities faced by rebel organisations. In doing so, it assumes that rebellions are caused primarily by greed. Paul Collier is one of the most widely quoted exponents of this approach, which focuses on the desire of rebel leaders to enrich themselves and their followers. Collier argues that 'a country with large natural resources, many young men and little education is very much more at risk of conflict than one with the opposite characteristics'.[28] Thus he posits such economic dynamics as key causal factors in most civil wars, other factors remaining insignificant or *ceteris paribus*.[29] On the basis of findings drawn from large-scale data sets gathered from examples of war-torn Africa, he argues that 'the true causes of much civil war are not the loud discourses of grievance but the silent force of greed'.[30] Warlords and rebel forces are driven by the opportunities of lootable resource rent as a means of survival and the perpetuation of the 'war economy'; Keen (1998) describes the latter as 'economics by subversion'.

Closely connected to the World Bank and multilateral projects such as the Natural Resource Charter, Collier's work has had considerable influence in policy circles. However, the claim for a more or less straightforward correlation between natural-resource wealth and increased risk of civil war is critiqued in academic circles as a simplistic and possibly misleading formulation.[31] For example, Ross (2004) suggests that rather than being caused by looting mechanisms, civil wars in resource-abundant countries are typically caused by various alternative mechanisms. Ross labels another causal factor, for which he finds some support in his study, the 'foreign intervention mechanism', whereby resource wealth increases the probability of civil war by increasing the probability of foreign intervention. This is connected to what Ross calls the 'booty futures mechanism', whereby resource wealth encourages or sustains civil war by enabling rebel groups to sell the future exploitation rights to minerals they hope to capture.[32] Nevertheless, other critics of Collier's work have also pointed to what they consider to be the highly arbitrary terminology of measurement on which his findings are based, including the restrictive definition of civil war as a conflict resulting in over 1000 combat deaths. This ignores the possibility of lower-level regional and sub-regional conflicts, or democratic contestation, focused on resource capture – forms of conflict and recidivism clearly emphasised in the 2011 World Development Report.[33] It also ignores the role of a series of other intervening variables, such as corruption, predation, prebendalism, lack of fiscal discipline, absence of rule of law, etc.[34] Moreover, the likely combination of these and other factors calls into question the plausibility of ruling them out, *ceteris paribus*, and targeting resource-related conflict, ahistorically, as an empirically isolated phenomenon. Indeed, as we argue in our conclusion, other factors cannot realistically be ruled out, and to do so appears to be one of the hallmarks of the sort of delimited knowledge production examined by Gustafson in Chapter 13.

Attempting to address some of these problems in order to provide a more nuanced approach to resource conflict, some authors have used a multidimensional perspective to capture the political ecology of resource-abundant states and the attendant implications for conflict.[35] To some extent these approaches also mirror moves by new-institutionalist scholars, such as Ostrom and Cox (2010), to build on rational-actor theories of environmental governance in order to develop a 'multi-tier framework'. Other approaches, such as Dunning (2008) or Humphreys (2005), also stress the significant variations that exist in the rentier dynamics of mineral-exporting states. Drawing on data from a much broader set of resource-abundant countries, including countries in Europe, Latin America and Asia, the results of this work conclude that previous analysis on predation has been too pessimistic, even dismissive of the states in the global south, which are castigated by northern powers despite their genuine efforts to break from the rentier web and conflict traps.[36] Naturally, the generalising tendency to assume that rentier states perpetuate underdevelopment becomes problematic when a greater range of exceptional cases (those relatively peaceful rentier states such as Malaysia, Botswana, Canada or Norway) are registered.

POLITICS AND HISTORY BEYOND TECHNOCRATIC REASON

Whilst some analysts have attempted to revise the analysis of the resource curse by adding more and more variables into the mix, other writers are currently questioning whether the ever increasing number of variables is not an indication that the whole discourse of the resource curse is in fact a 'red herring'.[37] There is increasing recognition that serious gaps exist in the kind and quality of the data on which the theories of the resource curse are built. Whilst research has provided considerable evidence that natural-resource abundance is associated with various negative development effects, as Rosser (2006) shows, the relationship is anything but as conclusive, or as direct, as the 'resource curse' terminology would suggest.

Although some efforts have recently been made to fill gaps in data through the use of new techniques, such as mapping techniques like GIS to study the spatial patterns of resources and violence within countries,[38] or economic modelling to test 'rent-seeking behaviour',[39] the resource curse thesis is still largely built on work focused on macroeconomic and national levels of governance. In matters of 'governance', the development community is long on national-level quantitative indicators, but short on exploring how and why effective local, regional, national, and international institutions actually work in particular times, places, and circumstances. Indeed, despite the large number of publications now available, resulting from macroeconomic data collected on the large scale, there is still a severe lack of depth and clarity to existing studies. Already in 1999, Ross suggested that the 'absence of careful testing has had two major consequences: scholars have been unable to produce a cumulative body of knowledge about policy failures of resource exporters; and with no apparent need to place their theories in testable form, their arguments are often left underspecified, with nebulous variables, ambiguous domains of relevant cases and fuzzy mechanisms'.[40]

Nor, as Rosser argues, have recommendations for overcoming the resource curse generally taken into account the issue of political feasibility.[41] Researchers have been too reductionist in positing a deterministic relationship between natural abundance, various pathologies (irrational behaviour and greed of elites, rent-seeking by social groups, weak institutions) and various negative developmental outcomes (poor economic performance, civil war, authoritarianism). As such, explanations for the links between natural resources and conflict do not adequately account for the role of social forces or external political and economic environments in shaping the developmental outcomes in resource-abundant countries, nor, as we have mentioned, do they pay due attention to those resource-rich countries which have done well in conventional terms of 'development'. In concluding a review of the resource curse literature, Rosser states that 'it will only be by further exploring the dynamics underpinning variation in resource abundant countries ... that we are likely to uncover the potential levers that might be employed to trigger the required policy, behavioural, institutional or social changes'.[42]

Recognising the weaknesses of current theories of the resource curse, not to mention the technocratic reasoning exhibited by writers such as Collier, there is a growing agreement that other approaches and methodologies are needed to study the political relationships involved in resource wealth governance. Efforts are now being made to expand a qualitative social geography and political economy of resource extraction which would incorporate the political dynamics of greed, as well as the characteristic complexity of grievances within resource-rich countries in the global south.[43] There is also a more general acknowledgement of the need to take account of the historical particularities of contexts under study. As Stevens and Dietsche highlight, 'parsimonious explanations that ignore time and historical context are unlikely to capture the dynamics of potentially more than one combination of a set of variables that can induce positive institutional change'.[44] Omeje highlights the lack of a firm historical foundation in most studies of resources and conflict, and argues for a 'trans-historical multi-regional anatomy of rentier politics in extractive economies that rigorously explores the accumulation devices and tendencies of key stakeholders in their interplay with the structures of domestic and international political economy'.[45] Omeje also argues that it is largely unexplored political mechanisms in extractive economies that seem to have the most decisive implication for dysfunctional conflict (or lack of it) in different countries and regions in the global south.

One of the major shortcomings of technocratic thought in this field is its unwillingness to address the full extent and influence of values, such as the entrepreneurial and competitive ethos, or the virtues of cooperation and solidarity, all of which it seeks to rationalise (globally) in utilitarian terms, rather than in terms of political and ideological praxis. Although aiming for equilibrium, this delimited liberal form of practical reason inevitably puts an artificial distance between economics and society – a gap which this book seeks to close. We argue that to address the socio-economics of oil and gas, a much greater sensitivity to the issues of historical temporality and the politics of growth is required.

TIME AND THE MARKET DISEQUILIBRIUM

As a country created by Spanish imperialism and now existing in the backyard of a less easily definable US empire, Venezuela may well encapsulate what is at stake in the whole symbolic economy of contemporary growth. The inclusion of formerly excluded 'popular sectors' through participatory politics and the consumption of collective goods (e.g. education, health and housing services) is now regarded as a proto-revolutionary task by proponents of such practical social goals. The background of this leftward shift was the not unforeseen failure of trickle-down economics. In the midst of the country's oil boom in the 1970s, the Venezuelan founder of OPEC, Juan Pablo Pérez Alfonso told Terry Lynn Karl to 'study what oil is doing to us ... Ten years from now, twenty years from now, you will see. Oil will bring us ruin'.[46] Give or take a few years, Pérez Alfonso was right. Karl's influential book took an eclectic theoretical approach to show that 'efficiency' is often merely a market 'code word to mask new power arrangements'.[47] However, whether it was oil, or more specifically a flow of petrodollars and the ranking up of fictive capital which brought ruin to Venezuela is an issue that is impossible to disentangle unless in counterfactual terms. The strength of Coronil's (1997) book *The Magical State, Nature, Money and Modernity in Venezuela* is that it offers an anthropological appreciation of the division of labour and the division of nature underpinning the modern symbolic order of economic progress.

In Venezuela both these divisions were reinforced by the liberalisation of markets and rise of speculative finance capitalism which Coronil saw effectively dividing the country in two. At a theoretical level the widening social schism recalls the customary divisions of labour and nature in pre-capitalist society, for example, in the way rights to the land and the sea may be subject to hierarchical social segregation.[48] However, with the introduction of speculative capitalism, any sort of social contract forged along such lines at the national level seems destined to fail. The decisive fracture between the financial economy and the productive economy came with the collapse of the banking system in 1994. As an angry depositor who had lost his savings remarked of Venezuela's business aristocracy, 'their country is money'.[49]

The proliferation of tax havens or 'anti-states', which make such a remark especially pertinent, was built into the complex tax avoidance strategies pioneered by oil companies like Standard Oil/Exxon. Offering substantial tax advantages to increasingly cosmopolitan national elites, these also opened the door to a range of speculative dealings at the international level.[50] It has been calculated that as much as 98 per cent of the international foreign exchange transactions are speculative, leaving the trade in real goods and services as a very slender part of the globalised economy.[51] Capital is nothing if not mobile. Resources, on the other hand, are territorially grounded. Therefore, in articulating the classic productive–exploitative relationship between *Monsieur le Capital* and *Madame la Terre*,[52] transnational companies face ideological difficulties in supplanting state enterprise. Appearing rather like economic philanderers, these companies often become the targets of civil-society campaigns. On the other hand, looking at the problem of rent-seeking behaviour, or the way governments all too often view the oil and gas industry as a 'cash cow', many studies make it abundantly clear that these issues cannot be viewed separated from the fiduciary relations arising from the nodal points in the global petroleum economy and its role in general capitalist expansion.[53]

As we have already highlighted, there is a wide range of answers as to why different governments have done so little to assert more meaningful control over what, in most cases, might be regarded as 'the people's property'. Acting on this principle is far from straight-forward, legally or politically. The issue is especially acute when the exploitation of oil and gas comes at the cost of workers' lives and at great social and environmental cost to citizens in general. In many instances, the promise of accelerated development, and indeed highly visible clusters of real activity, have dazzled elected political representatives no less than they did the Shah of Iran. The promise of economic advantage without the necessity of a democratic advance comes in the form of development projects presented to the state by a range of internal and external actors whose interconnections and political alliances are anything but transparent.[54] However, not-withstanding political hubris and corruption, and even the reputed sabotage of economic 'hit men', the context which ought to be borne in mind here (and which Venezuela exemplifies) is the schism in global capital between the productive industrial sectors and the finance, insurance and real estate sectors, i.e. the 'FIRE' sector. What understandably preoccupies many social democratic economists, such as Hudson (2005), is the parasitic and ultimately destructive impact the FIRE sector has on the productive sectors and therefore on general prospects for economic and technological diversification within nations. Indeed, the influence of the FIRE sector would provide as much of a poetic justification for our title, *Flammable Societies*, as the more obvious combustible properties of oil and gas or the often incendiary politics of energy resource extraction.

Going further than Hudson, Marazzi (2011) argues that the extent of the financialisation of the global economy means that the distinction between the FIRE sector and the productive sectors of the economy is now untenable. In line with Hardt and Negri's (2001) 'Empire' thesis, Marazzi argues that industrial production and international trade are themselves subsumed by the logic of finance capitalism, which has effectively restructured the nexus of capital, employment, production and consumption. From this theoretical perspective, consumers become the partial producers of the products and services they buy (for example in merging certain functions of warehouse/factory/shop, as done by Ikea) while employment is seen through the lens of rent (franchising, employment agencies, and university marketisation, etc.). Although the logic and mechanisms of finance capitalism may indeed be proliferating, the idea that a new *deterritorialised* 'Empire' has been constructed (the character of which is quite different from the typical asymmetric trade relations of imperialism) is highly questionable. At the very least, it appears to underplay the requirement of fictive capital to substantiate its own reproduction (even if only at a fractional level, as in the fractional reserve of precious metal) in the structures of state power.

In this respect, what has been argued by writers such as Boron (2005) and Harvey (2010) is that core capitalist states (the homes of finance capital and global corporations) remain very important imperial actors and power brokers. Contrary to Hardt and Negri's claim (taken up by Marazzi) that imperialism no longer has an 'inside', the asymmetric exchange of natural resources for technology and manufactured goods is still a very noticeable aspect of capitalist development. Moreover, the mega-accumulation of capital needed for technological development in the global north requires the sort of financial ingenuity advanced by finance capitalism in its home territories.[55] Resource-derived capital (such as interest drawn from oil-backed loans) and technological advancement in the global north are interdependent but increasingly divided aspects of capitalist technological development over time and space. Intellectual property rights are only the most obvious mechanism of a complex and embedded competitive status quo in which natural resources, the environment and human labour are vastly undervalued in real terms.

An obvious outcome of this undervaluing is the environmental irresponsibility in technologically advanced countries, where there is a striking reluctance to adequately research and develop renewable energy, despite massive accumulations of capital and the high level of consensus on the urgency of addressing climate change. Not only is there too much money to be made from energy scarcity, but the return on investment in renewable technology is inadequate in capitalist terms. This situation returns our attention to the 1970s, the last time 'energy saving' was a public mantra, and when a global economic catastrophe was predicted as a result of the 1973 oil embargo implemented by a group of Arab states, including members of OPEC (Organisation of the Petroleum Exporting Counties).

The much reported 'oil shock' in 1973 tended to obscure the memory of the 1971 'dollar shock' when US President Nixon abandoned the gold standard, leading to the rapid depreciation in the value of oil traded in US dollars. Oil regained its value in 1973, and the embargo provided the impetus for a much broader attempt on the part of developing nations to establish more equitable terms of trade under the banner of the New International Economic Order (NIEO) taken up by the United Nations General Assembly in 1974. However, an important factor in defeating this manifestation of resource (inter)nationalism was the rising power of fictive capital, supported to a great extent by petrodollar settlement, whereby oil and other major commodities are traded in dollars, thus allowing the United States to generate increasing deficits whilst preaching fiscal discipline to the rest of the world. As one of the critics of dollar hegemony put it in 2002: 'World trade is now a game where the United States produces dollars and the rest of the world produces the things that dollars can buy.'[56]

In this sense the tragedy of OPEC – obscured by the media and by occasional bouts of sabre-rattling in the United States – is that since 1975 it has functioned overwhelmingly as a consumer-friendly organisation, supporting dollar hegemony and accepting the dogma of market equilibrium delivered by the logic of international comparative advantage, even though the necessity of OPEC's creation was that market equilibrium had proved to be a false hope. As Paterson discusses in Chapter 12, this means that treaties and legal contracts between states tend to mask the failure of the free market to neutralise the strategic geopolitics of energy. As one can see from the work of political economists such as Hudson (2003, 2005), Naylor (2004) or Nitzan and Bichler (2002), cited above, in the absence of market equilibrium, capital flows (often illicit) and the politics of debt are historical factors which need to be taken into account. In 1986, Walter Wriston (1919–2005), a senior US banker and an influential neoliberal proponent of 'the information revolution', pointed out that the much vaunted oil crisis in the 1970s never really happened; rather, thanks to market networks OPEC surpluses were recycled through the Euromarket into loans to the least developed countries.[57] It was in the same period (1976–80), following the attempt to establish the NIEO, that the apparent benevolence of the World Bank also increased and Third World debt rose by an average of 20 per cent annually, providing enormous political leverage to the international financial institutions.

If not exactly a reward for compliance with the dogma of market equilibrium, petroleum-led capital flows have continued to give rise to clusters of accelerated development. If these clusters appear like islands of boom in seas of bust, it is largely because in the intervening decades the international division of labour and nature has grown year on year. As Manuel Castells, one of the most influential theorists of techno-social change, has pointed out, a year of intelligent and strenuous labour on the part of a farmer in the global south cannot compete with an hour of labour on cutting-edge software programming in the global north.[58] Because international comparative advantage does not deliver equilibrium, it would be a mistake to take this imbalance for granted, or belittle its moral significance for the aspirations of a global bourgeoisie whose sphere of operation (or whose 'country') is constituted by the same sliding scale. Notwithstanding the way in which marginalised communities go on the offensive using all possible means of networking, including the world wide web; as Castells acknowledges, they 'build their territorial trenches as their primary form of organisation'.[59] Thus, alongside the monocultural aspirations of an ethnically diverse global bourgeoisie, integrated with trade flows of capital and resources, market disequilibrium can also be seen as compelling forms of social territorialism.

THE INTERPLAY OF IDEOLOGY

It has been argued both popularly and academically that the struggle over resources in the twenty-first century has replaced the more ideologically orientated contests of the twentieth century (Klare 2001). For many people, it was not a contest between democracy and dictatorship, but the slogan 'No War for Oil' that captured the underlying dynamics driving the invasion of Iraq. However, as we show through our research, ideology has far from been erased by resource politics. Through the comparative and multidisciplinary study of hydrocarbon-rich countries, stretching from northern Europe to the Caucasus, from the Gulf of Guinea to Latin America, this book examines the way in which both the control of oil and gas resources and the conflict over their exploitation are loaded with incendiary ideological and epistemological issues.

An extension of theory and methodology away from rational-actor models and beyond quantitative research also heralds a return to a consideration of power, of social class, and of imperialist social relations and discourses. As within the wider study of global governance, critics of the resource curse thesis, such as Stevens and Dietsche (2008), recognise that assessments of institutions and development are based more on ideological perspectives than on scientific knowledge. Despite all the references by northern scholars, donor institutions and governments to the variables of legitimacy and capability in 'risk' indexes, there is no real agreement between them on the desired institutional or political design of resource governance. Indeed whilst the International Country Risk Guide's *political risk indicator* and the Journal of Foreign Policy's *Failed States Index* are widely used as proxies for institutional quality, their indicators rely on subjective expert interpretation of country risk components and have not been designed for comparative research purposes. Although international policy may be vague, it is still 'guided by models that are framed by certain norms of what states *ought* to look like, and how they *ought* to be run'.[60] As with the resource curse, concepts and indexes of fragile and failed states were originally formed as a means of identifying countries which, because of internal weakness, needed assistance. The generalisations borne out in policy by these various concepts fail to take account of different processes of state formation and have been all too easily manipulated by politicised efforts to discredit, and therefore exclude, countries undergoing momentous political change (Tedesco 2007). The discourses on the resource curse and fragile states are therefore related and they may be regarded as powerful ideological weapons, drawn upon by politicians and statesmen to legitimise policies and by opponents to criticise rulers.

FLAMMABLE SOCIETIES

The examination of varied histories of socio-economic development makes it obvious that states function in a variety of forms, and increasingly in relation to commerce and to the geopolitical interests of other states. However, if we are to go beyond mere pluralism, or cultural relativism, in this regard, it is not only the shining examples of success or those states mired in civil war that need to be studied. More attention needs to be given to the ideological struggles of a range of governments and actors. As this book highlights, it is important to realise that resource contestation more often takes the character of low-level sporadic violence and democratic, albeit sometimes militant, contestation than of full-scale civil war. So to understand resource conflict, or to design more appropriate policy responses and governance structures, we need to take account of these more mundane processes of confrontation and negotiation, and to appreciate their social dynamics. A key to a more nuanced understanding is the phenomenon of *social territorialism*, magnified by market disequilibrium as discussed above. The same factor can be seen in various responses to the contemporary limits of resource sovereignty, and indeed to the contested nature of national sovereignty *per se*. Conflict, in this context, is not necessarily a sign of instability or failure, however, and it may be an important and necessary route to a lasting solution to the issues of resource governance.

As this book makes evident, many countries, including Norway, are to be found between the two ends of what has been until now an oversimplified sliding scale between good and disastrous models for resource governance. In these mid-range examples there are positive and innovative experiences alongside problems of corruption and serious social divisions. Of course our studies are not exhaustive and are subject to the usual practical restrictions of research over a broad field of social and historical experience; however, it is the need to study a range of positive and struggling contexts which explains the choice of studies included in this volume. In this way the book shows how prescriptions for resource governance, and the problematic contexts of resource management to which they are directed, must be teased apart and studied in their own right. We argue, therefore, that more is obscured than revealed in currently popular policy approaches in terms of explaining the 'brute' facts of competition over resources.

In recognising the incomplete nature of processes of colonial government and the fluctuating influence of globalisation, it becomes evident that notions of state, market and law are frequently distant and distinct from those of the European ideal. Theory and methodology are in this way drawn in a more anthropological direction that seeks to disentangle the *orientalist* histories of 'development failure' or northern efforts to discredit resource nationalism in the south as populism. We are also obliged to consider the interaction between structure and agency, and to look beyond the formal trappings of functioning institutions, the economy and populations. In this process we discover differing and often contrasting languages of stateness and legality that compete and interact over long periods of time to define the state and basis of governance through varied dialectics of struggle.[61] Of specific relevance to this book is the way in which natural-resource wealth and competing languages of the state (nationhood, legality and identity) interact (violently or otherwise) to define ideas of social justice, such as 'our oil belongs to the people'.[62]

RESOURCE SOVEREIGNTIES

Resource wealth brings to the fore issues of political and social identity under the state and ultimately the ideological orientation and identity of the state itself. As we examine in this book, formal categories of geopolitical sovereignty overlap with informal and immanent sovereignties, and this jagged conjunction of different conceptions of sovereignty is exposed by the exploitation of natural resources. As a number of chapters in this book demonstrate, resource politics may expose, and even articulate, faultlines in sovereignty, but they do not cause them. Rather, a more complex series of interdependencies and social contracts are at play and this fact demands a pluralised discussion of 'sovereignties'.

The history of sovereignty from ancient times to the present, pursued by Agamben (1998), has generated a series of important insights, which rework the historicity of Foucault's earlier work on power and governmentality. In Agamben's work sovereignty is understood as an externality, an outside constitutive force that is independent of orders and of moralities. It is a wild power, which defines itself in its free unconstrained capacity to act independently of the rules it institutes. This sovereign power is also conventionally exercised against persons defined as outside the sovereign order. This externality, like the sovereign, is defined as an asocial, amoral being – in Agamben's analysis, as 'bare life' and beyond the protection of the sovereign order, open to being killed with legal and moral impunity. Arguing that this form of power is most apparent in its contestation or dispute, or in moments of the transformation or transmutations in the orders of power, Agamben argues that there has been a resurgence of *wild sovereignty* in the context of the recent 'war on terror' and that it is visible in contexts of legal and political contestation, such as Iraq and Afghanistan. Drawing on Agamben, Kapferer argues that wild sovereignties are also evident in the operation of corporate capitalism when corporations subvert state orders and institute their own regimes of war and violence.[63]

We touched on Hardt and Negri's (2001) controversial supranational theory of Empire in previous pages. As writers such as Boron (2005) argue, contra Hardt and Negri, the state and especially the US state (the ultimate guarantor of private property rights) remains a crucial structure for imperialism. In proposing a postmodern theory of imperialism, Hardt and Negri used the concept of multitude, 'as a poetic concept rather than as a factual one',[64] in an attempt to explain the rise of social movements and popular political transformations of recent years. According to their thesis, the multitude mirrors capitalism in so far as it looks beyond the state, but whereas the economic system diminishes citizenship, the multitude is implicitly striving for global citizenship. However, Sawyer (2009), in a study of the indigenous court case against the oil corporation Chevron, argues that care needs to be taken to explore the entangled, compromised and unfinished practices that form and give rise to sovereign power. The lawsuit against Chevron-Texaco suggests to Sawyer that the nation state – and the juridical regimes that buttress its existence – are increasingly prominent in both enabling the expansive reach of global capital as well as providing avenues through which 'subalterns' might rein in some of imperialism's more egregious tendencies.[65]

The meaning of the state, then, is still a point of struggle, in terms of both theory and practice. In this light, what passes as civil society is best 'conceptualised not as "below" the state, but as integral parts of a new transnational apparatus of governmentality' – that is, as constitutive elements for new forms of knowledge/power concerned with the conduct of conduct, the governing of people, resources and ideas.[66] Although many observers and political actors find the terms of sovereignty, and its boundaries, increasingly blurred, this does not diminish the significance of territory and land. Blom Hansen and Stepputat (2006) demonstrate how the ambiguity and contested nature of sovereignty is particularly marked in postcolonial contexts. Moving away from the straitjacket of state control, they emphasise sovereignty as an uncertain form of authority, grounded primarily in violence which needs to be repeatedly performed and redesigned to generate loyalty, fear and legitimacy that operates at different levels from the neighbourhood to the summit of the state and beyond. Blom Hansen and Stepputat argue that the sovereignty of the state is always idealised, and it is particularly tenuous in postcolonial societies in which sovereign power has been historically distributed among many forms of local authority.

Looking broadly across the constellation of sociological and legal theory concerning sovereignty (including politically diverse writers such as Max Weber, Carl Schmitt and Franz Neumann) also tells us that historically complex and, at root, unsettled configurations of sovereignty persist in many countries. Empirically, these faultlines are also evident in former colonial powers such as Spain or the United Kingdom and generally they give rise to a complex range of informal or immanent sovereignties which may call into question the state's ideological vocabulary, its belittling of conflicting internal interests, or its institutional appropriation of popular sovereignty. Ultimately, such local expressions of sovereignty also challenge the state's monopoly on violence.[67] Indeed, local expressions of sovereignty, i.e. of territorial power, ownership and identification, often structure the lives of ordinary people more profoundly and effectively than does the distant and far from panoptic gaze of the state. We argue that appreciating the fundamentally fractured character of sovereignty (exacerbated rather than ameliorated by capitalism) is crucial if we are to understand the debates and clashes surrounding the governance and benefits of energy resources. Sovereignty encapsulates not a singular but a series of contrasting, and at times overlapping, ideas about governance, law, and rights, territory and resources.

By comparing and contrasting experiences of the oil economy in the northern and southern hemispheres, we show in this book how contrasting expressions of social territorialism overlap with resource sovereignties. As Elden (2009) points out, sovereignty has been exercised by power elites over concrete territories. What can be taken from this deceptively simple point is that the ideal of popular sovereignty, or in other words the authority that resides with the people, should not be regarded in overly abstract terms (as writers such as Hardt and Negri would seem to do); rather, popular power also seeks to exercise itself over something tangible, not over an abstraction of itself. Resources may therefore be seen as sites upon which complex struggles for sovereignty are taking place. These struggles, however unfashionably 'modern' they might appear, should also be seen in the context of monetarism and the inherent rise of fictive capital that has propelled globalisation, not to mention postmodernity, for four decades now. It is in this rounded sense that we see the possession of natural resources such as oil and gas as having an increasingly inflammatory political meaning. Although resources are most frequently thought of as natural things, the use of the term *resource sovereignties* seeks to capture what is fundamentally both a social relationship, i.e. the attribution of value by social groupings to attributes and capacities that provide both functional and symbolic utilities, and a political relationship, recognising the larger settings and power structures in which both resources and social relationships are found.

THE NECESSITY OF SOCIO-ECONOMICS

By placing material meaning back in the equation of sovereignty, the stage is now set for a new *socio-economics* of natural-resource governance, and with it of oil and gas. The anthropologists Marshall Sahlins (1976) and Fernando Coronil (1997) both employ the metaphor of Minerva's owl to call into question the European critical wisdom which, like the owl that takes off at dusk, may only have awakened at the twilight of classical capitalist development. In other words, while capitalism had been apprehended by Marx and Engels in the radicalised terms of European political economy, the system developed differently in societies other than those witnessed by them. In expanding, not least by the imperial means, capitalism needs to be seen as part of a more complex world system organised around relationships of dependency between different societies. While this has been subject to a great deal of research and theorisation, notably from writers such as Janet Abu-Lughod, Giovanni Arrighi, Samir Amin, Etienne Balibar and Immanuel Wallerstein,[68] the arena of politics only appears more unpredictable and ideologically ambiguous when capital becomes socially integrated within hierarchies of kinship and community yet to be ideologically superseded by class and society, or where capitalism is adapted to regions where class and society are beholden to state-centred oligarchies. The rule of law, which Max Weber (1864–1920) regarded as an integral aspect of capitalist growth, was seen then by Franz Neumann (1900–54) to assume very different characteristics depending on the historical and political context in which it was established.[69] Similarly, at the micro level, capitalist market forces do not simply sweep away the extended family in favour of the nuclear family. Rather as Pierre Bourdieu saw it, the family is symbolically reordered and some of its relationships may be suspended to fit with the practical reason that belongs to the market.[70]

All these transformations, and the contradictions or tensions within them, make us particularly aware of the social obstacles encountered in political adaptation to the 'stark utopia' of the liberal free market, brilliantly examined by Karl Polanyi (1944) in *The Great Transformation*. In hindsight, the decades from the 1930s to the 1970s appear as the relatively brief period when a considerable degree of political consensus existed among political elites (albeit only at the level of identifying the problem) about the extent of market failure and the need for states to intervene to somehow realign the economy with society. The reordering of transformation in the opposite direction today, seen in the now commonplace political realignments of peoples towards the market economy, has various negative social effects. It may encourage political corporatism, disarming the working class, or it may result in *comprador capitalism*, a tyranny of middlemen stronger than the tyranny of the market and the productive drive of a nascent bourgeoisie. For Sahlins, in *Culture and Practical Reason*, the entire social and spatial shift of capital cannot be readily analysed in the embedded utilitarian terms which allowed Marx to distinguish use values from exchange values.[71] Nor would the shifting socio-economic values that give rise to modern practical reason suggest that an industrialised *homo economicus* can be put in the political spotlight as if already standing in the clear light of a new day.

Such Marxist 'short circuits' called for a materialist sociological poetics, and this was advanced in academia, most visibly by Bourdieu, who theorised the interplay of different species of economic, political, social and cultural capital. Like Sahlins, Bourdieu's work seeks a more universal, and therefore more differentiated mode of analysis than orthodox Marxism had been able to offer. Such a heterodox approach does not, however, undermine the significance of proletarian self-awareness, or the 'class war' fought from below in varied societal contexts. In recognition of a warmongering system, this would still appear to be the most benign and enlightened mode of economic struggle possible. However, if workers in strategic extractive industries feel themselves to be, or can still be thought to be, 'the shock troops of the working class', this myth easily gives way to a more reluctant epithet: 'the poor bloody infantry', to borrow the words of one oil workers' leader.[72] Notwithstanding their informal political leadership and the considerable achievements of oil workers' unions (seen for example in Nigeria under military rule, or in post-invasion Iraq) this epithet is much more telling of the socio-political divisions of organised labour and is suggestive of the intense debates about the structures of class struggle and its social and spatial contours. The theoretical arena of debate can be readily seen from the varied socio-political points of emphasis posed by anti-capitalist writers such as Murray Bookchin (decentralisation and municipalism), David Harvey (spatial/urban rights), Hardt and Negri (the recomposition of the *demos* through late capitalist labour), Chantal Mouffe (agonistic pluralism) and Slavoj Žižek (mass repoliticisation of the economic field).

In marked contrast to such radically minded trajectories, a great deal of research in socio-economics has instead gravitated towards the individuated rational-choice theorisation of Robert Putnam, Gary Becker and others, who have focused attention on social capital. In comparison with Bourdieu's analysis, this was increasingly presented in an aggregate form, essentially as the social glue which disinterested theory could discern among the otherwise disadvantaged. Conspicuous by its absence from this line of thought was, however, the role of political capital – highlighted by Logan in Chapter 4 – a missing link which now appears symptomatic of a broad attempt to offer a type of social theory that would be acceptable to institutions like the World Bank and which could be easily picked up by NGOs searching for funding.[73] Unsurprisingly, Bourdieu's more complex matrix of capital, class and social distinction was sidelined.

In a similar vein to Bourdieu, Sahlins does not see a radical social consciousness rooted in the European enlightenment, clearing away old values, even if only under the misleading guise of liberalism, and he argues persuasively for the existence of a 'more elaborate' and 'more dangerous' symbolic matrix. 'What is finally distinctive of Western civilisation is the mode of symbolic production, this very disguise in the form of a growing GNP of the process by which symbolic value is created'.[74] Because this non-reciprocal mechanism of economic growth is at one with the forms of cultural growth it generates, the two modes going hand in hand, growth is less subject to control. Arbitrary wants come to override actual needs and the distinction between relational goods and public goods becomes harder to distinguish in some instances. It may be argued that a consequence of this blurring is that the praxis of socio-economic justice becomes subsumed by discourses of inclusion and participation which can be seen as part of the development of a 'communicative capitalism', also embraced by the left and its intellectual cadres in advanced consumer societies.[75] In the end the market is left to its own devices as the final arbiter of growth.

One result of this massive deferral of political responsibility is that the most implausible notions of sustainability have symbolic currency while, at the very same moment, ways of life associated with Western modernity appear increasingly implausible to its greatest beneficiaries. Liberal economists such as Galbraith (1958, 1967) and Mishan (1967) raised an alarm about the politics of consumer sovereignty that is increasingly difficult to ignore. Nevertheless, the limit of economics as an academic field is arrived at when it is recognised that 'the values of life are not in the main, reducible to satisfactions obtained from the consumption of exchangeable goods and services'.[76] At this point the partisan positions taken in economic science come into view and economics collapses again into politics. While this may encourage a return to the ethical reasoning of classical political economy, a turn that is marked by welfare economics today, it must be done in a way in which theories of value and capital are re-examined, recognising the necessity of different social vernaculars and expression.

The methodological and theoretical challenges mentioned above are made evident by the socio-economic approach to political economy. Coming from different disciplinary backgrounds (history, anthropology, law, geography, sociology and political science) the contributors to this book all bring to light the need for qualitative analysis of the interface between the political and economic dynamics of global capitalism, on the one hand, and local processes of value formation, personhood, histories and relationships to resources, on the other. Our examination of linkages between different levels of decision making, the nuances of power relations and the interactions of institutional and non-institutional actors (which link the micro level to the macro) takes the position of 'global ethnography', in so far as oil and gas provide a key research context for the critical study of the governance of globally interdependent development. Although it may be obvious that interdependency is increasingly articulated by technocratic institutions operating at a great remove from everyday democratic processes, or from informal social contracts operating at the national level, it is much less clear how the discursive frameworks of global governance function to mediate, and indeed to construct, the asymmetric 'interests' of producers and consumers within the generalised logic of global economic growth.

THE STORY OF THIS BOOK

The extended case study method we have adopted brings to ethnography some of the reflexive insights gained from historical sociology. The aim is to extract the general from the unique, to move from the micro to the macro, and to connect the present to the past in order to predict the future, all by building on pre-existing theory.[77] Therefore, our approach does not focus on stable orders; rather, we emphasise historically changing social practices and conflicts and the competition of social actors over resources in the context of plural, or even contradictory, norms and rules.

The case study method utilised here furthermore highlights the interplay of structure and agency. As such, we draw attention to the basic observation that 'social theory can avoid many difficulties with concepts of structure and agency when it makes an effort to regard social life less in terms of individual agency "reproducing" structure in any mechanical sense and more in terms of ongoing dynamic interrelations between actors ... interacting with each other by reference to shared understandings'.[78] This basic premise helps to focus attention on micro–macro connections which (from the critical realist theoretical standpoint, argued for by writers such as Margaret Archer) are the 'genesis' of changing social structures.[79] It is on this basis that we question the plausibility of examining resource politics by ruling out other influences and factors, *ceteris paribus*. But just as importantly, and without conflating structure and agency, the interplay between (unreflexive) systemic structures and (reflexive) human agency means that ultimately we are concerned with the transformation of normative structures, not their reproduction or discursive validation.[80]

In research practice we have combined a diachronic focus (consultations, preparatory interviews, and analysis of secondary resources) with the sort of synchronic perspective gained, first from the considerable experience of the contributors to this book, and then through the course of several periods of fieldwork during the period of the actual research project between 2008 and 2010. Rather than relying on extended fieldwork periods alone, *Flammable Societies* has built on the contributors' knowledge of the research contexts, on the mutual trust between the researchers and informants, and more generally, from our concern with both oral and written documentation. This and other basic approaches to multi-sited ethnographic research have also been refined in recent years by a series of global ethnographers seeking to link study of large-scale processes with fine-grained observations of everyday life.[81]

As the following chapters amply demonstrate, the critical and theoretical scenarios outlined above ought to be compared and tested against the untidiness and contingency of real-world situations. Considering the reductionism we find in resource-curse-inspired studies, this point really cannot be overstated. The three parts of the book highlight certain key themes; 'Resource Sovereignties' (Part 1); 'States of Collective Consumption' (Part 2); and 'Supply-side Governmentality' (Part 3). Each of these parts brings out historical factors and social mechanisms that point to complex interdependencies, and therefore we have not sought to isolate causal factors. Rather, we have grouped the following chapters in a way which highlights three causal complexes, and it would be a mistake to see them in isolation from one another when they provide the means to critically evaluate interconnections.

In registering the complex social nature of resource politics, and also in highlighting the need for the reversal of technocratic models for resource governance discussed above, we advocate an integrative bottom-up approach to what we believe ought to be properly regarded as an expansive field that embraces, rather than sidelines, the examination of imperialism. Therefore we draw attention to the role of ideology, to the missing value of practical knowledge and to the construction of resource sovereignty under the idealisation of the free market. The reflexive requirements of this project lead us, inevitably, to the problematic capitalisation of academic knowledge as part of a nexus of governmentality in the context of energy production. By reversing the scales and approaches of common approaches to resource governance, the bottom-up structure of the book emphasises a desire by its authors to circumvent standard expectations of outputs in this field of research, in so far as we seek here to be instructive without being prescriptive.

The research for this book was conducted with funding from the Poverty and Peace Programme of the Research Council of Norway. The original subtitle of the project was 'The role of the oil and gas industry in the promotion of poverty reduction and social volatility'. Among other things, our research now tells us that such a neat formulation of pros and cons is untenable. Poverty cannot be measured separately from inequality, and, as anthropologists such as Sahlins (1972) and Escobar (1999) have argued, poverty is a social relation or status, which is constantly revised and constructed by institutions. The role of the oil and gas industry in political volatility may, at first sight, look like less of a relational issue. However, as we have suggested, there are problems with any attempt to examine social volatility within nations, separately from the competition between them. In the case of the invasion of Iraq, we now have a more reliable picture of the behaviour of oil companies as catalysts for the war, and what was deemed by governments to be normal expressions of *realpolitik* in negotiations which anticipated the invader's division of spoils.[82] Although the denial of the obvious oil interest can finally be laid to rest, what ought to stand out from the whole Iraq story is the strategic and joined-up reasoning which takes place behind closed doors between state and corporate actors. It is safe to assume that, one way or another, decisions made in the public interest will be kept from the public (at least until it is too late to make a difference), regardless of transparency initiatives. Therefore it seems just as important to consider the potential for joined-up strategic reasoning, from below, on a wide range of societal issues to do with natural resources.

The three parts of this book move from grassroots experiences and expressions of resource sovereignty to the details of regional and national petroleum *realpolitik* and to issues of resource related governmentality and discourse production at the international level. In Part 1, 'Resource Sovereignties', the book begins with McNeish's chapter focused on regional debates about revenue redistribution in the southern Bolivian department of Tarija. This chapter examines at close hand the character of local and regional contests over the distribution and control of oil and gas rents in a hydrocarbon-rich area of Bolivia. Such contests expose the fractures of popular sovereignty in the country, and McNeish argues that historic grievances between social groups are more important motivating factors than rent capture. In Chapter 3, Brotherstone highlights the interplay between local faultlines and imperial sovereignty, exposed by the politics of North Sea oil in the wake of the British Empire project. Comparatively, these two chapters draw our attention to the complex ways popular sovereignty becomes territorially anchored to contests over natural resources. By contrast, Chapter 4 by Logan examines historically and comparatively cultural expressions of consumer sovereignty that are now pervasive. Associated with the information age, and the ability of individuals to make informed choices, this neoliberal ideal is effectively unanchored from either territorial responsibility or a politics of production.

While Part 1 of this book points to some of the increasingly pronounced faultlines of sovereignty, Part 2, 'States of Collective

Consumption', explores their suturing at the meso level. As Manuel Castells (1983) shows, the politics of collective consumption has often hinged on the struggle of the working class for the reproduction of its labour power.[83] The Glasgow rent strike of 1915 was a key example in Castells' study of the production of public goods. There is a complex interplay of producer, consumer and citizen interests at work here and labour power is only one form of political capital that can be mobilised, or which may be taken into account, when it comes to the organisation of these goods. Part 2 highlights this process in four different states, showing varied attempts to democratise, renegotiate, or sustain social contracts that benefit, or are made possible, by resource revenues. In Chapter 5, Strønen's case study on the decision-making and working rationale of Communal Councils gives a detailed account of the communitarian roots of Venezuelan political and constitutional reform led by Hugo Chávez. In Chapter 6, Kjærnet examines a complex, and possibly fragile, political stand-off from the Nagorno-Karabakh conflict in the early 1990s. A period of relative peace (during which varying generational viewpoints have developed) appears to have been sustained by oil revenues in Azerbaijan, at least as much as the threat of conflict is also aggravated by the oil boom there. In Chapter 7, Wanderley, Mokrani and Guimarães question 'revolutionary rhetoric' in Bolivia through a comparative analysis of tax policies. The authors reveal the resilience of neoliberal limits and normative reasoning. In doing so they also show how the construction of social legitimacy and economic feasibility depends on the consolidation of an institutional framework capable of managing tensions and disputes amongst contrasting political agendas, differing social interests and conflicting visions of sovereignty and development.

In the context of the socio-economics of oil and gas, the mediating politics of consumption of collective goods often seems to dominate, or marginalise, political struggles at the sites of production – more so now that production in general appears dispersed and socially atomised by globalisation. However, it is the 'de-ideologised' aspect of this situation, rather than an actual structural condition, which comes across in Chapter 8, where Øverland and Kutschera address the transition from the social contract of Soviet communism to neo-feudal capitalism. Øverland and Kutschera argue that the removal of energy subsidies, in line with market liberalisation, is a point of considerable sensitivity for the avaricious Russian elite, even in the absence of substantial resistance.

Part 3 of the book addresses 'Supply-side Governmentality'. We expand here the discussion of resource sovereignties in Part 1, and the socio-economic mediation of political faultlines in Part 2, to consider some of the ways in which resource politics are delimited or constrained by the supply-side ethos, by which we mean the dominant practical reason of market-led growth which has been insinuated into various governance discourses, regardless of market failure or anti-free-market motives. This part of the book begins with Cumbers' account, in Chapter 9, of the role of the state in his analysis of divergent development in the UK and Norwegian oil economies. Cumbers argues that it would be a mistake to see states as powerless in the face of global capitalism. Rather, states have to make increasingly hard choices 'between prosecuting the interests of capital internationally and maintaining social cohesion and spatially balanced growth at home'. Cumbers' analysis of the intersection of state and civil society interests opens the way to the issues of state formation, interstate relations and state–corporate relations, also examined in this part of the book. The nuances of state formation are further explored in Chapter 10 by Folorunso, Hall and Logan, who call into question the discourse of the failed state in their account of the nexus of governmentality, knowledge and labour in Nigeria. The authors argue that the caricature of state failure conceals at least as much as it reveals about Nigeria, and through the analysis of the left and right hands of the state, this chapter aims to reopen the terms of debate with a realist approach to governmentality in a strategic 'petro-state'.

In Chapter 11, Zalik examines variations of state fiscal regimes internationally and demonstrates the manner in which liberal-inflected proprietor regimes have deepened the cultural and ideological alienation of residents in resource-rich countries, and cemented a direct interest and identification with the interests of extraction, in place of production. Nevertheless, in comparing 'landlord' roles of different states, Zalik offers a nuanced account of the emergence of social claims on petroleum revenues from the populations most affected by the erosion of agrarian society and ecology, and shows how resource sovereignty is inflected by varying claims to ownership. In Chapter 12, Paterson considers these issues of sovereignty from the legal perspective of interstate relations intended to increase energy security whilst, somewhat paradoxically, adhering to the free-market ideals.

There is an obvious propensity to view the issues of resource politics as a discreet category of geopolitics, removed from the internal politics of academia. In Chapter 13, Gustafson reminds us that the autonomy of universities and academic research has always been at stake in this field of study. If we are meaningfully to interrogate the international division of labour and the division of nature underpinning resource politics, then we also need greater critical reflexivity about the production of knowledge in this field, so that we may examine how public and private interests are articulated and how positions and values are formed. From this critical angle, one of the main pitfalls on the terrain of the natural-resource politics is its capacity effectively to naturalise politics, and the politics of market-led growth in particular. The final chapter summarises the findings of the book and its chapters and highlights the instructive significance of the book in relation to the tensions that exist between governance and growth.

NOTES

1. See www.ft.com/cms/s/2/99680a04-92a0-11de-b63b-00144feabdc0.html#axzz1 GwE0silL
2. See Ryggvik 2010, 2009.
3. Ibid. 2010, p.113.
4. As Ryggvik shows (ibid., p.50), there is 'a direct connection between local technological know-how and economic and political power'.
5. See Roll 1973, pp.318–42 on 'the break-up of the labour theory of value'.
6. See oral history interview with Paal Holme, in 'Lives in the Oil Industry', British Library Sound Archive.
7. See Mohan and Zack-Williams 2004.
8. See Coronil 2000, p.240.
9. E.g. Statoil's involvement in the Alberta Oil Sands; the Norwegian Oil Fund's investments in foreign energy companies, including the nuclear industry.
10. E.g. The operation of *Det Norske Oljeselskap* (DNO) in Afghanistan; the involvement of *Discover Petroleum International* in a corruption scandal that resulted in the firing of top Peruvian government officials in 2008.
11. In the 1950s, the geographer Norton Ginsburg argued that '[t]he possession of a sizeable and diversified natural resource endowment is a major advantage to any country embarking upon a period of rapid economic growth' (as cited in Higgins 1968: 222). Similar views were also expressed by mainstream economists during this period (see, for instance, Viner 1952 and Lewis 1955).
12. I.e. the World Bank and the International Monetary Fund; Bannon and Collier 2003; Sala-i-Martin and Subramanian 2003; Davis, Ossowski and Fedelino 2003; Leite and Weidmann 1999; Sarraf and Jiwanji 2001; Isham et al. 2002; Eifert, Gelb and Tallroth 2003; Gelb and associates 1988.
13. See Save the Children, http://reliefweb.int/sites/reliefweb.int/files/resources/74A 9739821EC309649256D4E000AFF36-scf-drc-17jun.pdf, Oxfam 2002: www. oxfam.org/policy/lifting-resource-curse
14. Auty 1993; Sachs and Warner 1995.

15. Collier and Sambanis 2005; Kaldor 1999; Kaplan 1994; Nafzinger and Auvinen 1996; Watts 2008.
16. Singer 1950; Prebisch 1950.
17. Nurske 1958; Levin 1960.
18. Rosser 2006, p.13.
19. Corden and Neary 1982; Bruno and Sachs 1982.
20. Le Billon 2008.
21. As Le Billon shows (2008, p.344), an economy can be fairly dependent on a resource that it hardly has an abundance of (e.g. Sierra Leone, where diamonds make up 17–18 per cent of exports but production is worth less than 100 USD per capita).
22. See Synder 2006.
23. Eifert, Gelb and Tallroth 2003; Rodrik 2003; Isham et al. 2002; Auty 2001a, 2001b; Torvik 2002.
24. See Rosser 2006, p.14.
25. Mitra 1994, p.295.
26. Krause 1995, p.322.
27. Karl 1997, p.16.
28. Collier 2000, p.97.
29. I.e. all other things being equal or held constant.
30. Collier 2000, p.101.
31. Indeed, this is also acknowledged in Collier's later work (e.g. 2010).
32. Collier and Hoeffler 2004, pp.57–8.
33. World Bank 2011.
34. Omeje 2008.
35. Le Billon 2001; Kahl 2006.
36. See Duncan Green's critique of Collier's 'The Plundered Planet': www.oxfamblogs.org/fp2p/?tag=paul-collier
37. Brunnschweiler and Bulte 2008; Wright and Czelusta 2007.
38. Buhaug, Gates and Lujala 2009.
39. Humphreys 2005; Kolstad and Wiig 2010.
40. Ross 1999, p.309.
41. Rosser 2004, p.3.
42. Ibid., p.25.
43. Watts, M. 2008, 2009; Peluso and Watts 2001; Kaldor, Karl and Said 2007; Ballentine and Sherman 2003; Arnson and Zartman 2005; Zalik 2009.
44. Stevens and Dietsche 2008, p.36.
45. Omeje 2008, p.2.
46. See Karl 1997, p.xv.
47. Ibid., p.xvii.
48. See, for example, Marshall Sahlins's account of these divisions in the Moalan and Lau Islands of eastern Fiji (1976, pp.23–50).
49. See Coronil 1997, p.381.
50. See Michael Hudson's introduction in Naylor 2004, p.xi.
51. See Lietaer 2001, p.314.
52. *Madame La Terre* is part of the influential 'trinity formula' through which Marx added a crucial dimension to the venal relations of capital and labour. Thus the critical nexus that Marx examines is between land–ground rent, labour–wages, capital–interest; in these relations Marx sees labour 'ghosted away' by the

illusion that capital and land are valuable in their own right. See Marx 1993, pp. 480, 953–71.

53. See for example Clark 2005; Coronil 1997; Harvey 2010; Hudson 2003, 2005; Nitzan and Bichler 2002; Karl 1997; Naylor 2004.
54. In this regard, see Perkins' 2005 influential exposé.
55. Notwithstanding evasion and avoidance, tax receipts to the United Kingdom from the finance sector over the past nine years amount to some £250 billion.
56. From ' Dollar Hegemony Has Got to Go', Henry C.K. Lui, *Asia Times*, April 2002.
57. See Wriston 1986, p.58.
58. See Castells and Ince 2003, p.31.
59. Ibid., p.60.
60. De Waal 2009.
61. Blom Hansen and Stepputat 2001; Santos 1995.
62. Coronil 1997; Apter 2005; Gledhill 2008.
63. Kapferer 2004, p.12.
64. Michael Hardt, quoted in Boron 2005, p.87.
65. Sawyer 2009, p.67.
66. Ferguson 2006, p.103.
67. Hansen and Stepputat 2006, p.305.
68. The Fernand Braudel Center, at Binghampton University, New York, and its journal *Review*, is an important hub for this work. Balibar and Wallerstein's (1991) book *Race, Nation Class, Ambiguous Identities* is a key publication in the field.
69. See Jayasuriya 1996.
70. See Bourdieu 1998, p.105.
71. See Sahlins 1976, p.163.
72. From the oral history interview with Ronnie McDonald in *Lives in the Oil Industry*, British Library Sound Archive.
73. See Fine 2010.
74. See Sahlins 1976, p.220.
75 See Dean 2009.
76. Frank Knight, quoted in Roll 1973, p.608.
77. See Buroway 2000.
78. See King 2005, p.230.
79. See, for example, Archer 2010, a critical realist engagement with the structuration theory of Anthony Giddens.
80. Margaret Archer, cited above, argues that the distinction made between structure, as *unreflexive*, and agency, as *reflexive*, is required if one is not to conflate structure and agency, or take the position of methodological individualism. Archer emphasises the need to reground 'collective reflexivity'. See 'Margaret Archer on Reflexivity', www.youtube.com/watch?v=bMpJ5wnuB64.
81. The ethnographies of Buroway (2000), Ferguson (2006), Scott (1998), Tsing (2007) and Ongh (2006) all demonstrate the possibilities of detailing what is happening in local settings without losing sight of the fall and rise of ideas, processes and positions, or shifts in the organisation and reach of capitalism. Importantly for a project aiming to take a 'cross-section' through the socio-economics of a global industry, these approaches to ethnography present the local and the global as mutually constitutive, and propose means to avoid

common pitfalls of other analytic tools that 'dominate', 'silence', 'objectify' and 'normalise' the experience and knowledge of others.

82. www.independent.co.uk/news/uk/politics/secret-memos-expose-link-between-oil-firms-and-invasion-of-iraq-2269610.html

83. See Castells 1983, pp.31ff.

REFERENCES

Agamben, G. (1998) *Homo Sacer: Sovereign Power and Bare Life* (Stanford, Calif.: Stanford University Press).

Apter, A. (2005) *The Pan-African Nation: Oil and the Spectacle of Culture in Nigeria* (Chicago: University of Chicago Press).

Archer, M.S. (2010) 'Morphogenesis Versus Structuration: On Combining Structure and Action', *British Journal of Sociology*, 61: 225–52.

Arnson, C.J. and Zartman, I.W. (2005) *Rethinking the Economics of War: The Intersection of Need, Creed and Greed* (Baltimore: Johns Hopkins University Press).

Auty, R. (1993) 'Natural Resources and Civil Strife: A Two-Stage Process', *Geopolitics*, 9(1): 29–49.

—— (2001a) 'Transition Reform in the Mineral-Rich Caspian Region Countries', *Resources Policy*, 27: 25–32.

—— (2001b) *Resource Abundance and Economic Development* (Oxford: Oxford University Press for UNU/WIDER).

Balibar, E. and Wallerstein, I. (1998) *Race, Nation, Class: Ambiguous Identities* (London: Verso).

Ballentine, K and Sherman, J. (eds) (2003) *The Political Economy of Armed Conflict: Beyond Greed and Grievance* (London: Lynne Riener).

Bannon, I. and Collier, P. (2003) 'Natural Resources and Conflict: What We Can Do', in I. Bannon and P. Collier (eds) *Natural Resources and Violent Conflict: Options and Actions* (Washington, D.C.: World Bank).

Beblawi, H. and Luciani, G. (eds) (1987) *The Rentier State*, vol.2 (London: Croom Helm).

Blom Hansen, T. and Stepputat, F. (2001) *States of Imagination. Ethnographic Explorations of the Postcolonial State*. (Durham, N.C.: Duke University Press).

—— (2006) 'Sovereignty Revisited', *Annual Review of Anthropology*, 35: 295–315.

Boron, A. (2005) *Empire and Imperialism: A Critical Reading of Michael Hardt and Antonio Negri* (London: Zed Books).

Bourdieu, P. (1998) *Practical Reason* (Cambridge: Polity Press).

Brunnschweiler, C. and Bulte, E.H. (2008) 'The Resource Curse Revisited and Revised: A Tale of Paradoxes and Red Herrings', *Journal of Environmental Economics and Management*, 55(3): 248–64.

Bruno, M. and Sachs, J. (1982) 'Energy and Resource Allocation: A Dynamic Model of the "Dutch Disease"', *Review of Economic Studies*, 49: 845–59.

Buhaug, H, Gates, S. and Lujala, P. (2009) 'Geography, Rebel Capability, and the Duration of Civil Conflict', *Journal of Conflict Resolution*, 53(4): 544–69.

Buroway, M. (2000) *Global Ethnography: Forces, Connections and Imaginations in a Postmodern World* (Berkeley: University of California Press).

Castells, M. (1983) *The City and the Grassroots: A Cross-Cultural Theory of Urban Social Movements* (London: Edward Arnold).

—— and Ince, M. (2003) *Conversations with Manuel Castells* (Cambridge: Polity Press).

Chaudhry, K. (1994) 'Economic Liberalisation and the Lineages of the Rentier State', *Comparative Politics*, 27 (October):1–25.

Clark, W.R. (2005) *Petrodollar Warfare: Oil, Iraq and the Future of the Dollar* (Gabriola Island: New Society Publishers).

Collier, P. (2000) 'Doing Well Out of War: An Economic Perspective', in M. Berdal and D. Malone (eds) *Greed and Grievance: Economic Agendas in Civil Wars* (Boulder: Lynne Reiner).

—— (2010) *Plundered Planet: Why We Must – and How We Can – Manage Nature for Global Prosperity* (Oxford: Oxford University Press).

—— and Hoeffler, A. (2004) 'Aid, Policy and Growth in Post-Conflict Countries', *European Economic Review*, 48: 1125–45.

—— and Sambanis, N. (2005) (eds) *Understanding Civil War: Evidence and Analysis – Africa* (Washington, D.C.: World Bank).

Corden, W. and Neary, J. (1982), 'Booming Sector and De-industrialisation in a Small Open Economy', *Economic Journal*, 92 (December): 825–48.

Coronil, F. (1997) *The Magical State, Nature, Money and Modernity* (Chicago: University of Chicago Press).

—— (2000) 'Towards a Critique of Globalcentrism: Speculations on Capitalism's Nature', *Public Culture*, 12(2).

Davis, J.M., Ossowski, R. and Fedelino, A. (eds) (2003) *Fiscal Policy Formulation and Implementation in Oil-Producing Countries* (Washington, D.C.: International Monetary Fund).

Dean, J. (2009) *Democracy and Other Neoliberal Fantasies: Communicative Capitalism and Left Politics* (Durham, N.C.: Duke University Press).

Dunning, T. (2008) *Crude Democracy: Natural Resource Wealth and Political Regimes* (Cambridge: Cambridge University Press).

Eifert, B., Gelb, A. and Tallroth, N. (2003) 'The Political Economy of Fiscal Policy and Economic Management in Oil Exporting Countries', in J.M. Davis, R. Ossowski and A. Fedelino (eds) *Fiscal Policy Formulation and Implementation in Oil-Producing Countries* (Washington, D.C.: International Monetary Fund).

Elden, S. (2009) *Terror and Territory, The Spatial Extent of Sovereignty* (Minneapolis: University of Minnesota Press).

Escobar, A. (1999) *Encountering Development: The Making and Unmaking of the Third World* (Durham, N.C.: Duke University Press).

Ferguson, J. (2006) *Global Shadows: Africa in the Neoliberal World* (Durham, N.C.: Duke University Press).

Fine, B. (2010) *Theories of Social Capital: Researchers Behaving Badly* (London: Pluto Press).

Frank, A.G. (1966) 'The Development of Underdevelopment', *Monthly Review*, 18(4): 17–31.

Fukuyama, F. (1992) *The End of History and the Last Man* (New York: Free Press).

Galbraith, J.K. (1958) *The Affluent Society* (Boston: Houghton Mifflin).

—— (1967) *The New Industrial State* (Boston: Houghton Mifflin).

Gelb, A. and associates (1988) *Oil Windfalls: Blessing or Curse* (New York: Oxford University Press).

Gledhill, J.E. (2008) '"The People's Oil": Nationalism, Globalization, and the Possibility of Another Country in Brazil, Mexico and Venezuela', *Focaal*, 52: 57–74.

Gunn, G. (1993) 'Rentier Capitalism in Negara Brunei Daussalam', in K. Hewison et al. (eds) *Southeast Asia in the 1990s: Authoritarianism, Democracy, and Capitalism* (Sydney: Allen and Unwin).

Hardt, M. and Negri, A. (2001) *Empire* (Cambridge, Mass.: Harvard University Press).

Harvey, D. (2010) *The Enigma of Capital and the Crises of Capitalism* (London: Profile).

Higgins, B. (1968) *Economic Development: Problems, Principles, and Policies* (New York: W.W. Norton & Co.).

Hudson, M. (2003) *Super Imperialism: The Origin and Fundamentals of U.S. World Dominance*, new edn (London: Pluto Press).

—— (2005) *Global Fracture: The New International Economic Order*, 2nd edn (London: Pluto Press).

Humphreys, M. (2005), 'Natural Resources, Conflict, and Conflict Resolution: Uncovering the Mechanisms', *Journal of Conflict Resolution*, 49(4): 508–37.

Isham, J., Woolcock, M., Pritchett, L. and Busby, G. (2002) 'The Varieties of Rentier Experience: How Natural Resource Export Structures Affect the Political Economy of Economic Growth', Middlebury College Economics Discussion Paper no.03-08R, Middlebury College, Vermont.

Jayasuriya, K. (1996) *Franz Neumann on the Rule of Law and Capitalism: The East Asian Case*, Working Paper 64 (Perth, Australia: Murdoch University).

Kahl, C.H. (2006) *States, Security and Civil Strife in the Developing World* (Princeton, N.J.: Princeton University Press).

Kaldor, M. (1999) *New Wars: Organized Violence in a Global Era* (Cambridge: Polity Press).

—— Karl, T.L. and Said, Y. (2007) *Oil Wars* (London: Pluto Press).

Kapferer, B. (2005) 'New Formations of Power, the Oligarchic Corporate State, and Anthropological Ideological Discourse', *Anthropological Theory*, 5(3): 285–99.

Kaplan, R. (1994) 'The Coming Anarchy', *Atlantic Monthly* (February).

Karl, T.L. (1997) *The Paradox of Plenty: Oil Booms and Petro-States* (Berkeley: University of California Press).

Keen, D. (1998) 'The Economic Functions of Violence in Civil Wars', Adelphi Paper 320 (London: International Institute for Strategic Studies).

Keith, M. and Pile, S. (eds) (1997) *Geographies of Resistance* (London: Routledge).

King, A. (2005) 'Structure and Agency', in A. Harrington (ed.) *Modern Social Theory* (Oxford: Oxford University Press).

Klare, M.T. (2001) *Resource Wars, The New Landscape of Global Conflict* (New York: Metropolitan Books).

Kolstad, I and Wiig, A. (2010) 'Is Transparency the Key to Reducing Corruption in Resource-Rich Countries?', in A. Wiig, L. Tøndel and V. Pinto de Andrade (eds) *Compendium of Natural Resource Management* (Bergen: Chr. Michelsens Institute).

Krause, L. (1995) 'Social Capability and Long-term Economic Growth', in B.H. Koo and D. Perkins (eds) *Social Capability and Long-Term Economic Growth* (Basingstoke: Macmillan).

Le Billon, P. (2001) 'The Political Ecology of War: Natural Resources and Armed Conflicts', *Political Geography*, 20: 561–84.

—— (2008) 'Diamond Wars? Conflict Diamonds and Geographies of Resource Wars', *Annals of the Association of American Geographers*, 98(2): 345–72.

Leite, C. and Weidmann, J. (1999) 'Does Mother Nature Corrupt? Natural Resources, Corruption, and Economic Growth', IMF Working Paper WP/99/85 (Washington, D.C.: International Monetary Fund).

Levin, J. (1960) *The Export Economies: Their Pattern of Development in Historical Perspective* (Cambridge: Harvard University Press).

Lewis, A. (1955) *The Theory of Economic Growth* (Homewood, Ill.: R.D. Irwin).

Lietaer, B. (2001) *The Future of Money: Creating New Wealth, Work, and a Wiser World* (London: Century).

Luciani, G. (1987) 'Allocation vs. Production States: A Theoretical Framework', in Beblawi and Luciani 1987.

Mahdavy, H. (1970) 'The Patterns and Problems of Economic Development in Rentier States', in M. Cook (ed.) *Studies in the Economic History of the Middle East* (London: Oxford University Press).

Marazzi, C. (2011) *The Violence of Financial Capitalism*, new edn (Los Angeles: Semiotext(e)).

Marx, K. (1993) *Capital: A Critique of Political Economy*, vol. 3 (London: Penguin/ New Left Review).

McGinty, R. (2004) 'Looting in the Context of Violent Conflict: A Conceptualisation and Typology', *Third World Quarterly*, 25(5): 857–70.

Mishan, E.J. (1967) *The Costs of Economic Growth* (London: Staples Press).

Mitra, P. (1994) *Adjustment in Oil-Importing Developing Countries: A Comparative Economic Analysis* (Cambridge: Cambridge University Press).

Mohan, G. and Zack-Williams, T. (eds) (2004) *The Politics of Transition in Africa: State, Democracy and Economic Development* (Trenton N.J. and Asmara, Eritrea: Africa World Press/Oxford: James Currey).

Nafzinger, W. and Auvinen, J. (1996) 'Economic Development, Inequality, War and State Violence', *World Development*, 30: 153–63.

Naylor, R.T. (2004) *Hot Money and the Politics of Debt* (Montreal: McGill–Queen's University Press).

Nitzan, J. and Bichler, S. (2002) *The Global Political Economy of Israel* (London: Pluto Press).

Nore, P. and Turner, T. (1980) (eds) *Oil and Class Struggle* (London: Zed Books).

Nurske, R. (1958) 'Trade Fluctuations and Buffer Policies of Low-Income Countries', *Kyklos*, 11(2): 141–4.

Omeje, K. (ed.) (2008) *Extractive Economies and Conflicts in the Global South: Multi-Regional Perspectives on Rentier Politics* (Aldershot: Ashgate).

Ongh, A. (2006) *Neoliberalism as Exception: Mutations in Citizenship and Sovereignty* (Durham, N.C.: Duke University Press).

Ostrom, E. and Cox, M. (2010) 'Moving Beyond Panaceas: A Multi-Tiered Diagnostic Approach for Social–Ecological Analysis', *Environmental Conservation*, 37(4): 451–63.

Peluso N. and Watts, M. (eds) (2001) *Violent Environments* (Ithaca, N.Y.: Cornell University Press).

Perkins, J. (2005) *Confessions of an Economic Hit Man* (London: Ebury/Random).

Polanyi, K. (1944) *The Great Transformation* (Boston: Beacon Press).

Prebisch, R. (1950) *The Economic Development of Latin America and its Principal Problems* (Lake Success, N.Y.: United Nations).

Rodney, W. (1972) *How Europe Underdeveloped Africa* (London and Dar es Salaam: Bogle L'Ouverture Publications).

Rodrik, D. (2003) (ed.) *In Search of Prosperity: Analytic Narratives on Economic Growth* (Princeton, N.J.: Princeton University Press).

Roll, E. (1973) *A History of Economic Thought* (London: Faber and Faber).

Ross, M. (1999) 'The Political Economy of the Resource Curse', *World Politics*, 51(2): 297–322.

—— (2001) 'Does Oil Hinder Democracy?', *World Politics*, 53(3): 325–61.

—— (2004) 'How Do Natural Resources Influence Civil War? Evidence from Thirteen Cases', *International Organisation*, 58(1): 35–67.

Rosser, A. (2006) 'The Political Economy of the Resource Curse: A Literature Survey', IDS Working Papers 268.

Rostow, W. (1960) *The Stages of Economic Growth: A Non-Communist Manifesto* (Cambridge: Cambridge University Press).

Ryggvik, H. (2009) *Til Siste Dråpe: Om Oljens Politiske Økonomi* (Oslo: Aschehoug).

—— (2010) *The Norwegian Oil Experience: A Toolbox for Managing Resources?* Senter for Teknologi, Innovasjon og Kultur (Oslo: Unipub).

Sachs, J.D. and Warner, M. (1995) *Natural Resource Abundance and Economic Growth*, National Bureau of Economic Research Working Paper 6398 (December) (Cambridge, Mass.: National Bureau of Economic Research).

Sahlins, M. (1972) *Stone Age Economics* (Piscataway, N.J.: Transaction).

—— (1976) *Culture and Practical Reason* (Chicago: University of Chicago Press).

Sala-i-Martin, X. and Subramanian, A. (2003) *Addressing the Natural Resource Curse: An Illustration from Nigeria* (Washington, D.C.: International Monetary Fund).

Santos, B. de Sousa (1995) *Toward a New Common Sense: Law, Science and Politics in the Paradigmatic Transition* (New York: Routledge).

Sarraf, M. and Jiwanji, M. (2001) 'Beating The Resource Curse: The Case of Botswana', World Bank Environment Department Papers, Environmental Economics Series (October) (Washington, D.C.: World Bank).

Sawyer, S. (2009) 'Empire/Multitude–State/Civil Society: Rethinking Topographies of Power Through Transnational Connectivity in Ecuador and Beyond', in E. Fischer (ed.) *Indigenous Peoples, Civil Society, and the Neo-liberal State in Latin America* (New York and Oxford: Berghahan Books).

Scott, J. (1998) *Seeing Like a State: How Certain Schemes to Improve the Human Condition Have Failed* (Durham, N.C.: Duke University Press).

Singer, H. (1950), 'The Distribution of Gains Between Investing and Borrowing Countries', papers and proceedings of the 62nd Annual Meeting of the American Economic Association, *American Economic Review*, 40(2): 473–85.

Stevens, P. and Dietsche, E. (2008) 'Resource Curse: An Analysis of Causes, Experiences and Possible Ways Forward', *Energy Policy* 36: 56–65.

Synder, R. (2006) 'Does Lootable Wealth Breed Disorder? A Political Economy and Extraction Framework', *Comparative Political Studies*, 39(8): 943–68.

Tanter, R. (1990) 'Oil, IGGI and US Hegemony: The Global Preconditions for Indonesian Rentier-Militarization', in A. Budiman (ed.) *State and Civil Society in Indonesia* (Melbourne: Centre for Southeast Asian Studies, Monash University).

Tedesco, L. (2007) 'The Latin American State: "Failed" or Evolving?', Working Paper 37 (Madrid: Fride Foundation).

Torvik, R. (2002) 'Natural Resources, Rent Seeking and Welfare', *Journal of Development Economics*, 67: 455–70.

Tsing, A. (2005) *Friction: An Ethnography of Global Connection* (Princeton, N.J.: Princeton University Press).

Vandewalle, D. (1998) *Libya Since Independence: Oil and State-Building* (Ithaca, N.Y. and London: Cornell University Press).

Viner, J. (1952) *International Trade and Economic Development* (Glencoe, Ill.: Free Press).

Waal, A. de (2009) 'How Can We Make Peace Without Functioning State Institutions?', Chr. Michelsens Lecture 2009, unpublished manuscript.

Watts, M. (2008) *Curse of the Black Gold: 50 Years of Oil in the Niger Delta* (Brooklyn, N.Y.: Powerhouse Books).

—— (ed.) (2009) *Dictionary of Human Geography*, 3rd edn (with R. Johnston, G. Pratt and D. Gregory) (Oxford: Blackwell).

World Bank (2011) *World Development Report: Conflict, Security and Development* (Washington, D.C.: World Bank).

Wright, G. and Czelusta, J. (2007) 'Resource-Based Growth: Past and Present', in D. Lederman and W.F. Maloney (eds) *Natural Resources: Neither Curse nor Destiny* (Washington, D.C.: World Bank and Stanford, Calif.: Stanford University Press).

Wriston, W.B. (1986) *Risk and Other Four-Letter Words* (New York: Harper & Row).

Zalik, A. (2009) 'Zones of Exclusion: Offshore Extraction, the Contestation of Space and Physical Displacement in the Nigerian Delta and the Mexican Gulf', *Antipode*, 41(3): 557–82.

Part 1

Resource Sovereignties

Mario Martinez Choque, trade union veteran of a divided workforce at the tin mines in Huanuni, Bolivia. Photograph by Owen Logan.

2
On Curses and Devils: Resource Wealth and Sovereignty in an Autonomous Tarija, Bolivia

John-Andrew McNeish

When the people of Tarija awoke on 1 June 2009 they discovered that all the roads in and out of their city had been entirely blocked. This was the start of a nine-day protest by a local peasant union organisation[1] demanding an increase in hydrocarbon rent payments by the departmental government – based in the city – to agricultural and rural development in the surrounding area. Following similar mobilisations in 2004 and 2005, when the oil installations of Isayachi and San Alberto were occupied, the departmental government had agreed to create a Solidarity Programme (PROSOL) in which 2 million bolivianos of the regional budget was set aside in order to make direct payments to assist the economic development of peasant families. The new protest focused on the long delay in releasing these funds, and a new demand that was made on the basis of growing departmental oil and gas rents for the triplication of the PROSOL funds in the 2009 departmental budget. In the face of the departmental government's apparent reluctance to support the provinces, the protesters also proposed that a revision of the departmental budget should lead to a reduction in controls by the departmental government and direct payments to peasant communities.

For the rest of the nine-day blockade over 20 different locations and 30 different routes were guarded. As the days dragged on the mood turned from resignation to frustration and then to anger, insults and violence. Fights were started and following refusals by the departmental government to enter into dialogue with the peasant union the protestors threatened to close national borders, important highways elsewhere in the department were blocked, and the local government offices in the municipalities of Villamontes, Padcaya and Bermejo were occupied by protestors. Reporting on the blockades, local media coverage in Tarija's newspapers and television channels characterised the rural population as uncouth devils and condemned the peasants' behaviour as both careless and brutish. The peasants 'threaten the right of citizens to free passage, and sow violence and grave risk', stated an editorial of the local El Nacional *newspaper. The road blockades were furthermore dismissed as an expression of the dependency of the peasant community and a cynical attempt by the rural population to extract more handouts from the departmental government.*

Remembering the widespread civic disruptions that led to Bolivia's transformation into a pluri-national state between 2000 and 2005,[2] it is clear that the blockades described above are more typical than remarkable episodes in the country's recent history. However, whilst 'stones on the road' are far from uncommon in Bolivia, it is argued here that studying the background of these events provides some important insights into the dynamics of resources and autonomy in a region of Bolivia that has been little considered in comparison to the more extremist campaigns and actions in neighbouring lowland departments.[3] Indeed, as well as pointing to the fractures in local civil society and the dynamics of a departmental power struggle, I argue that the blockades in Tarija in 2009 are important indications of the linkages which exist between the politics of autonomy and the politics of resources in the region. Moreover, it is proposed in this chapter that these linkages point to a broader and more profound reflection on resource politics.

The conflicting economic demands described in the confrontation above are only too clear. However, by developing the history and ethnography of the wider social relations in which these events have taken place, the chapter reveals that political contests in Tarija are driven by more than demands for improvements to incomes and material standards. A fuller account of the historic and social embedding of economic demands demonstrates that the blockades were incited by a combination of factors. Here we discover inescapable desires for more in an economic sense, but also the historical underpinnings of regional social identities, an elusive social contract, and conflicting but not always polarised relationships to land and resources. Whilst this chapter is limited to a regional study, I argue here that the dynamics of resource wealth in Tarija are suggestive of far reaching insights into current confrontations between states and local populations. Not only does it become evident that conflict is not only a question of 'rent-seeking', implying a critique of the influential resource curse thesis, but that the politically incendiary nature of resource politics is best understood and addressed by recognising its complex roots in multiple – often overlapping and sometimes contradictory – ideas and claims for resource sovereignty. Drawing on research into the background to the blockade, the chapter suggests that the idea of resource sovereignty effectively brackets together historic grievances, territoriality and the sense of ownership and value that different groups and individuals have in relation to local natural resources.

REGIONAL SOCIAL IDENTITY AND TERRITORIALISM

Tarija is one of nine departments in Bolivia and is located on the country's border with Argentina and Paraguay. It is Bolivia's smallest department, with a territorial extension of 37.623 km². The department is constituted by two topographical zones: the Chaco (13.208 km²) and the Andean zone (20.833 km²). In the Chaco – a sparsely populated, hot and semi-arid lowland region – productive land is largely dedicated to extensive livestock raising and national nature reserves. In the national census of 2001, 80 per cent of the population in Tarija identified themselves as non-indigenous[4] making it the department with one of the smallest indigenous populations in the country.[5] According to the same census, 51 per cent of the population in the department live in poverty: 86.6 per cent in the rural area, and 30.5 per cent in the urban area.

Whilst social divisions in Tarija are partially a product of natural and ethnic divisions, historical memory and economic experiences have also played an important role in defining the social character of the department. Basic ethnic categories were defined early on in the region's colonial history, in which new spatial and racial orders were produced and imposed through processes of expansion and conquest. It is in this period, and not the current day, that nascent notions of Tarijeño frontiers, and hence autonomy, were created. Here there is both the start of the difficult negotiation of regional power in relation to the colonial state, and the formation of clear social divisions based on a combination of racial typologies and political realities. In their military confrontation with the indigenous population (i.e. the now extinct Churumata and Tomatas peoples of the central Valley, and the Guaraní of the sub-Andean valleys and the Chaco) the Spanish settlers not only encountered a natural frontier, but constructed a social 'frontier' to be conquered and tamed.[6] With conquest the positioning of the indigenous population became fixed in the eyes of the ruling Spanish elites: they were vassals, workers and 'other'. The colonial system constructed a system of political control and economic production based on forts and *encomienda* estates, where private contracts were formed between the state and private individuals to rule these spaces for the crown. Luis Fuentes y Vargas, the founder of the city of Tarija in 1574 (then San Bernardo de la Frontera de Tarija) was granted rights of 'greater justice' by the Viceroy Don Francisco de Toledo. This was in essence a feudal contract for political control, including the ownership of lands, rights over the indigenous population and usufruct rights for the entire territory. The *criollo* descendents of the Spanish also become the inheritors of a notion of the ownership of space and of the social divisions engendered in it. Indeed, these notions are carried through into the present day – even recognising the processes of *mestizaje* (ethnic mixing) and legal changes with regards to citizenship rights produced in the course of key events in national history (the wars of independence, formation of the republic of Bolivia, the nationalist revolution of 1952, ratification of ILO 169 in 1992, etc.). The divisions between city and countryside, central valley and Chaco, capital and province, *chaqueño* and *chapaco* that are used today still echo colonial spatial and racial logics.[7]

To a significant extent the persistence of these categories into the present relates to the continuance of agriculture as a fundamental part of the departmental economy, in which the categories of landowner and peasant remain in use. In contrast to Santa Cruz, the development of the agricultural industry in Tarija has largely taken place without the assistance of the central government. Until the 1990s Tarija was, as one informant[8] described it, 'an island surrounded by mountains', and the economy in the department remained largely closed. The first asphalted road between Tarija and the border with Argentina was built in 1997. As a result, the elites in the department have formed closer relations with Buenos Aires than with La Paz. The divide between the central valley and the Chaco has also persisted under these conditions. Distant from the control of the departmental authorities and the state institutions of law and order, the land-owning elites were able to ignore developments in human rights and exploit indigenous resources and labour without limitation. Whilst ethnic distinctions and the traditional economy have been protected by physical isolation, this does not however mean that Tarijeño society remained entirely static and closed. Lying at the junction of high mountain, valley and subtropical lowland environments, Tarija has always been a waypoint for population movement.[9] Indeed, for the purposes of this chapter it is important to note two major regional events in near memory that ruptured what had long been the features of a near 'feudal' order.

The introduction of structural adjustment policies in the mid 1980s to control Bolivia's hyperinflation and restructure the economy along the lines of neoliberal new public management caused mines in the highlands of the country to be either closed or privatised. It is estimated that 60,000 miners were laid off as a direct result of these changes, and that between 20,000 and 30,000 families arrived in Tarija in the 1980s in search of work and new opportunities. As Miguel Castro Arce[10] described their arrival in an interview:

> These people arrived ready loaded with another social imaginary, unionised and organised ideologically. And all of this formation they had previously used to confront the state they now used to organise themselves and better their conditions of life. They started to petition and put pressure on the municipal and departmental governments. In return they were largely rejected by the townspeople here, being seen as *collas* (highlanders), *morenas* (dark skinned), and so were forced to form new neighbourhoods in the periphery of the city. Here they came into contact with the local peasant and indigenous community. There was a natural connection of 'skin' between these groups. Now the Tarijeño peasants feel more identification with the poor *colla* than with the Tarijeño elite. In this way a new social and political basis was formed in Tarija. (13 February 2009)

Congruent with this new sense of organisational radicalism, the other major force for change has been the rising importance of the hydrocarbon industry in the department. The first oil well in Bolivia was drilled in Tarija in 1928, and serious production began after the takeover of the operations of North American-owned Standard Oil and the introduction of the first nationalisation process following the conclusion of the Chaco War (1932–35).[11] With the foundation of the national oil company, *Yacimientos Petrolíferos Fiscales Bolivianos* (YPFB), Bolivia moved into a position where it was able to meet domestic fuel demands, and Tarija as a department started to benefit from the returns and rents of the industry. Yet it was not until the 'capitalisation' of the YPFB during the government of Sanchez de Lozada that the industry really gained its full importance for the department. Capitalisation opened the way for a large influx of private investment and activity in the department. This influx of private investment, coupled with the discovery of what are known as the gas *megacampos* (mega-fields) of San Alberto, Sabalo, Margarita and Itau, created a flurry of economic activity in O'Connor and Gran Chaco – provinces previously marginalised from investment. The increased presence of transnational firms and exploratory projects in these districts revitalised the moribund hydrocarbons sector.[12] This presence was accompanied by large infusions of capital and technology and generated excitement about the possibility of massive infrastructure projects related to the transport and distribution of these gas reserves, with an eye to exporting to international markets.[13] While the physical expansion of the sector – through seismic testing, the sinking of exploratory wells and the construction of hundreds of miles of oil and gas lines – was largely confined to the Chaco region, the gas bonanza also meant that natural gas steadily seeped into and captured Tarija's wider economic and political life. Tarija became what one informant termed 'a hydrocarbon addict'.[14]

The abrupt departure of President Sánchez de Lozada in 2003 followed by continued pressure from social movements eventually led to the passage of a new Hydrocarbons Law (No 3058) in Bolivia in 2005. The new law claimed to guarantee Bolivian society a greater share of the benefits of hydrocarbon extraction and led to the establishment of a mechanism to reassign more financial resources towards regional governments – both producing and non-producing – via a Direct Hydrocarbons Tax, known as the IDH (*Impuesto Directo a los Hidrocarburos*: Supreme Decree 28701).[15] These changes radically transformed the public financing available at the departmental level in Tarija. The Department of Tarija's revenues soared from around US$66 million in 2004 to over US$237 million in 2007,[16] with hydrocarbon revenues accounting for over 80 per cent of the department's income. This revenue bonanza, which is also in part attributable to higher prices for fossil fuels in the world market,[17] sparked a flurry of infrastructure work looking towards what departmental government hoped was a bright future for regional development. Work started on a number of spectacular projects, including a string of reservoirs, a network of paved highways to spur Tarija's integration with national and international markets, and an Olympic swimming pool. For political leaders in Tarija, as well as other sectors of the population (including supporters of MAS[18] and the FSUCCT), the struggle over rents and the IDH was now seen as fundamental to the department's ambitions for regional economic development. However, despite the expansion of the hydrocarbon economy in the department, the prefect and departmental elites in Tarija argued that a further proportion of the IDH should be paid to the departmental government in recognition of the origins of the resources being extracted and of the fact that they were non-renewable. Tarija's new place in the political economy of Bolivia is captured in an interview statement by Maria Lourdes Vaca, the departmental delegate for autonomy:

> Tarija has an interesting position. Ninety-five per cent of the hydrocarbon resources in the country are found in the department. It is here that there is the possibility to generate the economy necessary to raise levels in the rest of the country. When a mayor or representative of a municipality inaugurates the completion of public works in the country, they are doing this with resources drawn from Tarija. This is fine, but we think that in this moment of autonomy [a reference to the new constitution] we should have the right to decide what to do with our resources, to invest them ... The development of the region has been postponed for years because of centralism. (22 February 2009)

This new sense of strategic positioning was also evident following proposals by the central government to nationalise a series of local service providers,[19] and particularly the Tarijeño Gas Company (*Empresa Tarijeña del Gas*, EMTAGAS). EMTAGAS delivers gas to 30,000 users in the department of Tarija. Although an agreement was finally made on joint ownership of the company, members of the Civic Committee in Support of Autonomy (*Comité Pro-intereses del Departamento de Tarija*) interpreted the proposal as a direct threat to what they saw as Tarijeño heritage (*patrimonio*). Underlining this position, on 21 May 2009 the Civic Committee placed an announcement in the local newspaper *El Nacional* presenting their 'Manifesto for the Nation and People of Tarija'. In this the Civic Committee declared a 'state of emergency and permanent mobilisation to protect the Tarijeño institutions'.[20] Complaints were also made about the way in which further reforms and inaction by the central government had eaten into promised departmental coffers and hampered the competitiveness of the hydrocarbons industry as a whole.[21]

The departmental complaints and claims of resource autonomy were met with little sympathy from the national government in La

Paz. In the case of the blockade mentioned at the start of this chapter, the Bolivian minister of finance, Luis Arce, stated that protesters' demands were realistic given the 6 per cent rise in the departmental budget in 2008. Arce argued that as a result of the high oil and gas prices, Tarija was positioned to receive the highest level of public investment in its history. The provocation for the blockades, he stated, lay with the poor financial management and open corruption of the departmental authorities (i.e. the misuse of funds for political propaganda, and failure to pay for and complete public works). According to official statistics Tarija is the department with the most resources drawn from the oil rents – 2,445 million bolivianos.

Analysts at the national level highlight that Tarija receives a disproportionate share of the IDH, given its relatively small population. Tarija produces over 60 per cent of Bolivia's natural gas, but accounts for only five per cent of total population. However, it receives 30 per cent of all royalties and IDH. This disproportionate sharing of hydrocarbon wealth is criticised, and it has been argued that the current system of distributing what is constitutionally the nation's wealth will impede the central government's ability to direct these resources towards reducing overall poverty and building a new economy beyond hydrocarbons. On this basis, the argument is made that a more equitable per capita formula should be applied to contribute toward the development of a broad-based economy.[22]

AN ELUSIVE SOCIAL CONTRACT

Following years of militant demonstration and protest highlighting the lack of democratic legitimacy of both sitting administrations and governmental structures, efforts were launched with the election of the Morales government in 2005 to re-establish a new social contract between the state and citizenry. As well as the formation of a Constitutional Assembly,[23] other key elements in this process have been a series of referendums held on the question of autonomy at both national and departmental levels over the last few years. These popular votes have been held by both the national and departmental governments in efforts to foster support and 'democratic' legitimacy for their opposing positions and plans. Throughout their campaign for departmental autonomy the prefect in Tarija and his supporters in local government and the urban Civic Committee were keen to profile their unity, their mandate to represent all, and to deny that there were any relevant ethnic and social divisions. Indeed, great efforts were made by the departmental government to fund public assemblies to which they claimed all sectors of the population had been invited.

> This is not a campaign of the right or the left. Nobody is excluded in this process. All are involved, the middle classes and the poor. Our agreement on autonomy has been agreed by popular vote. We have met with the indigenous communities of the Chaco. They are part of this process of autonomy. (Oswaldo Flores, President of the Civic Committee, 22 February 2009)

Despite these claims of unity and inclusion, throughout the autonomy campaign in Tarija municipal political leaders from the Chaco have periodically marked their dissidence with the prefect largely on the basis of their historic and ongoing marginalisation from departmental funds. Prior to the departmental referendum on autonomy in 2008, chaqueño political leaders held a sub-regional vote to select a sub-prefect and departmental councillor. The election anticipated the departmental referendum and laid down the gauntlet for Tarija's prefect to follow through with promises for further intra-departmental decentralisation. The departmental government responded to the challenge by refusing to recognise the legitimacy of the election and by calling for departmental unity, not separatism. A further marking of these difficult relations came in February 2009, when leaders of the main municipalities in the Chaco (Yacuiba, Caraparí, Villamontes) refused to take part in an extraordinary meeting being held by the departmental government to finalise autonomous by-laws. In the press coverage of their decision, the leaders stated that they were tired of the city of Tarija deciding their future and the development of the region.[24]

As indicated above, the division between Tarija and the Chaco has deep historical roots stretching back to the colonial frontiers and the Chaco War. Although defended as an area of national importance for its oil deposits, there was little effort in the twentieth century to support wider processes of economic and social development in the area. The modern roots to the claim for chaqueño autonomy can be traced to 1983 and the signing of an agreement by representatives of 16 civic committees from Tarija, Chuquisaca and Santa Cruz (Pacto de Quebracho) in which they argued for the creation of a department on the basis of the failure of the attention by departmental governments and their common identity.[25] This was renewed in 2004. The departmental governments had also discussed the idea of the creation of a macro-region of the Chaco. However, this was before the discovery of the *megacampos* of gas in the area. With the discovery of large deposits of gas, these claims for regional autonomy were no longer entertained by the departmental government in Tarija, but promises had to be made to increase the budgets of the local governments in the region; 45 per cent of the oil rents were promised in this deal.

The failure to deliver the promised funds marked the start of a more focused campaign for increased funding to the provinces.[26] At present, the departmental prefect is held as responsible by chaqeño leaders for the failure to pay out the agreed rents to the province of Gran Chaco. They also claim that promised public works, most importantly road projects, have not been completed as promised. Moreover, they lament the failure of the Association of Municipalities in Tarija (AMT) to coordinate with the government in their favour. Following pressure by elected leaders in the Chaco to push for regional autonomy under the conditions provided by the new national constitution, a referendum on regional autonomy was held parallel to national elections in December 2009. The municipalities of the Gran Chaco area, i.e. Caraparí, Villamontes and Yacuiba, supported autonomy with over 80 per cent of the vote.

Although with their own particular character, the protests and campaign for the autonomy of the Chaco areas have also periodically picked up support from oil workers' unions in the region. Whilst supportive of the government's renationalisation policy, both employees and proponents of the national oil company criticise its implementation. This criticism is captured in a comment made in an interview by Mirko Orgaz, a prominent left-wing intellectual strongly allied with the oil workers' union, in his home town of Camiri:

> There has not been a process of nationalisation, there has not been a refounding of the company [YPFB], there has not been a substitution of international companies by a state company, there is no control of prices, of volumes or of export. Furthermore the rents of the country's hydrocarbons continue to rest principally in the hands of the transnationals. It represents a political transference of contracts. (22 April 2008)

In 2008/9 oil workers carried out a series of strikes and road blockades marking their disgruntlement with the failure of the nationalisation process to return real control to domestic hands and reductions in the percentage of hydrocarbon rents distributed to their communities. A number of these protests coincided with the sub-regional campaign in the Chaco to defend and express sovereignty over hydrocarbon resources.

Division and confrontation has also been seen elsewhere in the department and city. Whereas meetings and assemblies were sponsored by the departmental government to discuss and democratise understandings of autonomy, press coverage and informants highlighted that certain interest groups were not invited, or were falsely represented at such events. This is captured in comments by the Human Rights Ombudswoman in Tarija, Mariel Paz:

> The basic problem is that it is not a product of a pact. It is not fruit of the agreement of the different sectors in the department. It is a vision created from the perspective of a political and urban elite. There are large and important sectors that have not participated in its elaboration; peasants, indigenous populations, women's organisations, migrants, popular organisations such as those of neighbourhoods. Indeed, they have been marginalised. You will find names in the documents saying they represent these interests, but in reality they represent personal interest and not these bases. As a result they have created a discourse which is discriminatory, often racist and exclusive. They have often said that people who are not in agreement can go and live in the West. This is a discrimination of those that think differently, who have not been born in Tarija, or who have been born here, but do not think like them. It is the sectors allied with MAS, the poor in the main have been those who have been excluded from the process of elaboration. (26 May 2009)

This failure of inclusion and genuine dialogue underlies the proliferation of blockades and protest actions in Tarija. However, the militancy of marginalised groups must also be explained in light of early confrontations with serious and grave outcomes. One of the more serious confrontations between supporters of the departmental campaign for autonomy and marginalised sectors occurred in 2008. On 10 September civic leaders in the city of Tarija called on residents to maintain a permanent vigil and to defend their city. Responding to the denunciations of the mobilisations of city-based *Tarijeños* in the Chaco by peasant controlled radio stations and rumours that members of the peasant union (FSUCCT) were intending to march in protest of these actions to the city main square, they called on city residents to defend themselves. However, when the protesters failed to appear, a group of pro-autonomy supporters decided to look for a showdown by marching on the union office at the *campesino* market. According to the union's general secretary, Amil Carperez,

> [t]hey came with a lot of dynamite, many of them drunk. They destroyed doors, windows and did everything to be threatening. There were not many of us here. We were going about our normal activities when these *muchachos* [lads] arrived. Group after group arrived, throwing dynamite at the building of the union. A total assault! They fought all day, both sides. We were helped by our peasant comrades and families. (Amil Carperez, Secretary General FSUCCT, 27 May 2009)

Social movement organisations and local vendors then mobilised to defend their businesses and their public space. An angry and violent confrontation pitched students and other urban youth against market vendors and peasants.[27] Over 80 people were injured, including a young construction worker who lost his hand when he mishandled a stick of dynamite.[28]

COMPETING RELATIONSHIPS TO LAND AND RESOURCES

Apart from direct violence, the question of a contract on autonomy and its connections with hydrocarbon resources in the department has generated more long-lasting forms of violence. These take the form of everyday petty brutalities and terror[29] and are embedded in the structural fabric of the socio-economic relations in the region (humiliations and legitimations of inequality and hierarchy).[30] Indeed, as became evident in tracing the reasons for recent confrontations, their content is fused tightly with, and leads us towards an explanation of, the incendiary nature of peoples' competing socio-economic attachments to both land and resources. This has perhaps come most strongly to the fore in the tensions between indigenous populations and efforts to expand hydrocarbon production in the region.

With the discovery of the *megacampos* and the investment that came with capitalisation, new wells were established in indigenous territories in the provinces of O'Connor and Chaco. In 1998 Repsol established three wells in Puerto Margarita. The wells were bored within two or three kilometres of local settlements and at least on one occasion within a few metres of a Guaraní community.

Although Bolivia had signed the International Labour Organisation's Convention 169 in 1993, which states that indigenous people have the right to prior consultation, no effort was made by the company, or government, to consult or share benefits with the local community. Indeed, according to Centre for Regional Studies in Tarija (CER-DET), who were asked to come and represent the community in 2000, there was no environmental impact study done of the area. When CER-DET arrived they were presented with a study carried out in Chuquisaca, a neighbouring department. The company initially refused any responsibility for any social and environmental damage identified by the community and CER-DET in the area, passing the buck to their national filial Maxus. Through negotiation between CER-DET, the Assembly of the Guaraní People (APG) and Repsol, some settlements were eventually made out of court,[31] but other promises of further development assistance from the company never arrived. Over the last few years the APG have been looking to gather from NGOs and lawyers in Ecuador and Spain the financial and legal assistance needed to sustain a case in the international courts. Although a moratorium on opening new blocks in this area resulted from tensions with the APG, Repsol have recently managed to launch plans with government support for another 23 wells in the same area once tensions abate.

Improvements in the monitoring of hydrocarbon extraction in the department did not take place until the Mesa government and the introduction of the new Hydrocarbons Law forced a tightening up of the regulations and rights surrounding hydrocarbon extraction. However, despite these improvements in the formal systems of monitoring and international rights mechanisms,[32] Alipio Valdez, the coordinator for natural-resource issues at CER-DET, reports that the mistakes made in Puerto Margarita have been repeated throughout the department. The rights of indigenous peoples to public consultation under new laws, including the presence of state officials and comprehensive documentation of social and environmental impacts, continue to be ignored. Indeed, according to CER-DET and the leadership of the APG, conditions have failed to improve despite the arrival of the Morales government and nationalisation.

The government administration remains structurally incapable of responding quickly to individual cases of damage, or of following up on the findings of local social and environmental monitors. Moreover, corners are still being cut and important safeguards are being ignored in the push to increase production. There have been multiple examples of this within the department, including the recent widening of the gas pipeline between Villamontes and Tarija, part of the Juana Azurduy Integration Gas Pipeline (GIJA).[33] In another case in San Andita, a community close to Yacuiba in the Aguaragüe National Park, contracts for an exploitation block have been signed between YPFB and Chinese owned Petrogas, and between YPFB and Venezuelan–Bolivian Petroandina, without the local Guaraní being informed or the holding of a public assembly on the issue. In August 2010 this sparked off a series of protests by the APG resulting in a blockade by the community of the Park area. In a statement echoing the situation in many other communities in Bolivia and elsewhere, Alberto Viorel, the community leader or *capitán grande*, questioned how there could be 'so much extractive activity in a protected area'. In Resistencia, the Weenayek community have also halted plans for further extraction until the regulations of consultation and documentation are fulfilled and co-benefits agreed.

Responding to indigenous opposition to the opening of new gas blocks in the Chaco, the national government has suggested in media reports that indigenous communities are being manipulated by the opposition, and are standing in the way of necessary national development.[34] Echoing the historic claims and exclusionary policies of earlier Bolivian 'rentier' governments, recent government utterances suggest – perhaps counter-intuitively given the government's celebration of indigenous rights and identity – that indigenous populations simply do not understand the complex requirements and pressures of national modernisation and development. Similar comments have also been made to defend government actions elsewhere in the country (these notably resemble statements made by other less progressive Latin American governments confronting indigenous communities over access to resources and territory).[35]

During the Climate Conference held in Cochabamba by the Morales government to drum up support for a People's Accord (Universal Declaration on the Rights of Mother Earth), controversy arose when indigenous leaders from the Lowlands and Highlands proposed the organisation of a working group, Table 18, on social conflicts in Bolivia related to the environment. The government's response to the unauthorised working group was in the first place to deny that it existed, and in the second to denounce Table 18 as the work of 'opponents and capitalists'. On hearing of the responses of the government to their actions, the *capitán grande* of San Andita commented that the government had misunderstood their intentions. 'We are not against the exploitation of natural resources and development, but we ask that they respect our community and our rights.'[36] A similar war of words was produced by the large-scale protest march by the *Confederacíon de Pueblos Indígenas de Bolivia* (CIDOB) in June 2010, which, in addition to questioning the government's proposal for autonomy, largely focused on the right to be consulted regarding extraction (e.g. the Aguaragüe National Park) and infrastructure projects (e.g. the planned bio-oceanic highway through the Isobore Secure National Park). Although a compromise was eventually reached, the response of the government to the march was again to accuse CIDOB of having been manipulated by foreign NGOs (USAID, CEJIS) and of being out of step with the necessities of national development.

The public statements by Guarani representatives quoted in the press and the issues raised by Table 18 at the Cochabamba conference make it clear that whilst indigenous communities are supportive of the government's discourse on sustainable economic development, they see no evidence of change in the conditions of economic exploitation. Whilst rights and social benefits have been expanded in the country through nationalisation, referendums and the establishment of a new constitution, promises of consultation, benefits and the avoidance of environmental pollution were still distant. These issues have been pushed in public statements by APG, and were present alongside calls for an alternative vision of a 'mother earth'-friendly (*Pachamama/madre tierra*) development in the wider discussions that took place at Table 18 and the CIDOB march. Whilst the government has introduced indigenous concepts such as *el buen vivir* (*sumaq q'amana*, or well-being) into the national constitution and made claims to 'lead by obeying' (*mandar obedeciendo*), criticism is made by Guaraní leaders of the government's failure to adopt in practice the essence of these ideas, i.e. of social and natural inclusion and democratic consultation. In view of this, Guarani and Weenayek communities see no reason to desist in their claims of self-determination and control over their lands.

Similar tensions and contrasting ideas about the significance and value of hydrocarbon resources to development were also evident at the departmental level in Tarija. Indeed, at the departmental level general responses to these damage claims by the local government has either been indifference, or the assignation of blame to the indigenous communities themselves. In the case of the Juana Azurduy gas pipeline the departmental government threatened to take the

APG to court for loss of earnings. In talking about indigenous rights and damage claims, Gabriel Geita, ex-departmental secretary for hydrocarbons, had this to say:

> Why should they have to say when the pipeline is buried in the ground? They argue that there are sounds (seismic testing) that disturb the animals where they live, the gas changes our customs, there are environmental impacts. I see these as motives of negotiation and extortion. If you give the compensation of a million dollars to a community of a thousand people nobody knows what happens to this money. Nobody knows! The *capitán grande* takes the money, and nobody hears from him anymore. It is like this in all the country. The oil fields are unfortunately in the sub-Andean area in indigenous territories. This is another factor making investment in Bolivia insecure.[37] (20 May 2009)

Perhaps then it is not surprising that confronted with such attitudes and mistrust the APG are campaigning to utilise the new constitution in a claim for the indigenous autonomy of their traditional territory, Itika Guasu.[38]

RESOURCES CURSE AND SOVEREIGNTY

As the introduction to this book outlines, a new consensus is emerging in resource studies that further work needs to be done on the various political and social variables that mediate the relationships between natural-resource wealth and development.[39] My own work in Tarija looks to contribute to these theoretical and empirical departures and, in line with the overall message of this book, to emphasise the importance of a socio-economics of oil and gas. However, whereas previous studies have started forcefully to stress transformations at the level of the nation state and above, I argue here that the accounts above can also tell us more about related processes at the level of the nation state and below. Indeed, whilst in agreement with political economy approaches that see processes such as those above in the light of wider processes of political change in Bolivia (including a questioning of the rules of globalisation and a rejection of neoliberalism) I think that the above account is suggestive of a longer and more deeply embedded history of political positioning and thinking in the department of Tarija.

On this basis I argue there is need to disaggregate political economy understandings of resource politics through an awareness of the social articulation of resource politics over time. It should be clear from my account that within the department of Tarija confrontations over access to and the benefits of hydrocarbon resource are deeply rooted in Bolivia's social history. The regional conflict over resources relates not only to economic and material interests, but to ideas of land and ownership, position, ethnicity and class laid down before and after the *megacampos* boom in 2000. Indeed, it is possible to pick out from the details of more recent political dynamics in Tarija the traces of contrasting, as well as at times overlapping, values given to land and resources that push both debate and conflict. In this way we may talk about the existence and operation of differing resource epistemologies in the same context.

Recognising that epistemologies are linked to historical grievance is important because it reveals that local contestations over autonomy are as much about social relationships as they are about material interests. Moreover, this indicates the opportunity to diversify and expand recent social science efforts to rethink the significance of sovereignty to resource questions.[40] In particular Blom Hansen and Stepputat's (2006, 2001) proposal of an abandonment of sovereignty as a site of de facto source of power and order, when expressed only in law or through enduring theories of legitimate rule, appears to be particularly relevant as an approach to understanding dynamics in contexts like Tarija. Blom Hansen and Stepputat argue that sovereignty is always an unattainable ideal and is ideologically weak in postcolonial societies where sovereign power historically was distributed among many forms of local authority. This seems particularly relevant as a theoretical grounding of dynamics in Tarija, where autonomy and linked contestation of resources can be interpreted as expressions of the unfinished and contested nature of state sovereignty. Here lies the reason for the failure of efforts at both the national and departmental level to create a social contract. It is also useful in packaging together the structural rooting, revival and creation of competing counter-narratives of sovereignty in a period of wider change and uncertainty. Indeed, the contested nature of sovereignty and the persistence of counter-narratives makes sense of the fact that legal pluralism is a constitutionally recognised characteristic of the state of the nation (and the claims of Bolivia in its 2009 constitution now to be a 'Pluri-national State'[41]). Sovereignty is also a metaphor for the power, political rationality and threat of violence found in contrasting resource epistemologies.

In recognising the existence of multiple competing narratives of resource sovereignty in Tarija, it is also necessary to nuance what has been until now an overly simplified depiction of the causes for contestation in the region and beyond. In Tarija, as elsewhere in Latin America, resource contestation has commonly been described as resulting from the dichotomous positions of capitalist/socialist ideas of modernity and industrial development in opposition to indigenous/ecological efforts to conserve and protect the environment. Ethnography of the social dynamics surrounding resources in Tarija suggests that this picture is misleading. Many more actors are present than are commonly acknowledged. Moreover, the positions of different sectors such as the national government, departmental governments, peasant organisations, marginalised urban sectors, sub-regional elites, and different indigenous communities are also not easily defined, and we can often see indications of overlapping ideological standpoints as well as incoherency or outright contradiction. Indeed, as a result of its history and particular events such as the Chaco War and the National Revolution in 1952, the social categories of peasant and indigenous slide into each other, and with them distinctions between class and ethnicity have become opaque. Here we are reminded not only to pay attention to the old axiom that the devil is often in the detail, but of a need to revisit Michael Taussig's (1980) analysis of the 'devilish' ways in which local populations use cultural expressions to recognise and reconcile, or to fetishise, the destructive and productive forces put into work by commodities and capital.

This leads us to conclude that, contrary to the presumptions of politicians and ecologically minded academics, indigenous and peasant communities[42] in Tarija are not necessarily reducible to one-dimensional cartoon avatars[43] that are always opposed to the existence and operation of the oil and gas industry in their territory. In common with departmental and sub-departmental leaders representing the urban *criollo/mestizo* population they see the possible financial and developmental benefits the industry can bring, as well as its dangers. There is no outright 'rejection of an extractivist regime', as commonly attributed to the indigenous in recent writing on resource contestation.[44] However, in marked contrast to the claims of governmental and industry officials, indigenous cultural and economic rights are, for the most part, being ignored.

Rather than creating security, the industry has produced more insecurity and precarity. It has done so by opening economic competition over rents and by legally questioning indigenous control over land and resource. Equally important, it has done so by dismissing local peoples' rights to consultation and their active interest in decision making and by belittling the organisation and leadership on which subsistence patterns are based; and it is responsible for the physical damage to the local environment on which indigenous people still depend. This critical nuancing of the position of indigenous peoples is important, not only because it helps to dispel some oversimplifications, but because in a wider sense it also breaks with the distraction of arguments that suggest that some cultures are more natural than others. These arguments are misguided in suggesting that a sustainable way of life is a matter of 'going back', and unwittingly they do indigenous peoples an injustice by creating and reinforcing overly static and sharp social divisions that sustain racism and conflict.[45] What is seen in Tarija is the complexity and difficulty faced by the Guaraní and Weenayek in balancing an 'ecosophy' whereby the liberal division of European modernity between nature and culture, humans and animals does not exist, combined with an effort to claim the development and modernity offered by the state and shared by their neighbours. While the expressions of sovereignty and governance arising in this context might be different, the indigenous communities are involved in the same process of constructing and weighing up the relative values of nature and modernity as are other Tarijeños, and, perhaps, as we are.

CONCLUSIONS: ON CURSES AND DEVILS

This chapter has charted the roots and character of resource politics in the department of Tarija. In doing so I sought to explain the background of peasant blockades and to clarify the problematic dynamics which underlie the campaign for autonomy. What links recent protests and autonomy together is not only a desire by certain sectors in the department for a larger take of hydrocarbon rents and taxes, but their historical relationships and social identities. These have resulted in the expression of different outlooks and conflicting expressions of sovereignty over land and natural resources.

Historic grievances between social groups are a more important factor than rent-seeking behaviour, and this in turn explains the difficulty of forming a social contract in support of broad-based development in Bolivia. Tarija may be regarded as a microcosm in this regard. Despite the rhetoric of unity and inclusion in the autonomy campaign, the failure to respect vastly different social conditions has resulted in the fragmentation of support and the inability of departmental leaders to make use of high referendum support to firmly establish the acceptance of by-laws and determine recognition under the new national constitution.

Recognition of the complex social dynamics of resource politics – an arena of politics that stretches well beyond the economic into processes of social, legal and cosmological plurality in postcolonial contexts – demands a fundamental re-examination of current approaches to resource governance. Whilst technocratic solutions such as economic diversification and transparent governance may be important issues at the level of the nation state, recognition of the depth and persistence of different resource epistemologies that arise from the problems of commodity fetishism and which expose the fractures of popular sovereignty makes it clear that other approaches may be needed before peace and development can be established.

If lasting solutions are to be found to resource-based conflicts it seems appropriate to argue that a return must be made to basic questions of power and participation. Without a realistic understanding of power, participation is a misleading concept. Moreover, the real curses and devils are in the detail of powerfully contested ideas of resource sovereignty. Indeed, the facts of differing and overlapping epistemologies and sovereignties highlight the necessity of developing tailor-made solutions to different resource environments, understood as interlinked physical, social and historical entities and not as disparate abstracted sites on a world map of resource politics. They furthermore highlight the fact that the possible solutions to current tensions lie more with acceptance of the underlying problem of sovereignty than they do with the current tendency to stress entirely separate and incommensurable life-worlds, i.e. the problem captured in the title of this chapter.

NOTES

1. Federación Sindical Única de Trabajadores Campesinos de Tarija (FSUCCT).
2. For more on this, see McNeish 2006.
3. Focus on the ongoing political divisions in Bolivia has largely been directed in both academic work and international media coverage towards the separatist and racist expressions of the Civic Committee of Santa Cruz, the attack on peasants and pro-MAS marches by the Cruceñist Youth Union (Unión Juvenil Cruceñista, or UJC), the capture and deaths of right-wing mercenaries and the attack instigated by departmental authorities in Pando that left more than 30 peasants dead.

4. Instituto Nacional de Estadísticas 2001.
5. This indigenous population identify themselves as *Quechua*, *Aymara*, *Guaraní* or belonging to two other smaller indigenous groups (*Weenayeck*s and *Tapiete*s). However, the more widespread urban and peasant population of the department also identify themselves according to their roots in the central valley or Chaco by describing themselves as *Chapacos* and *Chaqueños*.
6. Lizárraga and Vacaflores Rivero 2007.
7. UNDP 2003, p.19.
8. Guido Cortez, 10 February 2009.
9. Preston, Macklin and Warburton 1997.
10. Avina Foundation, Tarija.
11. It is important to note that the Chaco War, called by some historians a world war due to the involvement of the US and European powers in support and supply of both the Bolivian and Paraguayan forces, was also largely focused on the control of the nascent oil economy and its future reserves. The Chaco War is also widely reputed in Bolivia to have been responsible for forging, through the grotesque conditions of fighting in the semi-desert of the Chaco, the Bolivian *meztizo/campesino* identity that would be so instrumental a force in driving the later National Revolution. The war needs also to be recognised as playing an important role in encouraging regional feelings of autonomy. At least urban *Tarijeños* remember the war as one in which they sacrificed all for the protection of *their* way of life and *their* resources.
12. Perreault 2008.
13. Hindery 2004.
14. Gabriel Gieta, 20 May 2009.
15. The advent of the IDH in 2005 meant that departments which had not received any income from the oil and gas sector began to receive large infusions of funds and those which had already received royalties saw large increases. The law further stipulated that a new system be formed for the redistribution of the resources produced by the IDH; 4 per cent to the departments involved in production and 2 per cent to all other departments in the country. At the same time the Executive Power are to be given the power to use the income of IDH to favour the National Treasury, indigenous communities, municipalities, universities, the armed forces and the police. As a whole, the departments saw their budgets triple in the space of three years, and oil and gas revenues channelled through the IDH made up a huge proportion of departmental budgets (78 per cent).
16. Includes royalties and IDH. Royalties account for most of the revenue, about US$175.5 million in 2007. Royalties are paid directly to the prefectural government. The IDH however is distributed to the Prefecture (US$35.2 million) to Tarija's 11 municipal governments (US$21.3 million) and to the University Juan Misrael Saracho (US$5.3 million).
17. This bonanza has now ended. As of 1 April 1 2009, gas prices have been renegotiated with Brazil and Argentina, with prices dropping some 33 per cent from their highs in 2008.
18. Movement for Socialism.
19. COSETT, COSAALT and SETAR.
20. *El Nacional*, 21 May 2009.
21. In a departmental economic report, 'Tarija Changes, the People Live Better', released to mark the third year of departmental administration by the prefect Mario Cossío Cortez, the section on the 'Destination of the Rents and IDH'

lists what are called a series of confiscations from the department budgets (Prefectura de Tarija 2009). These include the redistribution of departmental funds to the municipal governments, the payment of the new pension fund from 30 per cent of the departmental IDH, the failure to tax rents and IDH from transfers of gas to Brazil (105 million bolivianos), and changes to the law governing the timing of rental payments. It is claimed that this amounts to a total loss of 759 million bolivianos. As well as direct budgetary impacts, departmental leaders and supporters of the prefect also questioned the way in which the current government is handling the industry as whole, and the way in which this impacts on their development plans.

22. Wanderley 2008.
23. McNeish 2008.
24. El País, 11 February 2009, p.9.
25. Lizárraga and Vacaflores Rivero 2007.
26. This campaign has, however, wavered in its focus from time to time. Indeed, in 2008 an alliance was formed with the departmental governor to support the strikes and road blocks called by provincial leaders in opposition of nationalisation and in defence of local resources.
27. Bebbington and Bebbington 2009.
28. El Diario, 2008.
29. See, for example, Scheper-Hughes and Bourgois 2004.
30. See, for example, Bourdieu 1997.
31. US$180,000 dollars (for two years of monitoring), US$300,000 (settlement for lost earnings) and US$80,000 (community development project).
32. In particular the 2008 United Nations Declaration on the Rights of Indigenous Peoples.
33. See 'APG amenaza con paralizar proyectos energéticos en Tarija', El Diario, 29 August 2010, www.eldiario.net/noticias/2010/2010_08/nt100829/3_01ecn.php
34. See 'YPFB dice que indígenas traban las inversiones', La Razon, La Paz, Bolivia, 21 September 2009.
35. See for example the 2008 Colombian minga, the Belo Monte case in Brazil, Alan Garcia's response to the deaths at Bagua in Peru in 2009, confrontations over mining in Peru, Chile and Guatemala, the controversies surrounding REDD projects in Brazil and Guyana, and the Chevron oil case in Ecuador.
36. See Observatorio Boliviano de los Recursos Naturales, 1, Boletin Especial, August 2010.
37. Here he also referred to the 2009 Global Petroleum Survey published by the Canadian Frazier Institute, in which indigenous mobilisation together with progressive labour and employment legislation are cited as reasons for Bolivia being the least attractive country in the world for foreign investment in the oil and gas industry.
38. Interview with Benildo Vaca, 16 February 2009.
39. McNeish 2010.
40. Agamben 1998.
41. Estado Pluri-nacional.
42. Between which, as in the rest of Bolivia, there are as many social commonalities as ethnic differences – class and ethnicity slide into each other.
43. Bebbington and Bebbington 2010.
44. Ibid.; Gudynas 2010.
45. Milton 1996.

REFERENCES

Agamben, G. (1998) *Homo Sacer: Sovereign Power and Bare Life* (Palo Alto, Calif.: Stanford University Press).

Bebbington, A. and Bebbington, D. (2009) 'Anatomy of a Regional Conflict: Tarija and Resource Grievances in Morales's Bolivia', *Latin American Perspectives*, 37(4): 140–60.

—— (2010) *An Andean Avatar: Post-neoliberal and Neoliberal Strategies for Promoting Extractive Industries*, BWPI Working Paper 117.

Blom Hansen, T. and Stepputat, F. (2001) *Ethnographic Explorations of the Postcolonial State* (Durham, N.C. and London: Duke University Press).

—— (2006) 'Sovereignty Revisited', *Annual Review of Anthropology*, 35: 295–315.

Bourdieu, P. (1997) *Pascalian Meditations* (Stanford, Calif.: Stanford University Press).

Gudynas, E. (2010) 'The New Extractivism of the 21st Century: Ten Urgent Theses about Extractivism in Relation to Current South American Progressivism', *Americas Program Report*, January 21. See www.americaspolicy.org.

Hindery, D. (2004) 'Social and Environmental Impacts of World Bank/IMF-Funded Economic Restructuring in Bolivia: An Analysis of Enron and Shell's Hydrocarbon Projects', *Singapore Journal of Tropical Geography*, 25(3): 281–303.

Instituto Nacional de Estadísticas (2001) *Características Socio-demográficas de la Población* (La Paz, Bolivia: INE).

Lizárraga, A. and Vacaflores Rivero, C. (2007) *Cambio y poder en Tarija: la emergencia de la lucha campesina* (La Paz: PIEB, JAINA, Plural).

McNeish, J.-A. (2006) 'Stones on the Road: The Politics of Participation and the Generation of Crisis in Bolivia', *Bulletin of Latin American Research*, 25(2): 220–40.

—— (2008) 'Constitutionalism in an Insurgent State: Rethinking the Legal Empowerment of the Poor in a Divided Bolivia', in D. Banik (ed.) *Rights and Legal Empowerment in Eradicating Poverty* (London: Ashgate Publications).

—— (2010) 'Rethinking Natural Resource Conflict', background paper for the World Development Report (Washington: World Bank).

Milton, K. (1996) 'Cultural Theory and Environmentalism', in *Environmentalism and Cultural Theory: Exploring the Role of Anthropology in Environmental Discourse* (London and New York: Routledge).

Perreault, T. (2008) *Natural Gas, Indigenous Mobilization and the Bolivian State* (Geneva: UNRISD).

Preston, D., Macklin, M. and Warburton, J. (1997) 'Fewer People, Less Erosion: The 20th Century in Southern Bolivia', *Geographical Journal*, 163(2): 198–205.

Scheper-Hughes, N. and Bourgois, P. (2004) *Violence in War and Peace: An Anthology* (Malden, Mass. and Oxford: Blackwell Publishing).

Taussig, M. (1980) *The Devil and Commodity Fetishism in South America* (Chapel Hill, N.C.: University of North Carolina Press).

UNDP (2003) *Informe de desarrollo humano de Tarija* (La Paz: Plural).

Wanderley, F. (2008) 'Beyond Gas: Between the Narrow-Based and Broad-Based Economy', in J. Crabtree, and L. Whitehead (eds) *Unresolved Tensions: Bolivia Past and Present* (Pittsburgh: University of Pittsburgh Press).

3
A Contribution to the Critique of Post-Imperial British History: North Sea Oil, Scottish Nationalism and Thatcherite Neoliberalism

Terry Brotherstone

According to the memoirs of Margaret Thatcher's longest-serving chancellor of the exchequer, Nigel Lawson, 'defeatism' in Britain, 'although still endemic in many places' was 'on the retreat' in the 1980s. For Lawson, a committed Thatcherite writing soon after falling out with his leader and leaving office in 1989, free-market capitalism, the privatisation of state assets and the defeat of trade-union militancy (embodied for him by Arthur Scargill, the left-wing National Union of Mineworkers' leader) had by then reversed a tide of post-imperial 'decline'.[1] Beginning with the humiliating collapse of the Suez invasion in 1956, this had reached its nadir with the acceptance, by a Labour government 20 years later, of an International Monetary Fund (IMF) loan that was conditional on public spending cuts. In a 1982 lecture entitled 'What's Right with Britain?' Lawson, energy minister at the time, particularly 'castigated those who contrived to make even the discovery of North Sea oil [in 1969] into a curse'. Two years before, Michael Edwardes, the boss of the vehicle manufacturer British Leyland, had angrily told a Confederation of British Industries conference that, if the government could not act to prevent the North Sea oil revenues from strengthening sterling to the extent that British manufactures were priced out of export markets, they 'should leave the bloody stuff in the ground'. The reality, Lawson insisted, was that offshore oil arrived when it was of 'unprecedented value and strategic importance'.[2]

The strategy to which the oil revenues and years of energy self-sufficiency were so important is now referred to as neoliberalism, and, as Naomi Klein has argued in *The Shock Doctrine*, its implementation in the United Kingdom is of global importance.[3] Thatcherism showed that free-market doctrine could be imposed in an established Western democracy, without the sort of murderous 'shock' inflicted on the Chilean people in 1973 at the stadium in Santiago by the CIA-backed dictator Augusto Pinochet. Thatcher's slogan, 'There is no alternative' (TINA), was infiltrated into the 'common sense' of British politics when, after a catastrophic election defeat of 1983 and the unprecedented mobilisation of state force to defeat the 'Scargillism' of the mineworkers' union in 1984/5, the Labour opposition gradually accepted it. When Labour returned to office in 1997, it was as Tony Blair's 'New Labour', committed to nothing more radical than smoothing some of Thatcherism's roughest edges. Lawson attributes this success of neoliberalism essentially to what he and his co-thinkers regard as the correspondence of the ideology of free-market capitalism with 'human nature'.[4] But his account of how the policy was implemented in Britain is notable for its acknowledgement of the *strategic* importance of the offshore windfall. The largely self-serving memoirs of most of his former cabinet colleagues – including Thatcher's own – seldom mention it.[5]

Commenting on this, the journalist Andrew Marr surmises that Thatcher's amnesia could stem from her embarrassment that a crucial industry, dependent on the entrepreneurial spirit she espoused as her own, was something for which she 'could take absolutely no credit'.[6] But it also raises bigger questions. It is more realistically seen as concealment integral to a complacent account of British history since the 1980s (to which Marr's book for the most part contributes)[7] that played an essential part in embedding Thatcherite ideology in British political discourse.

'The only duty we owe to history is to rewrite it,' remarked Oscar Wilde;[8] and the global financial and economic crisis that began in 2007/8 provides a new vantage point for the overdue historical discussion about the significance of UK North Sea oil. Those who embraced TINA had good reason to treat the offshore story as a sideshow. It had to be free-market ideology – the acknowledgement of the final triumph of capitalism, which Francis Fukuyama later called (at first with a question mark but then without it) 'the end of history' – that, supposedly, had transformed Britain.[9] But the early twenty-first-century crisis exposed market fundamentalism, and, while it was quickly clear that it had produced no radical rethinking amongst the decision-making elites, it provided the stimulus both for a new period of mass actions against attacks on living standards and for a critical discourse about the significance of the period of neoliberalism's rise. One aspect of this was that questions about how the United Kingdom had earlier dealt with its offshore revenues began to be asked again.[10]

An 'official' two-volume history of UK North Sea oil and gas, by the energy economist Alex Kemp (published, dated 2012, since this chapter went to press), will provide a new foundation for historical interpretation, which must not be confined to retrospective profit-and-loss accounting. The rich diversity of experience – of personal and national aspiration, of entrepreneurial adventure and devastating tragedy – the UK North Sea story embraces can be sampled in the major University of Aberdeen 'Lives in the [UK North Sea] Oil Industry' [LOI] oral life-story collection.[11] It is perhaps not surprising indeed that journalists with a historical eye have been quicker than archive-bound academic historians to grasp the possibilities of such narratives; and that there is a journalistic quality to the only monograph on the history of North Sea oil to predate the official history.[12] A recent general study of the role of the 'black gold' in twentieth-century Britain provided important scholarly context but was not concerned with a wider debate about the role of North Sea oil in the interpretation of late-twentieth-century British history and the relevance of this history in understanding the global crisis of the twenty-first century.[13]

Helge Ryggvik's recent *The Norwegian Oil Experience* makes an important comparative contribution to such a discourse.[14] And the appearance – as this chapter was being revised – of Ian Rutledge and Philip Wright's edited volume on 'market fundamentalism' and UK energy policy provides a pioneering mainstream critique of 'the less than desirable role' of finance capital in determining 'UK public policy'. The editors focus on the argument of global management consultant Philip Ellis that '[t]he passive role ... government has played in energy security since the Thatcher–Reagan revolution is a luxury we can no longer afford';[15] and on the need for UK energy policymakers, 'having led the world in promoting free market dogma', to recognise the necessity to 'swing sharply away' from it.[16] But their book is also relevant to the development of a broader argument about the role played by the UK North Sea oil revenues in the origins of Thatcherism; and, thereby, in the history of neoliberalism as a whole.

My perspective derives from two main sources. First, I worked with Hugo Manson on the LOI oral-history project, listening to the stories of many usually unheard people who have worked in, or had their lives affected by, the industry; and reflecting that their experiences can mean as much for understanding the oil story as those of the decision makers who are conventionally deemed to 'make history'. Second, I arrived at Aberdeen University as a young history lecturer a year before oil was first discovered, so that my experience of the city coincided with its emergence as the 'Oil Capital of Europe'.[17] My ideas about rethinking this history are also conditioned by my having been a correspondent in the 1970s for the daily newspaper of a would-be revolutionary socialist party, when the theory behind my reporting was a conception of the predictive potential of Marxism that has been overtaken by the unpredicted realities of the intervening decades. For me revisiting the history of North Sea oil is linked with attempting a radical critique of historical and political theory, and, although my angle is personal, I think the project is of wider concern. There is a need for a contemporary history of the United Kingdom which, in demystifying Thatcherite neoliberalism, contributes to new theoretical foundations for those now looking beyond it – and, as the Marxist political philosopher István Mészáros puts it, in contributing to a 'theory of transition', 'beyond capital' itself.[18]

In seeking to contribute to such work, this chapter addresses the ways in which the prospect of oil wealth helped frame British political aspirations in the 1970s; elaborates briefly on how rethinking a theoretically misconceived 1970s approach to the wider historical significance of UK North Sea leads me, not to abandon the need for such theorising, but to approach it very differently today; and contrasts this approach with the lacuna in most conventional histories of post-imperial Britain where the story of North Sea oil should be. It concludes with some hypotheses to be tested in what I anticipate will be a new period of interest in that story.

THE COMING OF OIL: EXPECTATIONS AND CONCEALMENT

The two central themes in recent British history to which a critical narrative of North Sea oil and its economic and financial advantages for the Westminster government should contribute are the collapse of social democracy and the rise of neoliberalism; and the devolution of political decision making on domestic issues to the United Kingdom's peripheral nations, particularly Scotland. But these developments were not what was anticipated when the prospect of North Sea oil dawned. In 1973, for example, Laurance Reed, member of parliament for Bolton East, warned against under-estimating the significance of the discoveries, which had 'profound strategic, economic and political implications', with the potential to make the 1980s 'Britain's decade'. Far from being relegated further, the United Kingdom would be restored 'to the first division'. Britain's leaders would not have to go cap-in-hand to Washington: US presidents would be 'dropping in here to cultivate us'.[19]

Labour prime minister Harold Wilson, at the opening of the Forties field in 1975, claimed this was a rare moment at which 'without the benefit of hindsight' he could 'identify ... "the turning-point" beloved of historians and journalists'.[20] What he surely anticipated was the creation of economic conditions to underpin industrial regeneration, improved state welfare, and a redefined independent British role in world affairs, as the basis for maintaining the post-war, social-democratic political consensus – the revival, that is to say, of the vision of a technologically efficient social democracy that he had proclaimed in 1963, but which had proved beyond his power as premier from 1964 to 1970 to bring about.[21]

Twenty-one months earlier, in January 1974 – over a year away from first oil – the former Conservative prime minister Harold Macmillan told an aspirant politician, Alan Clark, on the eve of a crisis general election prompted by a coalminers' strike, that the poll 'would be a disaster' for Edward Heath's Conservative government. 'The working class [would] see it as a loyalty vote ... The miners had to be bought off until North Sea oil came on stream.' Then the trade unions could be 'outmanoeuvre[d]', and, Macmillan implied, the oil wealth could be used to underpin the restoration of the sort of Conservative rule he had presided over as premier for the six years after the Suez fiasco – 'One Nation' Toryism based on moderate social reform.[22]

The miners' power to provoke the February 1974 election had come in part from the Arab oil price hike following the Yom Kippur War, which in itself was a factor in the British government's decision to produce North Sea oil as quickly as possible, with little long-term planning.[23] Macmillan proved right about the election: Heath failed to win it or to recover office in a second poll in November. But his aspiration to see the oil windfall used for a social policy reworking the political relationship between government and the working class without deepening conflict foundered in 1975 when a right-wing reaction in his party against, not simply a twice-defeated leader, but also the perceived failure of post-war 'consensus' politics to safeguard the interests of capital, catapulted Margaret Thatcher into the Conservative leadership. By the time she became prime minister four years later, her influential free-market supporters, if perhaps not yet Thatcher herself or the majority of her party, were committed to a radically new economic strategy and were clear that defeating (not merely 'outmanoeuvring') the unions was necessary for the social discipline their policies required.[24] In 1984 Thatcher was to vilify the miners' union as 'the enemy within' – the domestic equivalent of the Argentinean *Junta* she had taken on abroad two years earlier in the conflict over *las islas Malvinas*.[25] From the beginning Macmillan was horrified by Thatcher's policies; but his memorandum cautioning the new prime minister against her destructive approach to the social infrastructure was ignored.[26] No patrician rebuke was to stand in the way of *her* Conservative government.

Shortly before the first 1974 election, the economist and government adviser Gavin McCrone prepared a 'secret' paper – initially for the Scottish Office but later sent confidentially to the Cabinet Office – about the Scottish National Party (SNP)'s claim that, with oil revenues, an independent Scotland would be economically viable.[27] Unionist politicians (both Labour and Conservative) claimed that the Nationalists were exaggerating the potential oil revenues, and McCrone's memorandum was given added relevance by the election results. In February an indecisive outcome resulted in a minority Labour government and in November Labour won a minuscule majority; but the SNP – first victorious in a fully contested Westminster election only as recently as 1967 – secured first seven, then eleven parliamentary seats (some 10 and 15 per cent respectively of Scotland's MPs) and, in November, over 30 per cent of the Scottish popular vote. Its key slogan was, 'It's our oil.'[28]

Most of the oil reserves were in what – had Scotland been an independent nation – would have been 'Scottish waters',[29] and the Nationalists claimed that oil wealth could make Scotland a prosperous Scandinavian-style social democracy. 'The case for Scottish nationalism' was not purely economic, McCrone pointed out, but 'it has been much more concerned with economic prosperity than nationalist movements in other countries', mainly because of 'persistent unemployment' in the industrial West and emigration. The SNP's argument that independence would solve these problems had 'until recently lacked credibility'. But the idea that Scotland 'derived more advantage than disadvantage from the Union' was called in question by North Sea oil more acutely 'than at any time since the Act of Union' in 1707 – although the 'full significance' of this remained 'concealed from the Scottish public'.

McCrone compared the British government's deals with the oil companies unfavourably with those done in Norway; and concluded that 'all that is wrong now' with the SNP's estimate of the potential oil revenues 'is that it is far too low'. Oil money could make Scotland superabundantly wealthy. McCrone thought there were other factors, to do with history, politics, financial governance and international affairs that militated strongly against independence. But it was not at all certain that a majority of Scottish electors, given full information about the oil's potential, would continue to vote against separation.[30] No UK government, in the midst of the post-imperial crisis soon to come to a head with the 1976 IMF intervention, could contemplate what was entering academic discourse as 'the break-up of Britain'.[31] Aside from the further political instability it would cause, the oil revenues were crucial to a UK recovery.[32] The McCrone memorandum was to remain confidential for 30 years.

In the USA the possibilities of oil money reviving (and perhaps dividing) a floundering Britain were followed closely. In 1973 Richard Funkhouser, a former ambassador with experience of the international oil industry, became US consul in Edinburgh, monitoring affairs in what might become another oil state with which his country had to deal; being a natural neoliberal proved no barrier to his developing considerable sympathy for the SNP.[33] In January 1975, Secretary of State Kissinger told President Ford that 'Britain is a tragedy; it has sunk to begging, borrowing and stealing until North Sea oil comes in'.[34] Later that month, Wilson and his foreign secretary, Jim Callaghan, visited the White House, in part to provide an upbeat account of Britain's energy prospects. In his 1974 election rhetoric Wilson had claimed, semi-seriously, that by 1985 'the Labour Secretary of State for Energy will be chairman of OPEC'.[35] In the Oval Office his aside, '[i]n six years, when Jim is Chairman of OPEC ...', drew from Kissinger the comment: 'A terrifying thought!'[36]

North Sea oil began to arrive in the United Kingdom in mid 1975 at an event we can revisit through two contrasting recollections. The British energy secretary was Tony Benn – a politician notable for his sharp move to the left in the early 1970s and for publishing voluminous diaries. Benn played a key part in the government that succeeded Heath's, settling the wage demands of the miners and embarking on the rescue of the United Kingdom from chaos by governing in alliance with the trade-union leaders. In the spring of 1975, he had been moved – as Wilson sought to reassure the City of London and international finance that his government represented no threat – from the Department of Industry, where, inter alia, he had promoted worker cooperatives, to Energy.[37]

On 18 June 1975 Benn attended 'the first landing of North Sea Oil' on a tanker in the River Medway, at a 'ravaged, desolate, industrial landscape' made to look 'quite beautiful' by fine weather and perhaps also by the sunny economic prospect the oil offered. But the thoughts recorded in his diary were dominated by disgust at the 'complete cross-section of the international capitalist and British Tory establishment' present. He was 'so glad [his wife] Caroline was there to talk to'.[38] Caroline Benn, however, was no passive companion. She left her mark on Frederic Hamilton, the American capitalist whose small Denver-based firm had beaten the majors in bringing the first UK North Sea oil ashore.

Hamilton told Hugo Manson he thought that Benn 'realised ... it was important to Britain what we were doing'.

He was very much union orientated, but we had to get along with him – and the only thing I remember specifically was the day we brought the first oil ashore ... [Benn] was saying ... 'We've got our own oil supplies now; we don't have to rely on the Middle East. This is the greatest thing that has happened to Britain!' ... Everybody was very positive ...

Except, he recalled, the 'American girl', Caroline Benn:

'Mr Hamilton ... I don't care about all that,' she said ... 'How many lives were lost to get this first barrel of oil ashore?' And ... I said: 'Is this your only comment?' She said ... 'That's all I care about.' So I said: 'Well, I don't have any idea; but it pales into insignificance compared to what this'll do for the economy of Great Britain and the rest of the world.'... I thought, 'Boy, maybe that's why Tony Benn is such a [*uncompleted*] ... as difficult as he is, he's got a wife who was just an absolute ... [*uncompleted*]! And she was an *American*!'[39]

Others too, interviewed for LOI, noted the casual attitude to safety. In the mid 1980s, Tim Halford, PA to Occidental Oil's Armand Hammer, accompanied his boss to the Piper Alpha platform north-east of Aberdeen. Hammer's comment that '[y]ou can just feel those dollars flowing underneath!' stayed with him. He told Manson that the remark was prompted by vibrations palpable on the platform deck – more rationally perceived as signs of danger than of profit.[40] On 3 July 1988, Piper Alpha exploded in the North Sea industry's greatest disaster, in which 167 workers and rescue-vessel personnel died.[41] By then North Sea oil had already delivered much of the economic benefit Hamilton had celebrated in 1975 and the strategic advantage to the Thatcher government Lawson had acknowledged in 1982; but, at the expense – it was now horrifyingly clear – of the failure to prioritise human life exemplified by Hamilton's dismissal of Caroline Benn's concerns.[42]

The policy of rapid exploitation meant dependence on overseas experience rather than developing the necessary expertise in the United Kingdom.[43] It was primarily the American majors, with their anti-trade-union culture, that were on hand. The unions were, at best, sidelined and were unable to play an effective role in health-and-safety policy – in contrast both to the industrial-relations culture established in the United Kingdom after the Second World War, when the trade unions were recognised in Winston Churchill's oft-quoted phrase as 'an estate of the realm', and to the role the unions played in Norway.[44] Yet this, like the story of North Sea oil generally, has struggled to find its way into histories of the period, which might have been expected to interrogate why so modern an industry should have risked such a major human disaster.[45]

In the 1970s, then, it was widely perceived that the arrival of North Sea oil represented a historic moment. Wilson and Macmillan, in different ways, envisioned the oil reviving the basis for social reform and consensus politics. McCrone explained that an important change in the economic balance of forces between the two largest (albeit unequal) component nations of the United Kingdom had taken place and argued that Scotland required particular consideration. But for the Thatcherites the oil was primarily to be a facilitator for neoliberalism. The change is symbolised by the English poet Al Alvarez, who, eager for adventure in the early 1980s, reported on the industry for the *New Yorker*.[46] One evening on the deck of an accommodation platform he was joined by a small man concentrating on his physical exercises, who 'nodded brusquely at the shimmering lights spread around us in the darkness' and, before marching quickly away, said, 'You know what that is? ... That's what keeps our country solvent.'[47] Participants still knew they were engaged in a vital economic enterprise, but it was one now largely concealed from public debate. The strategy to which its revenues had been committed was very different from the optimistic social perspectives of the discovery years.

THE NEED FOR THEORETICAL REORIENTATION:
A TROTSKYIST MISSES THE FULL STORY

When, in 1968, I arrived in Aberdeen, I had no idea it was about to become the urban base of the United Kingdom's most dynamic industry. The distinctively grey-granite capital of a beef- and whisky-producing region, its industries included fishing, fish processing, paper making, woollen manufactures and small-scale shipbuilding and engineering. It was seen as remote and parochial, liable to cede to the more central Dundee its status as Scotland's third city after industrial Glasgow and Edinburgh, the administrative capital. In 1969 a report on economic prospects by an Aberdeen University economist sought remedies for the problems of urban decline that made no mention of offshore energy.[48] That year the oil was discovered, and, though the city was slow to respond and was by no means certain to become the industry's onshore 'capital', its advantages – certainly when compared to Dundee – included an airport with space for development and a reputation for relatively untroubled industrial relations.

I had joined the Trotskyist Workers Revolutionary Party (WRP) and contributed to its daily newspaper.[49] My reports focused on declining industries where there were stories of working-class struggle, but, although my most direct experience of the offshore industry was on trains overcrowded with rowdy roughnecks and roustabouts, I tried to pay attention to some of its more accessible aspects. My writing, an editor told me, interested some newspaper people in London: it was 'different' in its stress on the negatives in the story. There was a Klondike atmosphere of hit-and-miss enterprise as Aberdeen's conservative gentility (and well-concealed poverty) faced boomtown frenzy and divisive social upheaval. There were fortunes for a few, impossible house prices for many; money-to-burn for passing-through offshore workers, diminishing opportunities for others dependent on declining industries.[50] I gave over-eager weight to business failures, seeing them as further evidence that British capitalism could not escape what 'the party' claimed was its terminal crisis. Signs that working-class militancy – very evident in the Scotland of industrial decline – might spread to workers in the new oil-and-gas-related enterprises were emphasised.

Social revolution, held back according to WRP thinking largely by working-class leadership 'betrayals', seemed briefly plausible. The possibility of Thatcherism went unanticipated; or, if contemplated, only showed the importance of averting that outcome by 'building revolutionary leadership'. Behind this was the idea that Lenin's 1916 pamphlet, 'Imperialism: The Highest Stage of Capitalism' (1964), whatever updating it might need, was the essential guide to the epoch. Lenin's analysis (as we understood it) told us that the First World War had signalled that the twentieth century would be capitalism's final epoch – with Britain entering it as the oldest, most decadent, finance-capital-dominated advanced economy. Surely even the oil windfall could not – whatever the optimistic rhetoric – reverse the tide of history. It seemed much less significant than the defeat, in its trial of strength with the trade unions, of the 1970–74 Conservative government – the most dramatic moment in times so far from the normality of British politics that they are tellingly described in the title of Francis Wheen's witty account of the 1970s as 'strange days indeed'.[51] On the political right there were those for whom Heath's fall in the heat of a class struggle presaged the descent into chaos; on the left it could be seen, not entirely implausibly, as a pre-revolutionary moment.

But it was not. A neoliberal world later, it can be seen that Britain was not ripe for revolution – although, as Mészáros argues, the late 1960s and early 1970s *were* critical in a new stage of crisis in the capital system.[52] I return in conclusion to how Mészáros's ideas lead me to suggest that rethinking historically the impact of North Sea oil on Scotland and the United Kingdom in the light of a critical reassessment of Lenin's characterisation of the twentieth century might contribute to the wider discussion I am arguing is needed.

FILLING A LACUNA IN CONTEMPORARY BRITISH HISTORY

North Sea oil and gas production is hidden from view. There are no oil communities as there were coalmining ones. Oil is produced, as very often are the facilities for its production, far from public view. The oil, unlike coal, remains underground, delivered largely unseen until pumped into vehicles, heating systems or whatever. And this has become an apt metaphor for a lacuna – the lack of attention to the industry – in academic histories of contemporary Britain. The trend is typified by Peter Clarke's in other ways exemplary *Hope and Glory: Britain 1900–2000* (2004), a much-admired scholarly popularisation. Even late-twentieth-century Scottish history has until very recently been written with little attention to the North Sea. In general, in explanations of the trajectory of post-imperial Britain, the offshore industry has had little part to play.[53] It is as though the amnesia of Thatcher and most of her key ministers has been allowed to set the historical agenda.

The situation, however, is changing. Even before Kemp's 'official history' furnishes comprehensive access to crucial evidence, historians have begun to show greater awareness. The relatively few references in Richard Vinen's *Thatcher's Britain* are penetrating on the role the oil revenues played, in line with Vinen's general emphasis on deconstructing oversimplified views of 'Thatcherism'.[54] In Scotland, Christopher Harvie's many contributions to national history have been influenced by his personal but pioneering study of the industry, tellingly entitled *Fool's Gold* (and published in the mid 1990s to coincide with 'Wasted Windfall', a Channel 4 TV history). John Foster's chapter on the twentieth century in the *New Penguin History* benefited from his work on offshore labour relations.[55] But of serious single-volume histories of twentieth-century Scotland, Catriona Macdonald's and Ewan Cameron's are the first to pay more than casual attention to North Sea oil.[56] Cameron in particular recognises that the Piper Alpha tragedy has to be confronted as a central event.[57]

A more profound challenge to conventional historiography is posed by the social historian Jim Phillips, whose book on the industrial politics of the 1960s and 1970s sets the movement for Scottish devolution in a class context, focusing on the social aspirations of working people and the problems of labour-movement organisations in representing them, rather than on the more conventional theme of the politicisation of 'Scottish identity'. He aligns himself with the thesis that the United Kingdom's oil wealth, instead of being invested in renewing the socio-economic and industrial infrastructure of the welfare state, was used to reassure world money markets in a period of financial turmoil; and later to foot a burgeoning social-security bill, which assisted with the containment of militant opposition as workers were made redundant in the transition from manufacturing to a 'consumer' economy. For Britain's working-class communities dependent on industry, it was indeed a 'wasted windfall'.[58] But there is also a more complex argument.

The potential of the oil revenues, by boosting the electoral fortunes of Scottish nationalism, pressured the Labour Party into accepting devolution, which in turn provided Scottish trade unionists with a pragmatic demand based on the not unfounded idea that Scotland's political culture was more rooted in social democracy than England's.[59] From the 1970s on, devolution came to look like a 'realistic' way of promoting working-class interests. An effect of 'Scotland's oil', therefore, was that it 'advanced devolution' as a potentially progressive social policy. Following Phillips, it can be argued that the oil money acted as an agent of the historic destruction of Scotland's (and of course the United Kingdom's) industrial society and the state-welfare policies that had alleviated its social problems; and, at the same time, as a promoter of devolution, which, it was hoped, might provide Scots with the ability to moderate the impact of UK-wide policies that threatened the future of the welfare state.

The revenues that in Norway were to be, in some measure at least, harboured as an 'oil fund' for future social and infrastructural investment, in the United Kingdom were, as Phillips puts it, 'dissipated', especially by Thatcher's Conservative governments, into 'tax cuts and social security payments'.[60] Only in the northern, culturally distinct Shetland Islands, where the local authority had gained a unique (for the United Kingdom) measure of control – including the right to negotiate separately with the oil companies – was a deal arrived at that, in its relatively small and isolated way, came close to the Norwegian approach to the long-term benefit of Shetland society.[61] For the United Kingdom as a whole the fate of the oil 'windfall', as Theo Nicholls noted at the time, was indicated by the fact that the trebled costs of unemployment benefit under Thatcher took the overall bill to a figure close to the North Sea oil receipts, and that 'more or less was where the revenue from North Sea oil [had] gone'.[62] Nor was this accidental: it was an element in the market strategy Lawson outlined in his 1982 lecture, to which, as he said, the North Sea 'windfall' furnished such a strategic contribution.[63]

The industrial and social unrest that eventually played its part in unseating Thatcher – if not Thatcherism – lasted throughout the 1980s.[64] But Thatcher's ministers succeeded in postponing the decisive showdown with the 'Scargillism' of the then still powerful National Union of Mineworkers – Britain's 'civil war part two' as it has been credibly described[65] – until 1984/5. By then the threat of a general strike or comparable challenge to the government's existence was offset by the fact that economic recovery – albeit on Thatcherite terms and at great social cost – was underway. Thatcher moreover had rid her ministerial team of its 'Wets' – the compromisers who baulked at the ruthless application of free-market economic and social policies. A major confrontation in the early 1980s could have had far more serious implications for the government even than the miners' strike, and, without the government resource to fund the burgeoning social security bill as unemployment mounted, it might have been difficult to avoid.[66] This is not to suggest that the crisis-ridden United Kingdom would have avoided neoliberalism – the Labour administration that held office after the crisis of 1976 had already reluctantly laid the foundations for it[67] – but it could have been more difficult to embed Thatcherite ideology into the 'common sense' of mainstream UK political–economic discourse. As the North Sea narrative acquires a larger presence in contemporary British history, such questions of detail can be readdressed. Nor should Klein's challenge to reinterpret the Thatcher years as international history be ignored. In seeing Thatcherism as the 'democratic' moment in the global neoliberalism's brutal global trajectory, Klein coaxes contemporary British history out of its accustomed national frame – incidentally giving ideological significance to Thatcher's friendship with Pinochet, manifested when the Chilean dictator was held in Britain in the late 1990s pending possible extradition to Spain to face charges of crimes against humanity. Against Klein, however, the actual history of the origins of Thatcherism needs to be asserted.[68] For her, the victory in the 1982 war against the Argentinian *Junta* in the so-called 'Falklands War' was the break that gave Thatcher – for whom, as an elected politician, the Chilean solution was not an option – the authority for driving on with the neoliberal offensive. The jingoistic hysteria generated, particularly in the south of England, was indeed a factor in the Conservatives' 1983 election victory, after which the privatisation programme and the war against the unions accelerated. But Klein's omission of North Sea oil means that she misrepresents the chain of events. Had Thatcher – aided by oil revenues – not been able to ride out the crises generated by the economic policies of her early years, she could well have been quickly out of office, or so preoccupied by domestic conflict that she would have been unable to embark on the South Atlantic campaign, far less, in 1984/5, to mobilise unprecedented state force in delivering what Klein acknowledges as the *coup de grâce* in the United Kingdom's 'shock treatment' – the ruthless defeat of the miners.[69]

Klein's account of the origins of Thatcherite neoliberalism, then, is wrong in detail. But it valuably points to the need for historians, in filling the lacuna in the narrative of contemporary Britain where North Sea oil should be, to recognise the extent to which Thatcher's success in embedding her ideology of no-alternativism in orthodox political discourse is a – if not *the* – main thing that gives the United Kingdom a continuing, important role in post-imperial world history.

TEMPORALITY AND CONTEMPORARY BRITISH HISTORY: CONCLUDING HYPOTHESES AND FUTURE WORK

This chapter set out to examine the impact of North Sea oil, exploited primarily by global corporations, on the United Kingdom and on Scotland particularly. Oil revenues helped make Thatcherite neoliberalism possible; Scottish working people and their communities were amongst its main victims; and the United Kingdom's social-democratic consensus – which had more deep-rooted, cross-class support in Scotland than in the most electorally significant parts of England – was dealt a death-blow, strengthening Scottish support for devolution. Thatcher's focus on making the United Kingdom a minimally regulated centre for global finance, at the expense of industrial production, was perceived most negatively of all in Scotland, which was where most of the oil was. Labour, the main UK social-democratic party, had majority Scottish support throughout the 1980s, but was powerless at the UK level to mount effective opposition to Thatcherism. Disillusionment in Scotland had the option of expressing itself politically through support for the Scottish Nationalists, who had been boosted in the 1970s – when Labour's UK-wide welfarist vision of the 1940s was already in deep crisis – by the potential of oil wealth.

When Blair's New Labour won a landslide victory in the 1997 general election, devolution – despite the new prime minister's own priorities – was one of the few policies inherited from the 'old' Labour Party to survive. Political credibility demanded that a referendum be held to authorise a Scottish parliament with responsibility for most domestic policy. It was established in 1999 and, until 2007, Labour–Liberal Democrat coalition administrations carried out policies on education and social welfare sufficiently distinctive to sustain the idea that devolution gave Scottish society some protection from the scarcely modified Thatcherite agenda in London.[70] But the growing unpopularity of the UK Labour government helped the SNP to secure a narrow plurality of seats in the 2007 Scottish election and form a minority government. Establishing an 'oil fund', while out with their power as a devolved administration, remained Nationalist policy, but it could no longer be supposed that it would be a one-shot solution to an independent Scotland's budgetary problems. The 2007/8 financial crisis, in which Scottish-based banks (and nations such as Ireland and Iceland, promoted by the SNP as models for Scotland) were heavily implicated, further limited the attraction of independence. Support for the SNP came to depend more on a perceived need to defend 'Scotland' against the effect of UK cuts in devolved budget allocations than nationalism *per se* – and this was confirmed by early analyses of what was widely hailed as a 'historic' triumph for the Nationalists in the Scottish election of 5 May 2011.[71]

In drawing up a balance sheet of the social impact of UK North Sea oil, the most obvious comparator is Norway, and its long-term strategy to harbour oil revenues to help meet the challenges of a post-oil economy. In 2010 a BBC Scotland reporter visited Norway to reflect on the contrast and on how a similar policy might have affected Scotland's – and the United Kingdom's – ability to weather the international financial crisis.[72] But the UK failure cannot be explained simply as a conjunctural 'mistake' in decision making: it has to be seen in the context of the historical determinations – the point arrived at in British post-imperial history – underlying the direction of policy not simply in the Thatcherite 1980s but in the whole period from the collapse of British social democracy during the Wilson governments of 1964–76 onwards.

Ryggvik's study of Norway's oil policies argues that they can be understood only in the context of Norwegian history and political tradition. There was 'no single Norwegian oil experience' easily emulated elsewhere, only the outcome of the often conflicting experiences of different interest groups. Norway's relative success in dealing with its oil windfall was 'the product of an active democracy' – one which has expressed itself 'not only through formal parliamentary representation, but equally through direct popular mobilisation'. And 'the greater the degree of openness and general popular oversight of political priorities and decisive technological choices, the better a society will be able to manage a strategic energy resource in a way which benefits society as a whole'.[73]

By this standard, Scottish politicians (whether nationalist or social democrat) might claim that the way North Sea oil helped – albeit indirectly – to change the pattern of Scottish politics ultimately produced a new parliament offering a greater measure of direct public access at least to the *process* of decision making, and that this outcome was in part the product of popular actions against Thatcherism in the 1980s. But the parliament had no control of key areas of policy, including the disposal of revenues from the offshore industry. It could not reverse neoliberal macroeconomic policy, which had dictated the short-termism of the early use of the oil money, or the industrial relations regime established in the 1980s, which New Labour left largely untouched. The highly restrictive 'anti-union' laws, justified precisely in the name of a democracy defined exclusively in terms of 'formal parliamentary representation', have substantially constrained the trade unions' role in politics by severely limiting their ability to organise industrial action – the foundation of their former strength within a more pluralistic conception of representative democracy. And, while Scottish Nationalists can claim that their moment of opportunity for independence was snatched from them in the 1970s by the undemocratic concealment of the real financial prospects of offshore oil, neither at that time nor more recently have they espoused a programme of radical opposition to the basic assumptions of neoliberalism.

In conclusion, there are two directions, I want to suggest, in which Ryggvik's caution about the limits of the Norwegian 'example' and about the need for historical contextualisation can usefully lead future evidence-based discourse about the 'lessons' (and international relevance) of the United Kingdom's (including Scotland's) offshore oil experience. First, more attention should be paid to the actions of offshore workers – the democracy of the industry – themselves. Second, the historical methodology that has in effect collaborated in establishing Thatcher's neoliberal ideology (TINA) in the underlying assumptions of much contemporary British historiography requires radical critique. Without recontextualising the historical moment in which North Sea oil came on stream and reached peak production – the last quarter of the twentieth century – debate about the use of its revenues cannot go far beyond subjective speculation.

In the late 1980s the UK offshore workers were forced to fight for a measure of democratic control over their industry. Their 1989/90 offshore sit-in movement followed the Piper Alpha tragedy and was inspired primarily by concerns about safety – about life itself – rather than traditional trade-union demands. The actions achieved only limited gains on wages: the anti-union regime the workers had to endure – encouraged by Thatcherite legislation and frustratingly different from what they saw in Norway – was not overcome. But they began to raise radical questions about the need for new dimensions in working-class organisation in the period of capitalist globalisation.[74]

A new body, the Offshore Industry Liaison Committee (OILC), led the action. It faced formidable difficulties, first in working within the established unions and then in organising independently of them until, in 2008, it became an autonomous part of the left-wing transport union, RMT.)[75] What is worth deeper examination is the extent to which OILC's difficulties lay not so much in conjunctural factors (tactical mistakes, trade-union rivalries, employer intransigence), as in the still dimly perceived change in historical circumstances. The offshore workers, this hypothesis suggests, were trying to establish trade unions on the basis of ideas about organisation and policy that had emerged in the nineteenth century when the class basis of society and industry and the national framework of economic organisation were much clearer, and the historical possibility of piecemeal reform was still real. But the offshore workers' demand for union recognition and a role in establishing a new safety regime challenged, not just a particular employer, but the managerial imperatives of a major global industry and even, implicitly, the social order within which it works. The offshore workers were fighting, that is to suggest, with weapons appropriate for a vanishing age of industrial relations. In Thatcherite Britain, where the oil corporations operated with minimal public oversight, the OILC's immediate battle could not be won; but it left a legacy of practical action and agonised debate, all the more relevant today as the need grows ever more pressing for new organisational forms to challenge and pose a real social alternative to neoliberal capitalism.[76]

To suggest that the offshore industrial actions of 1989/90 can be seen in retrospect to have been unwinnable at the time, but that they raised questions for the future, begs the question of how to understand the way in which the historically determined possibilities *then* are becoming different *now*. This is the point at which my personal attempt radically to revise the Leninism of the 1970s connects with the promotion of new thinking – much more generally significant – about the stage in its history at which humanity had arrived in the decades following the First World War and the Russian Revolution; and about how this can inform an emergent consciousness of the possibilities of realising the radical social transformation urgently needed in the twenty-first century.[77]

In an essay now republished in the context of his two-volume *Social Structure and Forms of Consciousness*, Mészáros elaborates on how Marx's conception of the contradictory forward movement of history is dependent on 'historical temporality' – the need, in interpreting events and making political prognoses, for analysis founded not on the abstraction of 'human nature' or the ahistoricity of postmodernism, but on penetration to the real human possibilities of development within the given determinations of a particular epoch.[78] As Cliff Slaughter, building on Mészáros, has written, the idea that the 1970s were understandable as part of Lenin's (and

Trotsky's) 'century of world socialist revolution', was, it is now clear, simply wrong.[79] But the tremors palpable in the 1960s and 1970s *were*, as Mészáros argues, indications of profound change and of the *beginning* of a process – laden with the *immanence*, though not the *imminence*, of revolutionary transformation – that is maturing in the early decades of the twenty-first century.

This has important implications for reinterpreting historically the attacks on the British welfare state that were mounted in the 1980s, as the idea that oil revenues could sustain and improve it was abandoned – attacks that have been re-engaged with a new and comprehensive vigour in the aftermath of the global financial crisis. As, in 2010 and 2011, mass opposition took to the streets of the United Kingdom in unprecedented numbers, it was striking that labour and trade union leaders had little to offer in the way of an analysis, beyond revamped versions of the neo-Keynesianism that had failed to halt the first neoliberal offensive in the 1980s. The alternative strategies that were offered were little more than different ways of implementing the cuts that global finance capital demanded. They did not challenge the fundamentals of the social system, the essence of which, rather than the accidents of individual greed and folly, had been disclosed by the crisis.

Mészáros writes of Marx's contempt for those 'who wanted to offer some limited and patronizing concessions about the forms of *distribution* to consumers prevailing in capital's socio-economic order while retaining its antagonist mode of *production* fetishistically intact'. The critique – with John Stuart Mill as Marx's main target in his own time – is all the more cogent today, he insists, when a century of experience has tested the 'highly absurd ... separation and contra-position of production and distribution' in a way that '*eternaliz[es]* the established reproductive order as a whole, by declaring its constituent of production' as having 'the character of *physical truths*'. The 'vacuous pseudo-concessions ... on distribution itself' that liberal theory allows can never resolve the fundamental problems created by capital's destructive hegemony over society, since, 'in this scheme of things distribution had to remain *locked into* the allegedly *physically unalterable* determinations of production as such'. Marx's analysis has been 'amply confirmed' by the failure, in the twentieth century, of everything 'from timid liberal reforms'

to the loudly proclaimed but in the end humiliatingly abandoned social democratic programme of transforming society – according to the recipe of 'evolutionary socialism' which was supposed to be established through the method of '*progressive taxation*' instituted within the framework of the '*Welfare State*'.[80]

Arguing in this way, we can say that, precisely when, in the United Kingdom, North Sea oil appeared to social democrats to offer the possibility of regenerating the welfare state without a transition to what Mészáros refers to as a radically new 'social metabolism', the capital system as a whole was arriving at the point at which even the possibility of 'pseudo-concessions' offered on the basis of accepting 'the allegedly *physically unalterable* determinations of production as such' was being superseded. Thatcher's notorious 'there is no alternative', in other words, should be redefined not as a serious political proposition but as the defensive manifesto of a historically outmoded social system, signalling the impact of the onset of a new period in the oldest imperial capitalist power. Struggles to defend the gains for humanity that advances in knowledge and technology have in the past made possible, even within capital's hegemonic social order, now have to be predicated on preserving these gains – *against* capital's increasingly unmediated and predatory human and environmental *destructiveness* – not only as important in themselves, but also as the necessary basis for transition to a new social order. Socialism cannot be built on scorched earth. And, within existing social relations, the transformatory potential for human intercourse and exchange inherent in the exponential expansion of information technology is – as widely perceived dangers to the environment and social life demonstrate – already being catastrophically turned against humanity itself.

To end on this note is in no way to belittle the struggles of workers – including the UK offshore workers after Piper Alpha – for their immediate demands, nor the critical empirical research that, as Ryggvik has shown, can illuminate the comparative experience of the oil industry in different countries. It rather proposes a way of contextualising both (and the other historical themes explored in this chapter) within a project of theoretical clarification on two related fronts. The first is the need for radical transformation to a new global social order, one in which all available resources, including oil, can be used for the planned satisfaction of human need and the urge for human equality. The second is the process by which the emerging forces of opposition to the policies being implemented to sustain existing social structures arm themselves with the mass consciousness necessary for these structures to be superseded by what Marx referred to, not as 'the end of history', but as the 'end of prehistory' – the point of social transition at which a 'truly human' history will *begin*.[81]

NOTES

1. For a critical account of the idea of 'decline' in British history, see Tomlinson 2009.
2. Lawson 1993, pp.58, 139.
3. Klein 2007, ch.6.
4. Lawson 1993, p.6.
5. Thatcher 1993, *passim*.
6. Marr 2007, pp.438–40.
7. Marr's book ends on a note exemplifying an almost nineteenth-century, whiggish complacency: 'In global terms, to be born British remains a wonderful stroke of luck.' Marr 2007, p.602.
8. Wilde 1945, p.102.
9. See Fukuyama 1989, 1992.
10. Even before the full impact of the global financial crisis on the United Kingdom became clear, Energy minister, Malcolm Wicks told a reporter in 2007: 'If you could replay history, the idea as in Norway of building up a national [oil] fund is actually quite an attractive one.' *Guardian*, 27 October 2007.
11. See Brotherstone and Manson 2007.
12. For example, Mackie 2004, 2006; Marr 2007; McGinty 2008; Beckett 2009. The monograph is Harvie 1994.
13. More 2009 has several chapters on the 'black gold' of the North Sea; see too Brotherstone 2010. Historical research will now also be facilitated by government records, increasingly available both through freedom of information and the normal 30-year release rules.
14. Ryggvik 2010.
15. Ellis 2005.
16. Rutledge and Wright 2010, pp.418, 430.
17. Newlands 2000, ch.5. See too Harris, Lloyd and Newlands 1988; and, for a bibliographical article on the impact of North Sea oil in northern Scotland, Newlands and Brehme 2007.
18. See Mészáros 1995.
19. Reed 1973 (unpaginated).
20. Beckett 2009, p.186; Wilson 1979, p.184.
21. See Wilson 1964; Pimlott 1993, esp. chs 14 and 25. A more recent account is Sandbrook 2006.
22. Clark 2001, p.40.
23. The principal academic critic of UK oil policy was Peter Odell. See Odell 2002, esp. pp.185–252, 277–88 and 517–72; and Odell 2010.
24. Beckett 2009, esp. ch.11; Vinen 2009, ch.4.
25. The right-wing commentator Charles Moore, in his *Daily Telegraph* review (23 March 2009) of Beckett and Hencke (2009) on the miners' strike, claims that Thatcher's phrase referred only to Scargill, not the striking miners as a whole. If so, the distinction was lost on the miners and the wider British public at the time.

26. The document was highlighted in a radio review of government documents from 1980 being released under the '30-year rule': 'UK Confidential', broadcast on BBC Radio 4, 30 December 2010. The original is in the National Archives at Kew.
27. McCrone 1975.
28. The Nationalists had briefly held Motherwell at the end of the Second World War, following a by-election when the 'wartime truce' between the main political parties limited competition for the seat, but they lost it in the post-war 'Labour landslide'. Their 'breakthrough' came in the Hamilton by-election of 1967 and their best UK general election performances in 1974. Histories of the SNP include Lynch 2002.
29. This is on the assumption that the maritime border would be based on an extension of the territorial border between England and Scotland that runs from north of Carlisle in the west to just north of Berwick-upon-Tweed in the east. The bulk of the oil in the UK sector as established (with undue haste by the British government, to the great advantage of Norway) by the Continental Shelf Agreement of 1964 is to the north of that line.
30. McCrone 1975, p.5.
31. See esp. Nairn 1977.
32. For the 1976–9 Labour government's economic difficulties as the benefits of oil were awaited, see Healey 1989.
33. See Harvie 1994, pp.51–2 and references *passim*; obituary in *Valley Reporter* 2008.
34. Accessible in the Margaret Thatcher Foundation Archive at www.margaretthatcher.org/document/110510
35. Beckett 2009, p.189.
36. Meeting on Thursday, 30 January 1975. Accessible in the Gerald Ford Archive at www.ford.utexas.edu/library/document/memcons/1552934.pdf
37. Benn 1990, pp.381–95.
38. Ibid., p.403; Benn's major social-democratic initiative in the running of the oil industry in Britain was the setting up, in 1975, of the British National Oil Corporation (BNOC), later effectively privatised by the Thatcher government: Benn 1991, esp. pp.4, 45, 171–4; Vinen 2009, p.194; Lawson 1993, pp.190–3.
39. LOI 1, interview with Hamilton.
40. LOI 2, interview with Halford.
41. Cullen 1990; McGinty 2008.
42. For the seminal analysis of this question, see Carson 1981.
43. See esp. Odell 2002 and N.J. Smith, 'North Sea Oil and Gas, British Industry and the Offshore Supplies Office 1963–1993' (Ph.D. thesis, University of Aberdeen, 2007, recently published as Smith 2011).
44. See Woolfson, Foster and Beck 1996; Gourlay 1998; Cumbers 2007 and his chapter in this volume; and Ryggvik 2010.
45. There is an ongoing debate about the extent to which the lessons of Piper Alpha enumerated in Lord Cullen's 1990 inquiry were seriously taken on board by the industry (e.g. Woolfson 2007). But there has to date been little effort to assess the part the flawed safety record should play in broader historical assessments of its significance.
46. See Alvarez 2002.
47. Alvarez 1986, p.40.
48. See Gaskin 1969; Newlands 2000.

49. The production of a daily newspaper from 1969 to the party's collapse in 1985 – first *Workers Press* and then *The NewsLine* – marks the WRP out as a more significant historical phenomenon than a realistic assessment of its political influence at the time (as opposed to its contemporary self-evaluation) would have suggested. Its best-known, though far from its most intellectually credible, member was the actress Vanessa Redgrave.

50. For a piece of political theatre, wildly popular in Scotland in the mid 1970s, which set the divisiveness of the oil boom in the context of a class-struggle view of Scottish history, see McGrath 1996. *The Cheviot, the Stag and the Black, Black Oil* was later adapted as a BBC TV 'Play for Today'.

51. See Wheen 2009.

52. See Mészáros 1995.

53. Brotherstone and Manson 2007, pp 28–32.

54. See Vinen 2009.

55. See Harvie 1994; Foster 2001.

56. See Macdonald 2009; Cameron 2010.

57. In many accounts, if not ignored, it appears simply as a blip in a general celebration of achievement, and when Stephen McGinty's *Fire in the Night* appeared on the twentieth anniversary of the tragedy, it received surprisingly little attention, certainly outside Scotland.

58. Phillips 2006, p.147.

59. The legacy of the industrial revolution in Scotland, a more rapid process than in much of England, left a legacy of acute social deprivation that persisted through the nineteenth and much of the twentieth century. And the ideology of social discipline that characterised the Calvinistic Presbyterian church was accompanied by a strong sense of social responsibility, supported by many in the prospering middle classes who feared social disorder and infectious diseases generated by urban poverty. The Scots attachment to the welfare state in the increasingly secular latter twentieth century has strong historical roots rather than signalling moral superiority.

60. Phillips 2006, pp.147–8.

61. Beckett 2009, pp.201–5; LOI 3: Ian Clark interview; Crawford 2005; and see Wills 1991 and 2010.

62. Phillips 2006, p.180; Nichols 1986, p.237

63. The Thatcher governments were also sustained by the split in a Labour opposition caught between working-class demands for a return to post-war social democracy and the emerging economic orthodoxy. Right-wingers committed to European union and hostile to trade-union militancy formed the Social Democratic Party, making electoral victory for Labour almost impossible. Within the Labour party a bitter conflict saw the right-wing former chancellor of the exchequer, Denis Healey, defeat the left candidate, Tony Benn, for the Labour deputy leadership by only the narrowest of margins.

64. For recent contrasting approaches to the narrative of events in Scotland in the Thatcher years, see Torrance 2009 and Stewart 2009.

65. Deller 2001.

66. The decision of the Conservative Party to dispense with their leader in 1990 was the result of many factors, notably the split in their own ranks over European policy and the growing frustration of her senior colleagues with her authoritarian personality. But ongoing industrial actions and especially the mass

protests against the regressive local government Poll Tax were a major factor in creating the impression of a government losing control.

67. There is a large literature on the crisis of the mid 1970s both in the British economy and in the Labour government, for example, Burk and Cairncross 1992; and, autobiographically, Callaghan 1987 and Healey 1989.

68. Klein 2007. The less convincing side of Klein's analysis is her attempt to make a direct link between the rise of neoliberal economics and a theory of torture, the source as she sees it of the use of 'shock treatment' to intimidate populations into accepting the new unmediated capitalism.

69. Ibid., pp.138–9.

70. See Macdonell 2009.

71. The results of the 2011 Scottish elections were being declared as this chapter was being finalised. The SNP's success exceeded all expectations, confirming that they were seen as the party best able to 'defend Scotland' from the impact of 'Westminster cuts'. Polling evidence suggested that this pragmatic concern, rather than commitment to Scottish independence, explained the result; but a consequence of it was that this issue will now be put to a referendum probably in 2014.

72. Fraser 2010.

73. Ryggvik 2010, pp.111–3.

74. Woolfson, Foster and Beck 1996 covers the history of OILC's origins; Gourlay 1998 provides insights into employer attitudes. See too Brotherstone 2011.

75. See Cumbers 2007.

76. See OILC 1989–90, 1991.

77. Mészáros 1989, 1995, 2008, 2010, 2011. A participant in the 1956 Hungarian revolution, Mészáros, when his most significant work began to be published in the 1980s, had behind him decades of rethinking the foundations of Marxism following the Stalinist experience. His prolific recent work forms a basis for radical new thinking. It can be contrasted with, for example, the unreflective restatements of better publicised Marxists like the historian E.J. Hobsbawm. Hobsbawm's recent title *How to Change the World* misuses Marx's thesis that the philosophers have only explained the world while the point is to change it, by merely pointing out that the new capitalist crisis of 2007/8 re-establishes Marx's relevance without grappling with how to relate this to oppositional practice or to interrogate the way in which the nature of the 'Communism' he himself espoused has made the word anathema to many. See Hobsbawm 2011, esp. pp.419–20.

78. Mészáros 1996, pp.251–92; and 2010/11, pp.101–48.

79. Slaughter, C. 2006, esp. pp.280–7.

80. Mészáros 2010, pp.286–8.

81. To conclude on this note is of course to recognise the complexity of the tasks in front and the urgent demands they make on historical theory, an awareness of which is signally absent from most of the often in other ways excellent work that is presented today in the United Kingdom as 'history'. This chapter pretends to have made no more than a stab at recognising these demands.

REFERENCES

Alvarez, A. (1986) *Offshore: A North Sea Journey* (London: Hodder & Stoughton).

—— (2002) *Where Did It All Go Right?*, paperback edn (London: Bloomsbury).

Beckett, A. (2009) *When the Lights Went Out: Britain in the Seventies* (London: Faber and Faber).

Beckett, F. and Hencke, D. (2009) *Marching to the Fault Line: the 1984 Miners' Strike and the Death of Industrial Britain 1984–85* (London: Constable).

Benn, T. (1990) *Against the Tide: Diaries 1973–1976*, paperback edn (London: Arrow).

—— (1991) *Conflicts of Interest: Diaries 1977–80*, paperback edn (London: Arrow).

Brotherstone, T. (2010) Review, '*Black Gold: Britain and Oil in the Twentieth Century*, by Charles More', *Twentieth Century British History*, 21(4): 570–3.

—— (2011) 'Energy Workers Against Thatcherite Neoliberalism, 1981–92. Scottish Coalminers and North Sea Offshore Workers: Revisiting the Class Struggle in the 1980s', unpublished paper presented at 'Strikes and Social Conflicts in the Twentieth Century', FCSH, Lisbon, 16–20 March 2011 (available from the author).

—— and Manson, H. (2007) 'North Sea Oil, Its Narratives and Its History: An Archive of Oral Documentation and the Making of Contemporary Britain', University of Aberdeen, *Northern Scotland*, 27: 15–42.

Burk, K. and Cairncross, A. (1992) '*Goodbye, Great Britain': the 1976 IMF Crisis* (New Haven and London: Yale University Press).

Callaghan, J. (1987) *Time and Chance* (London: Collins).

Cameron, E. (2010) *Impaled Upon a Thistle: Scotland Since 1880* (Edinburgh: Edinburgh University Press).

Carson W.G. (1981) *The Other Price of Britain's Oil: Safety and Control in the North Sea* (London: Robertson).

Clark, A. (2001) *Diaries: Into Politics 1972–1982*, paperback edn. (London: Phoenix).

Clarke, P. (2004) *Hope and Glory: Britain 1900–2000* (London: Penguin; first edn 1996).

Crawford, A. (2005) 'Field of Dreams: 30 Years since North Sea Oil Was First Brought Ashore in Britain. What Impact Has It Had on Scotland? Alan Crawford talks to key players', *The Herald*, Glasgow, 12 June.

Cullen, Lord W.D. (1990) *The Public Inquiry into the Piper Alpha Disaster* (London: HMSO).

Cumbers, A. (2007) 'Employment Relations and Union Recognition in the North Sea', University of Aberdeen, *Northern Scotland*, 27: 69–79.

Deller, J. (2001) *The English Civil War Part II: Personal Accounts of the 1984–85 Miners' Strike* (London: Artangel).

Ellis, P. (2005) 'The State Must Be Responsible for Energy Security', *Financial Times*, 10 September; at www.ft.com.

Foster, J. (2001) 'The Twentieth Century', in Houston and Knox 2001.

Fraser, D. (2010) 'The Viking Plunder that Keeps Giving', a report about Norway and North Sea oil, *Newsnight* Scotland, BBC2, 26 October; www.bbc.co.uk/blogs/thereporters/douglasfraser.

Fukuyama, F. (1989) 'The End of History?', *The National Interest*, Washington D.C., summer 1989; available at www.wesjones.com/eoh.htm.

—— (1992) *The End of History and the Last Man* (London: Hamish Hamilton).

Gaskin, M. (1969) *North East Scotland: A Survey and Prospects* (Edinburgh: HMSO).

Gourlay, D. (1998) 'Industrial Relations in the North Sea Oil and Gas Industry 1965–1995', Robert Gordon University, Aberdeen (unpublished Ph.D. thesis).

Harris, A.H., Lloyd, M.G. and Newlands, D. (1988) *The Impact of Oil on the Aberdeen Economy* (Aldershot: Avebury).

Harvie, C. (1994) *Fool's Gold: The History of North Sea Oil* (London: Hamish Hamilton).

—— (2001) 'Scotland After 1978: From Referendum to Millennium', in Houston and Knox 2001.

Healey, D. (1989) *The Time of My Life* (London: Michael Joseph).

Hobsbawm, E.J. (2011) *How to Change the World: Marx and Marxism* (London: Little, Brown).

Houston, R.A. and Knox, W.W.J. (2001) *The New Penguin History of Scotland: From the Earliest Times to the Present Day* (London: Allen Lane).

Kemp, A. (2012) *The Official History of North Sea Oil and Gas* (London: Routledge).

Klein, N. (2007) *The Shock Doctrine: The Rise of Disaster Capitalism* (London: Allen Lane).

Lawson, N. (1993) *Inside No.11: The Memoirs of a Tory Radical*, paperback edn (London: Corgi Books; first published 1992).

LOI, The 'Lives in the Oil Industry' oral history archive, University of Aberdeen Special Archives and Collections. LOI 1: Frederic Hamilton interview: F1-44-71/B, recorded 10 January 2007; LOI 2: T. Halford interview: F11285-F11287, recorded 22 November 2000; LOI 3: Ian Clark (Shetland County Clerk) interview. Restricted access.

Lynch, P.A. (2002) *SNP: The History of the Scottish National Party* (Cardiff: Welsh Academic Press).

Macdonald, C. (2009) *Whaur Extremes Meet: Scotland's Twentieth Century* (Edinburgh: John Donald).

Macdonell, H. (2009) *Uncharted Territory: The Story of Scottish Devolution 1999–2009* (London: Politico's Publishing).

Mackie, B. (2004) *Oilmen: The North Sea Tigers* (Edinburgh: Birlinn).

—— (2006) *The Klondykers: The Oilmen Onshore* (Edinburgh: Birlinn).

Marr, A. (2007) *A History of Modern Britain* (London: Macmillan).

McCrone, R.G.L. (1975) Letter from the Scottish Economic Planning Department, Edinburgh, to the Cabinet Office, London, attaching a memorandum on Scottish nationalism (written in 1974), 23 April, www.oilofscotland.org/mccronereport.pdf.

McGinty, S. (2008) *Fire in the Night: The Piper Alpha Disaster* (London: Macmillan).

McGrath, J. (1996) 'The Cheviot, the Stag and the Black, Black Oil', in *Six-Pack: Plays for Scotland* (Edinburgh: Polygon; first performed in 1972).

Mészáros, I. (1989) *The Power of Ideology* (Hemel Hempstead: Harvester Wheatsheaf).

—— (1995) *Beyond Capital: Towards a Theory of Transition* (London: Merlin).

—— (1996) 'Historical Temporality', in T. Brotherstone and G. Pilling, *History, Economic History and the Future of Marxism* (London: Porcupine).

—— (2008) *The Challenge and Burden of Historical Time* (New York: Monthly Review Press).

—— (2010) *Social Structure and Forms of Consciousness. Volume I: The Social Determination of Method* (New York: Monthly Review Press).

—— (2011) *Social Structure and Forms of Consciousness. Volume II: The Dialectic of Structure and History* (New York: Monthly Review Press).

More, C. (2009) *Black Gold: Britain and Oil in the Twentieth Century* (London: Continuum).

Nairn, T. (1977) *The Break-up of Britain: Crisis and Neo-nationalism* (London: New Left Books).

Newlands, D. (2000) 'The Oil Economy', in W.H. Fraser and C.H. Lee (eds) *Aberdeen 1800–2000: A New History* (Phantassie, East Linton: Tuckwell Press).

—— and Brehme, A. (2007) 'A Historiography of the Impact of North Sea Oil on Northern Scotland', University of Aberdeen, *Northern Scotland*, 27: 81–97.

Nichols, T. (1986) *The British Worker Question: A New Look at Workers and Productivity in Manufacturing* (London: Routledge & Kegan Paul).

Odell, P. (2002) *Oil and Gas: Crises and Controversies 1961–2000. Volume 2: Europe's Entanglement* (Brentwood: Multi-Science Publishing).

—— (2010) 'Managing the UK's Remaining Oil and Gas Resource: A Future Role for the State?', in Rutledge and Wright 2010.

OILC (1989–90) 'Blowout' (paper of the Offshore Industry Liaison Committee, Aberdeen).

—— (1991) 'Striking Out: New Directions for Offshore Workers and Their Unions' (Aberdeen: OILC).

Phillips, J. (2006) *The Industrial Politics of Devolution: Scotland in the 1960s and 1970s* (Manchester: Manchester University Press).

Pimlott, B. (1993) *Harold Wilson*, paperback edn (London: HarperCollins; first edn 1992).

Reed, L. (1973) *The Political Consequences of North Sea Oil*, Institute of Offshore Engineering (Edinburgh: Heriot-Watt University).

Rutledge, I. and Wright, P. (2010) *UK Energy Policy and the End of Market Fundamentalism* (Oxford: Oxford University Press, for the Oxford Institute of Energy Studies).

Ryggvik, H. (2010), *The Norwegian Oil Experience: A Toolbox for Managing Resources?* (Oslo: Senter for Teknologi, Innovasion og Kulture).

Sandbrook, D. (2006) *White Heat: A History of Britain in the Swinging Sixties* (London: Little, Brown).

Slaughter, C. (2006) *Not Without a Storm: Towards a Communist Manifesto for the Age of Globalisation* (London: Index Books).

Smith, N.J. (2011) *The Sea of Lost Opportunity: North Sea Oil and Gas, British Industry and the Offshore Supplies Office* (London: Elsevier Reference).

Stewart, D. (2009) *The Path to Devolution and Social Change: A Political History of Scotland under Devolution* (London: I.B.Tauris).

Thatcher, M. (1993) *The Downing Street Years* (London: HarperCollins).

Tomlinson, J. (2009) 'Thrice Denied: "Declinism" as a Recurrent Theme in British History in the Long Twentieth Century', *Twentieth Century British History*, 20(2): 227–51.

Torrance, D. (2009) *'We in Scotland': Thatcherism in a Cold Climate* (Edinburgh: Birlinn).

Valley Reporter (2008), Obituary of Richard Funkhouser (1917–2008), 22 May 2008, Red River Valley, Vermont; available at www.valleyreporter.com.

Vinen, R. (2009) *Thatcher's Britain: The Politics and Social Upheaval of Britain in the 1980s* (London: Simon & Schuster).

Wheen, F. (2009) *Strange Days Indeed: The Golden Age of Paranoia* (London: Fourth Estate).

Wilde, O. (1945) *Intentions* (London: Unicorn Press; first edn 1891).

Wills, J. (1991) *A Place in the Sun: Shetland and Oil – Myths and Realities* (Edinburgh: Mainstream).

—— (2010) 'The People's Oil? Community Involvement in Petroleum Revenue Sharing and Environmental Protection in the Shetland Islands of Scotland, 1972–2010', unpublished paper, University of Tehran (available from the author).

Wilson, H. (1964) *The New Britain: Labour's Plan Outlined by Harold Wilson* (Harmondsworth: Penguin Books).

—— (1979) *Final Term: The Labour Government, 1974–1976* (London: Weidenfeld & Nicolson and Michael Joseph).

Woolfson, C. (2007) 'The Continuing Price of North Sea Oil: Business Organisation and Risk Transfer Mechanisms in the North Sea Petroleum Industry', in A. Brannigan and G. Pavlich (eds) *Governance and Regulation in Social Life: Essays in Honour of W.G. Carson* (Abingdon: Routledge–Cavendish).

—— Foster, J. and Beck, M. (1996) *Paying for the Piper: Capital and Labour in Britain's Offshore Industry* (London: Mansell).

4
Where Pathos Rules:
The Resource Curse in Visual Culture

Owen Logan

Where pathos rules, where pathos is finally derived, a character has fought a battle he could not possibly have won.

Arthur Miller[1]

The resource curse in visual culture is the tale of two discourses, one academic and one cultural, which have found their ideal partners in each other. Recognising this, I want to begin with an image made before the correlation between natural-resource wealth and various socio-economic ills, including violent conflict, was studied and promoted.[2] The image I have in mind is Gilles Caron's 1968 photograph taken during the Nigerian Civil War (Figure 4.1). In keeping with the liberal–humanist tradition in photography that has provided the visual rhetoric for the resource curse, Caron's picture of war is imbued with a sense of pathos. Pathos invites audiences to identify with the photographer's perspective through his or her expression of pity. It is the most emotive aspect of classical rhetoric and to anyone attuned to political aesthetics, like the playwright Arthur Miller, it is also the most problematic.

Miller's most famous dramatic works were shaped by his experiences of economic depression, the New Deal and then cold war politics in the United States. In his lifetime he saw some under-appreciated victories in working-class politics as well as some unpredictable twists and turns, the history and impact of which I touch on in this chapter before returning to his insightful critique of pathos. In contrast to the shifting historical fortunes Miller witnessed, a 'curse' is, by definition, an inescapable affliction that bedevils human actions – a pathetic condition which inevitably calls upon the rhetoric of pathos and makes it seem fitting.

Whether or not 'curse' is a proper or accurate description of the problems associated with resource wealth, pathos offers

Figure 4.1 Ibo separatist guerrilla, near Onitsha, Biafra, Nigeria, April 1968. Photograph by Giles Caron, reproduced by kind permission of Contact Press Images.

audiences an ostensibly benign and humanitarian overview. Caron's picture of a gaunt young Biafran soldier is taken in such a way that we can hardly avoid sharing this vision. His subject appears to look piercingly at us, and without a conscious effort to disengage emotionally the viewer becomes part of a powerful rhetorical form. It should be asked then what is the significance of pathos in the context of resource curse discourse; what is the ethos (social credibility) and logos (form of reasoning) of this curse at a cultural and broader political level? To provide some answers, this chapter examines the resource curse in visual culture and the rise of consumer sovereignty.

ANTI-IDEOLOGY: THE RESOURCES OF PATHOS

The problematic rhetoric of positioning inherent in pathos can be gleaned from the response to remarks made in 2001 by Nigeria's President Obasanjo about the country's calamitous civil war (1967–70). The president, who fought for the Federal side, was quoted in the press stating that the war had been waged over the control of Nigeria's oil resources, a retrospective rationale rejected by Obasanjo's former Biafran opponents. The Biafran army commander, Alex Madiebo, wrote back with a counter argument in which he suggested that the president's remarks undermined the post-war unity of southern Nigerians in the face of their historic grievances with the northern Nigerian power elite. This elite was seen as responsible for the massive 'ethnic cleansing' of Ibo people the year before the outbreak of civil war.[3] Madiebo saw the war as one of the most divisive episodes imposed on southern Nigerians by the ambitions of the northern elite and he clearly resented the idea that the Biafran cause had ever been base or pathetic – the unavoidable implication of Obasanjo's utterances about resource control. In Madiebo's own words, 'Biafra to the Ibos, meant organised resistance against the first ethnic cleansing or pogrom on the continent of Africa'.[4]

There is more to this exchange than the mere fact that one person's defensive struggle for self-determination had become another person's 'oil war'. Rather, it is that the whole political and ideological basis of Nigerian sovereignty is still under review, as we discuss in Chapter 10 of this book. The Chaco War (1932–35) fought between Bolivia and Paraguay (with Standard Oil and Shell in respective roles as corporate backers) seems to be a clearer case of an oil war. Bolivia was defeated and the conflict was disastrous for both sides, yet despite this history it is increasingly argued by community leaders and anti-imperialists in Latin America that natural resources are a blessing and should be viewed as such.

One way to understand this alternative view is to see natural resources as sites *upon* which ideological struggles take place, and these struggles as bringing issues of collective rights and the common good to the fore. In the global mass media there is a plethora of images like Caron's photograph which propose a very different view. At the level of meta-narrative their pathos leads us towards the perspective of writers like the US academic Michael T. Klare, a professor of peace and world security studies. In his influential book *Resource Wars* (2001), he argues that 'conflict was until recently governed by ideological and political considerations', but that wars in the twenty-first century will 'largely be fought over the possession and control of vital economic goods – especially resources needed for the functioning of modern industrial society'.[5] This argument against the pertinence of ideology was Klare's central thesis and continues to inform his writing and public presentations. He is to resource conflict what Samuel P. Huntington is to civilisational conflict, a parallel Klare himself suggests.[6] In pointing to this connection, he makes explicit a particular brand of political reasoning that is only implied in the output of many other analysts and commentators.

Like that of Nigeria's former President Obasanjo, Klare's outlook on 'resource-related conflict'[7] appears increasingly partial the closer one looks into historical experiences. As an academic writer Klare also seems particularly unreflective about his own position in a country that gave us the term 'military–industrial complex' – a nexus which feeds both into and from one of the greatest state-funded higher education systems in the world.[8] In other hands this situation might present an ideological problematic of considerable significance, when one considers Klare's arguments that the United States is in need of a massive investment to develop renewable technologies if it is to measure up to a new 'global energy equation'. Seen in a context of dwindling world oil reserves, Klare argues that his country is on the threshold of a new world order wherein it is no longer the sole superpower and will be forced to compete with emergent 'petro-superpowers' such as Russia and Saudi Arabia for global supremacy. For Klare, the brute facts of this new situation would appear to strip away the significance of ideology.

What is the broader political and cultural role of such an anti-ideological conception of history? Interestingly, Klare's answer to competition over resources has shifted significantly over time. In the conclusion of *Resource Wars* he put forward proposals for the establishment of a new infrastructure at the level of global governance in order to create a cooperative and collaborative system for sharing of natural resources. Typical of the technocratic reasoning shared by other proponents of the resources curse, such as Paul Collier,[9] Klare's proposals did not include revisions to the one-sided institutional representation of global economic interests or address a system increasingly based on competition and market allocation in every other sphere of life. Predictably then, Klare's later work *Rising Power, Shrinking Planet: The New Geopolitics of Energy* (2008) adopts a starker realist position, and he has used this book to propose the merits of a strategic alliance between the

United States and China, arguing that without a Sino-American alliance China is likely to ally itself with petroleum rich Russia – the petro-state he regards as the greatest threat to international energy security.[10] What makes Klare's output a particularly telling introduction to the political culture explored in this chapter is the way he has also translated his geopolitical analysis into a storyline for a Hollywood movie, following James Cameron's success in 2010 with *Avatar*.

On its own, Klare's strategy to give leverage to the United States through an alliance with China hardly matches the original geopolitical ideology of the United States – namely the nation's 'Manifest Destiny'. However, his plotline for a prequel to Cameron's film, to be called *Avatar: Earth's Last Stand*, does recover the key aspects of that national ideology. Klare pitches his storyline as 'a harrowing tale of environmental degradation, resource scarcity, and perennial conflict in the twilight years of humanity's decline'.[11] Unlike US General Custer, of course, the earth cannot take a subjective 'last stand', and what Klare's futurological storyline really serves to do is to make resource conflicts *manifest* and the blurring of geopolitical boundaries into something nearing *destiny*.[12] In his narrative, a new sovereign order has already emerged and three competing powers, called the North American Federation, Greater China, and the North European Alliance, 'continually jockey for dominance in shifting alliances, while their armies face one another in the torrid, still relatively resource-rich parts of the planet'.[13]

This dystopian vision belongs to the epoch of the mass spectacle, but is no less ideological for that.[14] If we take up this line of critique, rooted in the work of Guy Debord, the real significance of Klare's storyline, or indeed a film like *Avatar*, is the way that the environmental meta-narrative is monopolised by some of the people who consume most of the planet's resources. This is no mere irony. It is a paradox that points to the gargantuan logic of consumer sovereignty, which is the underlying reason a liberal academic seeking to frame twenty-first-century conflict as part of a post-ideological epoch may with some seriousness, and no sense of irony, propose a 'global blockbuster' movie to elevate his viewpoint.

In the case of Cameron's *Avatar*, the film's extraterrestrial humanoids living on the mineral-rich planet of 'Pandora' belong firmly to the genre of the noble savage. This exposed the film to some criticism in the United States – from where *Avatar* derives its racial tropes – yet the film's global appeal depends on the inherent dichotomy drawn between an industrially driven culture (the human invaders) and a nature-driven culture (the indigenous Na'vi of Pandora).[15] Without this dichotomy Cameron's epic storyline would certainly flounder. True to their genre, the Na'vi live in perfect social harmony with nature, apparently untroubled by either oligarchy or class. It is when the liberal terms of citizenship and the mandate for consumer sovereignty are in doubt that these idealised, and profoundly ideological, settlements with Mother Nature appear most of all.

It is this misleading relationship which is called into question by the frontispiece of this book, showing an archetypal hunter–warrior sculpted as part of a process of industrial construction and deconstruction. And it is worth pausing to remember that a production such as *Avatar*, which instead envisages a natural social order, is, above all, a mammoth technical and industrial project conducted on the terrain of international comparative advantage. Moreover, competing in the market of global cultural commodities is not inimical to deeply held humanitarian ideas. In defending *Avatar* from accusations of racism, Cameron stated that it 'asks us to open our eyes and truly see others, respecting them even though they are different, in the hope that we may find a way to prevent conflict and live more harmoniously'.[16] What belies and undermines Cameron's intentions, however, is the inherent denial of difference at the heart of a risible conception of social harmony and total oneness with nature.

In drawing so heavily on the genre of the noble savage, Cameron's vision of the Na'vi – virtually free game to an invading army – may embody the concept of 'bare life'. The philosopher Giorgio Agamben (1998) traces this back to the paradoxical figure in Roman law of *homo sacer*. In coming to symbolise the state's power over life, *homo sacer* existed at a vanishing point between religious and secular authority. Both sacred and damned, he could not be sacrificed for religious purposes but could be killed with impunity by anyone. Agamben concentrates on the continuing saliency of *homo sacer* in the politics of citizenship by drawing attention to the way 'states of exception' and 'states of emergency' are normalised. Drawing on Michel Foucault's theorisation of bio-politics, the refugee, the camp, and the clinical/legal grey area between life and death are Agamben's main themes.

The key political problem that emerges from Agamben's history of ideas is 'the separation between humanitarianism and politics' experienced today as 'the extreme phase of the separation of the rights of man from the rights of the citizen'.[17] In a system which generalises the former but appears to undermine the latter, it is not going too far to argue that the modern significance of *homo sacer* may be nothing less than the disproportionate abstraction of countless deaths – the enormous collateral damage of a system which wages war and struggles opportunistically in the name of democracy and liberal rights. Seen at this scale, Agamben carries a dispiriting message to anyone not dogmatically committed to some future negation of the negation, or in other words a rediscovery of the very things which humanitarianism currently finds necessary or convenient to neglect. As Slavoj Žižek has argued, Agamben's work may rearticulate a particular form of surrender, as if only God can save us now from the bleak horizons outlined by advanced capitalism.[18]

Increasingly this system does not offer a democracy propelled by the positive liberties thought to be required to call the state to account to the public interest.[19] The system today seems more delicately underpinned by the negative liberties of liberalism, the future of which now hangs on consumer sovereignty. Perhaps the most obvious rhetorical example of the consumer sovereignty is the often repeated argument that 'lifting people from poverty' depends on the success of consumerist society, wherever it can be sustained or brought into existence. However, behind this rhetoric is a growing legal web reversing positive liberties and suffocating equalities in communication that were won by an organised internationalist working class. A landmark in this revisionary trend was the *Buckley* v. *Valeo* case in 1976, when the US Supreme Court found that 'money is speech', effectively reversing earlier egalitarian legislation on free speech.[20] The result of this growing commercial domination, according to writers such as Barnett (2003), Shiner (2003) and Compton (2004), is a reductionism and commodification of public discourse. This entails a process of discursive ring-fencing that creates what Compton and Comor (2007) call 'walled gardens' – a metaphor used to describe the political limits and corporate management of the Live 8 debt campaign.

In light of these critiques I argue that consumer sovereignty produces contemporary *homo sacer* in multiple forms, but always as the object of pathos. Through modern historical comparisons I want to show how the visual discourse associated with the resource curse has come to be ideologically laden with this form of victimhood. To do so I take the approach of sociological poetics, rooted in the Bakhtin school of genre analysis that looks 'to [the] actual political relations conditioned by and produced in discourse itself'.[21] In other words, what follows is the examination of languages in action.

FROM DIALECTICAL TO UNDIALECTICAL REPRESENTATION

Sociological poetics provides a means to locate historically the visual culture of the resource curse. To situate this discourse, and to compare different cultural hierarchies that have influenced world history, I map a shift from what we can call *dialectical* representation to the *undialectical* representation. The latter, I argue, is now a persuasive device of supply-side aesthetics, which asks viewers to position themselves as consumers and erodes earlier practices of representation that succeeded in portraying socio-economic relations. But I begin with what is now an anachronistic example of undialectical representation.

Drawing on Rodríguez and Böhrt, Haarstad (2009) points out how the mythical image of the *leyenda obrero* (Figure 4.2) served trade-union subjectivities in Bolivia's original nationalised oil company, YPFB.[22] Although the predominately male oil workers in YPFB today have elected a woman leader in Camiri, this masculine iconography in the style of socialist realism persists as a glorification of the essential nature of labour in Bolivia's old 'oil capital'. In the present day this form of representation remains a convenient patriarchal fiction for the much weakened union organisation in the new version of the nationalised company, in which workers employed directly by the state are far more poorly paid and trained than those doing similar work for YPFB's private subcontracting companies. The same iconography that promotes an abstract notion of the dignity of labour is therefore a convenient fiction for the new Bolivian pluri-national state too. Here one might recall the arguments against socialist realism that it was neither socialist nor realist and that this style of representation was more an outcome of the imposition of Taylorist doctrines on the working class in the Soviet Union.[23] Typically, the body and machine become one, in this case through all too obvious phallic symbolism. But what is important for my purposes is how *undialectical* this image appears when seen next to the less heroic and more comparative vision that came from an international movement for working class self-representation (Figure 4.3).

A movement for class self-representation was formalised in Germany in the 1920s under the auspices of the Communist International and centred mainly on photography, film, journalism

Figure 4.2 Leyenda obrero, the image of the 'mythical' YPFB worker. Adopted from Rivera, in Haarstad (2009).

and theatre. Interviewed in the 1980s, Erich Rinka, the former general secretary of the Association of Worker–Photographers, and one of the communist protagonists in this project of class self-representation, recalled its foundational discussions in 1927. Rinka said,

> We were quite clear that we could never accomplish this enormous task by exclusively relying on the communists who owned a camera. We therefore conceived a policy of the inclusion of all worker-photographers, regardless of their party affiliation ... We only wanted to win the largest possible number of photo-correspondents who regarded events from a working class point of view.

Rinka went on to suggest the importance of sympathetic mass-media publications in relation to the serial form of photography pursued by worker–photographers:

Figure 4.3 Covers from the British publication the *Sunday Worker* in the 1920s, showing the early, and in this instance, satirical use of juxtaposition. Headline captions read 'The Hunting Season Has Commenced for Both Classes'; 'Workers Hunting for Clothes: Idlers Hunting for Grouse' (adopted from Dennett 1981).

The concept of a series of photos was ... a new feature. As far as I know such series had not appeared in any photo studio, or at any photo-exhibition of bourgeois photography up to that time. The worker–photographers on the other hand had been orientated from the start towards series [of pictures] and photo reports by the *AIZ* (*Der Arbeiter Fotograf*) magazine.

Q. Was that based on, experience, or was it an original idea?

It was based on the awareness that a worker–photographer was class conscious [sic] needed the ability to see certain things in connection with certain others. That was the only way the broad public could be shown these connections and have explained its own situation as a class.

Q. There were surely no romantic concepts?

No there were not. We even said that if a photographer goes out into the landscape, the ragged shepherd, for example, should certainly not be the photographic subject. Look behind the scene: why is he in rags? A ragged appearance is in no way romantic, but a concrete indication of a social situation.[24]

The influence of this movement for class self-representation, especially its dialectical anti-naturalism, can be seen in the design and in the sequencing and captioning of images in different countries. It is only necessary to illustrate briefly some of the photo-essay projects and publications from left photography, especially in the interwar period of the twentieth century, to see how different they are from the liberal humanist tradition of photography I come to shortly (Figures 4.4 and 4.5). However, I cannot hope to illustrate fully or describe faithfully the aesthetic complexity of either political ethos in this short chapter. For conciseness and precision I want to highlight three distinctive points about the project of working-class self-representation before returning to the contemporary visual culture of the resource curse and its liberal humanist master frame.

(1) The working-class political aesthetics highlighted by Rinka helped give birth to a dialectical approach in representation which meant that this radical photography created its *other*. This is something that can be readily seen in photography by Lisette Model or Arthur Leipzig, both associated with the New York Photo League, which was originally formed in 1930 as the cultural wing of Workers' International Relief. I don't believe it would be an exaggeration to say that the radical sense of the *other* created a new contingent means to view oligarchy. Contradictory juxtapositions in the sequencing of photographs helped to construct a sense of non-identification that may still be with us today if confronted with an image like Arthur Leipzig's 'Opening Night at the Opera' from 1948 (Figure 4.6).

This new sense of *otherness* in visual culture was brought about by turning the camera lens on the rich and powerful while also looking at the everyday working conditions and political life of ordinary people. By focusing attention on the ruling classes, not only does this perspective effectively point viewers to *the other of*

Figure 4.4   Page from *Workers' Illustrated News*, December 1929.
Courtesy of the Gallacher Memorial Library, Glasgow Caledonian
University Research Collection.

the other, but it is also intended to unsettle the gaze and self-identity
of viewers. As a consequence the design of photo-essays and the
relationship between images and captions became an increasingly
sophisticated way of addressing the social whole. This was much
in evidence in the second, more pro-labour, phase of the New
Deal in the United States (Figures 4.7 and 4.8).[25] The potential
tension between emotional identification and non-identification has
underpinned a great deal of psychologically sophisticated modern
photography indebted to the working-class movement (Figure
4.9). Indeed, it was because of the potential appropriation of that

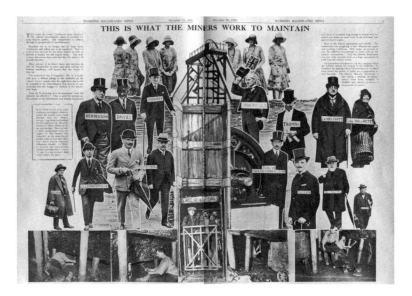

Figure 4.5 Double-Page Spread from *Workers' Illustrated News*, December 1929. Courtesy of the Gallacher Memorial Library, Glasgow Caledonian University Research Collection.

movement's rather sensational dialectical tactics that sections of the European avant-garde increasingly spoke, and acted, as if they needed to abolish aesthetic autonomy in favour of directly serving the communist movement.[26] The consequences of this were often tragic, as Stalinism increasingly took hold of communist politics internationally.

(2) Nevertheless, following on from the self-doubt on the part of some sections of the artistic avant-garde, we may also appreciate how dialectical representation was politically anchored to the networks which spawned it. In a social sense, dialectical representation could not flourish without the political capital articulated by the working-class movement. This is captured in interviews with surviving members of the New York Photo League which (characteristically of the relationships just described) provided discounted tuition to trade unionists. Lou Stettner, a former League member, amplified these practical connections when he was interviewed in 1978. Stettner said,

> People can only understand the Photo League when you take into
> context what was happening in America at the time historically

Figure 4.6 'Opening Night at the Opera', 1948. Photograph copyright Arthur Leipzig, reproduced by kind permission of the photographer.

Figure 4.7 Montage from the book *The Greatest Show on Earth: A Photographic Story of Man's Struggle for Wealth*, by S.A. Spencer, with art direction by Leslie Beaton, 1938. The caption of this section reads, 'So under the impartial guidance of Providence flourishes the much-debated miracle of men ... and machines ... the simultaneous movements that create consumers and eliminate producers ... the race between more employment and more unemployment ... the increasing standard of living ... the increasing ingenuity of the tools of industry and the increasing length of the lines of the unemployed'. Courtesy of Random House.

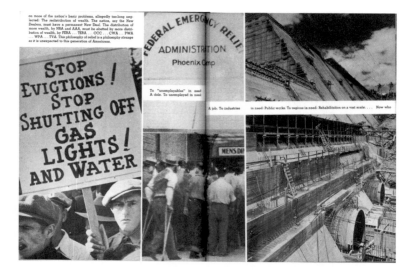

Figure 4.8   From *The Greatest Show on Earth: A Photographic Story of Man's Struggle for Wealth*, by S.A. Spencer, with art direction by Leslie Beaton, 1938. The closing spread of this book expressed ideological sympathy for 'New Deal America – pledged by the express will of twenty-seven million people to the control of capitalism!' Courtesy of Random House.

and socially ... the American working people were on the move, politically and socially. They were fighting the Depression and there was a huge progressive movement of hundreds of thousands of people and the Photo League was part of that movement.[27]

Another member, Walter Rosenblum, also said the League's work involved photographing 'our own flesh and blood. We're not ... tourists spying on the quaint mannerisms of the people.'[28]

In Germany workers had been proactively encouraged to differentiate their function from that of the artist, as Franz Hölerring stated in 1928: '[D]on't let yourself be misled into playful trifles which some try to play up by falsely alleging you are an artist of great dimensions – which in fact you are not. You are a worker. Be proud of it.'[29]

(3) Hölerring's cautionary remarks lead to my final point about the movement for class self-representation, namely that it involved the interplay of different species of cultural, social and political capital, a structural interdependency studied by Pierre Bourdieu (1993). This is well illustrated by the recollections of Photo-League

Figure 4.9   Photomontage by Karel Hajek, 1934. Adopted from Birgus (2002).

members like Walter Rosenblum who, when interviewed many years later, said,

> I owe the League everything. Without that organisation I might still have been a kid off the lower East Side who might have risen to the job of head shipping clerk at some dress factory. The League taught me about life, responsibility, photography, literature, art, relationships with people – everything.[30]

While I do not want to dehumanise Rosenblum's words, it is clear that the accumulation of social and cultural capital he describes was dependent on collectively networked political capital. This political capital stemmed in part from the League's connections with an increasingly militant labour movement in the United States. We may better understand the transference of political capital (as it surely would have appeared to Lou Stettner, quoted above) as the fruits of solidarity. This was demonstrated in the New Deal era, during which the League flourished to the benefit of many of its members. Although the pivotal role of political capital in relation to the acquisition of social and cultural capital seems difficult to avoid at a theoretical level, it has been blatantly ignored by researchers wishing to provide a capitalist-friendly theory of social capital.[31] In their desire to avoid class politics what is also bypassed is the all-important question of autonomy.

Despite its roots in the Communist International, the Photo League undoubtedly *had* autonomy and developed autonomously as part of the broader working-class movement. The rather vague term 'relative autonomy', employed theoretically by Louis Althusser, Bourdieu and others, might be better regarded here as an autonomy of scale, gained thanks to the level of democratic mobilisation to which the League belonged. Moreover, the degree of cultural autonomy enjoyed by the League (through which the organisation also moved away from socialist internationalism) was never quite 'a reversal' of the economic world, which is how Bourdieu envisaged the field of cultural production, creating an 'interest in disinterestedness' and something akin to a myth of autonomy.[32] As Bourdieu himself recognised, apparently disinterested aesthetic, literary or academic autonomy involves a game in which political and economic capital is disavowed or misrecognised.[33] Indeed, such a turnaround was attempted by the League when it became an avowedly 'aesthetic organisation' and aimed to be a 'Centre for American Photography'. However, in the eyes of the FBI during the McCarthy era, the organisation was still little else than an instrument of communism.

NEW LANGUAGES IN ACTION AND CONSUMER SOVEREIGNTY

In 1951 the New York Photo League closed down under pressure of 'blacklisting'. Magnum, a famous contemporary international photographers' cooperative, had already been founded in 1947 in the penthouse restaurant at the Museum of Modern Art in the same city. In contrast to the worker–photographers' movement, the exclusive Magnum agency has been interested in the professional autonomy of photographers, and not what we might today call media citizenship. Few Magnum members have pursued the critical realist approaches to photography begun in the working-class movement.[34] Overall the agency has distanced itself from what one of the organisation's foremost liberal proponents has called 'the dead hand of left aesthetics'.[35] In place of the attention given to dialectical relationships, both in photography and in society at large, Magnum has been very influential in bringing about and promoting a largely technocratic aesthetics that celebrates the sheer expressive power of images, and single images in particular. This ability to sell and resell iconic images is a key element in the visual culture of the resource curse, helping to articulate all the characteristic pathos upon which consumer sovereignty appears to thrive as a propaganda industry in its own right.

What is at issue here is made evident by an advertising campaign for the Lime Blue Diamond Store in Edinburgh in 2002. This campaign used photographs by the Brazilian photographer Sebastião Salgado, a former member of Magnum (Figure 4.10). The caption under one of Salgado's portraits used by Lime Blue reads: 'To find the perfect diamond he requires the help of a pushy over-eager sales assistant about as much as you do.' In fact, the photographs used for this campaign show impoverished Indian coal miners. The pictures were provided by Salgado in place of images of diamond miners who the advertisers felt did not appear sufficiently authentic.

Whereas workers' photography tried to construct the production of meaning in the interests of producers, what may be gleaned from this advertising campaign is the ability to manipulate the meaning of consumption through the plight of producers. As I've suggested above, the project of class self-representation often situated its ideal viewer in a position between different class interests, as if to ask, *Whose side are you on?* The aesthetics of liberal humanism, pursued by agencies like Magnum, invite viewers instead to identify directly with *the other* (as underdog) on a psychic level. No mutual and reciprocal strategy is either required or envisaged. Given that this visual reification superseded practices of reciprocity that still inform the ethos of enlightened self-interest in the labour movement today, and which underpinned the earlier realism of the workers' movement, we may understand this form of psychic identification as a type of synthetic solidarity fostered by images.[36] Indeed, the history of modern cultural institutions tells us that caring about images or being especially moved by them, has long been regarded by the power elite as a means to overcome and heal the politics of class.[37]

Of course, the attack on workers' autonomy and solidarity is first and foremost a political and legal assault on their civil rights. Nevertheless, once workers' social agency is substituted at a cultural

Figure 4.10   Photograph by Sebastião Salgado (ex-Magnum) used by Lime Blue Diamond Store for their advertising campaign in Edinburgh, 2002. The caption under the portrait reads, 'To find the perfect diamond he requires the help of a pushy over-eager sales assistant about as much as you do'. Author's photograph.

level by synthetic solidarity, it is not surprising to find that images become the sort of free-floating signifiers of postmodern repute. But the duplicity and the ambiguity of meaning evident in the last illustration is no historical novelty in visual culture, and ultimately, it should be asked if it really matters? The answer may be that it matters only if one is also interested in the underlying dynamics of spectacular society, which, according to Guy Debord's theory, is not made up by an ever growing collection and distribution of imagery, but more fundamentally is 'a social relation among people, mediated by images'.[38] It is from this standpoint, very close to that of sociological poetics, that it becomes possible to see the political culture of consumer sovereignty in the making.

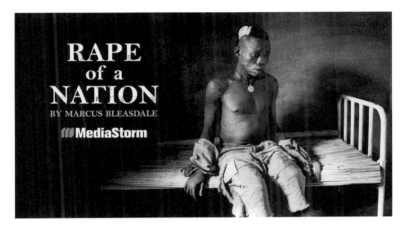

Figure 4.11   Media-storm webpage cover image of *Rape of a Nation*, photograph by Marcus Bleasdale, reproduced by kind permission of the photographer.

A morally earnest project done in the liberal humanist documentary tradition on the terrain of the resource curse is *Rape of a Nation*, by the photographer Marcus Bleasdale (Figure 4.11). As a vocal witness to the suffering of people in the Democratic Republic of Congo, Bleasdale draws a harrowing online narrative to a close with the following recommendations:

> I think there's one thing that we can do as consumers, and that is be aware of where our natural resources come from. When you're buying gold, when you're buying diamonds ask the retailer if they know where they're coming from. And that's one of the ways that we as consumers can maintain pressure on an industry that is sometimes not as diligent as it can be.
>
> One of the main things that will bring Congo out of the situation that it's in at the moment is education. There are great organizations that are working in DRC. Save the Children, UNICEF, Human Rights Watch is doing an enormous amount of work. And organizations such as UNHCR are providing the stability and the infrastructure to allow the children to receive some form of education ... A better-educated population leads to better questions, and better questioning population leads to a better government.[39]

At the time of writing, there are 114 comments about *Rape of a Nation*, mainly from people living in the United States posted at the

MediaStorm website, which hosts varied documentary projects. For the most part, the posted responses to *Rape of a Nation* are admiring and come from people clearly engaged by Bleasdale's work. Although his commentary attempts to construct particular audience responses, interestingly only five postings mention Bleasdale's emphasis on education and only six take up his call for ethical consumerism. Clearly not all of the correspondents are in a position to buy gold and diamonds anyway. Two complain about the emotional rhetoric and the unrealism of his proposals, while another two suggest some sort of larger organised 'boycott'. Fifteen voice support for humanitarian aid projects. Six call for some sort of major intervention; these include calls for military action and recolonisation. However, the vast majority of postings (at least 42) see the DRC's problems as a moral and spiritual dilemma of international dimensions, and around 36 concentrate on the documentary project itself as an important means of communication. Although the US-led invasion of Iraq is mentioned in eight responses, historic geopolitics and the troubles of African anti-imperialism are made almost invisible by Bleasdale's project, unless by default when a respondent from Washington asks: 'Why no mention of the "int'l communities" (US, others) support for the dictatorships alluded to in the film?'

What can be taken from these responses is the contemporary meaning of *homo sacer* which Agamben finds in the separation of humanitarian and political discourses. This appears to be more than the elision of complex political histories evident in humanitarian modes of address. The segregation also depends on constructing discursive 'walled gardens' in which audiences are invited to exercise politics through the logic of consumer sovereignty. Moreover, this is not limited to calls for ethical consumerism; and much more significantly it involves the consumption of a variety of media products sponsored by major corporations or elite-forming interest groups. In the case of *Rape of a Nation* online, the normative discursive frame here adheres to a network of bodies such as the US Council on Foreign Relations and the Asia Society, and the *Washington Post*, to which MediaStorm's work is linked.

If the phrase 'development porn'[40] has any purchase, it is because the type of representation which gains increasing visibility through this sort of network of political and cultural capital effectively positions viewers as autonomous consumers of information. Its audience is subject to a wholly voluntary politics that have nothing (realistically) to do with their own everyday conditions of life. This is, of course, why the mores of ethical consumerism are overwhelmingly business-friendly. At a theoretical level, the effect of this obscure cognitive project is that the public appears 'resubstantialised, as a single collective subject' and 'its presence is therefore not registered through open debate'[41] as Barnett (2003) has argued. Nevertheless a handful of critical comments made about Bleasdale's documentary project show that such paternalism never goes totally uncontested; but what is just as notable is an apparent impatience with critical reasoning, when, for example, one respondent complains about the comments of another: '[T]his is not a school and you're not the teacher. Go help someone.'

What is produced overall by the humanitarian frame exemplified by *Rape of a Nation* is a drama that makes labour politics and the enlightened self-interest of workers appear banal and amoral next to the extremes of suffering and exploitation. In keeping with the same melodramatic process driving discursive commodification, a law of diminishing returns or moral fatigue sets in that is met by a misleading inflationary trend in death counts asserted in Bleasdale's project.[42] Left to its own devices, it is difficult to see how the rhetoric of humanitarianism could have any other outcome but effectively to bring down a new moral 'iron curtain' around consumer sovereignty.[43]

The visual rhetoric of consumer sovereignty is surprisingly pervasive. In an apparently radically oriented book on Nigeria, *Curse of the Black Gold: 50 Years of Oil in the Niger Delta*, edited by the Marxian social geographer Michael Watts, the photographer Ed Kashi (2008) pursues the most undialectical uncritical traditions of photography. Therefore, despite the presence of sizeable white cantonments, Nigeria's oil economy appears to be almost wholly 'black'. Resistance to a petroleum-based hegemony is seen to hinge on violence in the Niger Delta rather than the less marketable politics of the Nigerian labour movement. And finally, the misery of Kashi's subjects is broken only by a few pictures showing the sort of 'local colour' intended to relieve the eyes, at least according to the thinking of picture editors at publications like the magazine *National Geographic*, where Kashi's photographs also appear[44] (Figures 4.12 and 4.13).

Indeed, the mores of *National Geographic* provide the master frame for Kashi's work, and any attempt to think through the costs of this from a Marxian perspective have been abandoned. Consequently the contemporary relationship between oligarchy and imperialism is again invisible, and the ruling class has vanished from the scene. This is a pity, since Kashi (a US citizen) would

Figure 4.12   Cover of *Curse of The Black Gold: 50 Years of Oil in the Niger Delta*, photographs by Ed Kashi, edited by Michael Watts, published by Powerhouse Books, New York (2008). Reproduced by kind permission of the photographer (original in colour).

have been well positioned to be a fly on the wall in Nigeria and (just as importantly for Nigerians) elsewhere in America or Europe. Unfortunately, his work offers no such conceptual space for any new pro-labour subjectivity to take root. If there is an implicit assumption behind *Curse of the Black Gold* that realism and political aesthetics are a lower priority compared to the task of disseminating political issues to civil society in consumerist economies it is a highly problematic one. It betrays the belief that democratic political and economic development is bound up with democratic cultural development and that these spheres should not be artificially separated. But to make this argument is not to assume that supposedly autonomous acts of representation should be avoided or that participation must be organised in order to remain

Figure 4.13   Photograph by Ed Kashi from *Curse of The Black Gold: 50 Years of Oil in the Niger Delta*, reproduced by kind permission of the photographer (original in colour).

faithful to the historic gains of class consciousness. It would be a mistake to assume that class self-representation and the relations of political and cultural capital I described earlier can be managed and brought to life at the very moment when the working class as the key international countervailing force against capitalism is most in doubt.

When the League photographer Walter Rosenblum said in 1948, 'We're not ... tourists spying on the quaint mannerisms of the people', he was already implying the subornation of realism in the public sphere to an increasingly spectacular and predatory culture that would create a social landscape to be surveyed from a position of economic and political disinterest.[45] If, we are not to sink into the pathos that ensued, what is needed today are clearer appraisals of the lack of cultural democracy and a renewed poetics capable of tackling consumer sovereignty and targeting the audience democracy at its core.[46] The turn to a participatory aesthetic, exemplified by the work of artists such as Renzo Martens in his film *Enjoy Poverty* (2009), looks ill-equipped to answer this larger problem of cultural industrialisation, because it is increasingly led by globally mobile artists and cultural entrepreneurs rather than communities facing the issues of their political rights and cultural democracy.[47] Indeed, in many instances, the social landscape of the 1950s has been revamped by the fashion for participatory art projects. However, none of this would seem to be a good reason for the surrender of critical realism that is typified by a project like *Curse of the Black Gold*.

PATHOS AND TRAGEDY

The languages in action explored above and their spectacular relationship to consumer sovereignty draw me to the distinction between pathos and tragedy. I cannot find a better commentary on this distinction than the source of the title of this chapter: Arthur Miller's dramaturgical essay 'Tragedy and the Common Man', written in 1949. What underlies tragedy for Miller is a struggle against injustice that makes tragedy cherished and plausible to humankind, whereas pathos is the truly pessimistic mode of address that dignifies a deeper apathy.

> The possibility of victory must be there in tragedy. Where pathos rules, where pathos is finally derived, a character has fought a battle he could not possibly have won. The pathetic is achieved when the protagonist is, by virtue of his witlessness, his insensitivity, or the very air he gives off, incapable of grappling with a much superior force.[48]

On the basis of the precautionary principle, climate change threatens to become *the* inescapable, and therefore true, resource curse. And perhaps it is in this context that we can best see how far the distinction between pathos and tragedy has been erased. We may also see in the example I now come to just how far the 'masculine virtues of magnanimity and generosity and courage', which feminists like Germaine Greer wanted to claim (against the strictures of matriarchy), have in fact been driven further away from both women and men.[49] The result, an unleashing of pathos, can be picked up in Mary Robinson's attempt to instigate a symbolic reordering in her role as president of the Ethical Globalization Initiative. In 2009 Robinson said, 'The image of climate change is the polar bear. I like polar bears, too, but that is the wrong image. The image of climate change is a poor farmer, and she is a woman and she is desperate.'[50]

Some of Robinson's interventions showing the positioning rhetoric of pathos might be comically suggestive of a matriarchal ethos at play in the public sphere (Figure 4.14). In promoting

Figure 4.14   Photograph by Photocall, Ireland, July 2009. Captioned, 'Mary Robinson helps Daniel Doyle put some final touches to his sculpture depicting the human impact of climate change'. Reproduced by courtesy of Photocall/Oxfam (orginal in colour).

human rights through her varied influential roles, Robinson, former president of Ireland, has taken care to emphasise 'the grassroots', and I do not want to call her sincerity into question. However, the grassroots Robinson speaks about are indistinguishable from the sort of 'NGOism' and the networks of neoliberal governmentality examined in more detail in Chapter 10. Perhaps the starkest example of the contradictory nature of these networks is the instance of an Indian GONGO (government organised non-governmental organisation) devoted to the cause of women's empowerment that sacked its women workers for unionising.[51] Indeed, Robinson's liberal mixture of feminism and human rights makes the linkage of labour and gender politics appear to be defunct in anything but a deradicalised corporatist political form. This crisis of feminism is not incidental to a matriarchal symbolism of moral interdependency that Robinson and others promote. The 'grassroots' thought among some workers and communities in oil-producing nations, that they could make better use of their natural political capital and express a much greater independence and strength in the marketplace than offered them by OPEC, is masked by the helpless icons of bare life which stand in for apparently powerless states.

It is not so much that the idea of holding avaricious customers to ransom is taboo, as that to seriously articulate a state policy to slow down production may only be a step away from igniting war or other forms of violent retaliation. The US Senate's bills threatening to sue OPEC show a belligerent attitude which is at odds with all the talk in the West about developing renewable energy technology.[52] Inevitably, the lurking threat of more violent courses of action on the part of major consuming nations forestalls a deeper and more strongly negotiated politics of development in oil-producing nations.[53] So when it comes to the hegemonic discourses of climate change, Agamben's critique of 'the separation between humanitarianism and politics' cannot be faulted. Intimidation, powerlessness and 'witlessness' all make up the pathetic order of the day. This makes Miller's argument all the more important: 'No tragedy can … come about when its author fears to question absolutely everything, when he regards any institution, habit, or custom as being either everlasting, immutable, or inevitable.'[54]

It might well be asked at this point if a multifaceted culture of pathos is masking the construction of a deeper and far-reaching political tragedy. After all, Michel Foucault's famous proviso, 'Where there is power there is resistance', may appear to anticipate tragedy as an objective condition. If so, this is countered by Lila Abu Loghod and others, who have argued that Foucault's maxim is insufficient, and by stating instead that 'where there is resistance there is power … we can begin to ask questions about precisely what relations of power are at play in different contexts'.[55] Unfortunately too many studies and reports of petroleum economies, including left-leaning portrayals like *Curse of the Black Gold*, exemplify 'walled gardens' in public discourse rather than prisms which capture the contemporary scope of resource-related politics. Therefore, some of the most powerful meanings, as well as important local nuances and weaknesses of political articulation, are driven out by an overarching discourse largely framed in the consuming nations.

CONCLUSION

Pathos is a rhetorical mode of address that is patronised and funded by power elites. Unlike the realism which emerged historically through the politics of working-class self-representation, pathos reasserts power relations, typically by calling us to identify with those who are in a position to show *their* pity. To truly understand such discourses as language in action, I have argued for an understanding of the interdependent relations of cultural and political capital and the ways in which these relations are rearticulated by consumer sovereignty. In photography, this rearticulation of cultural and political capital was carried forward by agencies like Magnum, which capitalised on the cold war and was able to gain professional autonomy and prestige as a purveyor of pathos in the public sphere.

In distinguishing tragedy from pathos in dramaturgy, and by reminding us of the possibility of victory that is inherent in tragedy, Arthur Miller was not of course proposing the sort of false optimism which characterises so much of the imagery sponsored by NGOs and development organisations, any more than he was advocating socialist realist glorifications. Nor does his classical critique corroborate the hasty celebratory impulses that overcome some left-wingers at the first sign of trouble or resistance today.

The communist Eric Rinka argued that it was only through the critical participation of the working class (regardless of workers' individual political affiliations) that the broad public could be shown its own situation as a class. This international movement for class self-representation blossomed all too briefly before it was swamped by the combined forces of fascism and Stalinism, leaving it to be virtually extinguished by cold war corporatism. Nevertheless, in laying emphasis on the social whole through its visual rhetoric, this movement was crucial in dismantling various 'walled gardens' in public discourse, which were barriers to social democracy. The main example I have given came from the New Deal in the United States, and without this same movement it would be impossible to imagine the second phase of the New Deal, which occurred when the forces of militant labour were combined with a plethora of groupings in support of progressive taxation. This was the basis of what economists such as Paul Krugman call 'the great compression', in which US society was equalised as never before.[56]

Consumer sovereignty resurrects the cultural barriers to a meaningful and empowered social democracy, and as long as these remain in place the processes of public reason will continue to be tainted by the rule of pathos. The resource curse in visual culture provides ample evidence of the way in which the underlying socio-economic relations are masked, a fact which becomes especially evident when one considers how this so-called curse has as much to do with accelerated growth as with social and environmental degradation. This paradoxical reality points to a quite different visual culture that is far more private and *not* apparently cursed, unless by conspicuous affluence (Figure 4.15). But the resource curse

Figure 4.15   Portrait studio, Santa Cruz de la Sierra, Bolivia. Photograph by the author (original in colour).

is one of several reductive categories, each of which allows poverty to be discursively repackaged and resold, and all of which add up to a minor boom in the industry of the spectacle.

The reconfiguration of class, or the understanding of class as a shifting set of structural antagonisms, surely demands that class politics and epistemological scope be seen as problematic interconnected issues, especially if the basis of consumer sovereignty is to be challenged. In the context of the resource curse, we can see how a combination of academics and cultural entrepreneurs succeed in narrowing public discourse and create the walled gardens which are so productive of Agamben's 'bare life' – a human condition denuded of substantial political rights. The examples I have given fundamentally call into question the conservative idea that the bourgeoisie is the universal class upon which democracy and development depend.

NOTES

1. From 'Tragedy and the Common Man' by Arthur Miller (1993).
2. See Rosser 2006.
3. Centred in south-eastern Nigeria the Ibo (also spelt Igbo) people are one of the three largest ethno-linguistic groupings in Nigeria.

4. See A.A. Madiebo, 'Obasanjo, the Civil War, and Resource Control', VANGUARD Lagos, 14 June 2001, accessed March 2010, www.waado.org/ nigerdelta/essays/resourcecontrol/Madiebo.html. Madiebo's assertion that this was the first ethnic cleansing in Africa overlooks episodes in colonial history, such as the genocide of Hereros in Namibia begun in 1904 by Lieutenant-General Lothar von Trotha.

5. See Klare 2001, p.213.

6. Klare 2004, p.x.

7. 'Resource-related conflict' is a qualifying term that Klare uses briefly at the outset of his book *Resource Wars* (2001). As a whole the book follows the more monolithic logic of the title.

8. See Giroux 2008.

9. See William Aal, Lucy Jarosz and Carol Thompson, 'Food Crisis Debates: Open Letter to Paul Collier', 2009, accessed November 2010, http:// concernedafricascholars.org/food-crisis-debates/

10. See Klare's public presentation at the Connecticut World Affairs Council on Fora TV, accessed March 2010, http://fora.tv/2008/04/22/Michael_Klare_Rising_ Powers_Shrinking_Planet

11. Klare 2010.

12. Although the discourse of Manifest Destiny dates back to the 1840s, when the term was used by US Democrats to justify war with Mexico, it is also an articulation of an earlier 'continentalism' which promoted the idea that the United States was destined to expand to the Pacific ocean and eventually encompass the entire north American continent. Stuart Elden gives a highly relevant account of 'fear, threat and division' in contemporary geopolitical map-making by the US political class; see Elden 2009, pp.1–33.

13. From 'Avatar: The Prequel', Klare 2010.

14. See Debord 1970.

15. Cameron's *Avatar* was criticised as racist and/or 'anti-white' from different quarters. See, for example, Gary Susman, 'Is *Avatar* Racist?', accessed March 2010, www.moviefone.co.uk/2010/01/11/is-avatar-racist/

16. Ibid.

17. See Agamben 1998, p.133.

18. Žižek points to Agamben's engagement with the work of Heidegger and the Frankfurt School. See Žižek 2008, pp.337–41.

19. See Bobbio 1990, p.89.

20. *Buckley v. Valeo*, 424 US 1 (1976). See Barnett 2003, p.122.

21. See Hirschkop 1986, p.111.

22. See Haarstad 2009, pp.244–5.

23. See Buck-Morss 2002, pp.98–111.

24. From 'The First Conference of Worker Photographers 1927: The Memories of Erich Rinka'. See Osman 1981, pp.71–2.

25. See Stein 1992 for an account of the evolution of design of photo-essays during the New Deal.

26. Examples of the avant garde crisis to which I refer can be seen in Vaneigem 1999, pp.31–2, and in the political trajectories of surrealists such as Karel Tiege, who exemplify artistic self-consciousness in the interwar period. See Birgus 2002, pp.24–5, 175–89.

27. From an interview by Colin Osman; see Osman 1983, p.1021.

28. Walter Rosenblum, 1948, quoted in Ollman 1994, p.157.

29. From A. Reuther, 'Leafing through the journal *Der Arbeiter-Fotograf*'; see Osman 1981, p.87.
30. Anne Tucker finds these sentiments echoed by other men and women associated with the League. See Tucker 1994, p.176.
31. See Fine 2010.
32. See Bourdieu 1993, p.40.
33. Ibid., pp.68–81.
34. An important exception here is the late Philip Jones Griffiths, a long time president of Magnum and a frank commentator on the shortcomings of the agency. Griffiths saw the agency as a beneficiary of cold war politics and he offers, quite unconsciously, an illustration of the issues of the indirect and complex transference of political capital theorised by Bourdieu. See Griffiths' interview by Bob Dannin in 2002, accessed July 2008, www.musarium.com/stories/vietnaminc/interview.html
35. This phrase is used by Michael Ignatieff, who argues that the world has been made transparent by press photography. See Ignatieff 2000, p.52.
36. This is not to imply that synthetic solidarity does not also exist in the arenas of labour politics; indeed it appears pivotal to corporatist style trade unionism. However, my focus here is on the infantilisation of relations between producers and consumers.
37. John Carey's book *What Good are the Arts?* explores 'the use of the arts as a means of raising the thoughts and improving the behaviour of the poor and so making them feel less antagonistic towards the rich'. See Carey 2005, p.133.
38. See Debord 1970, sec.4.
39. From www.mediastorm.org/0022.html, accessed March 2010.
40. For a discussion of the term 'development porn' as NGO sponsored imagery, see www.aidg.org/component/option,com_jd-wp/Itemid,34/p,488/
41. See Barnett 2003, p.200.
42. Thanks to Ingrid Samset for pointing out this inflationary trend to me. See Mack 2010.
43. My cluster analysis of online responses to *Rape of a Nation* is not exhaustive; mainly it shows the disparity between Bleasdale's stated aims and the terms of engagement of his online audience.
44. For a relevant content analysis study, see Lutz and Collins 1993.
45. For a close reading of the post-war social landscape in the United States see Vettel-Becker 2005.
46. See Mair 2006.
47. Some of the underlying problems here can be gleaned from Marten's provocative documentary film, *Enjoy Poverty* (2009).
48. Miller 1993.
49. See Greer 1970, p.330.
50. 'Euranet's European Development Days Blog', accessed March 2010, www.euranet.eu/eng/Dossier/European-Development-Days/Euranet-s-European-Development-Days-Blog
51. See Sharma 2006.
52. Bills passed by the US Senate in 2005 and 2007, designed to put pressure on OPEC to meet increasing demand, mark a historic role reversal. The Achnacarry Agreement of 1928, between Esso, BP and Shell, was designed to limit competition and counter overproduction and price crashes. 'Conservation' and 'wasteful production' were watchwords of the time. In the long run, OPEC

came on the scene partly to ensure production of neglected oil fields such as those in Iraq. Eventually, in 1961, Iraq nationalised all concessions that were not being exploited.

53. As the case of Norway would suggest, the state's control over the pace of production is a key to broad-based development policies and to the political contests over such policies. See Ryggvik 2010, pp.81–95.

54. Miller 1993.

55. Law 1997, p.112.

56. 'Paul Krugman: Income Inequality and the Middle Class', accessed March 2010, www.youtube.com/watch?v=5kwA-CwFK5A&feature=related. See Rauch 1944 for a close overview of the different forces at play during the two phases of the New Deal. Schwarz 1994 throws a more favourable light on the New Deal as a whole, concentrating on the legacy of a liberal technocracy which, Schwarz argues, advanced a generally beneficial state capitalist project until the 1970s.

REFERENCES

Agamben, G. (1998) *Homo Sacer: Sovereign Power and Bare Life* (Palo Alto, Calif.: Stanford University Press).

Barnett, C. (2003) *Culture and Democracy, Media Space and Representation* (Edinburgh: Edinburgh University Press).

Bobbio, N. (1990) *Liberalism and Democracy* (London: Verso).

Bourdieu, P. (1993) *The Field of Cultural Production*, ed. R. Johnson (Cambridge: Polity Press).

Birgus, V. (ed.) (2002) *The Czech Photographic Avant-Garde 1918–1948* (Cambridge, Mass.: MIT Press).

Buck-Morss, S. (2002) *Dreamworld and Catastrophe, The Passing of Mass Utopia in East and West* (Cambridge, Mass.: MIT Press).

Carey, J. (2005) *What Good Are the Arts?* (London: Faber and Faber).

Compton, J.R. (2004) *The Integrated News Spectacle: A Political Economy of Cultural Performance* (New York: Peter Lang).

—— and Comor, E. (2007) 'The Integrated News Spectacle, Live 8 and the Annihilation of Time', *Canadian Journal of Communication*, 32: 29–53.

Dennett, T. (1981) 'The British Film and Photo League', *Creative Camera*, 197/198 (London: Coo Press).

Debord, G. (1970) 'Society of the Spectacle', *Radical America*, 4(5) (Detroit: Black and Red).

Elden, S. (2009) *Terror and Territory: The Spatial Extent of Sovereignty* (Minneapolis: University of Minnesota Press).

Fine, B. (2010) *Theories of Social Capital: Researchers Behaving Badly* (London: IIPPE/Pluto Press).

Greer, G. (1970) *The Female Eunuch* (London: Paladin).

Giroux, H.A. (2008) *The University in Chains: Confronting the Military–Industrial–Academic Complex* (Boulder, Col.: Paradigm Publishers).

Haarstad, H. (2009) 'FDI policy and political spaces for labour: The disarticulation of the Bolivian *petroleros*', *Geoforum*, 40(2): 239–48.

Hirschkop, K. (1986) 'Bakhtin, discourse and democracy', *New Left Review*, 160 (November– December): 92–113.

Ignatieff, M. (2000) *Magnum Degrees* (London: Phaidon Press).

Kashi, E. (2008) *Curse Of The Black Gold: 50 Years of Oil in the Niger Delta*, ed. M. Watts (New York: Powerhouse Books).

Klare, M.T. (2001) *Resource Wars, The New Landscape of Global Conflict* (New York: Metropolitan Books).

—— (2004) *Blood and Oil: The Dangers and Consequences of America's Growing Dependency on Imported Petroleum* (New York: Metropolitan Books).

—— (2008) *Rising Powers, Shrinking Planet: How Scarce Energy is Creating a New World Order* (Oxford: Oneworld).

—— (2010) 'Avatar: The Prequel. Will "Earth's Last Stand" Sweep the 2013 Oscars?' www.huffingtonpost.com/michael-t-klare/iavatar-the-prequeli-will_b_473861. html.

Law, L. (1997) 'Dancing on the Bar', in M. Keith and S. Pile (eds) *Geographies of Resistance* (London: Routledge).

Lutz, C.A. and Collins, J.L. (1993) *Reading National Geographic* (Chicago: University of Chicago Press).

Mack, A. (ed.) (2010) *Human Security Report 2009: The Shrinking Costs of War*, Human Security Report Project (Vancouver: Simon Fraser University).

Mair, P. (2006) 'Ruling the Void? The Hollowing out of Western Democracy', *New Left Review*, 42 (November–December): 25–51.

Miller, A. (1993) 'Tragedy and the Common Man' (orig. 1949), in H.P. Guth and G.L. Rico (eds) *Discovering Literature* (New Jersey: Prentice Hall).

Ollman, L. (1994) 'The Photo League's Forgotten Past', *History of Photography*, 18(2): 154–8.

Osman, C. (ed.) (1981) *Creative Camera: Der Arbeiter Fotograf and The British Worker in Photographs 1839–1939* (London: Coo Press).

—— (ed) (1983) *Creative Camera*, 223 and 224 (London: Coo Press).

Rauch, B. (1944) *The History of the New Deal* (New York: Creative Age Press).

Ryggvik, H. (2010) *The Norwegian Oil Experience: A Toolbox for Managing Resources?* (Oslo: University of Oslo, Centre for Technology, Innovation and Culture).

Rosser, A. (2006) 'The Political Economy of the Resource Curse: A Literature Survey', Working Paper 268 (Brighton: Institute of Development Studies).

Schwarz, J.A. (1994) *The New Dealers: Power Politics in the Age of Roosevelt* (New York: Vintage Books).

Sharma, A. (2006) *Crossbreeding Institutions, Breeding Struggle: Women's Employment, Neoliberal Governmentality, and State (Re)Formation in India* (Middletown, Conn.: Division II Faculty Publications, Wesleyan University).

Shiner, R.A. (2003) *Freedom of Commercial Expression* (Oxford: Oxford University Press).

Stein, S. (1992) '"Good fences make good neighbours": American Resistance to Photomontage Between the Wars', in M. Teitelbaum (ed.) *Montage and Modern Life 1919–1942* (Cambridge, Mass.: MIT Press).

Tucker, A. (1994) 'A History of the Photo League: The Members Speak', *History of Photography*, 18(2): 174–84.

Vaneigem, R. (as J.-F. Dupuis) (1999) *A Cavalier History of Surrealism* (Edinburgh: AK Press).

Vettel-Becker, P. (2005) *Shooting from the Hip: Photography, Masculinity, and Postwar America* (Minneapolis: University of Minnesota Press).

Žižek, S. (2008) *In Defence of Lost Causes* (London: Verso).

Part 2

States of Collective Consumption

Reading the Constitution, Constitutional workshop, Miranda State, Venezuela. Photograph by Owen Logan.

5
Development from Below and Oil Money from Above: Popular Organisation in Contemporary Venezuela

Iselin Åsedotter Strønen

Caracas, spring 2010: 'Let's go into that house so you can see how bad it really is', Pedro suggests, pointing down the narrow street lined with red brick houses on both sides. We are wandering through the neighbourhood of Santa Maria in one of the larger shantytowns of Caracas. It is a warm Monday morning, and Pedro and other people from the community are showing technical employees from the municipality the problems with the inadequate drainage system. Pedro, a man in his forties, is one of the prime movers in the local Communal Council – the local decision-making organ sanctioned in law as a means to formalise resource distribution to local communities.

Pedro approaches an open door with a friendly 'buenas tardes' and a woman answers inside. He explains to her that that the public officials want to see 'las filtraciones' ('the leakages'). The tired-looking woman in her sixties, dressed in a pink blouse and red trousers, tells us to enter. As we cross the door step we are met with a dense, nauseating smell that makes my nose and throat tickle. The source of the smell is obvious; the wall in the back of the room is covered with black mould. The room, perhaps some 20 square metres in total, is filled with an old refrigerator, a washing machine, a sink and a laundry basket. The plates and glasses are cleaned and neatly stacked on a shelf next to a sink. In the back of the room are two mattresses, clothes and other household items. The wall next to the bed is also spotted with black mould. There are no windows in the back, only next to the door where we entered. As I take a few more steps into the room, the smell thickens. This is the home of a family with several children. The two beds are shared between the kids and the adults. 'The grandma in the house died last year from some respiratory illness', Pedro tells me.

The woman doesn't say much, she just listens and nods as Pedro talks and gesticulates and explains the direction of leakage to the men from the municipality. The Communal Council is trying to get an overview of which houses in the sector need repairing, which are beyond repair, and which inhabitants need to be relocated. When it rains, the sewage system in Monte Arriba, the sector above us, isn't capable of handling the downpour. Thus, the water runs downhill to Santa Maria, leaking into houses and flooding the streets. The main pipes in the area were laid some 50 years ago. Since then additional pipes have been precariously laid down as an increasing number of households have been hooked up to the under-dimensioned pipe system. Like other barrios in Caracas, the community expanded as people flocked to the capital in search of a better life. Little by little, cardboard shacks became brick stone houses, new homes were built on top of the older ones, streets were paved, electricity and water were piped in through the community's own efforts. Now, many sectors have become established communities, though new shacks are set up on the fringes with every passing year. For the woman and her family, the result of the inadequate infrastructure is that water keeps leaking into their house, causing disaster every time it rains. The dampness never leaves the walls, and as the building has several floors and is located on a natural slope in the hill, it is difficult to repair.

After a few minutes we thank the woman and leave. It is a great relief to fill our lungs with fresh air again, but for me the prickling sensation in my throat and nose remains for many minutes afterwards. Just the thought of sleeping in that room produces a feeling of asphyxiation.

This chapter focuses on Communal Councils in the *barrios* (poor neighbourhoods) in Caracas, the capital of Venezuela, based on several periods of research between 2005 and 2011. The analysis will be located in a context which illustrates the evolving nature of popular-sector organisation[1] during the past decade, and which takes into consideration the historical trajectories that led to the emergence of Hugo Chávez and the current political polarisation between supporters and opponents of the government.

Since 2006, Communal Councils have been the focus of government policy for the democratisation of local-level decision making and for the redistribution of wealth. Through these councils, organised communities are granted the legal right to plan, solicit funds, and execute local development projects based on the inhabitants' collectively agreed priorities. Communal Councils can be organised anywhere, but for the most part they have been formed in poor rural and urban neighbourhoods.[2]

The case of the Communal Councils is interesting for several reasons. First, because it represents a strategy to redistribute state resources that explicitly addresses formerly disenfranchised sectors of the population. Claims for sharing in the country's wealth stemming from natural resources have been a key factor for radical political mobilisation amongst impoverished groups during the past decade not only in Venezuela, but also in other countries, such as Bolivia and Ecuador. The case of the Communal Councils in Venezuela therefore illustrates a context-specific outcome of these *wider* struggles over the use of resource wealth. As I also demonstrate, the Communal Councils ought to be seen in the historical context of the social articulation of the political field between government and popular sectors. The foundations of this social alliance may be seen in the rejection of the legitimacy of the formerly dominant political sectors that are now in opposition, and which emerge mainly from the middle-and upper classes. This shift in political power and alliance building evidences the exhaustion of a political system that had monopoly in Venezuela for four decades, and raises important questions about the effects of neoliberalism and liberal elite democracy in Latin America.

However, I will argue that the case of the Communal Councils illustrates the inherent challenges, not only in altering a legacy of mass poverty, but also in fomenting new political spaces and cultures through which popular participation and collective aspirations are regarded as cornerstones of government policy. This is a process that involves not only changing the *modus operandi* of the state institutions, but it is also challenged by the persisting historical legacy of a socio-political culture that cultivated patronage, clientelism and individual dreams of consumption.

THE LEGACY OF SOCIAL INEQUALITY

Inequality in Venezuela has produced highly differentiated life worlds and social identities, resulting in a society that is increasingly articulated by class politics, albeit heavily nuanced by racial identities, gender issues and the politics of social space which I focus on in this chapter. A fair share of the middle-class votes for the government,[3] but by far the most vocal and visible group of Chávez's supporters was formed in the popular sectors. Although voting patterns are not purely class based, Chávez's popularity since the late 1990s reflects a historical polarisation of the Venezuelan polity along class lines.[4]

Social conflicts emerging from structural inequality are by no means features that emerged *because* of Chávez, although it is a conventional claim amongst opposition supporters that 'Chávez destroyed the harmonious society that we had before'. However, this perception is an illustration in itself of the diverging social realities that Venezuelan society is founded upon. A female informant in her late forties once commented to me that

> [t]hey [the middle and upper class opposition] never knew anything about the living conditions in the rest of the society. They didn't have to use public transport because they had their own cars. They didn't need to use public hospitals because they were insured at private clinics. They didn't have to care about pensions or social security because they had money. They didn't have to worry about crime because they had their private security firms. They knew nothing about all this and they don't understand what is happening here because they don't understand the background for it. It is like Chávez once said: even if we placed the opposition on a pedestal covered with diamonds, they would still hate us.

Social polarisation became more pronounced especially from the mid 1980s onwards. Racial democracy – a thesis postulating the absence of racial prejudices – and class compromise had been the prevailing national ideology after the 'birth' of the Venezuelan democratic period in 1958, following the ousting of the dictator Marcos Pérez Jiménez. Through a power-sharing agreement labelled the Punto Fijo Pact, the two dominant parties, Acción Democrática (Social Democrats) and COPEI[5] (Christian Democrats), sought to establish a centrist, developmentalist political hegemony. The material basis of the Punto Fijo Pact was 'the distribution of oil rents via clientelism';[6] a strategy that forestalled significant social unrest, tying both the peasant movements and trade unions to the political leadership and to Acción Democrática in particular.[7] The pronounced goal of the political elites was to create a sustainable diversified economy and a modernised country through 'sowing the oil',[8] a phrase that refers to using oil rents to create non-oil economic activities. However, ambitions to diversify the economy failed to materialise. The oil wealth created the so-called 'Dutch disease', dislodging other economic activities and creating economic and political structures associated with petro-states.[9] Venezuela's oil industry had gradually expanded since the 1920s in the form of a petroleum regime that privileged foreign oil companies and affiliated national sectors. The formation of the oil sector had crucial ramifications for the development of Venezuelan class structures, shaping a socio-economic stratum that siphoned off the oil revenues, with a large pauperised majority beneath. The OPEC oil bonanza in 1973 sparked off a spending frenzy, giving way to the expression 'Venezuela Saudita' (Saudi Venezuela). Middle-class Venezuelans went shopping in Miami and their own country's modernity and development was thought to wait just around the corner, symbolised by the potent skyscrapers that dominate Caracas' cityscape. However, as Judith Ewell notes: 'It is doubtful that much of the new wealth reached the poorest and least skilled of the population, but massive development projects encouraged the eternal expectation that soon the wealth would indeed trickle down to the poor.'[10]

But Venezuela Saudita didn't last. Hit hard by the global oil crisis in 1983, the government was forced to devaluate the *bolívar* and the country's economy descended into a downward spiral. Unable to pay back foreign loans taken up during the oil bonanza, the government succumbed to the neoliberal policies which the United States tutored in Latin America. On 28 February 1989, the country exploded in a popular riot unleashed by a new round of neoliberal reforms. The military was sent out to quell the riots, and between some hundreds and perhaps a thousand were killed.[11] This event marked the definite end to the appearance of social unity and class compromise. Escalating poverty, corruption and conspicuous consumption, and the use of state violence to control social unrest, all led to the discrediting of the political system and the elites that presided over it.

In 1998, Hugo Chávez was elected president on an anti-establishment platform. He had been arguing for social justice and the restoration of national sovereignty, though without presenting a clear electoral programme. Chávez, a career military officer, came dramatically into the view of the Venezuelan public after leading an attempt in 1992 to bring down the government of Carlos Andrés Pérez, who was responsible for 'el Caracazo', the 1989 massacre. Although the military uprising failed, it showed dissent within the military and Chávez, who was imprisoned, enjoyed enormous popularity amongst poor Venezuelans afterwards. The emergence of Chávez came as a shock to many observers and academics. In academic literature, Venezuela was treated as an exception in a Latin American context: rich in oil and politically stable, with an unbroken succession of elected governments since 1958.[12] Slipping under the academic radar, however, was widespread state violence and persistent poverty entrapping the majority of the population. Arguably, part of the reason why academics didn't emphasise the social faultlines of the 'Venezuelan exceptionalism' was that its political surface was so alluring and convincing. Since the start of the Punto Fijo period after 1958, successive Venezuelan governments had conjured up a powerful myth of national prosperity and social harmony, mediated through the riches of oil (Coronil 1997).

The major US oil companies dominating the oil sector were also actively projecting an image of oil production as the road to modernisation and development. Indeed, the companies legitimised their presence by presenting oil production as synonymous with the national interest.[13] As Tinker Salas writes, 'Although the control of oil by foreign interests inspired nationalist sentiments, they were muted by the country's dependence on oil and the lifestyle and benefits that it generated.'[14] Moreover, the organisation of the oil sector also led to a fundamental social and cultural reorganisation of Venezuelan society. Nascent working- and middle-class identities were formed in the oil camps where American and Venezuelan personnel worked and resided, shaping social values and class aspirations for parts of the Venezuelan population (Tinker Salas 2009).

However, the promises of social mobility, modernity and development were not produced and consumed in the same manner across all sectors of society. Today the popular historical narrative of the Punto Fijo period recalls the experience of state violence, neglect, and deceptive election promises. But above all, what is recounted is a struggle merely to get by in the midst of a sea of poverty. When it comes to oil, a typical remark from many people is, 'We didn't know much about oil, we didn't have anything to do with it.'[15] Oil was 'their business' – understood as the business of the wealthy and powerful. The poor existed on the margins of society, alienated from the projection of national prosperity conveyed and consumed by the architects of the oil-fuelled, capitalist-led modernisation.

Thus, the widening gap between lived realities and the radicalisation of social grievances eventually pulverised the myth of the Venezuelan exceptionalism. These social and political processes help explain the embrace of Chávez's leadership style and his unorthodox political proposals, as well as the anger still harboured against those associated with the old political elites and those perceived as belonging to the Venezuelan bourgeoisie.

THE MISSIONS AND BEYOND

Venezuela never had a strong and visible united popular movement representing the marginalised. However, that is not to say that the *barrios* were devoid of popular organisation. Indeed, urban popular organisation has a long and rich history in Venezuela, moving through different phases during the last half of the twentieth century as political and social dynamics in relation to the state changed.[16] These included, amongst others, radical networks having roots back to the clandestine guerrilla movements of the 1950s and 1960s, as well as groups and networks concerned with cultural and urban politics. Organisation in the *barrios* was also traditionally tied to church communities and neighbourhood associations; the latter holding clientelistic ties to the dominant parties. However, in spite of these organisational trajectories, there wasn't any unified popular movement to channel support for Chávez's political project when he moved into the presidential palace.

During the first few years of his presidency the government was predominantly preoccupied with organising the rewriting of a new constitution, the multiple elections[17] and the development of macro-reforms. In the *barrios*, people started to get organised in the so-called Bolivarian Circles[18] – small reading and activist groups that gathered to discuss politics and the new Bolivarian Constitution of 1999. These however gradually lost vigour as new forms of mobilisation emerged.

The so-called social missions[19] were launched with support from Cuba after the failed coup attempt in 2002, constituting a response to Chávez's promises of social justice. The purpose of these social programs was to attend to the urgent and multiple needs of the poor neighbourhoods by bypassing existing dysfunctional bureaucratic structures. Resources came directly from the national oil company PDVSA (Petróleos de Venezuela S.A.) which by this time was under government control.[20] The missions were based on a grassroots model: people would organise the services in their immediate surroundings, whilst the government would ensure material inputs and resources. An oil-for-doctors exchange with Cuba sent 30,000 Cuban doctors to Venezuelan urban slums and to remote countryside villages. Health committees were set up around each sector, mapping out the medical needs of the local population and helping the doctors. Educational programmes for literacy and primary and secondary schooling were set up inside the slums, organised around local educational committees and with the help of Cuban pedagogical material and Cuban teachers training local people to be educational 'facilitators'.[21] Cultural committees and sports committees distributed books and organised physical and cultural activities. Soup kitchens set up in private homes handed out free meals on a daily basis to the most impoverished, and small shops were set up to sell government-subsidised food. In 2003 Chávez also passed the Urban Land Law.[22] The law enabled people to organise in Urban Land Committees[23] through which they mapped their sector and were granted legal entitlements to houses and properties. This also made them eligible to apply for small credits for housing and infrastructure improvements. Many of these areas were previously marked as uninhabited spaces on the city map, despite the fact that thousands of people lived there. Additionally, work groups for electricity, gas and water supply were set up in coordination with relevant state institutions.[24]

These first forms of cooperation between the popular sectors and the state institutions were largely improvised, often chaotic, and corruption probably flourished. Despite these obvious problems, the launching of the missions had multiple effects: they created a mechanism for the immediate alleviation of pressing social needs. Furthermore, they created spaces for developing political consciousness and identity through the idiom of *el pueblo* or *los sectores populares*, linked to Chávez's political project. They also created a new sense of citizenship by socialising the popular sectors through new laws and political languages and in the dynamics and infrastructure of the state. Despite the shortcomings of the social missions, the poor were now being listened to and taken seriously for the first time. Moreover, they created organisational experience, expanded local networks in and between *barrios*, and fomented new local leadership figures. All these experiences also constituted the basis for what later emerged as the main form for community organisation: the Communal Councils.[25]

THE COMMUNAL COUNCILS

The Communal Councils were institutionalised in law in 2006 through the Organic Law for the Communal Councils (Ley Orgánica de los Consejos Comunales). The law was revised (following an extensive popular consultation) and reapproved by the National Assembly in November 2009. The institutional and legal mechanisms regulating them are complex, but, in short, the Communal Councils are neighbourhood groups organising between 150 and 400 families in urban areas. The borders between different Communal Councils are based on the inhabitants' perceptions of what constitutes 'natural' delimitations, based on the sector's social history, shared infrastructure and services and so on.[26] The Communal Council is divided into various working committees whose members are named spokespersons (*voceros*). The community elects spokespersons for a two-year term, and all major decisions must be voted over in a Citizen Assembly (*Asamblea de Ciudadano/as*) which is the highest instance of authority. Through carrying out a communitarian diagnosis (*diagnóstico communitario*), the community's primary character-istics, needs and resources are evaluated. The community is free to decide which working committees they want to form, depending on their needs. The missions and other forms of committees for local development, such as the water and electricity work groups, are supposed to be dissolved and merged into the Communal Councils so that all local community work is channelled through a democratically elected legal body. The main focus has so far been on housing and infrastructure, as these are the primary preoccupations in poor neighbourhoods. In addition, cultural arrangements, sports facilities and socio-economic projects have been given priority. The Communal Council may also have committees for security issues, the homeless, gender equality, single mothers, and so on. It is mandatory to have an electoral committee, an executive committee, an administrative and financial committee, and a committee for social comptrollership.

It is important to note that the state institutions do not actively form the Communal Councils. Rather; the initiative must be taken from within the community. Therefore, their formation, progress and dynamics are formed in relationship with the pre-existence of local leadership figures and already existing forms of organisation. Whilst in some areas the Communal Councils have reached an advanced stage, already having carried through a number of projects, other sectors have yet to constitute a Communal Council.

Funding for the Communal Councils is assigned through two government funds: FIDES (Intergovernmental Fund for Decen-tralisation) and LAEE (Law for Special Assignations Derived from Mines and Hydrocarbons). The resources are distributed through the state institution Fundacomunal, part of the Ministry of Popular

Power for the Communes and Social Protection. Additionally, the Communal Councils may solicit funds from parish and municipal authorities, the central government, and several state-controlled banks. Technical assistance for development projects can be called upon from the relevant state and government institutions, depending on the focus for the projects. For example, infrastructure projects are supposed to be subjected to quality control by the Ministry of Popular Power for Infrastructure.[27]

Fundacomunal is also in charge of administering the Communal Councils. Fundacomunal assigns each Communal Council a 'promoter',[28] whose task is to encourage participation, oversee elections, assist in administering and carrying out projects, control financial statements and report to state institutions. The promoters do not, however, exercise any form of authority over the Communal Council's decisions or priorities. The promoters come from the popular sectors themselves, many of them having been trained by Frente Fransisco de Miranda, a youth organisation set up in 2002 on the order of Chávez to educate a new generation of civil servants.[29]

THE COMMUNAL COUNCILS AND COMMUNITY DYNAMICS

There is not space here for a comprehensive analysis of every aspect of the Communal Councils. My purpose is to discuss some aspects of the dynamics between the Communal Councils and the state, paying particular attention to how communities constitute themselves as sovereign spaces in order to negotiate control over resources and local decision-making processes. According to Article 2 of the Law for the Communal Councils:

> The Communal Councils, within the constitutional framework of a participative and protagonistic democracy, are instances of participation, articulation and integration between the citizens and the various community organisations, social and popular movements, which allow the organised people to exercise [as a] communitarian government and [the direct exercise of] public policy and projects oriented towards responding to the communities' necessities, potentials and aspirations in the construction of the new model of a socialist society of equality, equity and social justice.

The text of the Law for the Communal Councils is part of the broad political–legal discourse articulated by the Chávez government in its attempt to constitute citizen organisations as cornerstones in the political architecture of Venezuela's transformation to a socialist society.[30] However, the extent to which the work of the councils is eclipsed by an ideological component varies from council to council, and depends on the political inclinations of local participants. Whilst some Communal Council participants primarily see the councils as mechanisms for mobilising resources for their own benefit or for the benefit of the community at large, others perceive the councils as part of an ideological process. Indeed, there is a broad spectrum of ideological positions, and many will engage in the councils perceiving them as a part of an ideological quest for broad societal change, implying a democratisation of society, social solidarity and redistributive politics. However, this does not mean that everyone who has an ideological perspective also adheres to Chávez's banner of 'Socialism for the Twenty-First Century'.

Recognising that the councils work in the interface between the state and popular organisations, it is useful to see them as a hybrid of public-service administration and popular-movement mobilisation. Put simply, they represent a mechanism to institution-alise and synthesise popular demands for economic redistribution and greater local autonomy. This understanding enables us to capture the complex intertwining of popular modes of aspiration and organisation, and the agency and rationality of the government and state institutions. The Communal Councils become a way to channel interaction between the population and the state in a direct manner, thus minimising the political distance between where the needs are and where priorities are set.

The reasons some communities successfully manage to constitute themselves as Communal Councils and carry projects through are complex. Of great significance is the social and political history of the area. Sectors with experience of organisation tend to have greater success, as well as sectors with a higher degree of politicisation in favour of the government. However, my research has shown that the actual topography of the sector is also crucial. Whether people perceive themselves as living within a common space and having a shared local history, and also whether they have natural meeting spaces which facilitate social interaction, contribute to fomenting socio-territorial cohesion. The delimitations between different Communal Councils are therefore highly important for whether people are able to identify common needs and constitute themselves as a social unit. Nor should one underestimate the extent to which social trust is involved in the formation of the Communal

Councils and the development and execution of projects. The very nature of the Communal Councils implies that the community must collectively decide which needs are to be prioritised. That can mean that if your neighbour's house is falling down over her head, her house must be prioritised in a housing project, even though your own home also needs fixing. Clearly, there are great complexities involved in fomenting and cultivating social trust in a culture that, according to widespread popular opinion, has privileged greed, individualism and private consumption – a culture that is by no means confined to the popular sectors.[31] As a consequence of this there are also many cases in which the community claims that the *voceros/as* of the Communal Councils steal the community's money through various manoeuvres. In some cases the rumours are true, whilst in others they spring up from a culture of generalised social mistrust.

Another determining factor for successful organisation is the extent to which the community has leadership figures who are able to inspire faith in the work of the Communal Council, and who can also mediate conflicts and conflicting interests. Often there are a few people from pre-existing groups, from the missions or other government-related forms of organisation, or from more autonomous popular organisations, who kick off the formation of a Communal Council. As I indicated earlier, the previous organisational forms that sprang up after the election of Chávez have played a central role in forming local leadership figures and cultivating organisational networks.

In general, debates about community projects emphasise the indigenous knowledge in the popular sectors about the community's needs, and how these needs can be resolved through local competency. Complex undertakings, such as planning the remodelling of houses or the fixing of roads, water, electricity and infrastructure, are resolved through drawing on the community's own knowledge base, even if 'expert help' also is brought in from state and government institutions when needed. In the case of Caracas, the city's supply of construction workers, electricians and carpenters live for the most part in the popular sectors, demonstrating the existence of a broad and relevant knowledge base.

Utilisation of the local labour force has been a central aim for the Communal Councils. As well as generating local employment, the enrolment of local labour is thought to improve the direction and control of resources and labour efficiency. By employing local people, social comptrollership (*controlaria social*), a central part of the statutes of the Communal Councils, can more easily be exercised by the community. Corruption is generally rife in construction projects, and on one occasion in particular I followed a prolonged discussion between a particular community and the municipality, which was to carry out a larger remodelling project in the area. The community insisted upon revising the accounts and employing their own people for the project, in order better to govern irregularities. Moreover, the communities frequently have a sceptical view of municipal and parish governments, as these historically have been the sites of corruption and clientelism. Often, people also claim that these institutions are trying to sabotage the work of the Communal Councils, because the councils are undermining the established institutions' traditional power base.[32]

NEGOTIATING SOVEREIGNTY

The general political discourse, articulated both by the state and the popular sectors, stresses that the work of the Communal Councils is part of a process of transformation rooted in popular power (*poder popular*), emerging from the principle of popular sovereignty. As García-Guadilla has noted, the 'Bolivarian' model of society as promoted by Chávez implied constituting 'the people as the sovereign'.[33] The perception of a separation between civil society and the state, as implied by the liberal political model, has, on a discursive normative level, been replaced by a model in which 'the people', through collective organisations, make the state adapt to their mode of organisation and articulation, in accordance with their needs. In the daily processes of interaction between the communities and state and government institutions, *la comunidad* (the community) is deployed as another idiom feeding into the political discourse centred on *el pueblo* (the people) and *poder popular* (popular power). The 'organised community' is constituted as a political unity that negotiates its autonomy vís-a-vís the state. However, giving prominence to the 'sovereignty of the people' in the context of a historical asymmetry of power can often give way to discontent and disillusionment at the grassroots. Needless to say, the interaction between the Communal Councils and the state and government institutions is a process of constant friction and negotiation.

These processes of struggle range from the broad ideological arguments and outbursts of frustration and anger at meetings between the community and high-level political figures, to small battles in the everyday evolvement in the work of the Communal

Councils. For example, a recurrent theme for the Communal Councils is a call for state representatives to come to the neighbourhoods to meet with the people, instead of the other way around. Moving the encounters 'out' from the state's spaces and 'into' the *barrios* becomes a way of negotiating the power balance between them, manifesting, at least on the surface, the degree to which the state is responding to 'popular power'. This change of site of interaction pushes the state to engage directly with the social realities and needs in the *barrios*, and to recognise the *barrio* and *barrio* inhabitants on their own terms.

In meetings and encounters, representatives from the state and government are often careful to underscore that they are respecting the popular will and the demands of the communities. Related to this is the fact that many people from the popular sectors have now moved up into state institutions and political offices. This is a central factor in shaping these encounters, as it lessens the perceived socio-economic status hierarchy between the state representatives and people from the *barrios*. Deploying 'popular terminology' becomes a way of negotiating a common ground for discussion. Moreover, the general reversal from the state of social marginalisa-tion implies that 'the poor' are no longer seen as 'the social others', and people will often react if they feel that they are treated by state representatives in a condescending manner.

Representatives from the state institutions also regularly make visits or arrange events in the *barrios* in order to communicate and underscore their 'popular responsiveness'.[34] However, there are also occasions on which state representatives overplay the 'horizontal' relationship to the point of mockery and deny the existing power imbalance between the communities and the state. For example, on two different occasions I witnessed high-level government figures addressing mass meetings, stating that 'it is just a coincidence that I am in this position today and you not. At a later point, the table can be turned, and I will go back and fight for my community [without a political position]'. That might very well be true; but it nevertheless rings hollow when high-level figures pretend that there aren't obvious asymmetries of power present, and thus deflate the conditions for people to articulate real conflicts and differences of interest.

However, the primary source of discontent in the communities and within the Communal Councils stems from the slowness and lack of responsiveness in the bureaucratic system. The reasons for the state's institutional shortcomings are manifold, and I cannot discuss them in depth here. However, a key factor to consider is that the state institutions working closely with the councils have not been able to increase their capacity to adapt to the work-flow generated by the creation and operation of the councils. Moreover, there are now approximately 40,000 Communal Councils registered in the country, and whilst not all are active, they present an enormous challenge if grassroots requests for engagement and assistance are to be taken seriously. The Communal Councils themselves frequently blame the institutional shortcomings on *la derecha endogena* (the endogenous right) within the state institutions and within the 'revolution' itself. By this, they refer to sabotage from within the state institutions, either because of political opposition to the Chávez government or because of individuals whose engagement in public service is opportunistic or careerist in character. The internal dynamics of the state institutions engages a whole series of complex issues, including the historical legacy of the Venezuelan state as a *rentier state*,[35] and cannot be adequately addressed here. However, suffice it to say that within the political and institutional spaces related to the Communal Councils there are both individual actions and structural constraints that produce inefficiency and conflicts between the Communal Councils and their institutional counterparts.

CONTRADICTORY PRACTICES

Venezuela has a long history of patronage and clientelism from which varied networks have been formed, and through which resources and influence is sought and accessed. There is nothing unique about Venezuela in this respect. Clientelism, here understood as the trade of votes and political support in exchange for goods, favours and services between hierarchically structured actors, is one of the most persistent, and one of the most studied traits in Latin American societies.[36] Clientelism is most commonly associated with vertical relationships between the poor and the elites, indicating that at its core, clientelism emerges from the inability to have needs fulfilled through regular social and political channels. As García-Guadilla (2002) has noted,

> the most economically and politically disadvantaged individuals tend to use the power of their vote (almost the only power that existing formal 'electoral' democracy allows them) and clientelist systems to ensure that their individual demands are included in the political system.[37]

In this sense, clientelism is not an anomaly, but an intrinsic part of the political system in contexts where claims to rights on the basis of citizenship are weak.

The Chávez governments have frequently been accused of fomenting clientelism through social programmes directed towards the poor. Penfold-Becerra (2007), for example, claims to have identified a weak but demonstrable link between the distribution of state funds through some of the missions in certain areas and the government's successful 'buying of votes'. This data is however of poor quality[38] and lacks empirical qualitative evidence to explain these dynamics in depths. García-Guadilla (2008) has criticised the Communal Councils in particular for fomenting clientelism, co-option, centralisation and exclusion based on political preferences.[39]

My field research indicates that the policies that have been implemented in the popular sectors under Chávez governments have provided opportunities for continuing a political culture of clientelistic practices; but they have also created spaces and mechanisms with the potential to moderate them. A central purpose of the Communal Councils is to break with the paradigm of individual gains through clientelism and patronage, as institutionalised in the political culture during the Punto Fijo period. Through constituting the community as a collective entity and joint beneficiaries, a more universalistic and collective mode of accessing resources can be transformed into the creation of a new political culture. Elected members in the Communal Councils are termed *spokespersons*, not 'representatives', and this is to signal that the councils are constituted by the community as a whole. The elected members are supposed to channel the community's decisions, not to act as agents on their own behalf. Apart from being consistent with the participatory ethos that dominates the political discourse, the change in terms is also directed towards underlining a rupture with the mechanisms associated with the former neighbourhood organisations, called Asociaciónes de Vecinos, which, historically, had operated as brokers within clientelistic networks between state institutions, political parties and local communities and networks.

Nevertheless, it is widely acknowledged that personal connections, and politics, undoubtedly play a part in the process of claiming resources. Yet, rather than being systematic discrimination, or 'vote buying', from the Chavistas, either at a local level or higher up in the system, what can be seen are local power struggles between customary friends and foes and amongst different political networks. Contrary to opposition claims, it is not the case that government institutions have been solely populated with diehard Chavistas. The government institutions are full of politically indifferent opportunists and careerists, draped in red but effectively opposed to the aims of the government, as well as more ideologically committed revolutionaries. Within the Communal Councils themselves, there are also small and large struggles fought between supporters and opponents of the government about whose hand is on the tiller. But in many cases, I also observed people with different political inclinations working together. It is in the everyday relationships that small and large struggles for power, resources and influence take place, and the 'traditional vices' of clientelism, patronage and kick-backs flow across political loyalties.

I have observed on various occasions that having connections or having the ability to make contacts with people within the state bureaucracy was a crucial factor in community projects being more quickly approved. Moreover, I regularly heard 'gossip' about people in state institutions who engaged in petty corruption or nepotistic practices. However, the reality of what transpires is, in many cases, difficult to identify. What is more clearly evident is that many people were concerned about reproducing the kind of political culture previous governments were criticised for. Indeed, there is a growing rage about bureaucratic inefficiency and dishonest practices. This might eventually create a pressure from below for modifying the prevailing political culture and practices, or the drive towards consolidating the Communal Councils as the sites for a new political culture will implode. It is still an open question where the pendulum will swing.

It is worth noting here that my research has never found evidence of any systematic exclusion of people from the social missions on the basis of electoral preferences, nor any cash-for-votes or the like. In contrast, an electoral strategy of Acción Democratica and COPEI in the past was to offer *barrio* dwellers a pile of bricks, for example, in exchange for a vote. A female informant in her late fifties in one of Caracas's western *barrios* told me with pride how she had dryly told the local party machinery of former president Jaime Lusinchi that if she wanted more bricks for her *rancho*,[40] she would buy them herself.

In any case, in tight communities such as these, people are well informed of their neighbours' electoral preferences. Whilst many would vote for Chávez, people also knew who were *adecos* or *copeyanos*,[41] or in other words, those who held ties to the old political parties through patronage and clientelistic loyalty. Even in the heart of the 23 de Enero neighbourhood, historically the most radical and leftist *barrio* in Caracas, there is a sector of the community that 'everyone knows' are *adecos*, mostly old people who had received their houses in an *adeco* housing project some 40 years ago. Customary political culture still holds sway over their sense of loyalty.

Analysts have also stressed the Communal Council's lack of autonomy in relation to the state.[42] However, as Steve Ellner also points out, Chavistas are a critical mass, even in the face of financial dependence on the state.[43] To varying degrees, both Communal Councils and other neighbourhood groups are consciously concerned about maintaining a critical distance from the government. To paraphrase a common attitude: 'We support Chávez, but the revolution must come from the people.'

The analysis of the Communal Councils is necessarily an ongoing process, and new theoretical instruments are also required in order to grasp their nature and dynamics. Focusing on the degree of autonomy enjoyed by the councils as an independent social movement is not necessarily the best analytical angle. It can obscure the particular dynamics that this particular form of organisation constitutes at the level of bottom-up reform. As mentioned above, I suggest that it is better to view the Communal Councils as a hybrid form of popular-sector organisation and public sector-organisation. Functioning in the intersection between the domains of the local population and the domains of the state, they shorten the distance between redistributive politics 'on paper' and real urgent needs. Undoubtedly, the state institutions were, and are, not prepared for the comprehensiveness of the task, and have frequently not responded in an adequate way to a vocal and assertive population. Moreover, customary political culture of clientelism and corruption are major obstacles that threaten to undermine the support and legitimacy of the government's redistributive policies if left unchecked. But it is nevertheless important to recognise that there are also numerous cases in which projects have been successfully elaborated, constituting significant improvements in people's living conditions.

Moreover, seen in a broader perspective, the most profound change is the mobilisation of political and social aspirations amongst the previously marginalised majority of the population. The alliance between the government and the popular sectors represents a rupture with the previous elite-domination of the state, and this rupture is experienced by many as a coming of age of a more inclusive polity. Despite the institutional shortcomings and persistent problems with the legacy of political favouritism, what is actually taking place is a redefinition and rearticulation of the social and political spaces from which power and agency are derived and dispersed. It is these processes, based on a complex interaction between self-interest, social position and genuine ideological commitment, that are reconfiguring the faultlines of Venezuelan grassroots politics.

CONCLUSION

In this chapter I have tried to draw some tentative lines between the historical legacy of poverty and social inequality in Venezuela, and the current endeavour, under the Chávez governments, of paying back 'the social debt' to the formerly marginalised part of the population.

In much of the academic literature and media reports concerned with characterising the dramatic shifts of recent Venezuelan politics, the poor are commonly condescendingly brushed off as 'the poor who support Chávez'. On the basis of my field research in poor neighbourhoods in Caracas, I would argue that this is a major error. First, by patronising 'the poor' and underplaying their political significance, the agencies and social histories formed in the popular sectors that led to the initial election of Chávez are ignored. Of course, from the right, Chávez is viewed as the culprit who has polarised Venezuelan politics. However, polarisation was in many ways predestined by a history of state violence, racism, classism, corruption and social neglect. Moreover, over the past years, the popular sectors have increasingly acquired a distinct agency of their own that cannot be ignored, whether Chávez stays in power or not.[44] Secondly: as there is an ideological proximity (though often partial, inconsistent and conflictive) between large parts of the popular sectors and the government, the government's ideologies and logics must be analysed in relation to the dynamics of the popular sector. This is particularly crucial when seeking to understand the complexities of the Chávez governments' policies for resource redistribution and popular participation.

However, there are evidently other factors that should be taken into consideration when analysing contemporary Venezuela. Across the continent, to varying degrees, there is pressure from below for participative forms of politics, though its national expressions and dynamics are context-specific. Thus, the ideologies, policies and discourses guiding popular mobilisation and participative politics in Venezuela cannot be studied as an isolated phenomenon; rather, they are part of a transnational shift in the perception of politics, democracy and citizenship. Identifying these linkages in the Venezuelan context must however be left for future studies. Moreover, Venezuela is facing numerous challenges linked to substantially overcoming structural inequality and entrenched poverty in the long run. This demands concerted efforts on various fronts, and the process has barely started. However, Venezuela cannot be studied in isolation from international geopolitics and global economic developments. As an oil-exporting country, Venezuela has long been vulnerable to external forces, and the question thus remains as to whether the current government is able to create a more stable economic base, evading the booms-and-busts that have previously had a destabilising effect on the country at large. Venezuela is not alone in facing this problem. It remains to be seen whether the Communal Councils will have a long-lasting presence as the nuclei for local organisation and community development. Aside from the broader processes just mentioned, this depends largely on the ability of communities to put pressure on the state from below to institutionalise this mode of citizen governance.

NOTES

1. Depending on context, 'the popular sectors' may refer to a social identity, a social stratum, or to geographical locations, or it may implicitly refer to them all. With reference to urban geography, it refers to the working-class urbanisations and *barrios* (shanty towns) that cling precariously to the hillsides surrounding Caracas. In the context of this article, it generally refers to the social stratum inhabiting the poor neighbourhoods.
2. Communal Councils have also been formed in more affluent areas, but to a much lesser degree. Because of the political connotation with the government, the Communal Councils have a limited appeal to opposition-minded middle- and upper-class neighbourhoods, and these sectors also have other channels of organisation more consistent with orthodox understandings of civil society organisations. Moreover, the poor neighbourhoods are obviously where social needs are greatest.
3. Lupu 2010.
4. See, for example, Herrera Salas 2005 or García-Guadilla 2005.
5. COPEI: Comité de Organización Política Electoral Independiente.
6. Hellinger 2001, p.1.
7. Ellner 1989.
8. The phrase 'sowing the oil' (*sembrar el petróleo*) was first used by the Venezuelan intellectual Úslar Pietri in 1936. It came to be, and remains, one of the most emblematic phrases in Venezuelan political discourse.
9. Central common characteristics for oil states are inequality and poverty, corruption and clientelism, rent-seeking behaviour by both private and public bodies, boom-and-bust cycles following the international prize of oil, and a

weak state and public sector unable to respond to changing economic conditions (Karl 1997). For an exhaustive analysis of the Venezuelan oil economy, see, for example, Karl 1997; Mommer 1996; Coronil 1997; Bye 1979; Tinker Salas 2009.

10. Ewell 1984, p.193.
11. The exact numbers were never established, and many were dumped in mass graves. The Chávez's government has launched an ongoing investigation that was not concluded at the time of writing.
12. For a critical review of the 'exceptionalism thesis', see Ellner and Tinker Salas 2005.
13. Tinker Salas 2009, pp.237–41.
14. Ibid, p.xiii.
15. From the author's research.
16. For a thorough account about urban social movements in Caracas, see Fernandes 2010.
17. Elections were held for a new constitution in 1999, with both presidential and parliamentary elections following in 2000.
18. In Spanish: Circulos Bolivarianos.
19. In total, 27 social missions have been launched since 2002.
20. One of Chávez's central goals was reversing the privatisation process of PdVSA, started by Rafael Caldera during his 1994–98 presidency. Both the 2002 coup attempt and the 2002/3 oil industry lock-out/sabotage were partly showdowns between the Chávez government and the former PdVSA meritocracy. In the aftermath of the lock-out/sabotage, the government fired around 16,000 (mostly white-collar) workers, and gained political control over PdVSA. Subsequently, contracts with multinationals ensuring that PdVSA became the main stakeholder were negotiated, and taxes and royalties from joint ventures increased. PdVSA was renamed *La Nueva PdVSA* (the new PdVSA) and rebranded with a social profile, destining large parts of its profit to the social programs.
21. In Spanish: Facilitadores.
22. In Spanish: Ley de Tierra Urbana.
23. In Spanish: Comités de Tierra Urbana.
24. A great many of the people involved in these programs were women. The sudden surge of community activism also meant that a collective negotiation and redefinition of gender roles took place in so far as men were confronted with a massive social mobilisation in which both men and women were encouraged to take part. This more inclusive political dynamic certainly helped to shift the perception of women's roles in the public sphere.
25. The impulse and judicial implementation of the Communal Councils were preceded by *Ley de los Consejos Locales de Planificacion Publica* of 2002, and *Ley Orgánica del Poder Público Municipal* of 2005; designed to oblige municipal and parish authorities to include local communities in the elaboration of local budgets (Machado 2009). However, these provisions had a limited mobilisation effect, and provided too much space for obscure backroom politics.
26. In reality, this issue is quite complex. In some cases, these borders are naturally given, such as a street, or a building complex or customary perceptions of natural borders. In other cases, the borders are not that clear, and can often be a source of dispute and conflicts. The formal definitions of borders between different sectors were to a large extent carried out by the aforementioned Urban Land Committees.

27. However, one of the main criticisms during the past years has been the lack of coordination between different state entities in the follow-up on the Communal Councils, and also the lack of capacity within the state institutions to follow up on projects.
28. In Spanish: Promotór.
29. Through Frente Fransisco de Miranda, thousands of people from across the country were trained in politics and public administration at educational facilities set up in Cuba, before the program was moved to Venezuela in 2007.
30. In 2005, Chávez declared that he was a socialist, terming his political project 'Socialism for the Twenty-First Century'.
31. The current political value-oriented discourse emphasises the need to foment 'new values' of collective well-being, solidarity and basic needs, explicitly denouncing the evils that capitalism has brought with it in terms of exclusion, egoism and greed. In effect, these new values are obviously neither easily imposed nor easily put into practice. However, the Communal Councils have become sites where social values are discussed and negotiated, often in very explicit terms. This will be further discussed elsewhere.
32. This is also related to a central tenet of the Chávez government's design for a new socialist governing model, namely that the Communal Councils will form the basis for a commune – a 'confederation' of various Communal Councils – which will be the new territorial authority, thus undermining the authority and resource base of the parish and municipal authorities. Many thus perceive these institutions as 'trying to hold down' the community organisations in order not to lose their power base.
33. García-Guadilla 2005, p.113.
34. The content of these meetings can range from events with a real political and social substance to political spectacles with more propaganda effect than actual value. This discussion will however be dealt with in forthcoming publications.
35. Here, I specifically refer to the feature of the state becoming the centre of gravity for rent-seeking dynamics, often leading to an over-dimensioned and underachieving state apparatus, permeated by practices of corruption, patronage and nepotism.
36. For a review of different academic approaches to clientelism, see Javier Ayuero 2001.
37. Garcia-Guadilla 2002, p.106.
38. Penfold-Becerra 2007, p.78.
39. García-Guadilla 2008, p.19.
40. Informal way of referring to *barrio* shack houses.
41. Terms used to refer to supporters of *Acción Democratica* and COPEI.
42. García-Guadilla 2008 for example identifies one of the struggle for the Communal Councils as either constituting themselves as a para-state clientelistic instance, or as a social movement. See also Machado 2009.
43. Ellner 2009, p.4.
44. The next presidential election is scheduled for 2012.

REFERENCES

Ayuero, J. (2001) *Poor People's Politics: Peronist Survival Networks and the Legacy of Evita* (Durham, N.C. and London: Duke University Press).

Bye, V. (1979) 'Nationalization of Oil in Venezuela: Re-defined Dependence and Legitimization of Imperialism', *Journal of Peace Research*, 16(1).

Coronil, F. (1997) *The Magical State: Nature, Money, and Modernity in Venezuela* (Chicago: University of Chicago Press).

Ellner, S. (1989) 'Organized Labor's Political Influence and Party Ties in Venezuela: Accion Democratica and Its Labor Leadership', *Journal of Interamerican Studies and World Affairs*, 31(4).

—— (2009) 'A New Model with Rough Edges: Venezuela's Community Councils', *NACLA: Report on the Americas*, May–June.

—— and Tinker Salas, M. (2005) 'Introduction: The Venezuelan Exceptionalism Thesis Separating Myth from Reality', *Latin American Perspectives*, 32(2).

Ewell, J. (1984) *Venezuela: A Century of Change* (Stanford, Calif.: Stanford University Press).

Fernandes, S. (2010) *Who Can Stop the Drums? Urban Social Movements in Chávez's Venezuela* (Durham, N.C. and London: Duke University Press).

García-Guadilla, M.P. (2002) 'Decentralization and Clientelism: New Relationships and Old Practices' (trans. Carlos Pérez), *Latin American Perspectives*, 29(5).

—— (2005) 'The Democratization of Democracy and Social Organizations of the Opposition: Theoretical Certainties, Myths, and Praxis', *Latin American Perspectives*, 32(2).

—— (2008) 'Poder popular y limites de la democracia participativa en Venezuela: la experiencia de los consejos comunales', paper delivered at the Second Conference of the Venezuela Section of the Conference for Latin American Studies Association (LASA), Caracas.

Hellinger, D. (2001) *Nationalism, Globalization and Chavismo*, Paper delivered at the Conference for Latin American Studies Association (LASA), Washington, D.C.

Herrera Salas, J.M. (2005) 'Ethnicity and Revolution: The Political Economy of Racism in Venezuela', *Latin American Perspectives*, 32(2).

Karl, T.L. (1997) *The Paradox of Plenty: Oil Booms and Petro-States* (Berkeley, Calif.: University of California Press).

Lupu, N. (2010). 'Who Votes for Chavismo? Class Voting in Hugo Chávez's Venezuela', *Latin American Research Review*, 45(1).

Machado, M.J.E. (2009) 'Participación social y consejos comunales in Venezuela', *Revista Venezolana de Economía y Ciencias Sociales*, 15(1).

Mommer, B. (1996) 'Integrating the Oil: A Structural Analysis of Petroleum in the Venezuelan Economy', *Latin American Perspectives*, 23(3).

Penfold-Becerra, M. (2007) 'Clientelism and Social Funds: Evidence from Chávez's Misiones', *Latin American Politics and Society*, 49(4).

Tinker Salas, M. (2009) *The Enduring Legacy: Oil, Culture and Society in Venezuela* (Durham, N.C. and London: Duke University Press).

6
Living under the Bullet: Internal Displacement in the Azerbaijani Oil Boom

Heidi Kjærnet

The conflict over Nagorno-Karabakh was one of several ethnic conflicts that emerged from the breakup of the Soviet Union. The largely Armenian population living there claimed the right to self-determination and independence in 1991. Azerbaijan, which had jurisdiction over this autonomous region during the Soviet period, repudiated the proclamation, and the resulting conflict sparked ethnic violence on both sides, leading to the displacement of several hundred thousand people. Armenians who had lived in Azerbaijan during the Soviet period fled to Armenia, and Azeris living in Armenia or in Nagorno-Karabakh fled to Azerbaijan. This chapter focuses on the community of approximately 580,000 Azeris who fled Nagorno-Karabakh, and the seven other regions that ended up under Armenian control after the war, for Azerbaijan. Nagorno-Karabakh was at the time an autonomous *oblast* within the Azerbaijani Soviet Socialist Republic of the USSR, which means that the refugees from Nagorno-Karabakh did not cross an international border. They are therefore defined as 'internally displaced persons' (IDPs) instead of 'refugees'.[1] Nagorno-Karabakh's independence has not been recognised by any state, and along with seven other Azerbaijani regions it has been under Armenian control since the 1992–94 war.

Since their initial exile, displaced people have been kept in limbo by the Azerbaijani government. Maintaining that all IDPs shall return to Nagorno-Karabakh either upon a peaceful resolution of the conflict or upon a military defeat of Armenia, the government separates the displaced from local communities. Therefore the internally displaced communities remain largely segregated from the rest of the population, and although poverty in Azerbaijan is widespread their displacement and their liminal status aggravates the issues of poverty and inequality. Moreover, not only are the displaced caught on the wrong side of the widening social gap associated with Azerbaijan's oil and gas boom, they are also at the crux of developments related to the country's oil-fuelled military rearmament and the issue of the settlement of the Karabakh conflict. Since 2005, Azerbaijan has been overflowing with oil and gas revenues coming as a result of the country's success in attracting foreign investment to develop its petroleum resources and secure their transportation to international markets. Parts of the petroleum revenues have been spent on building new settlements for the IDPs, as well as on increasing the monetary benefits they are receiving. The construction of new settlements close to the ceasefire line has given some of the refugees a chance to move from tent camps and shelters to newly built houses. The IDPs in the new settlements described their move there as small comfort while they could not return to their ancestral lands. Although they are now living closer to their native lands, and have better housing conditions, they are still clearly uprooted. The government's policy is, and has been for almost 20 years, that the IDPs shall return to Nagorno-Karabakh upon resolution of the conflict. Furthermore, the displaced describe the proximity to the ceasefire line as a stressful and difficult situation. They know that if conflict flares up they are likely to be hit first, in which case they might have to flee again. A group of male refugees in a new government-built settlement in Agdam described their situation, where they claim to hear shootings every night from the ceasefire line only some two or three kilometres away as 'living under the bullet' – hence the title of this chapter.[2]

Also, as Azerbaijan is getting richer, the social gap between the small urban elite and the displaced community and other poor people is widening. The quality of life among the displaced people has improved only marginally. Meanwhile, growing petroleum revenues have fuelled increased military expenditure, which is a factor that influences the prospects of reaching a negotiated solution of the conflict over Nagorno-Karabakh. President Ilham Aliyev has repeatedly stated that war is the last resort to restore Azerbaijani territorial integrity. His regime's policy on the IDP situation is shaped by foreign-policy issues, but most importantly by its policies on Nagorno-Karabakh. Indeed, to make it clear that Azerbaijan intends one day to reassert control over the area, displacement is regarded as a temporary phenomenon and this is why the government strives to keep displaced people separate from the rest of Azerbaijani society.

In official rhetoric, the plight of the refugees signifies, above all, the national trauma of Azerbaijan's loss of territory.

For the IDPs, whose initial displacement took place 20 years ago, the wait for what the government calls the 'Great Return' is becoming long. For this reason, the international community has started encouraging the Azerbaijani government to focus less on IDP status, but rather on alleviating general poverty issues. For the government, it is taboo to ask how many generations of refugees are to remain segregated from the rest of society before they are considered 'ordinary' Azerbaijanis. Yet, for the young generation of IDPs, some of whom have few or no memories of the region they are told is their ancestral land, and many of whom were born after the flight, the promise of a 'return' to these areas is perhaps not as comforting in today's situation of deprivation as for the older generations. And because of the lack of integration which results from Azerbaijani government policy, the government runs the risk of creating groups of unsatisfied young people who could in turn be mobilised by radical ideas.

Nagorno-Karabakh holds high symbolic value to the Azerbaijani population. As long as negotiations over Nagorno-Karabakh are not bringing a peaceful resolution of the conflict, the question must be how long the Azerbaijani regime can go on without delivering on the promise to return Nagorno-Karabakh to Azerbaijani control. This chapter discusses the Azerbaijani policies on Nagorno-Karabakh and its IDP population in light of the recent oil boom, and the ways in which the resource revenues are affecting domestic as well as regional dynamics in the South Caucasus.

The chapter proceeds in the following manner. The first section shows the IDPs' pivotal role in any negotiated solution. It is demonstrated that the resource revenues in Azerbaijan have fuelled a military rearmament. This makes up one of several links between Azerbaijan's oil boom and the situation of the refugees. Approaches to internal displacement are then discussed from the point of view of international norms on displacement and the government's response to the displacement situation in Azerbaijan. The main part of the chapter is about the lives of the internally displaced people in Azerbaijan. This involves a discussion of how the socio-economic situation of the internally displaced is influenced by the oil boom. Resource revenues have been spent on improving the IDPs' living conditions. The extent to which the marginal improvement of living conditions is really what the internal refugees want and need in their prolonged displacement is, however, questioned. The discussion is informed by interviews with displaced people carried out in June 2008, which among other things shed light on how the displaced people view their own situation and their prospects for the future in the context of Azerbaijan's oil and gas wealth. This part also contains a discussion of research insights from other conflicts that have caused protracted displacement situations (Palestine and the Western Sahara). Despite significant differences, these conflicts bear some relevance for an analysis of Azerbaijan's outlook. For instance, these unresolved conflicts have produced several generations of refugees who are born outside the areas they have allegedly fled from. The Azerbaijani government keeps a group of people uprooted and segregated from the rest of society for several generations, and even maintains that people born outside Nagorno-Karabakh are refugees from there. There seems to be a generational divide among the internally displaced in terms of the desire to return. As Azerbaijan is spending its resource revenues on military rearmament and building new temporary settlements for the displaced, the question is whether the Azerbaijani government should not rather open up the way for integration of the displaced people into society. The chapter's conclusion discusses the implications of the protracted displacement for social stability and government IDP policies in Azerbaijan.

RESOURCE REVENUES AND CONFLICT DYNAMICS

Although a ceasefire was signed in 1994, there has been no peace agreement between Armenia and Azerbaijan. There are also still frequent skirmishes along the ceasefire line. The Minsk Group of the Organisation for Security and Cooperation (OSCE) has taken the lead in facilitating peaceful resolution to the conflict. Although no agreement has been signed, the talks seem to focus on three elements of a peace plan, namely Armenian withdrawal from the districts surrounding Nagorno-Karabakh, return of displaced persons under some kind of international security presence, and a referendum to determine the final status of Nagorno-Karabakh.[3] The role of the IDPs in such a chain of events would be pivotal. Their eligibility to vote in a prospective referendum on the final status of Nagorno-Karabakh could not only tip the results, but would be crucial for the legitimacy of the result.[4]

Return of the displaced people is perceived to be impossible in the absence of a peace agreement.[5] Furthermore, the desire to return may in fact be influenced by the final status of the territory, and some IDPs may not want to make that decision until the status of the territory is decided[6] – even though the prospective referendum would be likely to take place only several years into the phased-package peace approach. For the time being, however, the peace negotiations have not brought tangible results, and leaders of both countries continue to make public statements that fuel nationalist sentiments and undermine trust in the negotiation process. For example, President Aliyev has frequently threatened that war will be the solution if all else fails. In December 2010, at an OSCE summit held in Kazakhstan, the president of Armenia, Serzh Sarkisian, countered that Armenia would be the first state to recognise Nagorno-Karabakh's independence if Azerbaijan resorted to military aggression.[7]

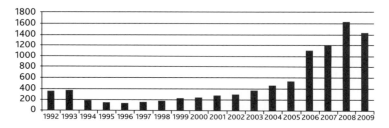

Figure 6.1 Azerbaijani military expenditure in million USD (2008 constant)

Sources: Information on military expenditure from the Stockholm International Peace Research Institute (SIPRI) database on military expenditure, http://milexdata.sipri.org/result.php4 (last accessed 6 December 2010)

However, Aliyev's belligerent statements are generally thought to be more about pressuring the Armenians into making concessions at the negotiating table than as being real threats. His emphasis on making the Azerbaijani military budget bigger than Armenia's total state budget serves the purpose of pointing out the economic differences between the two polities. As shown in Figure 6.1, Azerbaijani military expenditure has increased rapidly since the revenues started flowing in when the BTC (Baku–Tbilisi–Ceyhan) oil pipeline came online in 2005/6, followed by the SCP (South Caucasus Pipeline) gas pipeline in 2006. In comparison, Armenia's economy is weak. Azerbaijan has become a strong regional player through the construction of oil and gas pipelines that transport its resources to world markets, while Armenia is largely isolated. Despite diplomatic efforts in 2007–09 to normalise relations with Turkey, Armenia still has closed borders with two of its neighbours (Azerbaijan and Turkey), and its economy largely depends on transfers from the numerous Armenian diaspora and trade with Russia. In this context, it is possible that the Azerbaijani leadership might be fooled into thinking that a supposedly short and victorious war might be possible. However, Russia backs Armenia militarily, and the Georgia crisis in August 2008 does make clear to the Azerbaijani leadership the risks of a military challenge to the geopolitical status quo.

APPROACHES TO INTERNAL DISPLACEMENT

This section looks at different approaches to internal displacement. Internationally, the situation of IDPs is managed through ascribing them rights which national governments are responsible for upholding. The government of Azerbaijan, however, is not fully safeguarding the rights of its displaced people. Rather, in Azerbaijani political rhetoric, the refugees are symbolically laden victims, as the following discussion of the Azerbaijani government's response to the situation of the IDPs shows.

International Norms on Internal Displacement

While the status and rights of refugees are regulated by the 1951 Geneva Convention and the 1967 protocol relating to the status of refugees,[8] there is no international convention that relates specifically to internal displacement. A set of guiding principles on internally displaced persons was recognised in a 2005 UN resolution as 'an important international framework for the protection of internally displaced people'.[9] According to these guidelines, there should be no discrimination towards IDPs on the basis of that status, and they should have the same rights as other citizens, including the right to free movement. In Azerbaijan, however, there is a limited acceptance of these rights. According to representatives of humanitarian organisations, the authorities dislike references to the guiding principles.[10] The authorities prefer to frame the problem of displacement within the context of the conflict with Armenia, rather than accepting universal principles that point to their responsibility for their own population. To make matters more complicated, the UN High Commissioner for Refugees has stated that there is no 'discernible discrimination' in Azerbaijan against IDPs, who 'generally enjoy the same rights as other citizens'.[11] However, Amnesty International emphasises how the refugees' right to freely choose between return, integration or permanent resettlement is restricted by the violation of a number of their other rights.[12] The discrimination experienced by people displaced in Azerbaijan stems primarily from several practical obstacles to their right to move freely within the country: for example, education of their children and their healthcare are provided only in their registered places of residence. On the other hand, IDPs in Azerbaijan do receive special economic benefits, as is elaborated later.

Domestic and International Response to the IDP Situation in Azerbaijan

As mentioned in the introduction, the Nagorno-Karabakh issue has become central to Azerbaijan's national identity. The outbreak of conflict was closely linked to national sentiment, and the war was fought in parallel with Azerbaijan's path to independence. Conflict resolution policies have therefore become an integral component of the country's foreign policy, and the adoption of an uncompromising position on the conflict has been crucial to the government's legitimacy among the Azerbaijani population. Given the highly political nature of the Nagorno-Karabakh conflict, IDP issues are a sensitive area for the Azerbaijani government. While it has previously been criticised by international donors for keeping the IDPs in camps and temporary shelters as a 'showcase of misery', there are some indications that the government is now slowly adopting a more pragmatic approach to the refugees. One indicator is that the official numbers of IDPs have been adjusted downwards; another is that resource revenues have been spent on alleviating their situation. There can still however be no doubt that Azerbaijan has failed to integrate the displaced communities into society, in order to use their presence as evidence in propaganda about the 'results of Armenian aggression'.[13]

In 2008, Azerbaijani government officials revised their estimate of the number of the country's IDPs, reporting a total of 572,531 to the Internal Displacement Monitoring Centre.[14] Prior to this, the government had been unwavering in its account that 680,000 individuals had been uprooted in the initial displacement. Although international humanitarian organisations believed this figure was exaggerated, there were no independent assessments and it was difficult to challenge the official figures.[15] The new figure seems more realistic, and from the point of view of the international agencies it signifies that the government may be moving away from the use of number-inflating propaganda, feeding the view of Azerbaijan as the 'victim of Armenian aggression', and towards a more fact-based policy on its IDPs.

The new figures are among several indicators that the government is moving in a more pragmatic direction in its policies on displacement. In the 1990s, the government focused primarily on return; little was done to address the housing and economic needs of the displaced.[16] As the head of one international humanitarian organisation said, 'I assume it is beneficial for the government to keep the IDPs uprooted. If they were integrated, there would be nothing to point to, and nothing to blame Armenia for.'[17] However, since the inflow of resource revenues, the government is increasingly taking more responsibility for the IDP situation and relying less on international donors.

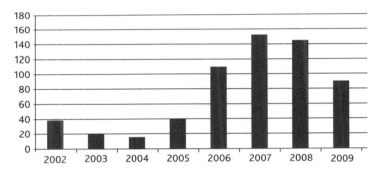

Figure 6.2   Funding for IDP programmes over the State Oil Fund of the Republic of Azerbaijan (billion AZN)

Source: The annual reports of the State Oil Fund of the Republic of Azerbaijan 2002–09 (the figures for 2002–05 are converted from AZM to AZN at a rate of 5000/1)

Note: In addition to the funding over the State Oil Fund, the government also has IDP-related expenses over the state budget. The reason why the IDP programmes over the State Oil Fund is singled out here is to show how the petroleum revenues are used to target the IDP issue, and how the inflow of resource revenues since 2005 has increased the state's financial commitment to these programmes.

The funding for the relocation programme has come from oil and gas revenues. As petroleum revenues have increased, so has the funding for IDP-related programmes over the State Oil Fund of the Republic of Azerbaijan, as shown in Figure 6.2.[18] During the same time period, the international aid community has been downscaling their programmes in Azerbaijan, and some of them, such as the Norwegian Refugee Council, have withdrawn from the country. For comparison, the international community allocated AZN (Azerbaijani manat) 25 million in 2008 for humanitarian and development programmes focusing on IDPs.[19] While the government of Azerbaijan encourages the continued engagement of international organisations,[20] these organisations have found it increasingly difficult to justify the spending of donor money in a country that had the world's strongest economic growth in 2006, 2007 and 2008.[21] Still, there is the concern that, while the government may have the financial means, it lacks the skills, knowledge and competence to implement effective development programmes. The greatest concern is over job creation and agricultural development, two areas in which the displaced communities require most help.[22] The government seems partly aware of its own limitations and has turned to international expertise in government-funded projects – for example, the UNDP has implemented several projects within these spheres.

Although the government has now taken the financial lead in providing support to the IDPs, it continues to emphasise the number of international humanitarian organisations working in the country (approximately 70). One could ask why the government needs their presence if its own response is adequate and the oil and gas money is increasing its own capacity to remedy the situation. Informants in Baku working closely with the government on IDP issues indicated that the government feels that the presence of international humanitarian agencies increases the visibility of the refugee problem, which in turn may increase support for Azerbaijan's view of the Nagorno-Karabakh conflict internationally.[23]

DISPLACED LIVES AND THE OIL BOOM

The internally displaced people in Azerbaijan are living symbols of Azerbaijan's national trauma, the loss of Nagorno-Karabakh. Yet, we seldom hear their perspectives or views on their own situation or their desires for how to deal with the displacement. This section describes the living conditions and socio-economic situation of the refugees in Azerbaijan and conveys their perspectives on the present and future of their communities in light of the oil boom in Azerbaijan. It draws on reports on IDP living conditions to show that the displaced people depend on oil-funded welfare benefits for their livelihood and hence have less control over their livelihood than the local population.[24] Their experiences as beneficiaries of a petro-state's welfare spending show the risks of resource-rich states becoming over-reliant on resource revenues. The review of the refugees' socio-economic situation therefore tells us a lot about the resource-centred economy and the state which oversees it. The issue of the political orientation of the refugees is also discussed, with a view to explaining the lack of radical mobilisation among them. Finally, it is argued that the generational divide among the displaced can cause problems for the government's policies in the longer term, as insights from other conflict areas with significant protracted refugee situations are shown to have relevance for Azerbaijan.

The Socio-economic Situation of the Displaced People

Poverty is widespread in Azerbaijan. A comparison of the living standards of the displaced communities relative to those of other citizens helps illustrate the implications of displacement. The World Bank found that the incidence of poverty among IDPs is about the same as among the general population.[25] The displaced people are however more vulnerable than the local population, because they depend more heavily on livelihood sources outside their control.[26] Family incomes are lower among the IDPs than in the local population: the average monthly family income of local residents was AZN 196 as compared to AZN 144 for displaced families.[27] A total of 48 per cent of local families reported earning less than AZN 150 per month, compared to 64 per cent of IDP families. And while a similar proportion of local families and IDPs fall within the middle income range of AZN 151–250, IDPs are significantly less likely to earn more than AZN 250 per month and significantly more likely to earn less than AZN 150.

What really links the Azerbaijani petroleum economy to the socio-economic situation of the displaced community is however their dependence upon government benefits, which are increasingly being financed by resource revenues. The most common sources of income for displaced people are in-kind and cash allowances.[28] IDPs are exempt from paying tax, and are supplied with water, gas and electricity free of charge – even though it should be noted that since the majority of IDPs still live in non-residential areas, their access to these utilities is poor.[29] Displaced people do not pay rent, and many receive food aid. In addition, all IDPs get a monthly allowance of AZN 15 from the government, commonly referred to as 'bread money' (the amount was increased in a presidential decree in September 2010). The increase in IDP benefits, in keeping with the minimum wage increase, is 'just enough to keep us from starvation', said several refugees in 2008.[30] Compared to local families, the displaced people are less likely to have employment, permanent or temporary, and they report receiving lower income from their employment.[31] In the World Bank survey, about half of the IDPs surveyed were not working or seeking work, compared to 36 per cent of the general population.[32] Even the entrepreneurial efforts of some refugees are negatively affected by their displacement. IDPs are just as likely to run private businesses as the local residents, but their businesses generate less than half as much income as those belonging to local families.[33] This illustrates the lack of IDP integration into local economies, and confirms the importance of integrating the displaced people with locals for their economic success. My own interviews with refugees living in the new government-built settlements support this finding. Respondents said that their biggest problems were unemployment and difficulties in engaging in agriculture. These issues were closely linked to the isolated location of the settlements in areas with little economic activity, few local residents and a general lack of infrastructure.

These benefits that IDPs enjoy have two important implications. First of all, they mean that IDP households are in some cases marginally better off than some locals, who might earn slightly more but do not receive government support. One study found that IDP households were more likely to receive state support than non-IDP households in both 1995 and in 2002, and that the share of state support in total household income had increased for IDP households during the intervening period.[34] However, the overall reality is that, despite government assistance, displaced people have a lower per capita income than the local people, and a standard of living lower than that of locals who do not get such assistance. This is connected to the second important implication. Although more refugees receive government support, these families generally have lower incomes and are therefore dependent on government subsidies. In contrast, locals are more economically active and able to support themselves and their families.[35] IDPs were found to rely on government transfers and exemptions for more than half of their income. This makes the displaced communities vulnerable to any future changes in government policy and weakens 'the resolve of IDPs to strive for self-reliance'.[36]

The largely oil-funded resettlement programmes for the displaced people have had a negative impact on the resettled refugees' livelihood. In the now demolished tent camps, subsistence agriculture was an important way of life for the refugees, and there was access to transport to nearby towns and villages where they could seek work. That is not the case with the new settlements. Agriculture is complicated by the lack of access to land, and local employment is made difficult by the location of the settlements close to the line of contact and far away from everything else. In Fizuli region, parts of which are occupied, local aid organisations in 2008 claimed that only 5 to 10 per cent of the population were employed.[37] The state resettlement programme includes a job creation component – but at the time fieldwork was carried out for this study (June 2008), unemployed IDPs were still waiting for this component to be implemented. Neither private nor public investors are keen to invest in locations close to the military zone. One example is Tazakent in Agdam region, located 2 or 3 kilometres from the line of contact, close to military barracks and an easy target if the situation were to reignite.[38] Pending a solution to the conflict, it is difficult to imagine any investors willing to take the risk of trying to create a thriving local economy in such a location.

The government programme was also supposed to provide land and facilitate agriculture in the new settlements. The programme promises all resettled IDPs a one-hectare plot – but for most of the resettled IDPs this has not materialised. The political will to provide land seems to exist, but practical matters, such as unclear property rights following the post-Soviet land privatisation, still need to be resolved. In Agdam, many refugees have been provided with land, but there are complaints about its poor quality and lack of agricultural potential.[39] The success of the government resettlement programme depends to a large extent on the implementation of the job creation and agriculture components. Government agencies tasked with implementation of IDP projects, however, did not seem to fully take in these problematic issues connected to moving upwards of 80,000 people. The State Oil Fund, for example, announced the success of the resettlement programme in its 2007 annual report:

> 2007 was also marked with major results achieved in improving the social and living conditions of refugees and internally displaced persons, which represent a substantial item on the State Oil Fund's expenditure budget. Tent camps for IDPs were completely eradicated during the reporting year, and the IDP settlers were relocated into new housing. This is yet another success of the economic policy conducted by the President of the Republic of Azerbaijan.[40]

The way the government so triumphantly proclaims the success of a programme that has uprooted a large community and complicated its opportunities for an independent livelihood, thereby making this community ever more dependent on government aid, shows the disconnect between the resource-rich Azerbaijani government and those affected by its policies. The petroleum-fuelled welfare programmes have to some extent relegated the displaced community to a second-hand dependence on oil and gas revenues. The feeling of lack of control over their own lives may aggravate their situation, not least given the considerable uncertainty as to when the displacement will come to an end.

Displacement and Political Perspectives: Insights from Other Protracted Conflicts

The previous section showed that the displaced community in Azerbaijan is dependent on petroleum-funded welfare benefits for their livelihoods. Government policy stresses return to the occupied territories at an unknown point in time, but for the foreseeable future it keeps the IDPs segregated and uprooted. The refugees themselves have little say in the development of the government policies that affect them. In this context, political or religious radicalisation seems conspicuously absent among the refugees. The lack of mobilisation from within the displaced community itself can however be explained by the lack of cohesion of the displaced community, whose settlements are spread throughout the country, with little networking between them. Another reason seems to be that the displaced people do not blame the government for their difficult situation. Armenia and Russia, both external enemies, are blamed by the IDPs for the conflict and their displacement. A recurrent argument in all my interviews with displaced people in Azerbaijan in June 2008 was that everything was the fault of Armenia and its ally Russia. Therefore, they do not mobilise against government policies. Also, outside groups that might conceivably mobilise among these communities, such as independent Islamic groups or the political opposition, are not known to try to garner support among the refugees.[41]

The author's interviews with displaced people in Azerbaijan revealed a generational divide. The older generations expressed a strong desire to return to the occupied territories, and complained that a new house in the new settlements was meagre comfort as long as return to Karabakh was unfeasible. One refugee waiting for his roadside house to be demolished and his family to be moved to a new house in a government-built settlement said, 'If they cannot offer me my ancestral home, I would rather stay here. I do not need a new house, I want my land back.'[42] Young IDPs, however, were less eager to return. One young IDP living in a public building in Sumgait said he was six years old when he left his birthplace, and that he did not remember anything from there. Apparently ill at ease with my questions about returning, he ended the interview.[43] The government policy of emphasising return while keeping the displaced people segregated and in poverty might therefore result in the creation of a segment of young dissatisfied IDPs who do not see the promise of a future 'return' to areas where they have never been as a compensation for their current difficult situation.

Although the conflict in the Middle East should be seen as a specific context, and the displacement of the Palestinians is quite unique, it is worth noting that this conflict also resulted in 'second- and third-generation refugees' growing up and living their lives in refugee camps. As long as the Nagorno-Karabakh conflict remains unresolved, it is only a matter of time before the displaced communities in Azerbaijan also produce several generations of refugees who have never seen the areas they have allegedly fled from. Among the 580,000 IDPs in Azerbaijan are 230,000 children under the age of 17 who have acquired the IDP status of their fathers – and who have never been to the areas from which they are considered to have been displaced.[44] For the Palestinian refugees, oral history has become an important tool for making children form strong connections to the lands their parents and grandparents were forced to leave.[45] The Azerbaijani exiles similarly hear stories of Nagorno-Karabakh and the occupied regions. Research on the Palestinian refugees has revealed that the younger generations of refugees differentiate between their political standing and improving their livelihood – in contrast to their elders, who refused to renovate their shelters for fear this would be interpreted as acceptance of their situation.[46] Similarly, one might expect the younger generations of Azerbaijani IDPs to have a different political outlook from that of their parents – perhaps differentiating more between blaming external enemies for the initial displacement and demanding more of the government in terms of their current livelihood.

The low level of political mobilisation among Azerbaijani exiles is in stark contrast to both the Palestinian case and another example of a protracted displacement situation, namely that of the Sahrawi refugees of the western Sahara. The Sahrawi refugees' political identity is seen to be even stronger than their humanitarian status as refugees.[47] Their liberation movement, the Polisario, which in 1976 established a state-in-exile, and its success in mobilising collective action, does not have a counterpart among Azerbaijani IDPs.

Obviously, the Azerbaijani IDPs' cause is not that of liberation, but nevertheless it is striking how, aside from rather weak committees of IDPs in the various settlements, whose function has been to mediate between the displaced people and various aid agencies, the Azerbaijani refugees have not organised. Again, the contrast with the Palestinian situation is stark, as the refugee camps there have functioned as bases for the Fedayeen, and the refugee populations have had a pronounced emphasis on armed struggle.[48] That we have not seen them mobilise until now does not however mean that the Azerbaijani refugees might not protest in the future – if, for instance, government policies in Azerbaijan were to create a mass of dissatisfied young people receptive to radical ideas.

In neighbouring Georgia we have seen displaced people from that country's breakaway regions Abkhazia and South Ossetia protest against the government's policies on IDP resettlement. Georgian IDPs protested against the government's plans to resettle IDPs from Abkhazia in a remote region with no employment prospects.[49] The August 2008 crisis in Georgia resulted in a new wave of approximately 26,000 internally displaced persons, adding to the country's community of approximately 220,000 people who were displaced in the early 1990s. This surge sparked a renewed focus on IDP issues in Georgia, and, it would seem, a dynamic in which the larger group of long-time displaced people are dissatisfied with their own living conditions, given that the group of new IDPs have benefitted from generous amounts of international aid. A similar dynamic is not entirely unlikely in Azerbaijan, since the government's resettlement programme has created disparities in living conditions between different groups of IDPs. All in all, the present stability of the displaced community in Azerbaijan should not be taken to mean that the refugees cannot become a factor in domestic politics in the future.

CONCLUSION: CURRENT POLICIES AT ODDS WITH PROTRACTED DISPLACEMENT

As there continues to be no solution to the Nagorno-Karabakh conflict, there appears to be no imminent end to displacement. The promise of return is a key element in the authorities' policies, which insist that all government efforts to improve the living conditions of IDPs are temporary measures pending return. This stance is 'increasingly at odds with the protracted nature of displacement'.[50] As time passes, there is reason to believe that the 'Great Return' is becoming less of a priority for many of the displaced, particularly for the younger among them. This generational divide might gradually undermine the government's IDP policies.

Oil and gas revenues have caused only limited improvements in the standards of living of the displaced people in Azerbaijan, and there is no sign of change with regard to the conflict that caused their displacement. Modest improvements in IDP living standards through resettlement have also come with some negative side-effects: the resettlement amounts to a second displacement; the refugees' employment opportunities have worsened; and their dependence on petroleum-funded government benefits has increased. It is harder to assess what influence Azerbaijan's affluence has on the peace negotiations, but it is only too obvious that Azerbaijan is trying to make its economic strength a factor in the negotiations. The increased military expenditure and the belligerent statements of the Azerbaijani leader seem to be a way of boosting Azerbaijan's position.

Even if the political leadership is only talking about the military build-up and the country's new military and economic strength vis-à-vis Armenia out of a need to cater to anti-Armenian sentiments among the public, or in order to translate the resource wealth into a strong hand in the negotiation processes, a number of questions nevertheless arise. How long can promises of war be made before it becomes necessary to deliver on them? Will the refugees demand war? Will they eventually take action themselves? How long can the petro-revenues function as a disincentive to go to war? During my interviews, I did not meet a single displaced person who believed the current negotiations would lead to success. Nevertheless, most of my respondents emphasised the importance of finding a peaceful solution to the conflict. Some, however, were more impatient: 'Azerbaijan should start a war not tomorrow, but today, because tomorrow it may be too late to take back Karabakh.'[51] One community leader said she did not believe that what had been taken away by force could be returned peaceably.[52] Some IDPs said five years would be too long to wait, others said they could wait forever to go back to their native lands, while for some young IDPs the idea of going 'back' was altogether strange. There was no consensus about these issues among the displaced, but it was clear that the issue of conflict resolution was crucial to their future. And while they are waiting for resolution, the resource wealth, as well as government policies and rhetoric, are not only affecting their livelihoods, but creating certain expectations. The Azerbaijani government may thus be creating a problem for itself: if the IDPs and other people are told for many years that the final resort is military 'liberation', then at some point they may be held to that promise. The displaced community may thus become a factor in domestic politics. In authoritarian Azerbaijan, the government has shown little concern for how its policies on conflict resolution affect the future prospects of the internally displaced; but the growing generational divide in the displaced community will increasingly make it harder for the authorities to maintain their policies on displacement.

NOTES

1. This chapter will however for sake of variation refer to the IDPs in Azerbaijan as IDPs, displaced people, refugees and exiles.
2. Author's interview with male IDPs in a government-built IDP settlement chaikhana (tea house) in Agdam region, 11 June 2008.
3. See Johansson 2009, p.126.
4. The ethnic Armenians outnumber the ethnically Azeri IDPs from the former autonomous region of Nagorno-Karabakh, but if the IDPs from the other occupied regions were eligible to vote in a referendum, they would outnumber the ethnic Armenians. Patrik Johansson therefore argues that it would be in Azerbaijan's interest to include the occupied regions as well as Nagorno-Karabakh in the territory that is voted on in a referendum, in order to have the IDPs from these regions take part in it. See Johansson 2009, p.135.
5. This is the opposite situation of the peace process in Bosnia where repatriation was held to be a precondition for peace. See Johansson 2010, p.31.
6. Johansson 2009, p.136.
7. See RFE/RL 2010b.
8. UNHCR 2007.
9. UN 2005, p.30.
10. Author's interview with several humanitarian organisations in Azerbaijan, June 2008.
11. UNHCR 2009, p.7.
12. Amnesty International 2007, p.46.
13. This is a term frequently used by government organs and officials. One example is the only map I have been able to find of IDP settlements throughout Azerbaijan: it has been prepared by the government and is titled 'Results of Armenian aggression against Azerbaijan in 1988–1993'. See ECORES 1997.
14. In my meeting with the Head of Department for Problems of Refugees, IDPs, Migration and Work with International Organisations, Gurban Sadigov, on 13 June 2008, he cited the figure of 680,000. See IDMC 2008.
15. Author's interview with UNHCR representative in Azerbaijan, William Tall, 13 June 2008.
16. IDMC and NRC 2008, p.197.
17. Author's conversation with programme manager of the Danish Refugee Council in Azerbaijan, Dmitry Medvev, Baku, 12 June 2008.
18. The Oil Fund was established in 2002 and is ruled by presidential decree. The funding of IDP-related programs over the State Oil Fund was ordered via the presidential decrees no.562 (dated 22 August 2001), 577 (7 September 2001),

700 (13 May 2002), 132 (1 October 2004), 346 (28 December 2005), 505 (28 December 2006), 687 (26 December 2007), 68 (26 February 2009) and 204 (25 December 2009), as well as directives no.80 (4 February 2004), 298 (1 July 2004) and 2475 (1 October 2010).

19. UNHCR 2009, p.18.
20. Ibid., p.7.
21. Author's interviews with several international and domestic aid organisations in Azerbaijan, June 2008.
22. Author's interviews with several international and domestic aid organisations in Azerbaijan, June 2008.
23. As the head of an international humanitarian organisation pointed out, it might even seem that the government is artificially keeping the number high, since even though several organisations have left the country, the official number of international humanitarian organisations has remained unchanged.
24. Calling the non-IDPs 'local population' is problematic, as this implies the IDPs are not local in places where they have lived for over a decade. For the purposes of this chapter it is necessary simply as a term that distinguishes between IDPs and non-IDPs living in the same place.
25. World Bank 2010, p.36.
26. Ibid., p.37.
27. DRC 2007, p.17.
28. Ibid., pp.22–3.
29. World Bank 2010, p.35.
30. Author's interview with middle-aged female IDP living in a government-built IDP settlement in Fizuli region, 10 June 2008.
31. DRC 2007, pp.18–19.
32. World Bank 2010, p.35.
33. DRC 2007, p.18–19.
34. Lücke and Trofimenko 2008, p.149.
35. DRC 2007, p.23.
36. World Bank 2010, p.37.
37. Author's interviews with local aid workers, June 2008.
38. Author's interview with Elnur Nasibov, head of Azerbaijani legal aid organisation Praxis, Baku, 12 June 2008.
39. Author's conversation with programme manager Dmitry Medvev, Danish Refugee Council, Baku, 12 June 2008.
40. State Oil Fund of the Republic of Azerbaijan 2007, p.5.
41. There is no evidence that the few outlets of independent Islam that do exist, like the Abu-Bakr mosque in Baku, have mobilised, particularly from among the IDP communities, nor does the imam focus on the Nagorno-Karabakh issue. Author's interview with anonymous expert on independent Islam in Azerbaijan, 20 June 2008. For a longer discussion of the reasons for the lack of protest among the IDPs, see Kjaernet 2010.
42. Author's interview with middle-aged male IDP living in makeshift house along a roadside in Agdam region, 11 June 2008.
43. Author's interview with young male IDP in public building in Sumgayit, 18 June 2008.
44. Children of IDP women and non-displaced men do not acquire IDP status and are thus not entitled to state benefits. According to the Internal Displacement

Monitoring Centre, these children are discriminated against on the basis of the sex of their IDP parent. See IDMC and NRC 2010, p.3.
45. Farah 2009, p.84.
46. Ibid., p.89.
47. Ibid., p.82.
48. Ibid., p.86.
49. RFE/RL 2010a.
50. IDMC and NRC 2010, p.8.
51. Author's interview with male IDPs in an IDP settlement *chaikhana* (tea house) in Agdam region, 11 June 2008.
52. Author's interview with community (*obschina*) leader in urban IDP settlement in Xirdalan, 17 June 2008.

REFERENCES

Amnesty International (2007) 'Azerbaijan: Displaced then Discriminated Against – the Plight of the Internally Displaced Population' (London: Amnesty International).

DRC (2007) 'IDP Livelihood Assessment: Azerbaijan. March–May 2007' (Baku: Danish Refugee Council).

ECORES (1997) 'Refugee map', *Azerbaijan International*, 5(1) (Spring), available at www.azer.com/aiweb/categories/magazine/51_folder/51_articles/51_refugeemap. html.

Farah, R. (2009) 'Refugee Camps in the Palestinian and Sahrawi National Liberation Movements: A Comparative Perspective', *Journal of Palestine Studies*, 38(2): 76–93.

IDMC (2008) 'Total Internally Displaced People in the Government-Controlled Territory: 572,531 People' (Geneva: Internal Displacement Monitoring Centre).

—— and NRC (2008) 'Azerbaijan: IDPs Still Trapped in Poverty and Dependence. A Profile of the Internal Displacement Situation' (Geneva: Internal Displacement Monitoring Centre and Norwegian Refugee Council).

—— —— (2010) 'Azerbaijan: After Some 20 Years, IDPs Still Face Barriers to Self-reliance' (Geneva: Internal Displacement Monitoring Centre and Norwegian Refugee Council).

Johansson, P. (2009) 'Putting Peace to the Vote: Displaced Persons and a Future Referendum on Nagorno-Karabakh', *Refugee Survey Quarterly*, 28(1): 122–39.

—— (2010) 'Peace by Repatriation: Concepts, Cases and Conditions', Ph.D. thesis (Umeå University).

Kjaernet, H. (2010) 'Displacement in a Booming Economy: IDPs in Azerbaijan', in I. Øverland, H. Kjaernet, and A. Kendall-Taylor (eds) *Caspian Energy Politics: Azerbaijan, Kazakhstan and Turkmenistan* (Abingdon: Routledge).

Lücke, M. and Trofimenko, N. (2008) 'Whither Oil Money? Redistribution of Oil Revenue in Azerbaijan', in B. Najman, R. Pomfret, and G. Raballand (eds) *The Economics and Politics of Oil in the Caspian Basin: The Redistribution of Oil Revenues in Azerbaijan and Central Asia* (Abingdon: Routledge).

RFE/RL (2010a) 'Self-Immolation Incident Highlights Desperation of Georgian IDPs', *Radio Free Europe/Radio Liberty*, 29 October.

—— (2010b) 'Armenia Threatens to Recognise Disputed Karabakh Region', *Radio Free Europe/Radio Liberty*, 3 December.

State Oil Fund of the Republic of Azerbaijan (2002) 'Annual Report for 2002' (Baku: State Oil Fund of the Republic of Azerbaijan).

—— (2003) 'Annual report for 2003' (Baku: State Oil Fund of the Republic of Azerbaijan).

—— (2004) 'Annual report for 2004' (Baku: State Oil Fund of the Republic of Azerbaijan).

—— (2005) 'Annual report for 2005' (Baku: State Oil Fund of the Republic of Azerbaijan).

—— (2006) 'Annual report for 2006' (Baku: State Oil Fund of the Republic of Azerbaijan).

—— (2007) 'Annual report for 2007' (Baku: State Oil Fund of the Republic of Azerbaijan).

—— (2008) 'Annual report for 2008' (Baku: State Oil Fund of the Republic of Azerbaijan).

—— (2009) 'Annual report for 2009' (Baku: State Oil Fund of the Republic of Azerbaijan).

UN (2005) 'General Assembly Resolution A/60/L.1', 15 September.

UNHCR (2007) 'Convention and Protocol Relating to the Status of Refugees, with an Introductory Note by the Office of the United Nations High Commissioner for Refugees' (Geneva: United Nations High Commissioner for Refugees).

—— (2009) 'Azerbaijan: Analysis of Gaps in the Protection of Internally Displaced Persons (IDPs)' (United Nations High Commissioner for Refugees).

World Bank (2010) 'Azerbaijan: Living Conditions Assessment Report' (World Bank, Human Development Sector Unit, Europe and Central Asia Region).

7
The Socio-economic Dynamics of Gas in Bolivia

Fernanda Wanderley, Leila Mokrani and Alice Guimarães

Bolivia has faced structural problems in its economy throughout its history as a republic, i.e. a pattern of accumulation supported by non-renewable extractive activities with little connection to sectors that generate employment, and which are dependent on external variables and vulnerable to marked cyclical trends. The various management models applied intermittently in the country – both liberal and statist – have not been able to break free from the system of non-renewable extraction that has resulted in low average growth and high levels of poverty and inequality.

The liberal model, which was in place for the first two decades of the twentieth century, consolidated the 'tin-dependent' development model. In 1937, with the nationalisation of Standard Oil and the creation of Bolivia's national oil company, Yacimientos Petrolíferos Fiscales Bolivianos (YPFB), the pendulum swung towards nationalisation of the extractive model. This was completed with the nationalisation of the tin sector and the birth of the Bolivian mining corporation, Corporación Minera de Bolivia (COMIBOL), in 1952. In the 1960s, there was a brief period of liberalisation with new private investments in mining and hydrocarbons. However, this was interrupted by the nationalisation of Gulf Oil in October 1969.[1]

In 1985 the pendulum swung back towards a liberal model that, among other things, resulted in the reform of the hydrocarbon sector in 1996, which implemented an aggressive policy of attracting private foreign investment. This reform began the 'era of gas' in Bolivia – a phase characterised by increased economic dependence on exporting this natural resource. After less than ten years, in 2005, a new cycle of statist reforms began with the passing of the Hydrocarbons Law, which was very quickly subjected to two processes of adjustment. First, the nationalisation decree (Decreto Supremo de Nacionalización) in 2006 and secondly the approval of the new Political Constitution of the State by referendum in 2009. This process has yet to be fully concluded.

Between 1996 and 2005, in a highly conflictive political context, the shift took place from a clearly liberal model towards a model based on state management. Political struggles connected the issue of hydrocarbons to other key issues in Bolivian politics, recovering distinct historical horizons and adopting modalities for collective action that ranged from open confrontation and conflict with the state to the formulation of alternative projects and intense debates in institutionalised public spaces.

Seeking a greater understanding of the process of reforms over the past 15 years, this chapter proposes a reading of the socio-political context in which these reforms took place. Our focus is on the articulations between the technical–economic and political–symbolic dimensions of oil and gas management in Bolivia, and their setting within networks of social, political and economic relations. These set the stage for broader questions about the models of development, the meaning of sovereignty and the model of state, society and economy.

We argue that the production of meaning and value of natural resources constituted a fundamental aspect of a crisis of legitimacy with the liberal model and efforts at state reform. During this period, the ideological debate on the model of state, society and economy was dominant in the framework of different modernisation projections. This debate obscured consideration of more specific questions relating to the socio-economic outcomes of distinct proposals for the management of the sector. These ongoing efforts at reform reflect the difficulties of the Bolivian political system in achieving a necessary balance between legitimacy on the one hand and sufficient levels of investment and production as well as the capture and use of economic rents by the state, on the other.

In countries that are highly dependent upon natural resources, as is the case of Bolivia, it is essential to define sustainable domestic models for the political and economic management of hydrocarbon resources. This is particularly important in the process of constructing a development model that moves towards fulfilling expectations for sustainable growth in terms of wealth and improved living conditions for the population (through the eradication of poverty and the equitable distribution of resources and opportunities) and a democratic and intercultural framework for social coexistence and environmental responsibility. The Bolivian case illustrates the difficulties of constructing public spheres that establish legitimate and economic sustainable collective accords on how to 'govern oil and gas'. These difficulties characterise the development trajectories of many countries that are dependent on these resources. As such, Bolivia runs the risk of repeating the past mistakes of policies that were exhausted as a result of economic limitations and an inadequate understanding of the social mandate.

This chapter is organised in the following manner. The first section outlines the neoliberal model that was implemented in 1985 onwards. The second analyses the specific reform of the hydrocarbon sector in 1996 and its main economic impacts. The third section discusses how the increase in investments and production in the industry was accompanied by the growing discontentment of the population in a context of increased precariousness of labour, continuing poverty and increasing inequality. With this as background, in the fourth section our attention turns to the issues of politics and symbolism that shaped the national debate and resulted in the profound crisis of the neoliberal model's legitimacy. In the fifth and sixth sections of the chapter, historic events and the complex process of reformulating hydrocarbon policy are discussed. The chapter concludes by considering how the Bolivian experience illustrates the complexities and multifaceted nature of oil and gas management in countries that are highly dependent on these resources.

THE NEOLIBERAL MODEL

Bolivia abandoned the model of state capitalism in 1985[2] and made the private sector principally responsible for carrying out productive investment. As such, the state took on the role of regulating and guaranteeing macroeconomic stability and promoting public investment in health, education, sanitation and infrastructure. The stabilisation plan of August 1985 incorporated measures recommended by the International Monetary Fund, such as the reduction of public spending, a contractive monetary policy, the reduction of public employment, the opening of internal markets and the elimination of price and wage regulations.[3]

From 1993 on, these structural reforms were deepened and a process of capitalisation (a variation of privatisation in which partial public ownership is retained) was pushed through, transferring the main state enterprises to private administration. Public ownership of 49 per cent of the shares was maintained, however; the shares were to belong to all citizens over 21, and were placed in a trust called the Fondo de Capitlización Colectiva (Collective Capitalisation

Fund). Upon turning 65 years old, all Bolivians would have the right to collect their individual dividends, made available through a universal old age insurance scheme, the 'Bono Solidario' (Solidarity Subsidy – Bonosol).

The defenders of the capitalisation system based their arguments on the liberal principle of minimising the state's role in the economy and saw it as the beginning of a modernisation project based upon the free market. The government of the time stated that capitalisation was the 'answer for Bolivian development',[4] and in the words of President Sanchez de Lozada, the measure 'gave a face to the goal of hastening development'. According to him, if the YPFB was not capitalised, Bolivia would lose 'the possibility of being a viable country with growth and social justice'.[5] Juxtaposing capitalisation with underdevelopment,[6] the president connected economic reforms not only to economic development but also to social development and to Bolivia's very viability as a nation. However, as time demonstrated, these promises were left largely unfulfilled, predominantly due to the failure of economic policies to prioritise employment-intensive sectors or coordinate with wider social policies.

During this period, economic policies were centred on sectors that were capital-intensive such as hydrocarbons, telecommunications, transportation and electricity. The hope was that the liberalisation of markets, the creation of regulatory bodies and the privatisation of public enterprises in these sectors would offer the necessary conditions to stimulate the economy and generate employment. Specific policies for other labour-intensive sectors, for example agriculture, food production and the incipient Bolivian textile industry, were not developed in coordination with these changes. In the end, the structural reforms ended up reinforcing a model for growth that was concentrated in the exploitation of natural resources, and inhibited the development of the employment-generating sector. The result was increased employment in the informal sector and the increasing vulnerability of salaried and unsalaried labour.

Parallel to, but formally disconnected from economic policies, new social policies promoted the expansion of the population's access to public services in education and health. This expansion included the implementation of universal programmes of social protection, such as the Bono Solidario, and other programmes directed towards the poorest segments of the population through social investment funds. Moreover, during this period there were ambitious institutional reforms aimed at the decentralisation of the state and the expansion of popular participation in politics. These reforms gave judicial and political recognition to historically marginalised social actors in Bolivian society, such as indigenous peoples, and opened spaces for participation in the design and implementation of social policies.[7]

Despite the breadth of the social programmes introduced, there was little effort to articulate these policies within a common framework. Institutions responsible for policies in each sector (health, education, housing, work, pensions, among others) developed their activities with very little coordination. The precarious financial sustainability, fragmentation and insufficient coordination among institutions can be explained to a large extent by their overdependence on external resources, in particular international cooperation,[8] and the pro-cyclical character of their programmes. These problems were further compounded by low levels of state institutionalism, marked by the discontinuity of public policies and of technical teams among governments and even among ministers of the same government.

THE LIBERAL REFORM OF THE HYDROCARBON SECTOR OF 1996

It is in this context that the reform of the hydrocarbon sector was passed in 1996.[9] The Sanchez de Lozada government introduced an aggressive package of institutional restructuring, the objective of which was to eliminate the vertical integration that characterised Bolivian industry. The branches of the hydrocarbon's industry were separated into units of exploration and production, pipeline transport, and refining and distribution, which allowed for private participation in their operation. The goal was to demonstrate public will for efficient energy-sector ordering and transparent rules for the conduct of business.

This model assigned responsibility for the administration and supervision of plans in the sector to the Ministry of Economic Development. These also applied to the plans for downstream regulation and auditing by an autonomous body, which would act as an arbitrator in resolving the appeals that might arise when faced with possible acts of normative damages. The possibility for the resolution of conflicts through international arbitration was also established, subject to Bolivian legislation.

One of the fundamental changes in the new institutional structure was an effort to limit the role of the YPFB. It had previously acted as a representative of the state, exercising total control over the chain of production,[10] and had directed the operation of various business units up to that moment. As such, it had occupied a central position in the national productive apparatus. From that position, the company became dedicated to fulfilling functions solely related to the control and administration of contracts and upstream auditing. This measure had a significant impact on public opinion. Indeed, it was seen as limiting state participation in a strategic activity and state influence in decision making over what was considered a sovereign issue.

The hydrocarbon sector reform of 1996 structured the operating rules of exploration and exploitation activities through a standard concessionary contractual model or 'shared risk contract'. This model had its conceptual basis in the principles of economic liberalism that placed full responsibility for activity on private initiative. Instead of taking responsibility for production, the state would receive a 'counter-provision' – or royalty – for the right to exploit a non-renewable resource, in addition to other taxes established by law.

In commercial terms, the reform defined by Law 1689 of 1996 summarises the liberal spirit of the model at the conceptual level: 'There is free import, export and internal marketing of hydrocarbons and their derivative products, subject to the dispositions of this law' (Article 5), and 'those who sign shared risk contracts acquire the right to prospect, exploit, extract, transport, and commercialize the production obtained'. These rules of the free market included a single supply safeguard, the disposition contained in the final part of Article 24, which established that 'the volumes required to satisfy internal consumption of natural gas and to fulfill export contracts agreed upon by YPFB that predate this law, are exempt from the free market'.

As part of the packet of reforms to attract investment, the 1996 reform established a new tax regime. It differentiated between oilfields discovered before the establishment of this law (existing hydrocarbons) and those discovered after the law's approval (new hydrocarbons). The former were subject to the payment of approximately 50 per cent of their production for royalties and participation in the national treasury, while the latter were subject to an incentive that translated into a lower 'blind' tributary charge[11] of 18 per cent of production on the same terms. The framework was complemented with a set of standard taxes[12] on new hydrocarbons. This system obliged oil companies to pay rates of 25 per cent for utilities, 12.5 per cent on remittances abroad, a 3 per cent transaction tax on commercialisation in the internal market and a 15 per cent value added tax (VAT). In addition, a tax of 25 per cent on extraordinary utilities (surtax) was applied only in the case of extractive industries.

The differentiated tax structure for existing and new hydrocarbons, accompanied by a system of general taxes, made it difficult for the population to understand this system. There was also lack of clarity amongst political actors with regards to the effective rate of contribution to the state. As a result, the collective imaginary focused on the idea that the total participation of the nation had fallen from 50 per cent to 18 per cent. In actual fact, the system of state appropriation of economic rents had not been 50 per cent in the period prior to the reform,[13] nor was it 18 per cent under Law 1689. To illustrate the new tax situation and to establish ranges of magnitude, we cite the results of the Medinaceli (2007) simulation. According to this simulation,[14] actual state participation in benefits from oilfields were in the range of 50 per cent, 61 per cent, and 64 per cent for small, medium, and large fields respectively. If the results of the model are referenced to gross income or to the value of wellhead production, these indicators would remain of the order of 42 per cent, 53 per cent and 56 per cent respectively.

Whilst noting the previous assertions, we do not claim to make a value judgment about to what extent this system was reasonable. Instead, we wish to establish that behind the tax regime there was complex engineering that was not widely understood, not at least at the level of public opinion or even amongst those responsible for creating sectoral policies. In light of the complexity of the variables at play (levels of risk, and high volatility of the market), it is important to consider the difficulty of defining an optimum formula for a sectoral tax regime that would allow adequate participation of the state and at the same time establish reasonable returns for investment. This situation is also complicated by the capacity of citizens to adequately interpret the amount collected by the state.

THE EXCELLENT SECTORAL RESULTS OF THE REFORM AND THE POOR EFFECTS ON THE QUALITY OF LIFE OF THE POPULATION

The sectoral reform of 1996 created the conditions for the signing of a contract between YPFB and Petrobras SA for the export of natural gas to Brazil. This contract began the second and most significant cycle of natural gas exportation in the country. The most notable result of this situation was Bolivia's positioning as the country with the largest reserves of free gas in Central and South America, according to the certification of reserves in 2005,[15] and the second largest after Venezuela in terms of natural gas. In that year, Bolivia achieved the certification of 48.7 trillion cubic feet proved and probable reserves; an increase of more than 700 per cent over those registered in 1997.

This finding had an impact on the confidence of the industry in Bolivia and gave new encouragement to the energy sector in the country. It not only indicated that the country had the volumes of natural gas needed to meet the commitments it had made to Brazil, but offered the possibility for Bolivia to consolidate itself as the energy centre in the southern cone.

The legal regime at this time can be seen then to have achieved its main goal: the consolidation of important sources of international private investment, both for exploratory activities and for operations. For example, the regime resulted in the construction of the Gasbol gas pipeline that connects with the transport pipeline on the Brazilian side to the market of Sao Paulo. Sectoral investment reached a figure of approximately $4.1 billion between the implementation of the law in 1996 and 2005. This included obtaining record capital contributions in 1999 of $1.06 billion according to the referring rubrics.[16]

Nonetheless, although expectations were growing with respect to the sector's contribution to the structure of production and to generating income, there was also a growing public feeling that this spectacular growth was only possible at a high fiscal cost. The concern was that the historic tendency of not using strategic resources to benefit society would be repeated.

Contrary to the expectations of sustained improvements in living and working conditions, this period was characterised by the further informalisation and precariousness of salaried work and an increase in formal non-salaried workers at the margins of the short and long-term social security system (see Figure 7.1). Whilst 45 per cent of the working population were in urban areas and 61 per cent of working women were unsalaried in 1992, in 2003 this number had climbed to 51 per cent of the working population (61 per cent among women and 43 per cent among men). This was a situation that did not change significantly in subsequent years. In urban areas, the informal family sector absorbed more and more jobs, both male and female, and its importance in terms of the provision of employment increased from 37 per cent in 1985 to 39 per cent in 1992, and to 45 per cent in 2003.

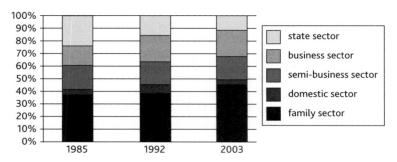

Figure 7.1   Composition of urban employment

Sources: CEDLA, and created by the authors with data from surveys carried out by the National Statistics Institute (INE)

Note: The semi-business sector is made up of units that employ fewer than five salaried workers or cooperativists and in which the owner of the establishment participates actively and directly in the productive process. These units are not typically covered by labour legislation and social security. The family sector is made up of pieceworkers and unpaid family members.

Furthermore, as a result of the policy of open hiring and unrestricted salary negotiations, the practice of temporary or short-term hiring was extended. Indirect labour costs and salaries for non-skilled workers were reduced.[17] As can be seen in Figure 7.2, the average income of non-salaried workers experienced a decline throughout the period, while the average income of salaried workers shows improvements from 1995 to 2003.

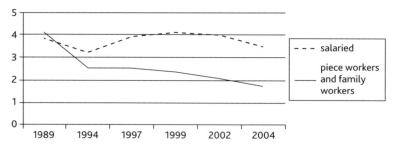

Figure 7.2   Average incomes (in multiples of the poverty line)

Source: CEPAL, 'Panorama Social de América Latina 2006'

While working conditions were deteriorating, progress was made in expanding basic social service coverage. In this manner, although public social spending decreased from 1985 to 1990, it once again increased from 12.4 per cent in 1995 to 19.9 per cent in 2002 in relation to GDP. Social investment, including health, education and culture, basic sanitation, urbanism and housing, increased from 18 per cent of total public investment in 1990 to 35 per cent in 1995 and 43 per cent in 2002.[18]

The improvements in health and education facilities and attendance had a significant impact in terms of expanding the percentage of the population with access to services. However, there was little change in the uneven quality of public and private service provision. In primary education, gross registration was maintained at 104 per cent from 1998 to 2005. (The figure is greater than 100 per cent due to the inclusion of older students who were past the official enrolment age.) In secondary education it increased from 50 per cent in 1998 to 76 per cent in 2005.[19] The differences in access among boys and girls were not significant, although male access remained slightly higher. Although the Bolivian school system has difficulty retaining students, the dropout rate fell in the 1990s.

With regards to health, according to data from the National Demographic and Health Survey the free public insurance programmes for mothers and children contributed to raising the proportion of births in clinics or hospitals from 27 per cent in 1995 to 61.9 per cent in 2003. The rate of prenatal check-ups also increased. Maternal mortality fell from 416 per 100,000 live births in 1989 to 229 in 2003, and the rate of infant mortality fell from 89 per 1000 live births in 1989 to 54 in 2003. The free medical insurance programme for seniors also increased coverage among this group, reaching 217,000 registered and insured of the 650,000 seniors in the country in 2006.

Despite the advances linked to concrete programmes, the overall coverage of the public health system remained low: 59 per cent of the sick population covered their health costs through private means – 49 per cent through pharmacies, at home or other and 10 per cent in private establishments. Household health spending increased from 32 per cent to 36 per cent of the total between 1995 and 2002. Business and institutional spending also increased from 39 per cent to 45 per cent while state spending decreased from 18 per cent to 12 per cent and international aid from 10 per cent to 7 per cent.[20] The majority of household spending was on medication and only 15 per cent was spent in a clinic or a private practice.

The economic model of the time relied upon increasing public service coverage and direct resource distribution, but lacked policies directed towards transforming the production structure and, as such, the creation of employment. As a result, average levels of poverty measured by income were maintained, inequality increased, but poverty measured by basic needs was reduced (see Table 7.1) from 85.5 per cent in 1976 to 70.9 per cent in 1992 and to 58.6 per cent in 2001, a process that was concentrated in urban areas. In rural areas, 91 per cent of the population still did not have access to any basic health service or basic sanitation. Nonetheless, poverty measured by income did not register a decline and inequality increased. The Gini coefficient increased from 0.54 in 1989 to 0.61 in 2002.

Table 7.1   Poverty and inequality indicators

	1976	1989	1992	1994	1997	1999	2001	2002	2004
Incidence of poverty (%) (unmet basic needs)	85.5	...	70.9	...	...	...	58.6	...	...
Urban	66.0	...	53.1	...	...	...	39.0	...	...
Rural	98.0	...	95.3	...	...	...	90.8	...	...
Incidence of poverty (%) (income)	...	...	...	...	62.1	60.6	...	62.4	63.9
Urban	...	52.6	...	51.6	52.3	48.7	...	52.0	53.8
Rural	...	...	...	...	78.5	80.7	...	79.2	80.6
Incidence of extreme poverty (%) (income)	...	...	...	...	37.2	36.4	...	37.1	34.7
Urban	...	23.0	...	19.8	22.6	19.8	...	21.3	20.2
Rural	...	...	...	...	61.5	64.7	...	62.9	58.8
Gini coefficient	...	0.538	...	...	0.595	0.586	...	0.614	...

Sources: Compiled by the authors based on 'Bolivia: Mapa de Pobreza 2001, INE 2002 y Estrategia Boliviana de Reducción de la Pobreza', referenced in the UNDP 'Human Development Report' of 2002 and CEPAL, 'Panorama Social de América Latina 2006'.

Though the notable increase in productive capacity in the hydrocarbon sector raised expectations of its contributing to significant improvements in social well-being, the population experienced vulnerability in access to employment and segmented expansion in access to public services and goods. In this socio-economic context, social dissatisfaction with the neoliberal model grew, and the proposal for 'the recovery of gas for Bolivians' developed, a process that we analyse below.

THE CRISIS OF THE LIBERAL REFORM OF THE HYDROCARBON SECTOR

Looking at historical events, one can see that the crisis of the liberal model was not founded on a broad discussion of the management design used to steer the hydrocarbon industry, but instead concerned the political basis of its conception. What was experienced was fundamentally the political crisis of the legitimacy of the neoliberal model as a whole.

The downplaying of more technical and economic questions relating to hydrocarbon management and the feasibility of distinct sectoral proposals in favour of ideological debates is a characteristic that is constant throughout the processes of reform the country has experienced over the last decade. Although technical–economic questions were not absent, they were largely obscured by what was predominantly an ideological debate on the model of the state, economy and society in the framework of different modernisation projects.[21] To understand the crisis of the 1996 model, it is absolutely essential to look back to the very moment of its conception and the symbolic constructions that were confronted in this context: on the one hand capitalisation was associated with liberal modernisation and on the other this measure was juxtaposed with the defence of national sovereignty. Let us look at the political stage upon which these two positions unfolded.

The Senate president, Juan Carlos Duran, of the party in government, stated that there were two positions on capitalisation: 'the government's position, which is trying to change the old structure for a modern one', and that of the opponents 'who say no to everything'. He stressed that opponents were 'contrary to the neoliberal model, to the government, to capitalisation and to modernisation' while the government sought 'modernisation of the country with the goal of improving the well-being of the Bolivian people'.[22] So the government declared that reducing the role of the state in the economy was the recipe for Bolivia's economic and social development, as well as for its modernisation.

The minister of capitalisation at the time, Alfonso Revollo, defended the 'social' character of the structural reforms. He indicated that transferring administration of the productive sector to private initiatives would not only achieve economic advances, but would also reduce the weight of the 'gigantic investments needed in those companies in the state's hands'. It could then 'focus on its social role, especially in the areas of education and health'.[23] Capitalisation, the minister stressed, was not about a simple economic plan, but instead had 'social characteristics that signified benefits for all the Bolivian people'.[24]

Opponents played off sentiments of nationalism, recalling tragic historic moments[25] with regard to state sovereignty and proposing a state that promoted development and that was active in the national economy. In their arguments there were not only economic and political considerations, but also a mix of deep-rooted feelings and passions. As such, YPFB carried a powerful emotional weight, which was largely derived from the association made between the company and the events in Bolivian history. It had particular power in activating nationalist sentiments, and provided the basis for collective action against capitalisation.

To understand the social mobilisation that took place in defence of YPFB, it is important to rapidly review its history. The company was created in the wake of the nationalisation of Standard Oil's holdings in Bolivia in 1937. The official reason for this measure was that the company traded contraband Bolivian crude to Argentina, but there were also other underlying reasons. There was a perception in Bolivia that the Chaco War had been a conflict over control of the oil wells in the Chaco region. So the 50,000 Bolivians who died 'in the sands of Chaco' did so in a heroic defence of the most important national resource: oil.[26]

Diverse sectors of civil society opposed capitalisation. The Comité de Defensa del Patrimonio Nacional (CODEPANAL: Committee for Defence of the National Patrimony)[27] suggested that the move would relinquish 'the national and collective patrimony of the country' and open 'the doors to political power being held in private hands', since 'foreign enterprises would have all the economic power', and consequently, 'all the political power'.[28] The manifesto of the Comité Departamental de Defensa del Patrimonio Nacional (CDPN) of Tarija played upon this collective memory by declaring that 'history painfully shows us, in the cases of the Sea, Acre, and the Chaco, that whoever controls the economy, controls the sovereignty of the nation'.[29] Playing upon the 'tragic national memory' in this fashion also brought together ex-combatants from the Chaco, who declared that it would be absurd for a government to 'step over the 50,000 Bolivian corpses that were left in the Chaco, in defence of oil wealth'.[30]

The civic committees in Bolivian cities also played upon the nationalist imaginary and the notion of the state sovereignty by declaring that it was the duty of 'every Bolivian to protect the territorial and economic sovereignty of the country'.[31] According to the Federación Departamental de Centros Provinciales de La Paz (Departmental Federation of Provincial Centres of La Paz), control over hydrocarbons was closely related to the 'independence of the country', since 'economic prosperity, political independence and national defence of the people' are based upon petroleum wealth. Moreover, it declared that the absolute control of the state over this wealth was imperative to the nation's existence and to the real exercise of sovereignty. It defended a call for popular consultation on the issue, since 'the people are the owners of sovereignty' and, as such, they are 'the only ones who can legitimately make a valid decision on the transcendental aspects related to the future of the country'.[32]

The Central Obrera Boliviana (COB: Bolivian Workers' Central) also denounced capitalisation as the 'alienation of national patrimony'. It called on the population to defend 'the hydrocarbon resources of the country'[33] and 'national sovereignty in the face of the anti-national policies that the government is implementing'.[34] In the National Defence Debate Forum of YPFB, participants emphasised the unconstitutionality of the project. They stressed that capitalisation of YPFB would put 'national resources in private and foreign hands'. In giving them economic power, they would also gain political power, so that national politics would be managed from outside, 'in support of interests that are not those of the nation'. They further argued that the intention to capitalise YPFB was 'an attempt against the nation' and 'a betrayal of the homeland'.[35]

As can be seen, the mobilisation of ample social sectors against the capitalisation of YPFB was based upon the vision of hydrocarbons as the national patrimony and the perception that opposing capitalisation was equivalent to defending the sovereignty and interests of the country. Moreover, arguments against capitalisation made reference to the illegality and illegitimacy of the process: it was incompatible with the Political Constitution of the State. As such, the two sources of support and justification for state authority, legality and legitimacy, were questioned, putting democratic stability in jeopardy. Finally, opponents defended the role of the state in promoting national development by participating directly in what was a strategic sector of the economy.

In this scenario of strong ideological polarisation, the accumulation of these events created the conditions for new sectoral reforms. The first event to highlight is the change of government that followed the first presidential period of Gonzalo Sanchez de Lozada. In August 1997, Hugo Banzer Suarez assumed the presidency of Bolivia with a fragile political presence. He was supported by a weak coalition of traditional parties in a context marked by adverse conditions in international commodity prices and a significant fiscal deficit.

It was this government that began to formally introduce and bring to light the problems of hydrocarbons. Government discourse constantly denounced the process of capitalisation, the fiscal reform and the loss of state control that this process generated as justification not only for the problem of public finances, but also for the internal policies of fuel prices.

In this atmosphere, the parliamentary opposition – with strong support of social organisations – began to win ground on the national political stage. An important fact to note is the creation of the National Coordination for the Defence and Recovery of Gas (CNDRG) in 2002, led by Evo Morales and Filemon Escobar. This movement encompassed a broad spectrum of interests, from military personnel to anti-globalisation activists, neighbourhood organisations, retirees, union organisations, peasants from the altiplano and coca growers.[36]

Although they began by questioning the tax system, the critiques of the liberal model of hydrocarbon management, both from social organisations and from the formal political system, adopted greater intensity with time and created a new national debate. Within this debate two voices – with different emphases – emerged: on the one hand, those that stressed the necessity of modifying the system of ownership of production, and on the other hand those that referred to a process of nationalisation.

The reform of 1996, in terms of the increase in the productive capacity of the country, had a significant impact. It generated high expectations about the role of the sector as the engine of economic and social development and brought into question the very orientation of the industry's policies. In this manner, the demand of social organisations was centred on the principle of 'recovering gas for Bolivians' through a reversal of the process of privatisation.

This position went so far as to argue against exporting natural gas as a raw material. This proposal was in stark opposition to proposals for a large-scale LNG (liquefied natural gas) export project to the United States – through the Chilean port of Patillos – designed by the companies Repsol YPF, British Gas and British Petroleum (operators of the Margarita field in Tarija). This project touched a nerve with the Bolivian population, given the historical antecedents and the conflictive diplomatic relationship between Chile and Bolivia.[37] In light of this initiative, the opposition revived the rhetoric of a defence of sovereignty and of national patrimony, calling for uprisings demanding the nationalisation of hydrocarbons, in what has been called the 'gas war' of 2003. This uprising led to confrontations between the forces of government and peasant and marginalised populations of peri-urban and rural areas. A series of roadblocks established by protesters left the city of La Paz completely isolated. The conflict exploded into violence when the government ordered military action to unblock the entrance to the city, resulting in the death of at least 70 civilians and bringing about the resignation of Sanchez de Lozada in October 2003.

BEGINNING A NEW PROCESS OF REFORM

Faced with the resignation of President Sanchez de Lozada in 2003, Carlos Mesa, the vice-president, assumed the presidency. Events had made it clear that the country needed to solve two problems as quickly as possible: that of sovereignty, associated with the issue of ownership of hydrocarbon production, and that of the structure of state participation in hydrocarbon rents.[38] Ex-president Mesa recognised this fundamental challenge when he stated:

A referendum on hydrocarbons was essential because the export of gas and the law had become the great problem that was at the brink of setting the country on fire … not only was the issue of exportation on the table, but also the central ideological question of our natural resources. Two visions faced off against one another.[39]

Once again, the two confronting visions were the liberal and the statist.

The intensity of the events that had taken place meant that one of the priorities of the new government was to call a referendum. Nonetheless, this happened without sufficient public debate to allow citizens to make decisions based on clear conceptual principles and accurate technical and economic knowledge.

Five questions were asked in a national referendum. These focused on (1) disapproval of Law 1689 of 1996; (2) the return to state ownership of hydrocarbons at the wellhead; (3) the refounding of the YPFB, giving it the capacity to participate in the entire hydrocarbon productive chain; (4) the use of gas as a strategic resource to recover sovereign and useable access to the Pacific Ocean; and (5) the export of gas in the framework of a national policy that (a) covered Bolivian gas consumption; (b) promoted industrialisation of gas in the national territory; and (c) charged taxes and/or royalties on petroleum companies, reaching 50 per cent of the value of gas, and directing it principally towards education, health, roads and jobs.

Although the consultation brought together issues of national interest, it left open a wide range of possibilities for its solution, which indicated the absence of a project to direct discussion. In short, there was consultation on the elimination of one model of management without taking the time necessary to create the basis for what would be the new model of management and development of the hydrocarbons industry. Moreover, no position was taken on the role of investment and the objective possibilities of exposing the state to financial risk.

Support for the principles formulated in the consultation nonetheless brought to light a manifest desire, at the national level (a) to strengthen YPFB and promote its active participation in the hydrocarbon chain, and (b) to establish a regime of more equitable state participation in rents, supported by a structure of direct capture (better understood and conceived by the population as an element to guarantee greater revenue collection).

Faced with this scenario, it was up to the political system not only to collect, but also to 'interpret' the national will, and 'process' this will into a legal body. Supported by the results of this consultation, Mesa presented a bill to Congress that included a proposal for direct and progressive complementary taxes. Although this bill sought to adapt to the differentiated characteristics and the economies of scale of the fields, it was rejected.

At the heart of Congress, politicians were more inclined to accept a tax fixed at 50 per cent of wellhead production or production at the point of inspection. In this sense, the principle of 50 per cent versus 18 per cent was paramount, since these were numbers that had been adopted by the social imaginary, centring the internal debate on the problem of whether the additional 32 per cent ought to be conceptualised as a tax or as royalties. This last option had the support of the Movement towards Socialism (MAS).

With regard to contractual issues, some interests sought a service contract, in which the operator assumed the risk and the productive activity instead of exclusive monetary retribution. Other voices considered it important to open the possibility for the YPFB to create production-sharing and association contracts. These were considered more attractive to business initiatives and avoided compromising the principle of state ownership of hydrocarbons.

In May 2005, Congress approved the new Hydrocarbons Law no.3058,[40] in which different visions appeared to take priority. It had not been possible to construct a project that had been debated and accepted as legitimate by all sides, including by the government. This law contains conceptual ambiguities in its management model: in some of its articles it suggests that YPFB retains not only ownership at the wellhead, but is also considered to be the exclusive vendor of hydrocarbon production;[41] in others it appears to refer to a mixed management system.[42] With regard to the structures of contracts in the law, YPFB can sign production-sharing (PSC), association and operation contracts. Companies are thus obliged to adapt to these modes despite having signed shared risk contracts under the previous regime. These contractual terms have, as a common characteristic, the provision that the investor assumes financial responsibility for the risk of exploration and exploitation. YPFB is thus allowed to opt for associating itself with private enterprise once the field is declared to be commercial.

With regards to the tax system, the new law of 2005 creates the Direct Tax on Hydrocarbons (IDH), complementary to the system of royalties and contributions. The IDH taxes the measured production of hydrocarbons at a fixed rate of 32 per cent. At the same time, the law determines a system of co-beneficiaries of this tax. It is directed towards departments, municipalities, universities, the Indigenous Fund and the armed forces, among others – with the remainder going to the national treasury. On the other hand, it also eliminates the existing hydrocarbon tax regime and surtax. With this new regulatory framework, the state participates in the gross income at the point of inspection, with a fixed total charge of 50 per cent, in addition to general taxes by law.

The application of this new structure took place in a context in which international commodity prices experienced spectacular growth, contrary to the depressed prices that had characterised the decade of the 1990s. Adding the impact of this reform to the price effect meant that Bolivia reached unprecedented levels of tax revenue. By way of example, and only related to what has taken place with the system of blind charges, in 2006 the total collection, including royalties, contributions and IDH, was registered as approximately US$1.077 billion.

It is useful to establish a framework that can offer comparative references between the Law 3058 of 2005 and the Law 1689 of 1996. According to simulations carried out by Medinaceli (2007), with the application of the operational contracts for natural gas that were signed in 2006 (in a context of high prices), this new system translates into a state share of the benefits of 80 per cent, 74 per cent and 88 per cent for small, medium, and large fields respectively. These parameters in the case of participation on gross incomes or the value of wellhead production would be of the order of 67 per cent, 64 per cent, and 77 per cent.[43]

THE MODEL OF STATE MANAGEMENT

Enacting Law 3058 in 2005 did not mean the end of a historic cycle. Exactly one year after it was passed, and whilst the law was still being regulated, the government of president Evo Morales introduced the nationalisation decree ('Heroes of the Chaco', no.28701) in May 2006. This new decree reflects the fact that the political results of the law had not fulfilled the expectations of an important sector of the population.

The new operational contracts with all the companies that ran the hydrocarbon fields in the country, signed in October 2006, were based on a philosophy of state management of hydrocarbon resources. These contracts belonged to the category of 'risk service contracts', in which the investor assumes the risk for the operation of the field in exchange for financial return. The state retains ownership of hydrocarbons and also has the full responsibility for the commercial management of hydrocarbon production.

The breadth and depth of the principles of the 2005 law were greatly extended by the nationalisation decree, which, together with the operating contracts, translated into a new legal mandate for YPFB in the business arena. YPFB now acted in the name of the state as the only and exclusive vendor of hydrocarbons produced in the country.

The most recent and final event we think important to highlight is the approval, on 7 January 2009, of the New Political Constitution of the State, which endorses the principles of the aforementioned decree. However, instead of the compensation of exploration and production contracts, a service modality was adopted, in which the signing of contracts can never result in a loss for YPFB or the state. Whether these are risk service contracts, or 'pure' service contracts is not explicitly defined. In the case of the latter, we would be faced with a new reform in terms of contractual relations. There would no longer be business operators but instead petroleum service providers; and the state – through YPFB – would take absolute control over operating the fields, including risks and responsibility for the injection of capital.

An analysis of the general regulations of the constitution may be premature or speculative, because laws that establish the reach of this and other issues pertinent to the sector, such as the economic regime of the Social Unitary State of Pluri-national Communitarian Law, have still to be still enacted. The new management model for the sector also remains to be fully defined.

Although perhaps premature, the consolidation of state hydrocarbon management clearly faces multiple challenges within the framework of the broader political project of the current government. The first challenge is the consolidation of a management framework that accompanies the recovery of state control over the entire productive chain and attracts foreign private investment. Faced with a future scenario of depressed prices, the model in place does not appear to be sustainable. According to the study by Medinaceli (2007), in the case of low or even medium prices (less than US$4/MMBTU) state participation in profits could be close to or even higher than 110 per cent. By creating this scenario, not only would foreign direct investment be compromised but the very viability of YPFB.[44]

Stagnation of investments, decreasing production and the closure of markets in the region are worrying signs regarding the sustainability of generating hydrocarbon profits in the medium term. Hydrocarbons rent currently represents approximately 50 per cent of taxes collected by the Bolivian state, making it the economic base of the current government's development strategy and a prerequisite for the viability of the social policies of the rent's direct redistribution (through bonuses and subsidies).

Secondly, there is tension between the need to expand non-renewable natural-resource extractive activities to finance new economic and social policies, and fulfilling the constitutional commitment to respect the rights of indigenous populations that live in the territories of extractive industries, while honouring principles of environmental sustainability.[45] Thirdly, there is the ongoing political dispute over hydrocarbon surpluses among sectors and social organisations, which deepens rent-seeking and clientelist practices and pressures the government to make decisions on assigning public spending based upon short-term political calculations rather than on strategic management principles.

It is in this context that we see the repetition of past cycles, in which an over-reliance on non-renewable resource rents deepened social struggles for the distribution of those resources. In these cases, attention was once more diverted from policies that would lead to strengthening the employment-generating sector and the redesign of systems of social protection for the inclusion of the majority of the Bolivian population. In this sense, the state continues to face the challenge of implementing policies that change an engrained culture of rent-seeking and prebendalism. What is at stake is the construction of public institutions with the capacity to increase tax collection, combined with progressive, transparent and sustainable distribution of non-renewable resource rents that avoids the negative effects on productive and income-generating sectors.

FINAL CONSIDERATIONS

The formulation of public policies – as well as their criticism – always brings with it a complex web of interests, perceptions and objectives. As such, it can be observed that policies are symbolically constructed and structurally situated. Recognising this, we consider that the analysis of the ideas, perceptions, meanings and values behind the formulation of public policies often allows for a better understanding of these policies and of the processes of construction of social legitimacy.

In the same fashion, we recognise that despite their ideological claims, public policies are not exempt from tests of economic sustainability. In the end, these define whether objectives can be obtained or not. The definition of coherent and workable objectives in policy design, consideration of costs and their financing, inclusion of principles of effectiveness, efficiency and transparency in decisions, and mechanisms of monitoring and evaluation in the process of implementation are some of the elements that make up the economic sustainability of public policies. Sufficient balance of all these elements has never been present in either the liberal or statist models of the Bolivian past.

A review, such as that outlined above, of recent reforms in the hydrocarbon sector in Bolivia negatively demonstrates that the construction of social legitimacy and economic feasibility depends on the consolidation of an institutional framework capable of managing tensions and disputes amongst contrasting political agendas, differing social interests and conflicting visions of sovereignty and development. Attempts must be made again in Bolivia to move towards a free, plural and informed public debate on resource management and ownership; towards the consolidation of relatively stable and sustainable collective accords. The absence of a grounded public accord explains to a large extent the perpetual change in the rules of management of the sector and the disconnection between optimum levels of investment and production on the one hand and the capture and use of the economic rents by the state on the other.

In this manner, the liberal restructuring of 1996 resulted in an important flow of investments that increased the productive capacity of the reserves and consolidated the energy sector as the most dynamic sector of the national economy. However, implementing this model did not give similar levels of success with regard to a social mandate, tax revenue or social improvement. As a result, when proposals for reforms began in 2005, they had a wide level of support and social acceptance, which allowed tax revenue to reach unprecedented levels in the country. Nonetheless, the country entered a phase of investment stagnation, which put the reproduction of the surplus at risk and with it redistributive policies and policies of energy self-sufficiency.

It is beyond the scope of this chapter to evaluate the ex-post objective results of these programmes. However, we have demonstrated that it is important to reconsider the basis for historic trends. The Bolivian political system has not been capable of incorporating past lessons and experiences in order to take advantage of opportunities – largely afforded by years of high commodity prices – to construct a national energy sector that builds upon the interests of citizens and demonstrates judicial, technical and economic sustainability.

As such, we argue there is still need for the development of a sustainable model for hydrocarbons management in Bolivia. This model must be based on our country's rich experience in the sector, on the objective technical and economic conditions of the industry in our country, and on an adequate reading of the social mandate. If Bolivia is unable to take significant steps towards a wide-ranging institutional process, all indications are that it will not achieve its long-sought-after ambition of successfully consolidating the hydrocarbon industry. Nor will it be able to use rents successfully to sustainably overcome its historic addiction to a model of growth entirely reliant on resource extraction – a model that has failed to stimulate economic growth and continues to generate, despite the revolutionary rhetoric of the time, high indices of poverty and social inequality.

NOTES

1. Wanderley 2008.
2. For a deeper analysis of the model applied in Bolivia between 1952 and 1988 see Wanderley 2009.
3. For more on the stabilisation plan and the first (structural or neoliberal) reforms see Jemio and Antelo 2000.
4. Advertisement of the Ministry of Social Communication, *La Razón*, 28 April 1996.
5. *Última Hora*, 4 January 1996. It is important to stress that, in the end, YPFB was not capitalised.
6. Advertisements of the Ministry of Social Communication, *La Razón,* 28 April 1996.
7. For more on the social reforms and policies of the period, see Instituto Prisma 2000 and Wanderley 2009.
8. Aid to Bolivia represented an average of 10 per cent of the annual GDP during the 1990s.
9. See Mokrani 2010.
10. Including processes of exploration, exploitation and commercialisation of hydrocarbons.
11. The term 'blind' tax or charge is used in the theory of oil regimes to refer to the entire fixed tax participation that is not related to the economic utility of the field and that generally considers production to be taxable.
12. Contained in Law 843 of the tax system.
13. For more information on the tax system in the period prior to the 1996 reform, see Mokrani 2010.
14. Assuming a high-price scenario of US$4/MMBTU for gas and US$60/Bbl for oil.
15. Latest official estimates, released by an international certifying company, DeGolyer and MacNaugthon.
16. Cámara Boliviana de Hidrocarburos, 2007. Available at www.cbh.org.bo, accessed in 2008.
17. With the structural adjustment plan of 1985, the union movement entered into crisis. This crisis could be seen in the fragmentation of demands and the deterioration of the capacity of the Central Obrera Boliviana (Bolivian Workers' Central: COB) to convene its membership. In the following years, worker–owner negotiations were more and more restricted to the realm of businesses.
18. Institute of Social Studies, 2003.
19. UDAPE, 2007.
20. Cardenas 2004.
21. See Guimarães 2010.
22. *El Deber*, 23 January 1996.
23. *Hoy*, 9 January 1996.
24. *El Deber*, 17 January 1996.
25. The loss to Chile of access to the sea, the War of the Pacific (1879–84).
26. Klein 1984; Mesa Gisbert 2007.
27. Created in 1994 to bring together diverse social and political actors that opposed capitalisation of state enterprises, with notable members such as army retirees, engineers, lawyers, workers in the hydrocarbon sector, and the YPFB among others.

28. *Presencia*, 1 January 1996.
29. 'Manifiesto del Comité de Defensa del Patrimonio Nacional Filial Tarija', *Presencia*, 10 January 1996.
30. *Los Tiempos*, 2 April 1996.
31. 'Documento de los Comités Cívicos de La Paz, Potosí, Chuquisaca, Santa Cruz, Cochabamba, Oruro y Tarija', *Hoy*, 26 January 1996.
32. 'Manifiesto de la Federación Departamental de Centros Provinciales de La Paz', *Presencia*, 28 February 1996.
33. *Presencia*, 8 January 1996; *Los Tiempos*, 10 January 1996.
34. Lucio González, leader of the COB, *El Mundo*, 12 January 1996.
35. 'Conclusiones del Foro Debate Nacional', *Los Tiempos*, 14 February 1996.
36. Kohl and Farthing 2007.
37. This project began to be structured and managed during the government of Banzer and Quiroga, and in the midst of escalating oppositional voices of social movements. It was formalised and put on the negotiating table during the government of Sachez de Lozada, who came into office for the second time in August 2002.
38. For further details on the sectoral reform projects, see Mokrani 2010.
39. Mesa Gisbert 2008.
40. For further information on the tax, economic and institutional systems of Law 3058, see Mokrani 2010.
41. Article 22 of Law 3058.
42. Article 86 of Law 3058.
43. To compare the reform of 1996 and the reform of 2005, see the simulation in the section 'The liberal reform of the hydrocarbon sector of 1996'.
44. Which must act in the capacity of a business and which, within this new model, would be subject to paying these taxes.
45. This issue was also discussed at the Summit on Climate Change that took place in Cochabamba, Bolivia in 2010. See Bebbington 2010.

REFERENCES

Bebbington, A. (2010) 'Extracción, territorio e inequidades: el gas en el Chaco boliviano', *UMBRALES*, 20 (La Paz: CIDES–UMSA and Plural Editores).
Cardenas, M. (2004) *Cuentas nacionales de financiamiento y gasto en salud* (La Paz: DFID).
Guimarães (2010) 'La capitalización de los hidrocarburos y la modernidad: un análisis de las ideas subyacentes al modelo de gestión y de sus críticas', *UMBRALES*, 20 (La Paz: CIDES–UMSA and Plural Editores).
Institute of Social Studies (2003) *Bolivia: evaluación y monitoreo de estrategias de reducción de la pobreza – 2003* (The Hague, Netherlands: Sida), www.sida.se/publications.
Instituto Prisma (2000) *Las políticas sobre la pobreza en Bolivia: dimensiones, políticas y resultados (1985–1999)* (La Paz: Instituto Prisma, Plural Editores).
Jemio, L.C. and Antelo, E. (eds) (2000) *Quince años de reformas estructurales en Bolivia: sus impactos sobre inversión, crecimiento y equidad* (La Paz: CEPAL and Universidad Católica Boliviana).
Klein, H. (1984) *Historia general de Bolivia* (La Paz, Editorial Juventud).

Kohl, B. and Farthing, L. (2007) *El bumerán boliviano: hegemonía neoliberal y resistencia social* (La Paz, Plural Editores).

Medinaceli, M. (2007) *Impuesto directo a los hidrocarburos: origen y destino* (La Paz, IDEA).

Mesa Gisbert, D. (2007) *Presidencia sitiada* (La Paz: Plural Editores and Fundación Comunidad).

Mokrani, L. (2010) 'Impacto de las recientes reformas estructurales en Bolivia, en el modelo de gestión del sector de hidrocarburos', *UMBRALES*, 20 (La Paz: CIDES–UMSA and Plural Editores).

UDAPE (2007) *Dossier estadístico*, vol.17 (La Paz, UDAPE).

Wanderley, F. (2009) *Crecimiento, empleo y bienestar social: ¿Por qué Bolivia es tan desigual?* (La Paz: Plural Editores and CIDES–UMSA).

—— (2008) 'Beyond Gas: Between the Narrow-Based and Broad-Based Economy', in J. Crabtree and L. Whitehead (eds) *Unresolved Tensions: Bolivia Past and Present* (Pittsburgh, University of Pittsburgh Press).

8
Subsidised Energy and Hesitant Elites in Russia

Indra Øverland and Hilde Kutschera

Russian energy subsidies make up the largest gross sum of any country in the world,[1] totalling US$50 billion in 2007.[2] About half of all Russian energy, equal to the annual primary energy consumption of France, is lost in production, transport, transmission or inefficient consumption – much of this due to artificially low prices which reduce incentives to improve efficiency.[3] Included in this figure is potential saving of 240 billion cubic metres (bcm) of natural gas, equivalent to 51 per cent of Russia's total gas consumption in 2006.[4]

Russian decision makers have on numerous occasions committed themselves to cutting subsidies and raising gas prices. The government's 'Energy Strategy of Russia through 2020', which forms the backdrop for many of the events and developments discussed in this chapter, recognised the need to reform domestic pricing arrangements.[5] The newer 'Energy Strategy of Russia through 2030', adopted by the government in 2009, further ramps up the emphasis on energy efficiency and repeatedly states that prices should gradually rise to market levels.[6] At the G20 summit in Pittsburgh in September 2009, Russia signed the 'Leaders' Statement', pledging to phase out energy subsidies 'in the medium term'.[7]

As Ahrend and Tompson have noted, however, higher gas prices are difficult to absorb, both for industry and for households.[8] Higher gas prices would affect household consumers through several channels: district heating, electricity generation, employment in the industrial sector and gas for cooking. Of these channels, only the last one involves the direct use of gas by household consumers. In all the others, households use natural gas indirectly, which increases the complexity and unpredictability of the impact of changes in gas pricing – including consumer reactions.[9]

As Martusevich points out, the government has encouraged the regions to achieve full recovery of utility costs by raising tariffs.[10] As a result, utility services have already become unaffordable for a large and growing part of the population, and yet the full costs are still not covered. According to the OECD, the cost of water supply and sanitation (which are part of the utility payments) is considered a burden if it exceeds 3–5 per cent of a household's income.[11] Applying a threshold of 3.5 per cent, Martusevich finds that in 2001, water and sanitation were very expensive for the poorest 10 per cent of Russia's households; and by 2006, water and sanitation were an economic strain for 70 per cent of the households in Russia.[12] This example indicates the dramatic impact likely from any further increase in utility tariffs driven by higher gas prices. Only a small minority of Russian households, it seems, have sufficient income not to be affected by rising utility tariffs.[13]

Ahn and Jones note that, despite pressure from Gazprom, 'the Kremlin remains reluctant to raise prices for fear of provoking economic and social stresses'.[14] Similarly, Hanson argues that, although the proposed price rises are significant, there might not be sufficient political determination to carry them through, as they would certainly prove unpopular with the population.[15] There have been numerous instances of the Russian authorities vacillating between, on the one hand, expressing the intention to cut subsidies and raise energy prices, and, on the other, pulling back from such price increases. For example, compare and contrast the following statements:

[B]y 2011… domestic sales of gas will be equally profitable as sales in foreign markets. (Prime Minister Fradkov, 30 November 2006)[16]

If the principle of equal profitability were to be applied immediately, it would be necessary to raise the price of gas in Russia by 95–100% … A compromise was reached. We keep the emphasis on netback … but at the same time, in essence, the transition period is extended for several years. In practice we will go over to netback in 2014–2015. (Deputy Minister of Economy Klepach, 30 May 2008)[17]

Wholesale prices for natural gas for the population will rise by 25% in 2009, 30% in 2010 and 40% in 2011. (Federal Tariff Service, 13 February 2009)[18]

The Ministry of Energy is not prepared to cancel state regulated prices until 2012 at the earliest…Gazprom in 'some cases' abuses its dominant position, therefore liberalisation of domestic prices on gas ... is 'extremely risky'. (Praim-TASS, 20 October 2009)[19]

Raising gas prices is a particularly daunting task because, during the Soviet period, energy was considered a social good to which the entire population should be guaranteed access. Lenin proclaimed that 'communism = soviet power + electrification'.[20] Access to cheap energy was a notable achievement of the Soviet industrialisation effort, becoming a particularly engrained component of the Soviet social contract. Although the current rulers may have scant regard for that social contract, they cannot easily sweep it away.

And on that note it might be possible to conclude this chapter: the Russian government wants to remove energy subsidies, but the population is used to cheap energy, so decision makers are hesitant to carry through this project. However, we believe that this perspective on Russian energy pricing is worth exploring further because it contradicts much of what is being said and written about Russia. Two assumptions in particular are questioned here.

Firstly, in much of the broader academic literature and media coverage of Russian politics, the government is explicitly or implicitly portrayed as a bunch of brutal ex-KGB spies[21] – carrying out genocide in the North Caucasus,[22] permitting a dramatic increase in human rights violations since the fall of the Soviet Union,[23] imprisoning and ignoring the human rights of innocent business people and targeting its perceived opponents for criminal investigation (mainly Russia's formerly richest man, Mikhail Khodorkovsky),[24] and not caring about the socio-economic situation of the population while the elite fills its own pockets, free of control from society.[25] The government is also seen as impervious to domestic as well as international criticism on all these accounts.[26]

Secondly, several prominent Russia scholars have suggested that social unrest any time soon might result in the government's 'inability to control the discontent',[27] in mass repression by the government,[28] or in a crisis 'the exit from which would not be possible within the framework of the current constitutional system'.[29] Thus, such commentators seem to assume that Russia is on the verge of a revolt, or coup d'état.

Taking into account these widespread assumptions about the imperviousness of the government to socio-economic discontent and criticism and the likelihood of social upheaval, this chapter explores the ongoing interaction between Russian decision makers and public opinion over gas subsidies, seeking to show that both assumptions are overly simplistic.

OTHER PROTESTS

The chapter builds on the understanding that gas price reform is not only a function of stable economic facts and their interaction, but must also be understood as the next phase in the long-term, path-dependent trajectory of relations between the population and decision makers over socio-economic issues. That is why we proceed to examine previous cases of public protest linked to major changes in government policy or the national economy. From the lessons learned from these cases, we try to say something about the likely reactions to major reductions in subsidies for natural gas.

For the purposes of this chapter, 'protest' is defined as public expressions of socio-economic discontent, such as demonstrations, pickets, rioting or strikes. Such protests have been relatively rare in Russia during the last decade, so the reactions of decision makers to the few major protests that have actually taken place become important in setting a precedent for similar cases in the future, even if they are in disparate social sectors.

Three cases are covered here: the protests against the 'Law on Monetisation' in 2005, demonstrations against high petrol prices in 2008, and the wave of rallies in connection with the financial crisis in 2008 and 2009.[30] The great complexity of reform in these areas and the delays in its implementation, highlighted in research by the Moscow Institute for Urban Economics, make it clear that these cases are particularly relevant for understanding the prospects for price reform in the natural gas sector.[31]

MONETISATION

In January 2005, thousands of Russians took to the streets in protest against the implementation of Federal Law 122 F-3, the 'Law on Monetisation'. In order to understand this law and the protests it generated, the concept of *lgoty* must be explained.

Rasell and Wengle define *lgoty* as 'special benefits or privileges that entitle eligible recipients to the free or discounted use of various public services'.[32] 'Eligible recipients' include such diverse groups as military veterans, disabled people, pensioners and residents of the High North. They are entitled by the *lgoty* system to benefits like free or reduced payment for public transport, housing, utilities, medicines and stays in sanatoria.[33]

In the 1990s, as a measure against runaway inflation, the Soviet-era system of *lgoty* was expanded by broadening the ranges of the in-kind benefits and their recipients. With their wages eaten up by inflation, many households became increasingly dependent on *lgoty*. Wengle and Rasell refer to estimates that 10–15 per cent of the budgets of poor households consisted of *lgoty* in 2003.[34] Though accurate data is not available, the figure was probably even higher in the 1990s. It was becoming clear that the *lgoty* system was ill-suited for handling the social challenges of post-Soviet Russia: the system was underfinanced, and the focus on in-kind benefits rather than money disempowered the beneficiaries and led to wastage.

On 22 August 2004, the Duma passed law 122-F3, replacing *lgoty* with cash. When the law came into force in January 2005, major protests broke out. Those who had been receiving *lgoty*, the so-called *lgotniki*, held that the financial compensation would not even pay for the services previously provided free of charge. In addition, many feared a situation similar to that of the 1990s, when inflation zeroed out wages and pensions.

Protests took place in most major Russian cities, with roads and in some instances government buildings occupied by protesters.[35] Though initially provoked by the 'Law on Monetisation', the rallies included both *lgotniki* and other sections of the population and evolved into a display of general dissatisfaction with the decision makers. The protests had a spontaneous quality, although some were organised by parties and organisations.[36] Certain opposition politicians, among them Oleg Shein (Spravedlivaya Rossiya) and Galina Khovanskaya (Yabloko), used the monetisation to rally political support against the government. The protesters had solid popular support: according to a survey carried out by the Levada Centre, 81 per cent of the population either supported the protests or said that they understood them and could relate to them.[37]

The reaction of the decision makers to these protests was multifaceted. Initially, the government maintained that the reform was a success and largely ignored the protests, while the state media portrayed them as being driven by marginal groups. Protesters were detained by the police, and several were reportedly beaten.[38] In February, the government seemed to change tactics, however, and gave an official response to the protests. President Putin publicly criticised the government and regional governors for inadequately implementing the Law on Monetisation, and acknowledged that the reform had not been properly prepared.[39] Concessions were made to reduce the loss of benefits of the *lgotniki*; pensions and salaries for some groups were increased ahead of schedule, and other social reforms were delayed. However, implementation of the reform itself continued.

PETROL PRICING

Russia does not have the same tradition of subsidising petrol as it has with natural gas. Gas, the country's main source of heat and electricity production, has traditionally been provided by the state, whereas petrol is for those who own cars – which were luxury items until recently.

Without directly subsidising petrol prices, however, Russian decision makers have occasionally put pressure on petrol retailers to keep prices down. This happened during the second half of 2006, after prices had increased by 11 per cent in the previous months, thereby surpassing the price in the USA.[40] German Gref, the minister of economics, called on oil firms to avoid price hikes. Subsequently, prices stayed flat, despite a 15 per cent rise in wholesale prices in April 2007.

One year later, the situation was quite different. World oil prices were rapidly approaching an all-time high, and between February and July 2008 petrol prices rose by almost 40 per cent.[41] This price hike resulted in a nationwide outburst of protest on 24 May. These protests were not unique to Russia, but took place in many parts of the world. The Russian Motorists Association organised protests in cities across the country. Its main argument was that, as citizens of one of the world's major oil-exporting countries, Russian car owners should have to pay less for petrol than they were currently doing.

Police reactions were severe, but the decision makers showed no other public reaction to the protests, and did not put the same pressure on oil companies as in 2006. Quite the contrary: when oil prices decreased and petrol prices across the world started falling in late 2008, Russian oil firms were not pressured by the government to follow suit.[42]

THE FINANCIAL CRISIS

Russia was hit hard by the global financial crisis. By April 2009, the unemployment rate was growing rapidly, and €1 cost 44 Russian roubles, up from 36 roubles in October 2008.[43] At a meeting on 23 April 2009, First Deputy Interior Minister Mikhail Sukhodolsky reported that more than 2,500 protests related to the socio-economic conditions had taken place in Russia since the beginning of the year.[44]

One area where protests had been building up was the car import business. The government raised tariffs in order to protect the domestic car manufacturing industry during the financial crisis, and in December 2008 Russia saw the first wave of protests related to the higher import tariffs on cars. The increase was highly unpopular in broad sections of society, particularly in the Russian Far East, where many jobs are connected with the import of second-hand cars from Japan.

The first significant protests against higher car import tariffs occurred on 13 and 14 December. There were demonstrations in several Russian cities, but the initial rallies were in Vladivostok. These protests received additional attention because of the way decision makers reacted to them: riot police were flown the 9,000 km from Moscow to Vladivostok to confront the demonstrators, beating them up and detaining over 100.[45] Despite the firm reaction from the federal authorities, the protests continued to spread. On 21 December there were new demonstrations in Vladivostok, in which the riot police reportedly beat and detained several participants. Parallel protests took place in Moscow, where hundreds of people denounced the higher tariffs. Despite this wave of protests, the government went ahead and implemented the tariff hike in full.

December 2008 also saw protests related to other economic issues. In the city of Izhevsk, thousands rallied against rising housing and utilities fees.[46] By January 2009, the protests seemed to channel a more general dissatisfaction with the economic and political situation in the country, and with the way the decision makers were handling it. On 30 and 31 January, thousands of people across Russia protested against the government's economic policies. Among these were about 2,000 communists protesting in Moscow, and an estimated 2,500 protestors in Vladivostok, where vehicle import tariffs were again among the main issues. These protests too were broken up by the police.[47]

Another category of protests occurred in the mono-industrial centres, the so-called 'mono-towns'. Closure of a factory in such a town can be catastrophic for the local community, which depends on it not only for employment, but often also for electricity, district heating and various cultural activities. The impact is further exacerbated by the fact that such industrial sites are located near the natural resources on which they are based, often far from other population centres. Getting a new job and commuting to a nearby town is seldom an option for sacked mono-town residents.[48]

Approximately 12 per cent of Russia's population live in mono-towns,[49] and several of these towns saw protests and civil unrest during the spring of 2009. The most noted of these took place in Pikalevo, where over half the workforce had lost their jobs by the beginning of May.[50] In reaction to unemployment and underpayment, thousands took to the streets, protesting against what they saw as the shutting down of their entire community. Prime Minister Putin then visited the town and ordered the owners of factories to resume production. The owner of the main factory, and formerly the richest man in the country, Oleg Deripaska, was humiliated on television – at the same time as he was discretely provided with credits worth billions of US dollars by the Russian state to save his indebted business empire from bankruptcy. Putin's appearance in Pikalevo may have been a smokescreen for the state aid to Putin-friendly Deripaska, as some commentators have insinuated,[51] but the fact that Putin made the effort to travel there and stage an elaborate television performance nonetheless shows that such protests can indeed matter for the government.

COMPARISON

The protests over *lgoty* and petrol prices were both expressions of popular discontent with Russian decision makers, but these protests differed in several ways. Whereas the monetisation case involved protests *against* a specific government reform, the petrol pricing example concerned protests urging the government to *take action*.

The two incidents also differed in their participants. The anti-monetisation demonstrations saw participants from a broad range of social groups, as well as those specifically affected by the reform. The petrol price protests, by contrast, involved almost exclusively young male car owners. General societal involvement in the rallies was thus far more significant in the monetisation protests, most likely boosted by feelings of solidarity with the *lgotniki*. Moreover, higher petrol prices naturally concern those who already own cars and can be assumed to have certain economic resources. This group includes people involved in shuttle trade with second-hand cars from western Europe and Japan, taxi drivers and haulage companies. These differences may help to explain why the monetisation protests drew in larger segments of the population than was the case with petrol price protests.

As for outcomes, there are both similarities and differences between the two events. The demonstrations against monetisation did yield some results, including higher pensions and wages. The petrol price rallies, on the other hand, saw no change of policy as a direct result; petrol prices did eventually decrease as the oil price fell, but the effect came later in Russia than in many other countries. However, both examples show situations where government policy in general has appeared to be little affected by popular protests.

Some of the protests related to our third case, the financial crisis, are more similar to the petrol price example than to the *lgoty* example, as they reflect frustration with lack of policy engagement rather than negative reactions to an implemented policy. The protests against the tariff hike on car imports, which seem to have been the most large-scale protests related to the financial crisis, were directed precisely at a specific government policy. Thus even in connection with a crisis that permeated Russia and put stress on all parts of society, socio-economic discontent still revolved around sectoral issues.

Where then does organised labour fit into this picture? This question is particularly pertinent in light of Russia's communist past. It would appear that organised labour is currently weak in Russia and has not played a significant role in the events we have examined here. This is also reflected in the fact that the three waves of protest examined here have involved few strikes of any magnitude: they have mostly been about people taking to the streets and protesting.

The reasons for this are multiple, and include the tradition of non-independent trade unions in the Soviet period, their intensified co-optation during the post-Soviet period and the general de-ideologised state of post-Soviet society. This reflects the degree to which post-Soviet society now finds itself in an ideological vacuum – it is an atomised society in which the mores and solidarity of the Soviet period have been swept away, without yet being replaced by anything else. This in turn helps to explain why the back of Russian organised labour is broken, and why no revolution is likely in the short term (say, the coming three years). On the other hand, it also helps to explain why today's situation is an anomaly which has arisen at a very peculiar historical juncture (the collapse of Soviet communism) and which is bound to change, sooner or later.

THE PROTESTS' SIGNIFICANCE FOR GAS SUBSIDIES

The three cases examined here show that protests may have influenced the speed and degree of policy implementation, without stopping it. Russia's policymakers ultimately move ahead with their plans regardless of public opinion. Some sensitivity towards popular reactions is combined with the will to continue pragmatically with reform, all the same.

These recent cases of socio-economic protest indicate patterns along which popular reaction to gas price reform might develop. Monetisation and the global financial crisis share several features with the issue of gas pricing: they are related to governmental economic reform (or the lack thereof); they concern a large part of the population; they are all likely to have the greatest impact on the lowest-income groups; and they fundamentally challenge the socio-economic inheritance from the Soviet period.

We have seen how decision makers have often responded by trying to stop or limit protests (detaining people protesting against increased petrol prices, or dispatching special police forces from Moscow to Vladivostok to handle protests against import tariffs on cars), and have branded the protesters as 'marginal groups' (as with the monetisation protesters) or 'opportunists' (as with the financial crisis protests in early 2009). At the same time, they have calmed protesters by offering partial concessions, slowing down reforms and putting pressure on local and regional authorities to alleviate problems. It is also worth noting that protests have not been banned altogether – perhaps in order to ensure a safety valve for letting off socio-economic steam.

In all three cases discussed above, the decision makers seem to have achieved their objectives – in the sense that their policy was ultimately implemented. It therefore seems likely that any protests against higher gas prices might be met with similar tactics. As for the role of potential protests in the planning of gas price reform, earlier cases have shown the decision makers that, although protests may be unpleasant, they are not synonymous with policy failure. Reforms can be implemented even if the population shows its discontent.

FURTHER IMPLICATIONS

The three cases of previous protests in other sectors covered in this chapter were selected for their relevance. Although the government has been relatively ineffective in its reform efforts since the year 2000 and has achieved little in terms of reducing Russia's dependence on commodity exports or addressing corruption, that does not mean that the Russian economy and society have not seen dramatic changes. Since December 1999, when Vladimir Putin became acting president, Russia has undergone significant federal,[52] judicial,[53] foreign policy[54] and tax reforms,[55] amongst others. Considering the deep and often painful changes Russian society has experienced, the number of protests during this period has not been great. Understanding this lack of protest is perhaps just as relevant for the strategy of decision makers as analysing those protests that have taken place.

The limited public expression of popular discontent could be linked to the idea of a special social contract between the population and policymakers in Russia: Give us political stability and economic welfare, and we will not meddle in the way you run the country. Thus the social contract of Soviet communism has in practice been replaced by something akin to neo-feudal capitalism. During 2009, the mass media referred frequently to this contract theory, with journalists and academics alike speculating whether the financial crisis might invalidate the contract, finally causing Russians to turn against their rulers in earnest. As mentioned at the beginning of the chapter, prominent Russia scholars Baev, Gontmakher and Kupchinsky are among those who have seen such protests as the beginning of a possible revolution.[56] Could demonstrations against a rise in the price of natural gas become the final straw?

Previous examples have supported the view that gas prices have the potential to generate discontent and public protest, and the developments during the financial crisis showed that concerns related to the overall economic situation could be linked to sector-specific dissatisfaction with, for example, import tariffs on cars. However, two points should be borne in mind here: despite the severity of the financial crisis and its consequences for the population, most Russians did *not* protest, and the most prominent decision makers retained their popularity.

Surveys conducted by the Levada Centre in March 2009 show that 26 per cent of the Russians interviewed considered it likely that they would take part in protests against current price levels and the general standard of living if such protests were to occur in their hometown. That was only 2 per cent more than in March 2008, and 1 per cent less than in March 2005, the year of the uproar against monetisation. Of those questioned, more than half had not even heard of any recent protests over deteriorating standards of living.[57]

The limited support for public demonstrations is mirrored in the stability of popular support for Russia's rulers. In April 2009, surveys indicated that 68 per cent of the Russian population approved of President Medvedev's work, and 76 per cent approved of that of Prime Minister Putin.[58] These rates are high by the standards of most countries. These surveys, made after the financial crisis hit Russia, indicate that it did not cause the country to teeter on the brink of revolution.

This is not to imply that the Russian population is not concerned about issues like the financial crisis or higher gas prices. In another survey conducted by the Levada Centre, between 26 and 29 March 2009, Moscow residents were asked what they worried about. Rising municipal utility bills was the most common concern mentioned. As many as 55 per cent said they worried about utility bills (up from 19 per cent in 1999), whereas only 27 per cent said they worried about unemployment.[59] In sum, issues such as utility bills and the price of natural gas are major concerns for the population – but even taking into account the skyrocketing hardship of the Russian population after the unravelling of the Soviet Union, they are unlikely to be the last straw that could provoke a revolution under current circumstances. Commentators predicting imminent revolution are therefore probably jumping the gun.

The financial crisis may not have sparked a revolution, but it did have significant impact on how decision makers and consumers alike think about socio-economic matters such as gas price increases. The declared goal of the Russian government has been to bring domestic gas prices up to West European levels, excluding transport costs and export taxes. Under most current contracts, gas prices are indexed to the oil price, with a lag of approximately six months. For gas, however, there is no world price, and it makes sense for Russia to use West European prices as its benchmark, since that is where it exports most of its gas and gets the highest price.[60] The financial crisis, shale gas and LNG have brought West European price levels for natural gas closer to Russian prices – at least temporarily.

However, the fact that the target has come closer does not necessarily mean that it has become easier to attain. Gas is priced in US dollars, and, with a Russian rouble that is weaker than the dollar, closing the gap between Russian and European prices might become more difficult. As revenues from the European market decrease due to falling demand and sinking prices, potential income on the domestic market will become increasingly important to the finances of Gazprom, and thereby also those of the Russian state. On the other hand, further economic pressure on household consumers raises the likelihood of negative reactions against decision makers, as shown by the recent protests concerning other issues. The general economic situation in Russia also makes it more difficult to increase prices and raises the potential political cost of gas price hikes. Thus, from a decision maker's point of view, both the potential gains and the costs of increasing gas prices are raised by the economic downturn in Russia under the financial crisis. The overall result of the financial crisis for the prospects of removing subsidies for natural gas is therefore one of raising the stakes, rather than increasing or decreasing the probability of successful implementation.

For a Russian gas pricing reform to be implemented all the way down to the end users, it will have to be carried out in conjunction with structural reform. The economic downturn of 2008–10 may have a negative impact on the ability and willingness of decision makers to make the investments necessary for such comprehensive reform. Prime Minister Putin's speech to the Duma on 6 April 2009 demonstrated the intention to cushion the effect of higher utility prices through more generous benefit schemes.[61] However, with the impact of the financial crisis, there might not be sufficient funds for both financial cushioning and structural reform. Taking recent popular discontent and protest into consideration, Russia's decision makers may therefore be forced, at least in the short term, to choose between assuaging the population and implementing their gas pricing reform in full.

CONCLUSIONS

We have seen that Russia's decision makers have demonstrated some sensitivity towards the possibility of socio-economic discontent in their policymaking on gas prices so far. Nevertheless, they have retained their ultimate goal of reducing subsidies. We should recall that protests have still been the exception rather than the rule. The numerous occasions on which protests have *not* occurred are also an important part of the reaction pattern of the Russian population.

The material examined in this chapter indicates that there is reason to expect significant interaction between government and household consumers on the issue of gas pricing. If the decision makers decide to raise gas prices rapidly, that might well trigger major protests. Similarly, discontent and the prospect of public protest may affect policy, even though previous protests do not seem to have changed policy drastically, although they may have modified or delayed it.

Interestingly, the *possibility* of protests seems to have a more significant impact on the strategies of decision makers than do those protests that actually take place. This is to a certain degree mirrored in the empirical material of this chapter: we have seen that, once protests occur, they have not led to major policy changes. When protests actually take place, it seems that decision makers cannot allow themselves to be too greatly influenced – perhaps they believe that would be considered a weakness, or fear that giving in to one protest would encourage protest on other issues as well. On the other hand, they are certainly aware of the negative influence each protest has on their popularity and on the democratic image of the country's political system. That makes it more important to avoid protests in the first place than to bow to them once they occur.

It has become commonplace to assume that the socio-economic situation of the population is not a factor in the Russian government's decision making, and that the government is impervious to criticism. We have shown that these assumptions are at best oversimplifications, and at worst wrong: Russian politics is more complex and dynamic than is often assumed.

ACKNOWLEDGEMENT

This chapter is based on research carried out under both the Flammable Societies project and the RussCasp project, which is financed by the PETROSAM Programme of the Research Council of Norway.

NOTES

1. See World Bank in Russia 2008.
2. See Victor 2009.
3. See Ahrend and Tompson 2005.
4. See EIA 2009.
5. Ministry of Energy 2003.
6. See Government of the Russian Federation 2009, pp.2, 4, 16, 18, 21, 22, 33, 50, 52.
7. See White House 2009.
8. See Ahrend and Tompson 2005.
9. IEA/OECD 2006, pp.40–1.
10. Martusevich, R. 2008 p.2.
11. See OECD 2003.
12. See Martusevich 2008.

13. In 2001, household expenditure on all utilities services represented 10.1 per cent of the average disposable income of the poorest 10 per cent of households in Russia. District heating made up 1.8 per cent of this expenditure, water supply and sanitation 3.5 per cent. See Martusevich 2008.
14. See Ahn and Jones 2008.
15. Hanson 2009, pp.38–9.
16. See Grivach 2006.
17. See Grivach 2008.
18. See Federal Tariff Service 2009.
19. See Praim-TASS 2009.
20. In Lenin's original Russian formulation, 'Soviet power' was 'sovietskaya vlast'. Thus there is in the English translation a word play on 'power' that did not actually exist in the Russian version. See Lenin 1977, p.280.
21. For an overview of the literature which posits the Russian government as a power grab by members of the security forces, see Renz 2006.
22. See, for example, Moshe 2002.
23. See, for example, Weiler 2004.
24. See, for example, Kvurt 2007.
25. See, for example, Schröder 2005.
26. See, for example, Trenin 2006.
27. See Baev 2009.
28. See Kupchinsky 2008.
29. See Gontmakher 2008.
30. On these three protests, see Øverland and Kutschera 2011.
31. See Andrianov et al. 2003.
32. See Rasell and Wengle 2008.
33. See Wengle and Rasell 2008; Alexandrova, Kusnetsova and Grishina 2005, p.117.
34. See Rasell and Wengle 2008.
35. See Wengle 2005.
36. See Rasell and Wengle 2008.
37. Wengle 2005, p.7.
38. See Corwin 2005.
39. Wengle 2005, p.7.
40. See Reuters 2007.
41. See Ministry of Economic Development and Trade of the Russian Federation 2008.
42. See *Russia Today* 2008.
43. Currency rates 1 October 2008 and 15 April 2009, from xe.com (accessed 9 December 2010).
44. See Interfax 2009.
45. See Chernyshev 2008.
46. See Coalson 2008.
47. See Parfitt 2009.
48. Other mono-towns are based around the former Soviet automotive industry, most famously the AvtoVaz plant in the city of Togliatti. There were recurrent protests in such towns from 2006 onwards. Although they were sometimes combined with demands for government intervention and subsidies to maintain jobs, such protests have mainly been triggered by downsizing aimed at improving profitability at specific factories, not by broader socio-economic policy. We have

therefore chosen not to focus on them here, although they became a significant part of the wave of protests in connection with the financial crisis.
49. See Whitmore 2008.
50. See *Rossiya* 2009.
51. See Latynina 2009.
52. See Hyde 2001.
53. See Solomon 2002.
54. See Lo 2003.
55. See Åslund 2004.
56. See Baev 2009.
57. See Levada Centre 2009a.
58. See Levada Centre 2009b.
59. See Levada Centre 2009c.
60. In Vladivostok, which according to plan is to receive gas from 2012, West European gas will be less appropriate than in the western part of the country, where the vast majority of the population lives and most of the gas is consumed.
61. Putin 2009.

REFERENCES

Ahn, H. and Jones, M. (2008) 'Northeast Asia's Kovykta Conundrum: A Decade of Promise and Peril', *Asia Policy*, 5.

Ahrend, R. and Tompson, W. (2005) 'Unnatural Monopoly: The Endless Wait for Gas Sector Reform in Russia', *Europe–Asia Studies*, 57(6).

Alexandrova, A., Kuznetsova, P. and Grishina, E. (2005) 'Reforming In-Kind Privileges at the Regional Level in Russia: Political Decisions and their Determinants', in M. Cain, N. Gelazis and T. Inglot (eds) (2005) *Fighting Poverty and Reforming Social Security: What Can Post-Soviet States Learn from the New Democracies of Central Europe?* (Washington, D.C.: Woodrow Wilson International Center for Scholars).

Andrianov, V., Sivaev, S., Struyk, R. and Askerov, E. (2003) *Russia's Winter Woes: Tariff Setting for Local Utilities in a Transition Economy* (Moscow: Institute for Urban Economics).

Åslund, A. (2004) 'Russia's Economic Transformation under Putin', *Eurasian Geography and Economics*, 45(6).

Baev, P. (2009) 'Russia's Sinking Economy and Wandering Politics', *Eurasia Daily Monitor*, 6(16).

Chernyshev, A. (2008) 'Perekati-poshilny', *Kommersant*, 23 December, http://kommersant.ru/doc.aspx?fromsearch=c950791d-c187-4531-b3b5-ddbcdf969bee&docsid=1098723, last accessed 12 July 2010.

Coalson, R. (2008) 'Russian Protests a Danger in System Without Safety Valves', *Radio Free Europe/Radio Liberty*, 16 December, www.rferl.org/content/Russian_Protests_A_Danger_In_System_Without_Safety_Valves/1360495.html, last accessed 10 December 2010.

Corwin, J. (2005) 'Moscow Does Not Believe in Pensioners' Tears', 25 January, www.cdi.org/russia/johnson/9034-1.cfm, last accessed 12 December 2010.

EIA (2009) *International Energy Data and Analysis for Russia* (Washington, D.C.: Energy Information Administration).

Federal Tariff Service (2009) 'Kakov rosta tarifov na prirodnii gaz i elektricheskuyu energiyu na 2009 g. v protsentakh dlya promyshlennykh prepriyatii?', 13 February, www.fstrf.ru/tariffs/answers/gas/4, last accessed 28 November 2010.

Gontmakher, E. (2008) 'Scenario: Novocherkask-2009', *Vedomosti*, 6 November; available at www.insor-russia.ru/en/_news/analytics/3236.

Government of the Russian Federation (2009) 'Energeticheskaya strategiya Rossii na period do 2030 goda', Decree no.1715-r, adopted on 13 November 2009.

Grivach, A. (2006) 'Teorema Khristenko: Pravitel'stvo obsuzhdaet liberalizatsiyu rynka gaza', *Vremya novostei*, 30 November 2006, http://gasforum.ru/news/2006/301106_prav.shtml, last accessed 12 July 2010.

—— (2008) 'Ekonomika Rossii trebuet', *Vremya novostey*, 28 May 2008, www.vremya.ru/2008/92/8/204789.html, last accessed 12 July 2010.

Hanson. P. (2009) 'The Sustainability of Russia's Energy Power: Implications for the Russian Economy', in J. Perovic, R. Orttung and A. Wenger (eds) *Russian Energy Power and Foreign Relations: Implications for Conflict and Cooperation* (Abingdon: Routledge).

Hyde, M. (2001) 'Putin's Federal Reforms and their Implications for Presidential Power in Russia', *Europe–Asia Studies*, 53(5).

IEA/OECD (2006) *Optimising Russian Natural Gas: Reform and Climate Policy* (Paris: IEA).

Interfax (2009) 23 April, www.interfax.com/8/Products.aspx, last accessed 26 November 2010.

Kupchinsky, R. (2008) 'The Price of Gas and Russian Democracy', *Russian Daily Monitor*, 5(240).

Kvurt, Y. (2007) 'Selective Prosecution in Russia: Myth or Reality?', *Cardozo Journal of International and Comparative Law*, 7(53).

Latynina, Y. (2009) 'Sledite za ruchkoi prem'yera', *Novaya gazeta*, 8 June, www.novayagazeta.ru/data/2009/060/00.html, last accessed 27 November 2010.

Lenin, V. (1977) *Lenin Collected Works*, 3rd English language edn, vol.42 (Moscow: Progress Publishers).

Levada Centre (2009a) 'Potentsial protesta v marte 2009', 23 March, www.levada.ru/press/2009032602.html, last accessed 28 November 2010.

—— (2009b) 'Otsenki Rossiskikh liderov i polozhenia del v strane', 24–27 April, www.levada.ru/press/2009043003.html, last accessed 27 November 2010.

—— (2009c) 'O tom, chto bespokoit moskvichei', 26–29 March, www.levada.ru/press/2009040803.html, last accessed 28 November 2010.

Lo, B. (2003) *Vladimir Putin and the Revolution of Russian Foreign Policy* (Oxford: Blackwell).

Martusevich, R. (2008) *Regional Disparities in the Utility Sector in Russia: Does the Reform of Local Self-governance Help Reduce Them?* (Greenwich: Public Service International Research Unit).

Ministry of Economic Development and Trade of the Russian Federation (2008) 'Uroven inflyatsii i dinamika tsen', July, www.budgetrf.ru/Publications/mert_new/2008/MERT_NEW200807301758/MERT_NEW200807301758_p_003.htm, last accessed 12 November 2010.

Ministry of Energy (2003) *Summary of the Energy Strategy for Russia up to 2020* (Moscow: Ministry of Energy).

Moshe, G. (2002) 'Nationalism and History: Rewriting the Chechen National Past', in B. Coppieters and M. Huysseune (eds) *Secession, History and the Social Sciences* (Brussels: VUB Press).

OECD (2003) *Key Issues and Recommendations for Consumer Protection* (Paris: Organisation for Economic Cooperation and Development).

Øverland, I. and Kutschera, H. (2011) 'Pricing Pain: The Politics of Natural Gas for Russian Households', *Europe–Asia Studies*, forthcoming.

Parfitt, T. (2009) 'Russia Rocked by Financial Crisis Protest', *Guardian*, 1 February, www.guardian.co.uk/world/2009/feb/01/russia-protests-vladivostok-moscow, last accessed 29 November 2010.

Praim-TASS (2009) 'Gosregulirovanie tsen na gaz sokhranyat minimum do 2012 g.', 20 October, avaliable at www.prime-tass.ru/news/articles/-201/%7B78D994A5-ECF4-4112-9B51-5C8230F7C860%7D.uif, last accessed 12 July 2010.

Putin, V. (2009) 'Prime Minister Putin's Speech to the Duma', 6 April, premier.gov.ru/eng/events/2490.html, last accessed 30 November 2010.

Rasell, M. and Wengle, S. (2008) 'Reforming the *Lgoty* System: The Future of In-Kind Benefits in Post-Soviet Russia', *Russian Analytical Digest*, 37.

Renz, B. (2006) 'Putin's Militocracy? An Alternative Interpretation of *Siloviki* in Contemporary Russian Politics', *Europe–Asia Studies*, 58(6).

Reuters (2007) 'Russian Petrol Price Seen Capped till 2008 Election', 2 May, http://uk.reuters.com/article/oilRpt/idUKL2866042720070502, last accessed 5 November 2010.

Rossiya (2009) 'Izbezhat' uvol'nenii pikalevtsam ne udastsya', 3 June, www.vesti.ru/doc.html?id=290032, last accessed 12 December 2010.

Russia Today (2008) 'Fuming Drivers Set to Drive Petrol Price Scrutiny', 2 December, www.russiatoday.com/Business/2008-12-02/Fuming_drivers_set_to_drive_petrol_price_scrutiny.html, last accessed 7 December 2010.

Schröder, H. (2005) 'What Kind of Political Regime Does Russia Have?', in H. Pleines (ed.) *How to Explain Russia's Post-Soviet Political and Economic System*, Forschungsstelle Osteuropa, Bremen, *Arbeitspapiere und Materialen*, 69.

Solomon, P. (2002) 'Putin's Judicial Reform: Making Judges Accountable as well as Independent', *East European Constitutional Review*, 11(1/2).

Trenin, D. (2006) 'Russia Leaves the West', *Foreign Affairs*, 85(4).

Victor, D. (2009) *The Politics of Fossil Fuel Subsidies: The Global Subsidies Initiative* (Geneva: International Institute for Sustainable Development).

Weiler, J.D. (2004) *Human Rights in Russia: A Darker Side of Reform* (Boulder, Colo.: Lynne Rienner).

Wengle, S. (2005) 'The Monetisation of *L'got*: Politics of Welfare and Institutional Change in Russia', *Newsletter of the Institute of Slavic, East European, and Eurasian Studies*, 22(3).

—— and Rasell, M. (2008) 'The Monetisation of *Lgoty*: Changing Patterns of Welfare Politics and Provision in Russia', *Europe-Asia Studies*, 60(5).

White House (US) (2009) 'Leaders' Statement: The Pittsburgh Summit', 25 September, www.pittsburghsummit.gov/mediacenter/129639.htm, last accessed 20 November 2010.

Whitmore, B. (2008) 'Is Russia's Social Contract Breaking Down?', *Radio Free Europe/Radio Liberty*, 28 December, www.rferl.org/content/Is_Russias_Social_Contract_Breaking_Down/1364119.html, last accessed 31 October 2010.

World Bank in Russia (2008) *Energy Efficiency in Russia: Untapped Reserves* (Moscow: World Bank).

Part 3

Supply-side Governmentality

The church under the Enron Building Houston, Texas, USA. Photograph by Owen Logan.

9
North Sea Oil, the State and Divergent Development in the United Kingdom and Norway

Andrew Cumbers

There has been growing recognition in recent years of the continuing variation in the way that states and national economies negotiate with and mediate broader processes of global economic integration.[1] Despite an increased deepening of processes of economic globalisation, and the heightened flows of capital, information and people linking places and countries together, there continue to be marked differences in the economic trajectories, institutions and policy arrangements operating at the national level. The diverse experiences and responses of developed economies and their governments in the wake of the recent financial crisis – compare the United Kingdom and the United States against Germany and France for example – provides powerful evidence of this, while the fate suffered by less powerful states such as Greece and Ireland also reminds us of the uneven 'geometries of power' that characterise the relationship between nation states and broader political institutions such as the European Union (EU) and the International Monetary Fund (IMF) in the current global order.[2]

This diversity in the relations between states and broader processes of global integration becomes particularly apparent when considering the experiences of countries in relation to oil development. Those that have been blessed (or cursed?) with vast oil resources show markedly different economic trajectories that on the one hand are related to the relations between a state and the national economy and its insertion within the broader global economy. The United States and the United Kingdom clearly play very different roles in the geopolitics and geo-economics of oil compared to the Nigerian state, or compared to the Venezuelan state under Chávez or the Saudi or Iranian states. On the other hand, domestically, the nature of oil-related development reflects the contingent, historically constructed relations between the different elements of business, labour and broader civil society interests that shape state policies and governance. Compare the current Venezuelan or Bolivian approaches to oil development, with their broad redistributional aims, with those of so-called 'failed' states such as Nigeria and Angola, where oil revenues have been squandered, mismanaged and appropriated by wealthy elites or foreign multinational corporations (MNCs). The entangled connections between a state's external and internal relations have a fundamental bearing on which groups and places benefit from oil development and which are exploited or marginalised.

In this chapter, the recognition of state variety embedded within broader processes of uneven development is used to interpret UK and Norwegian experiences of developing their oil and gas resources in the North Sea. Both countries became major oil producers in the 1970s – the first discoveries having been made in the 1960s. While there are commonalities in the two countries' experiences of oil developments over the past 40 years or so, what is more striking is the contrasting trajectories of oil development and what these reveal about the nature of the two states' relationships to the broader geographical political economy of oil. In each country, the state has played an active role in oil development – but it is also noteworthy that these roles have been very different, and in turn reflect a different balance in the power relations between the competing interests that make up the state in the two countries and the way that these interests themselves interact with broader spatial actors and processes.

Following this introduction, the chapter is divided into six sections. The next section draws upon insights into the relations between states and broader processes of capital accumulation, to understand changing state–economy–society relations in the context of globalisation. The following three sections then detail the divergent trajectories taken by oil developments in the two countries, framing these in terms of past and ongoing contingent state–society–economy relations and the varied balance of social forces at work in the two countries. The penultimate section deals with the issues of resource maturity in the two countries; the conclusion then reflects on the broader implications of these contrasting experiences for our understanding of economic development and state policy in the global oil industry.

STATE, SOCIAL RELATIONS AND DIVERGENT TRAJECTORIES IN THE GLOBAL ECONOMY

Although the role of the national state may be changing in the context of globalisation, the state remains an important actor in regulating and managing the economy, and in determining economic opportunity and outcomes between different social groups.[3] There is not the space here to develop a full perspective on the state under globalisation, but a couple of points are critical for the argument that follows. The first concerns our understanding of what the state represents in a global capitalist society. Following Jessop (2002), the state can be considered as an institutional form or 'social relation' that attempts to resolve the contradictions inherent in securing the conditions for sustained capital accumulation. However, compared to some more orthodox Marxist interpretations, the state does not operate automatically in the interests of a capitalist class, but, following Gramsci and Poulantzas, should be considered as an

> ensemble of socially embedded, socially regularized and strategically selective institutions, organizations, social forces and activities organized around (or at least actively involved in) making collectively binding decisions for an imagined political community. State power can be understood in turn as a power relation that is mediated in and through this institutional ensemble.[4]

Variations in actually existing state forms between different countries reflect the outcome of historically contingent social forces competing and contesting state power through the various institutions and mechanisms, but fundamentally the state is a social relation that is reflective of the balance of power between competing interests and groups.[5]

Geographically, the state has always had to balance the competing interests of advancing the needs of capital and business to roam geographically in search of profit and those of its citizens concerned with the provision of national wealth and the jobs and income opportunities that go along with this: a decent health system, housing and public services, etc.[6] Put simply, we might think of this as the contradictions running through the state in relation to space and place. But globalisation is arguably exacerbating these contradictions (ibid.). Accepting that the state continues to be a critical player in the context of an increasingly global economy and that it faces these geographical tensions between spatial mobility and place-based governance, national governments are becoming even more important players in mediating between the interests of multinational capital, both at home and overseas, and social and community groups within national territories. This results in a variegated terrain of state–society–economy relations between different nation states, giving rise to discussions about varieties of capitalism: Anglo-Saxon or liberal market versus Rhenish or social democrat, the Asian developmental state, etc.[7] While dominant policy agendas can develop at international scales (e.g. Keynesianism or neoliberalism), these take different forms in different places and are influenced by the existing balances of power between different social groups.

The second point is that while it is something of a myth to think that there was ever a time (pre-1973, for example) at which there was a hermetically sealed system of national capitalisms over which the state played an important role in the distribution of resources, there has nevertheless been a considerable re-scaling of state power through broader global processes in the last 30 years.[8] The growing hegemony of neoliberal economic policy dominance, with all that this means for deregulation and the opening up of economies to broader market forces, means that national economic spaces have been opened up in an unprecedented manner to forces of global capitalism. As part of this shift, the post-war period of state national economic management has given way to a more multi-scalar mode of governance with considerable deterritorialisation and reterritorialisation of state strategies downwards to the local and regional scales and upwards to supranational (e.g. EU, NAFTA) and global scales (e.g. IMF, WTO, G20).

Following on from these two key points, it is clear that the state is neither a passive victim, nor a neutral arbiter of globalisation processes, but, through economic strategies and other policy tools at its disposal, dictates which fractions of capital and which social groups are prioritised over others under conditions of increasing international competition and globally uneven development. Under these circumstances, the national state is doing what it has always done; making political choices about economic development and redistribution policies, which will benefit particular groups and regions at the expense of others. To provide a quick example from the United Kingdom, the internationalisation strategies of many UK-based corporations during the 1980s were contingent upon their ability to free capital of its place-based restrictions through the sale or disposal of assets tied up in the national economy.[9] The ability to do this was far greater than for German or French firms, which were more firmly embedded within their own national economies. In the United Kingdom, the greater mobility of firms and the fewer restrictions (e.g. lower redundancy payments, fewer restrictions on the transfer of capital) involved the closure of older and less profitable plants in some of the United Kingdom's more peripheral and economically depressed regions and the reinvestment of capital overseas. This was not a new trend, but in fact dated back to the period after the First World War when British firms were able to take advantage of imperial markets to generate higher profit levels overseas than in domestic operations. Nevertheless, the ability of firms to pursue such strategies was made substantially easier by a government that was on the one hand committed to relaxing capital exchange controls, while on the other opposed to the introduction of tighter constraints on factory closure or to policies that provided greater employment protection. The costs of relocation decreased significantly for UK firms in the 1980s compared to many of their counterparts in other western European countries.

More generally, increased global economic integration (without accompanying political integration) has intensified the pressures under which state strategies are being made; capital is making greater claims on the state in its internationalisation strategies, for example through attempts to enforce a global regime of free trade under the WTO, lobby for more integrated European or North American economies, or impose market-friendly conditions on loans through the IMF and the World Bank, which in turn may come into conflict with national and local development priorities.[10] However, to the extent that the state itself remains the site of contested social relations, the nature and direction of state policy cannot simply be read in terms of the pressures of global capital, but is likely to vary between states.[11] This reflects differences in the balance of power between class forces, between different fractions of capital (financial versus industrial) and between the geographical centre and the periphery.

DIVERGENT DEVELOPMENT IN THE NORTH SEA: OIL-RELATED TRAJECTORIES IN THE UNITED KINGDOM AND NORWAY

Geometries of Power and Differential State Positioning in the Evolution of Global Capitalism

My central argument here is that to understand the very different oil development trajectories in the United Kingdom and Norway, we have to understand the nature of the state in each country and the playing out of relations between competing interests, both domestically and internationally, that have shaped government policy towards oil. This also means recognising the way the two states are differently implicated in relation to broader geographical structures of power, or what Doreen Massey (1993) has termed 'power geometries', in theorising how places are connected up to broader power relations in the global economy.

A simple but important difference relates to the make-up of the two states and their historical evolution in relation to the international oil industry. As Radice (1995) has cogently argued, British capitalism has, from the very outset, been global in character, with the growth of the domestic economy being heavily bound up with the growth of empire and international trade connections from the eighteenth century onwards. For almost the same length of time, the UK domestic economy has been open to external influences in a way that has not been paralleled in other developed countries. By the 1990s, Radice argues that, as far as the United Kingdom was concerned, '[t]here [was] no longer a viable "national capitalism", based on an alliance between national capital, labour and the state, waiting to be freed from the dominance of financiers and foreign investors'.[12]

The United Kingdom was the first country to industrialise fully, and the global hegemonic power in the nineteenth century was in many senses the progenitor of globalisation processes in the oil industry and the wider economy. London became the primary centre for trading in oil stocks and shares as well as being home to British Petroleum (BP) and Shell. British Petroleum, originally created as Anglo Persian (the name in itself invoking its broader geopolitical significance), was largely a creation of the British state, which retained a 51 per cent shareholding up until 1979. Internationally, the British government's imperial interests were closely aligned and at times were indistinguishable from the interests of the two MNCs. This is noticeable in Britain's foreign policy in the Middle East in securing access to cheap oil resources in the 1920s and 1930s, and its role in the overthrow of the Mossadegh regime in Iran in the 1950s, which had threatened to nationalise the oil industry.

In contrast, Norway's relatively late industrialisation and relatively recent independence have meant that there has been a more underdeveloped capitalist or business class historically, although this has changed in the past 20 years. From the perspective of globalisation, the early twentieth century was for Norway a period of negotiating with foreign MNCs over its rich abundance of natural resources. In this respect, the state has tended historically to play the role of entrepreneur, stimulating industrial development through negotiating joint venture deals and technology transfer agreements with foreign companies.[13] A strong thread of 'Norwegianisation' has therefore tended to underpin the state's economic development strategy in recognition of the perceived vulnerability of the country's economy to foreign control; in this sense, Norway, although being a relatively rich Western country, had more in common structurally with many oil-rich third world countries. The 'developmentalist' state perspective has therefore also shaped the Norwegian state's dealings with foreign oil companies in the 1970s and 1980s, most notably through insistence on Norwegian ownership throughout the oil industry and its supply chain and the establishment of Statoil, with the intention of developing a fully fledged national oil champion.

The contrast with the United Kingdom also extends to the broader macroeconomic relationship between Norway and the world economy, which traditionally has been a much more closely regulated one. Internationalisation strategies in a few key export enclaves have taken place alongside high trade tariffs protecting domestic markets from foreign competition, and (until the 1980s) tight control over flows of financial capital. Although it is important not to overemphasise the differences – both countries underwent phases of market liberalisation and deregulation in the 1990s – these basic differences in the social and political forces driving oil developments in the two countries do remain and continue to shape different approaches with regard to North Sea oil developments.

Initial Reflections on Three Decades of Oil Development

In charting the different trajectories taken by the two states in relation to North Sea oil, it is important to start with a few basic indicators, which are important in illustrating the very different types of state and national economic trajectories in the United Kingdom and Norway. Both countries constitute liberal European democracies that have important trading connections with the rest of the European Union. Although Norway remains outside the EU, to secure access to the large single European market for its firms it has adopted a large number of EU standards and economic regulations. Despite these commonalities, the two countries are characterised by very different trajectories of development. Although the countries are not directly comparable – given that the United Kingdom is a large, diverse and multinational state of 60 million people, whereas Norway is a much smaller, more homogenous nation of 4 million people, which has only been independent for just over a century – a few basic economic and social indicators give an impression of the different balances of social forces in the two countries and the outcome of conflicts between different groups that shape state policies.

After three decades of oil development, the United Kingdom is a far more unequal society than Norway, as measured by the OECD's index of inequality.[14] While taxes in Norway are lower than in the rest of Scandinavia, they remain higher than in the United Kingdom as a proportion of GDP, when income, sales and other taxes are included. In the United Kingdom, oil revenues in the mid 1980s were critical in allowing the Conservative government to cut business and income tax rates for the very richest in society. In the 1988 financial strategy, the top rate of income tax was cut from 63 to 40 per cent.

Norway also scores better on a range of other indicators. A critical factor in Norway has been the strength of the labour movement and the broad social democratic consensus that has underpinned the country's development since 1945. Over half of the workforce in Norway is unionised, with nearly 75 per cent of workers covered by collective bargaining agreements, compared to only around 25 per cent in the United Kingdom. Although the United Kingdom had a strong labour movement in the 1970s, there was never quite the social consensus achieved in Norway; at the same time business and financial interests have always been stronger in the United Kingdom. UK employment relations remained largely voluntaristic, while in Norway, unions became much enshrined as social partners in the formal state apparatus.

In the United Kingdom, oil developments in the period after 1979 took place against the backdrop of the return to power of a Conservative administration committed to an aggressive neoliberal ideology that espoused laissez-faire economic policies and market deregulation.[15] This government also introduced some of the toughest anti-trade union laws in the developed world and was successful in defeating organised labour in a number of landmark disputes, most notably the miners' strike in 1984/5. In comparison, oil-related developments in Norway since the late 1970s have continued to be underpinned by a strong social democratic consensus. Although this has come under pressure in recent years from neoliberal ideology and the increasingly aggressive national business elite, social consensus has remained a dominant feature of economic policy, most evident in the tripartite incomes policies of the 1990s.[16]

MULTINATIONAL POWER, NEOLIBERALISM AND THE GLOBAL EMBEDDING OF UK NORTH SEA OPERATIONS

The very different historical contexts of state–economy–society relations have been critical in the evolution of oil policy regimes in the two countries[17] (Table 9.1). Policy in the United Kingdom since 1979 has been driven unashamedly by the interests of the United Kingdom's own well-established multinational oil companies, BP and Shell. Together with their foreign partners, they have been allied to the requirements of the internationally-oriented financial centre, the City of London, whose short-termist investment priorities have been critical in the development of a regime of rapid depletion of North Sea resources. Although there was some attempt to encourage foreign oil companies to use British suppliers in the North Sea, through a somewhat ambiguously titled 'Full and Fair Opportunities' policy, this was scrapped in 1991. In practice, even this policy was flexible enough to allow foreign companies to set up their own subsidiaries, with no requirement for the development of specific local skills or expertise in oil technologies. Any policy that could be seen as interventionist or anti-competitive has remained firmly off the agenda under both Conservative and Labour governments in the recent past.

On the whole, oil development in the United Kingdom has been driven by the desire to use oil revenues to bolster macro-economic policies rather than to pursue an interventionist industrial strategy. An important element of this has been to provide a 'friendly and accommodating' environment for foreign companies with the appropriate expertise to develop North Sea resources as fast as possible.[18] Against this backdrop, there has been a marked absence of debate about the local and regional development implications of North Sea activities. This is despite the fact that oil developments have resulted in the build-up of significant local industrial complexes in hitherto economically marginal regions in the north of England and Scotland.[19] Multinational companies and their proxies have dominated policy discussions and official forums, with other interests being excluded.[20] Not only were trade unions left out of the policy loop between 1979 and 1997; local communities affected by oil development and local business interests were also given little voice.

The prevailing UK political economy of North Sea oil has therefore resulted in a situation in which local oil developments have become embedded within much wider global networks, predominantly those

Table 9.1   Divergent oil development paths in the United Kingdom and Norway

	United Kingdom	Norway
Economic geography of oil development	Strong clustering around 'oil capital' Aberdeen, which becomes transnational hub for offshore operations beyond North Sea	Stavanger and Rogaland region becoming centre of industry and corporate headquarters for Statoil and some limited supply firms
	London and South East England playing key role in HQ and R & D activities	Attempts to spread industry to other (northern) regions in 1970s, important secondary centres (e.g. Bergen)
		Oslo: centre of government, corporate headquarters and some R & D activities
Nature of state regulation	1970s: some limited attempts to develop industrial and regional policy (e.g. BNOC)	1970–mid 1980s: strong regional and industrial policy, creation of Statoil, indigenisation of technology and training
	1979–present: light tax and regulatory regime, no regional and limited industrial policy	Protectionist policy to oil supplies industry in early years
	Anti-union strategy by government after 1979; dominance of MNC interests (Piper Alpha disaster)	Strong union and labour movement though tensions between corporatism and more independent unions
Key social relations and tensions	Government–MNC (BP, Shell, City of London financial interests)	Social democratic forces (Labour Party, LO trade union organisation), state bureaucracy and Statoil
	Post-1997: incorporation of moderate trade unions into management strategies; devolution settlement attempt to deal with tensions between uneven development in south east and rest of United Kingdom	1990s onwards: growing influence of business class and discourse of modified neoliberalism
		Tensions between state modernisers and elites v. left in labour movement, rural communities and greens
General oil strategy	Rapid depletion policy driven by government interest in oil revenues, and MNC profits	Managed depletion driven by local development concerns and welfarist objectives
	Maintenance of low taxation regime and use of revenues to finance tax cuts for richest groups	Use of tax revenues to create social welfare fund
		Early 1990s onwards: more business-oriented approach around internationalisation and national competitiveness (e.g. part privatisation of Statoil)
Ownership characteristics and structure of national oil complex	Dominated by foreign and London-based MNCs but development of some local supply capabilities and evidence of broader global role for Aberdeen-based industries	Mix of national firms and foreign MNCs, development of strong national champions (e.g. Statoil, Kvaerner) but over-reliance on national resource base

dominated by foreign multinational interests. The situation has been accentuated by recent trends in which cost-reduction strategies within the industry have led to the standardisation of many supply contracts, favouring larger foreign-owned contractors over more innovative local firms.[21]

Despite such concerns, what we might term the 'global embedding' of the UK oil complex within broader networks of knowledge and power has brought some important local development benefits. Scotland has an estimated 195,000 jobs supported by oil development[22] and the city of Aberdeen has become the principle focus of oil-related activity in the United Kingdom, with around 20 per cent of the United Kingdom's total direct oil-related employment, according to one recent estimate.[23] In this respect, it has become home to substantial numbers of relatively highly skilled and well-paid oil workers, with a standard of living amongst the highest in the United Kingdom. There is also evidence that oil developments have created a significant number of small, independent UK firms that have benefited from global links established through supplier relationships with larger foreign firms, forged in the North Sea. A significant number of UK firms, both from Aberdeen and its wider region, are now competing in export markets, although the more technologically innovative activities still tend to be dominated by foreign firms.[24]

THE DEVELOPMENTAL STATE, SOCIAL DEMOCRACY AND THE NORTH SEA OIL EXPERIENCE IN NORWAY

In contrast to the United Kingdom, the Norwegian state has played a much greater developmental role in the North Sea, more akin to the type of state–economy relations apparent in Asian developmental states than to those of the Anglo-American liberal democratic state.[25] Indeed, more broadly, Vartiainen even talks of an East Asian–Nordic model of late industrialisation (1995: 137–69). In the Norwegian case this involved the establishment in 1972 of a state oil company, Statoil, to protect domestic interests. This initially took place through joint venture arrangements with foreign oil companies as well as through the establishment of the state's direct financial interest (SDFI) in 1985. The latter means that the Norwegian state has a direct financial investment in oil and gas developments. This was valued at NOK834.8 billion (about £80 billion) in 2008.[26] Another departure point marking out Norwegian oil operations from those of the United Kingdom was the establishment in 1990 of a state oil fund known as the 'Government Pension Fund – Global', which is currently worth around £214 billion.[27] Foreign oil companies were also required to cooperate with Statoil in the transfer of industry-specific knowledge, skills and expertise – known as 'goodwill agreements' – so that by the early 1980s Statoil was able to pursue its own oil and gas field developments independently of any foreign involvement. Whilst in recent years the Norwegian state's direct involvement in the oil industry has declined, it remains an important strategic presence and arbiter of oil developments. It retains considerable power to shape North Sea developments – in comparison with the United Kingdom – though successive Conservative and Labour-led administrations have been wary about using this power for fear of frightening off foreign investment.

A concerted protectionist infant industry strategy has been applied through using its two national oil companies (partially state-owned Norsk Hydro, originally a petro-chemical company that entered the North Sea sector, but especially Statoil) to develop a domestic supplier base.[28] To provide some direct comparative evidence, research conducted in the early 1990s estimated that 45.9 per cent of all contracts awarded by the Norwegian domestic oil companies in the North Sea between 1979 and 1993 went to Norwegian suppliers.[29] These figures compare with a figure for Scottish contractors from UK oil companies of only 9 per cent. Over time, it is clear that this strategy has succeeded in creating some sizeable Norwegian companies in key areas of the offshore industry.[30]

Subsequently the close relationship between the Norwegian oil companies and their domestic suppliers was extended into international markets, with the development of long-term frame agreements for the supply of the new generation of subsea equipment on a worldwide basis.[31] In 1995 these relationships were formalised with the establishment of INTSOK, an export initiative involving the three Norwegian oil companies, the government and the domestic supplies industry. Although the links between Norwegian oil companies and their suppliers have become less formalised in the 2000s, the evidence suggests that local companies continue to benefit from the ability to supply oil companies. A survey conducted in 2003[32] suggested that 55 per cent of SMEs (small and medium enterprises) in the Norwegian oil capital, Stavanger, believed collaboration with national oil companies to be important in stimulating technological development, compared to much lower levels on innovation support (around 33 per cent) among Scottish-based SMEs.[33]

In common with wider economic strategy, oil policy has been accompanied by a strong regional development dimension, with attempts to decentralise the impact of oil development being particularly pronounced during the 1970s. This has happened in a number of ways. First, Statoil and the government's Petroleum Directorate were located in Stavanger to create an alternative economic growth pole to Oslo. Second, there was a strategy of building up separate service bases for each new field development, in an effort to spread the benefits of oil-related employment northwards to more peripheral areas. Examples included a major Shell base at Kristiansand, a Statoil operations centre near Trondheim and Mobil at Haarstad. Third, during the 1970s a number of smaller shipyards in the north of Norway received significant subsidies to help them diversify into the offshore industry.[34] Fourth, and finally, there has also been an effect through the regional dimension of national technology policy, whereby Trondheim, as the location for the country's main technical university (NTNU) has become an important centre for energy-related research. Such developments have meant that the benefits of oil-related employment have been dispersed more widely than in the United Kingdom.

While state intervention has been important in encouraging and enabling such localised initiatives, it is important not to overstate the integrity and agency of Norway's local oil complexes. The principal focus of policy has been to establish a nationally based oil cluster, which has mitigated against the creation of strong locally based and contained agglomerations. In line with other sectors of the Norwegian economy, the oil-related sector has become increasingly delocalised and incorporated within national-level corporate networks.[35] Oslo still dominates the country's labour market for higher-level management and engineering skills. While Stavanger has enjoyed considerable oil-related growth and prosperity – in a similar fashion to Aberdeen – it is not clear whether it contains the local innovative capacity to generate self-sustaining growth as oil activities begin to decline. Despite having Statoil and the Petroleum Directorate located there, the city does not appear to have attracted similar higher-level decision-making and technical activities from other companies;[36] whilst a recent study comparing Aberdeen and Stavanger found that both cities continued to be heavily dependent upon oil and thus far displayed little evidence of moving into new markets, such as sustainable energy development.[37] Nevertheless, the state remains committed to a regional innovation strategy in the south-west with substantial investment in the local research and higher-education sector. The Rogaland Technical College was recently granted university status, and there is continued encouragement of the shipbuilding yards in Haugesund and other smaller local boatyards with contracts for North Sea equipment. The leading Norwegian offshore contracting firm Aker has also established a technical centre north of Stavanger.[38]

During the 1990s the contradictions between developing an internationally competitive 'national' oil cluster on the one hand and sustaining local oil-related employment on the other have become increasingly apparent, with a number of Norwegian firms seeking to expand their global operations. In such circumstances the commitment of Norwegian firms to their domestic supplier bases may well diminish, although the evidence above suggests that these links are comparatively strong. At the same time, the Norwegian state has relaxed, although not completely discarded, its protectionist stance as part of an 'internationalisation' strategy, geared towards improving efficiency and enhancing competitiveness.

DEALING WITH RESOURCE MATURITY: DIVERGENCE OR CONVERGENCE IN OIL TRAJECTORIES IN THE EARLY TWENTY-FIRST CENTURY?

Despite the divergent trajectories apparent in the two countries' experiences of North Sea oil, we should not overstate the differences. Both countries are dealing with the same underlying pressures, and the same conflict that arises under a global capitalist system between providing the right incentives for private companies to secure profits from oil, and attempting to extract a 'social' share in the oil revenues. Both are grappling with the wider contradictions of securing the conditions for capital accumulation while maintaining the social and political integrity of national spaces in the context of global economic integration.[39] The broader global oil industry context and the locally contingent circumstances in the North Sea mean that the contemporary dilemmas facing the United Kingdom and Norway are similar. The passing of peak oil production points in the 1990s means ensuring maximum extraction and benefits from North Sea oil as a declining resource amidst more attractive investment options elsewhere for globally oriented oil companies, in Latin America, West Africa, the Caspian Sea region and the Middle East. Meanwhile, it is fair to say that neither the United Kingdom nor Norway is taking seriously the need to frame oil developments within broader concerns about global warming and environmental destruction. Statoil and the rest of the Norwegian oil industry are currently putting considerable resources and political pressure into extending offshore developments into the Arctic, with a new series of cooperation agreements with Russia opening the way for exploitation. A particularly intense battle between oil interests, environmentalists and the fishing industry is centred upon the opening up of Vesterålen and the Lofoten islands in the far north of Norway. Overall, a business-as-usual attitude of extracting oil and gas when and wherever possible, to contribute to state and corporate revenues, seems to be prevalent, with climate change policy happening somewhere else in the government jurisdiction. Hardly joined-up thinking!

Both Norway and the United Kingdom were subjected to deregulation and marketisation policies during the 1990s, and whether there was much substantive difference between the politics of New Labour and that of the Norwegian social democrats is a moot point. The election of a centre-right neoliberal government in 2001 merely accentuated a developing trend in this respect (Wahl 2010). In Norway, the state itself has become more like other western European states, with tensions developing between a more traditional Norwegianisation agenda with elements of protectionism, a fracturing social democratic consensus, and the emergence of a business lobby and a pro-European Union political elite.[40] In this sense, the Norwegian state is faced with the dilemma of reconciling its long-standing commitment to balanced interregional growth and social cohesion with that of enhancing the interests of a small, but increasingly influential, number of multinational actors.

While the hegemony of business interests and the ability of UK Conservative governments to construct stable governing coalitions on the basis of a south-east and 'middle England' bloc at the expense of the outlying regions and nations enabled a neoliberal agenda to be pursued vigorously in the 1980s, this came unstuck in the 1990s. From the perspective of North Sea oil, two significant changes occurred to the United Kingdom's political economy with the election of the Labour Government in 1997. First, there has been a new Employment Relations Act, giving unions legal rights to organise the workforce in the North Sea for the first time. Although this has led to several new collective-bargaining agreements, this has not challenged the existing policy regime, largely because of the pliant attitude of the unions involved, which have been prepared to sign no-strike agreements with the oil companies.[41] Nevertheless, there is greater recognition of unions as social actors in the oil sector; and the growth of a more militant grassroots trade unionism to challenge the established unions, spearheaded by the Oil Industry Liaison Committee (OILC),[42] which has subsequently become part of the National Union of Rail, Maritime and Transport Workers (RMT), may lead to shifts in the balance of power. As evidence of this, in November 2006, 900 divers and support staff, backed by RMT, undertook successful strike action, securing a 40 per cent pay increase over two years with additional holiday entitlement.[43]

A second development has been the Labour Government's devolution programme, which has resulted in the setting up of a Scottish Parliament and a renewed debate about the role of oil in Scottish development.[44] Although thus far there has been little shift in the overall governance position regarding North Sea oil, the arrival of a Scottish National Party minority government in 2007 has resulted in renewed demands for more local control of oil revenues. Using international maritime boundaries, the SNP government has estimated that an independent Scotland would have property rights over 90 per cent of remaining North Sea oil production.[45] While the SNP – as a centre-left party broadly committed to neoliberal market policies, with a slight social democratic tinge – is unlikely to challenge the dominance of corporate interests over oil development, it has nevertheless initiated a debate over the control of government oil revenues. One proposal has been for the setting up of an oil fund to promote welfare and infrastructure funding.[46] Although North Sea oil and gas production peaked in the late 1990s, it has been estimated that oil revenues will still generate £45 billion in tax receipts for the United Kingdom between 2009 and 2014.[47] This is a significant figure considering the total devolved Scottish Government budget of an estimated £33.5 billion for 2011/2.[48]

Regarding the specifics of North Sea oil and gas developments, the period since 1997 has seen more continuity than change in established relations. The continuation of a relatively light-touch regulatory and tax regime has enabled BP and Shell to divest themselves of their less profitable and increasingly marginal fields to facilitate the foreign expansion and intensification of activities in Africa, Russia and other former Soviet states, such as Azerbaijan, and Latin America. While Aberdeen continues to thrive as an oil hub with connections beyond the North Sea, this is clearly time-limited, as North Sea resources decline further. Meanwhile, having rapidly used up North Sea resources, the United Kingdom is once again moving to a situation of being a net energy importer. Indeed, it is already dependent on gas supplies from the Norwegian sector.

There is also little expectation that the new Conservative–Liberal Democrat coalition will change tack. Because of its smaller population and more gradual depletion policy, Norway will continue to be a large net oil and gas exporter for many years to come. It is both more dependent on oil than the United Kingdom and likely to continue to receive greater benefits: a recent estimate put revenues from the oil and gas sector at 33.5 per cent of government revenue for 2008.[49] The election of a centre-left coalition government in 2005 on a platform opposing further privatisation signalled a shift leftwards in government policy,[50] though currently the governing coalition of social democratic Labour Party, Socialist Left Party and agrarian centrist Centre Party is continually tested by converging tendencies, i.e. a continuing commitment to a version of neoliberalism among the moderate social democrats, and the desire for greater social protection and national control of resources among other elements. So far, there has been little change in direction in the overall approach to oil, and even the extreme right of the political spectrum in Norway, the Progress party (Fremskritsspartiet), emphasises – albeit to a quite different degree and with a different set of intentions – the utilisation of Norway's oil revenues to fund a generous welfare state.

CONCLUSIONS

My purpose in this chapter has been to highlight the varied role of the 'national' state in shaping economic development prospects despite current trends towards the internationalisation (if not quite globalisation) of capital. All countries are to some extent facing the pressure of increased global competition and the imperative to deregulate and privatise their economies; this has certainly been the case in the oil industries of both the United Kingdom and Norway. But the examples of these two countries highlight the different possibilities and prospects that are available to oil-rich states and nations. Both countries have derived considerable local benefits from oil, but from a progressive perspective of dealing with issues of distributional justice, Norway clearly represents the better example.

Whilst it is clear that Norwegian oil policy has come under the influence of a neoliberal 'globalisation' discourse in recent years, the context, in terms of historically constructed state–society relations, remains very different to that of the United Kingdom. At a wider level, the rejection of EU membership in the 1995 referendum is a reminder of the continuing requirement for the Norwegian state elite to balance internationalisation strategies with social cohesion and redistribution domestically. This contrasts dramatically with the United Kingdom, where a Labour Government, elected in 1997 with a large and secure majority, became a willing convert to a neoliberal macroeconomic strategy privileging the City of London and finance capital over a more balanced industrial and regional policy. The commitment to an extreme variant of neoliberalism by both Conservative and Labour governments, and the squandering of North Sea oil revenues on tax cuts for business and middle-class groups, are now coming home to roost.

At a deeper analytical level, an important part of the divergences reported here relate to the character of the state – in Jessop's sense of representing particular social relations (2002) and the balance of power of interests that operate through it. Clearly, while both UK and Norwegian state elites have signed up to the neoliberal project, the opposition of labour and other social forces in Norway has moderated the effects of market liberalisation and deregulation better than in the United Kingdom, where the business agenda has been heavily dominant. Norwegian trade unions remain important actors (beyond the wildest dreams of their UK counterparts) both in the political sphere, through their influence on the ruling Labour coalition, and in the economic sphere, through their continuing role as social partners. In this respect, an increasingly critical issue facing progressive politics in Norway has been the complicity of much of the Labour and trade union establishments with neoliberal measures such as the privatisation of Statoil and the projection of a Norwegian model of oil development overseas, whilst turning a blind eye to some of the threats to the strong labour protection laws at home.

In the United Kingdom, the interests of internationally oriented capital continue to be prioritised over modernisation of the domestic industrial base or an assessment of the needs of local and regional economies; these are neglected in favour of a macroeconomic strategy designed to satisfy financial interests in the City of London. In Norway, the state's commitment to industrial modernisation, social justice and regional balance remains, but will continue to come under pressure from the very business interests that it has stimulated in the past. To a large extent I would argue that the current dilemma facing nation states is not that they are necessarily powerless – although some are clearly more powerful than others – but that they face increasingly hard choices between prosecuting the interests of capital internationally and maintaining social cohesion and spatially balanced growth at home. A final word is reserved for future developments. Because of the divergent trajectories taken by the two countries, their governments face very different priorities in relation to future developments. Whilst the United Kingdom's oil and gas reserves have dwindled considerably through its rapid depletion policy, Norway retains considerable resources (although as I have noted earlier both countries are past peak oil). Further exploitation in more environmentally sensitive areas could lead to conflict with green and fishing interests. The UK Government is faced with trying to maximise output and revenue from its remaining North Sea resources through cost-saving and incentivisation for foreign firms, often through tax incentives. Neither the British nor the Norwegian government currently appears to be inclined to develop oil policies that might address concerns about climate change. Both countries seem to be content to offset continued oil production through climate change measures in other areas – in particular through their commitment to the REDD (Reduced Emissions on Degradation and Deforestation) mechanism.[51] This market-based model effectively allows them to export their responsibility for dealing with the most pressing issue facing the world: climate change caused by the production of hydrocarbons.

NOTES

1. Peck and Theodore 2007.
2. Massey 1993.
3. Martin and Sunley 1997; Jessop 2002.
4. Jessop 2002, p.6.
5. Jessop 1990.
6. Harvey 2003.
7. Albert 1991; Boyer and Hollingsworth 1997; Hall and Soskice 2001; Peck and Theodore 2007.
8. Jessop 2002.
9. Cumbers 2000a.
10. Harvey 2003.
11. Jessop 1990.
12. Radice 1995, p.235.
13. The industrial giant, Norsk Hydro, a conglomerate with interests stretching from metal production to oil, gas and chemical fertilisers, is perhaps the most celebrated product of this development process.
14. Norway has a Gini index of 25.8 as against 36.0 for the United Kingdom. UNDP 2009.
15. Gamble 1988.

16. Dolvik and Stokke 1998.
17. See Cumbers 2000a for discussion in greater depth.
18. Woolfson, Foster and Beck 1997.
19. See Cumbers 1995, 2000b.
20. Cumbers 2000b.
21. Cumbers et al. 2003.
22. Scottish Government 2009.
23. Hatakenaka et al. 2006.
24. Cumbers 2000b; Cumbers, Mackinnon and Chapman 2003.
25. Weiss 1998.
26. NPD 2009.
27. Scottish Government 2009.
28. Hydro and Statoil were recently merged.
29. Howie and Lipka 1993.
30. Cumbers 2000b.
31. Statoil, for example, negotiated a 5-year agreement with the Norwegian firm Kongsberg Offshore, in which the latter supplied it with subsea equipment in all its geographical markets up until the year 2000; similar agreements were also made between ABB and Saga and between Norsk Hydro and Kvaerner in the 1990s. These agreements enabled the three suppliers to develop longer-term market strategies.
32. See Hatekenaka et al. 2003.
33. Cumbers, Mackinnon and Chapman 2003.
34. An example is Aker's offshore construction site at Verdal, near Trondheim.
35. Cumbers 2000b.
36. Cumbers 2000a.
37. Hatakenaka et al. 2006.
38. John-Andrew McNeish, personal communication, December 2010.
39. Jessop 2002; Harvey 2003.
40. Like many other western European countries, Norway also faces the pressures of the growth of an extreme right politics, capitalising on popular fears of immigration.
41. Cumbers 2005.
42. More details of these developments are contained in Cumbers 2005.
43. Cumbers 2007.
44. The discovery of oil in the 1960s boosted the Scottish National Party and led to considerable public debate in the 1970s regarding the economic case for an independent Scotland. Although the election of the Thatcher government in 1979 closed down demands for more Scottish autonomy regarding oil development, the issue fuelled much of the anti-Conservative sentiment that developed in Scotland during the 1980s.
45. Scottish Government 2009, p.19.
46. Scottish Government 2009.
47. Ibid., p.10.
48. Scottish Government figures accessible at www.scotland.gov.uk, last accessed 3 January 2011.
49. NPD 2009.
50. Wahl 2010.
51. Thanks to John-Andrew McNeish for the reminder about this point.

REFERENCES

Albert, M. (1991) *Capitalisme Contre Capitalisme* (Paris: Le Seuil).
Boyer, R. and Hollingsworth, J.R. (1997) 'From National Embeddedness to Spatial and Institutional Nestedness', in J.R. Hollingsworth and R. Boyer (eds) *Contemporary Capitalism: The Embeddedness of Institutions* (Cambridge: Cambridge University Press).
Cumbers, A. (1995) 'North Sea Oil and Regional Economic Development: The Case of the North East of England', *Area*, 27: 208–17.
—— (2000a) 'The National State as Mediator of Regional Development Outcomes in an Era of Globalisation', *European Urban and Regional Studies*, 7: 237–52.
—— (2000b) 'Globalisation, Local Economic Development and the Branch Plant Region: The Case of the Aberdeen Oil Complex', *Regional Studies*, 34: 371–82.
—— (2005) Genuine Renewal or Pyrrhic Victory? The Scale Politics of Trade Union Recognition in the UK, *Antipode*, 37(1): 116–38.
—— Mackinnon, D. and Chapman, K. (2003) 'Innovation, Collaboration and Learning in Regional Clusters: A Study of SMEs in the Aberdeen Oil Complex', *Environment and Planning A*, 35(9): 1,689–706.
Dolvik, J.E. and Stokke, T.A. (1998) 'The Revival of Centralized Concertation', in A. Ferner and R. Hyman (eds) *Changing Industrial Relations in Europe* (Oxford: Blackwell).
Gamble, A. (1988) *The Free Economy and the Strong State: The Politics of Thatcherism* (Basingstoke: Macmillan).
Hall, P.A. and Soskice, D. (2001) *Varieties of Capitalism: the Institutional Foundations of Comparative Advantage* (Oxford: Oxford University Press).
Harvey, D. (2003) *The New Imperialism* (Oxford: Oxford University Press).
Hatakenaka, S., Westnes, P., Gjelsvik, M. and Lester, R.K. (2006) 'The Regional Dynamics of Innovation: A Comparative Case Study of Oil and Gas Industry Development in Stavanger and Aberdeen', MIT IPC Working Paper 06-008.
Howie, D. and Lipka, J. (1993) *Contracts in the Offshore Oil Industry: A Comparison of the UK and Norwegian Sectors* (Glasgow: STUC).
Jessop, B. (1990) *Putting Capitalist States in their Place* (Cambridge: Polity Press).
—— (2002) *The Future of the Capitalist State* (Cambridge: Polity Press).
Martin, R.L. and Sunley, P.J. (1997) 'The Post-Keynesian State and the Space Economy', in R. Lee and J. Wills (eds) *Geographies of Economies* (London: Arnold).
Massey, D. (1993) 'Power-Geometry and a Progressive Sense of Place', in J. Bird, B. Curtis, T. Putnam, G. Robertson and L. Tickner (eds) *Mapping the Futures: Local Cultures, Global Change* (London: Routledge).
NPD (2009) *Facts 2009: The Norwegian Petroleum Sector* (Oslo: Norwegian Petroleum Directorate).
Peck, J. and Theodore, N. (2007) 'Variegated capitalism', *Progress in Human Geography* 31(6): 731–72.
Radice, H. (1995) 'Britain in the World Economy: National Decline, Capitalist Success?', in D. Coates and J. Hillard (eds) *UK Economic Decline: Key Texts* (London: Harvester Wheatsheaf).
Scottish Government (2009) *An Oil Fund for Scotland: Taking Forward Our National Conversation* (Edinburgh: Scottish Government).
UNDP (2009) *Human Development Report 2009: Overcoming Barriers, Human Mobility and Development* (New York: United Nations).

Vartiainen, J. (1995) 'The State and Structural Change: What Can Be Learnt from the Successful Late Industrialisers?', in H.J. Chang and R. Rowthorn (eds) *The Role of the State in Economic Change* (Oxford: Clarendon Press).

Wahl, A. (2010) 'How New Social Alliances Changed Politics in Norway', in A. Bieler and I. Lindberg (eds) *Global Restructuring, Labour and the Challenges for Transnational Solidarity* (London, Routledge).

Weiss, L. (1998) *The Myth of the Powerless State: Governing the Economy in a Global Age* (Cambridge: Polity Press).

Woolfson, C., Foster, J. and Beck, M. (1997) *Paying for the Piper: Capital and Labour in Britain's Offshore Oil Industry* (London: Mansell).

10
A Country Without a State? Governmentality, Knowledge and Labour in Nigeria

Femi Folorunso, Philippa Hall and Owen Logan

It has been suggested that Nigeria's infamously corrupt state structure is so weak that it could become 'a country without a state'.[1] The fact that this issue can be considered in all seriousness should call for more cautious consideration of contemporary discourses of the state, how they are arrived at and where they lead us. It is not only African politicians who have been accused of instrumentalising disorder to 'maximise their returns on the state of confusion'.[2] It has also been argued that unfettered access to Africa's resources depends upon notions of state failure; and a discourse of 'saving Africa' has become the dignifying rhetoric of a twenty-first-century scramble for the continent's resources, led by the United States and China.[3]

In this scenario resource wealth that could otherwise be used to spearhead a renaissance of African development is being carelessly depleted to sustain aggressive consumer capitalism elsewhere. It is widely estimated that the Gulf of Guinea will account for 25 per cent of all crude oil exports to the United States by 2015. This production will be crucial if petroleum is to continue flowing quickly, and therefore relatively cheaply, to US consumers. In 2000 Olusegun Obasanjo (then president of Nigeria) stressed the need to keep production levels high at the Organisation of the Petroleum Exporting Countries (OPEC) Heads of State Summit in Caracas, when Saudi Arabia unilaterally pledged to increase production.[4] Indeed, the pace of production appears to be determined less by the OPEC cartel than by the political might of key consumer nations and their allies. In 2009 OPEC secretary-general Abdalla el-Badri was reported as saying that the time was not right for a reduction in output, because '[w]e see people who are out of work, we see people in tents in the most rich countries'.[5]

Many Nigerians will feel that this is an unusually generous attitude when the conditions of poverty are of a much greater magnitude in African producing countries. And some will warn that the invasion of Iraq was partly intended as a lesson that the United States will not tolerate erosion of its economic hegemony. Apparently regardless of geopolitical threats, militants in the Niger Delta succeeded in significantly reducing Nigeria's official oil production. Therefore, under the imperative of putting an end to 'oil bunkering' (illegal siphoning) and getting production back to normal, the Nigerian government negotiated amnesty settlements for repentant militants, some of whom were already on surprisingly good terms with the authorities. As for the 'rich countries', public opinion in them might be fairly evenly divided and would certainly not wholly concur with the idea that a rise in oil prices would be a bad thing after the disappointment of the Copenhagen Summit on Climate Change in 2009. Increasingly, what is at issue is the slow pace of transition to a more prudent and mixed-energy framework. This situation raises the question of why a country like Nigeria does not institute longer-term depletion policies rather than remortgaging production with exorbitant oil-backed loans? Would conserving finite energy resources and thereby turning the tables on some grasping customers not be that rare thing – something that makes sense both commercially and environmentally? And if Nigeria followed such a course, would the consequent increase in the price of oil help ordinary Nigerians? What we address in this chapter is the underlying social and political composition of the state, upon which all such questions depend.

Angola (a key oil supplier to China) and Nigeria are presently highly ranked as fast-growing economies, but their poverty indicators are testaments to the abject failure of neoliberal 'trickle-down' economics. To pro-labour demonstrators the conspicuous consumption in a planned city like Abuja (the federal capital of Nigeria since 1991) signals the corruption and greed of a ruling class intent on building a world for themselves. Indeed the city provides ample evidence of sovereign resource wealth being exploited in a rapacious and wasteful manner instead of being used as a strategic component of a broad-based development agenda. Nevertheless, Abuja is also a celebration of modern statehood, and its creation had support from the different wings of Nigerian politics. Official accounts of a 'death economy' in the oil producing Niger Delta,[6] the obscure political commerce of armed militancy there (only partly exposed by the amnesty process mentioned above), as well as the continual gas flaring conducted illegally by multinational oil companies, may all be taken as signs that an effective economic and environmental 'apartheid' is being managed by the state. As the regional analyst Ricardo Soares de Oliveira observes, 'the lingering benefits of statehood are privatised while its drawbacks and failures are "public", to be shouldered by the masses'.[7]

From the above perspective, private success and primitive accumulation appear intertwined with state failure – the latter provides better opportunities for the former. Moreover, de Oliveira (2007) regards Nigeria, thanks to the cushioning effects of oil revenues, as 'a successful failed state', on a continent where more catastrophic colonial legacies of nation building are to be encountered. More generally, a paradoxical aspect of crisis-ridden states is the way in which a cosmopolitan 'development set' thrives on them. Their lifestyle and influence has been the target of radical journalists, following Graham Hancock's lead in his 1989 book *The Lords of Poverty*. In short, there are private fortunes to be made and fast-track upwardly mobile careers to be had from the apparent incapacity of the state. However, one cannot claim that this is a peculiarly African situation. Neoliberalism places a general emphasis on think tanks, consultancies and a plethora of NGOs, which all amount to a development technocracy. Recent academic studies posit this as a highly ambiguous global phenomenon of historical proportions.[8]

Notwithstanding its chaotic character and without eschewing critiques of its mythic ideological content, we should remember that Nigeria is legally embodied as a state. So to answer straightforwardly the question borrowed for the title of this chapter: without doubt Nigeria remains a state; and if this were to disappear then, like Czechoslovakia or Yugoslavia, so would the country.

The notion that a country could gradually become totally denuded of its state and continue to exist ignores a distinction, made by Pierre Bourdieu, between the left and right hands of the state.[9] The issue for us is how an ideologically one-dimensional view of the state eclipses meaningful political discussion of human development and well-being. For example, not only are serious expectations of the state in the provision of education, health, welfare and public goods superseded, there is also a virtual silence about the role of taxation in articulating relations between citizen and state. Indeed, these primary matters often seem to be obscured by the uses or abuses of resource revenue. So in this chapter, recalling Bourdieu's analysis of governance, we seek to unravel the perpetuating structures and discourses of the 'successful failed state'. We take this as a useful term in so far as it suggests the exhaustion of failed-state discourse. This is evident from the relative ease with which Noam Chomsky redirected this discourse towards the United States. In his polemic, Chomsky (2006) regards the United States as the greatest failed state of all.

While the different sides in the conflict over the exploitation of Nigeria's oil resources hold contradictory views of what is wrong with Nigeria (either caught between 'big oil and big government' or hidebound by a reluctance to embrace modernity via international comparative advantage) there is now an increasingly common tendency to portray Nigeria's failures as symptoms of a postcolonial variation of the resource curse. This tendency has moved public discussion further away from academic/political debates which continued to rage from the 1970s to the 1990s about the social fabric of African states and the development of class politics *through* these states.[10] Our emphasis here is informed by the political economy of those decades, which showed that the emergence of an African ruling class (defined in Marxist terms by ownership of the means of production) was contingent on its subservience to the requirements of international capital. On this premise, class relations have a necessary fluidity, which might not be captured if one were to speak of class politics *within* Nigeria. Nor do we imply that a small native ruling class is necessarily unified on its home turf, which remains an ideological patchwork stitched together by the imperial imagination. What is much more striking is the willingness of this ruling class to collude with foreign interests. But in place of these perennial issues, resource politics often presents a simpler set of problems, to which technocratic thought will advance remedies which typically fail to embrace the true scope of the issues they purport to address. Tagged as a 'petro-state', Nigeria has been vulnerable to this sort of reductionism. Within the space we have here, the following three sections reopen the terms of discussion, portraying the interwoven politics of governmentality, knowledge and labour respectively.

THE ROOTS OF GOVERNMENTALITY IN NIGERIA

From a theoretical point of view governmentality asks us to cut off the king's head and examine how a 'headless body often behaves as if it indeed had a head'.[11] This is certainly an approach well suited to the life of a postcolonial nation. The continuation of uneven development within independent Nigeria poses a challenge to rational-choice theories of the state.[12] When applied to developing countries, these theories generally assume the existence of a national elite capable of transcending divisions to create consensus on development. Predictions made about Nigeria before independence also call into question the mores of resource-curse discourse, which portray Nigeria as afflicted by oil rather than by the reservoirs of its political history.

In a book written in 1946, the same year that marked the beginning of the Nigerian state, albeit under colonial rule, Obafemi Awolowo, one of the nation's independence leaders warned:

> There is a popular illusion among educated young Nigerians about self-government. They believe that it is like the 'Kingdom of God and His righteousness' which, once attained, brings unmixed blessing. They, therefore, seek it as the first objective. It is a clever way of evading the immediate problems which confront the country.[13]

As many passages in *Path to Nigerian Freedom* reveal, Awolowo saw self-government as nothing more than a preliminary stage of national development. Self-government would become an expression of sovereignty only if it was able to escape atavistic tendencies by paving the way for a 'thoroughgoing rationalisation of social life'.[14] This enlightenment project was no small preoccupation in a country 'the size of France, Belgium, and the United Kingdom put together' and whose ethnic faultlines were as distinct as those 'between Germans, English, Russians and Turks, for instance'.[15] The hubris of this imperial agglomeration was the basis of his oft-quoted statement that Nigeria was not a nation, but merely 'a geographical expression'[16] – articulated at the behest of the British for the purposes of colonial exploitation and self-aggrandisement.

Awolowo's cautionary book was in preparation when the Richards Constitution (1946–51), which created the first 'Nigerian' administration involving Nigerians, was being crafted. The constitution was colonialism's first attempt to impose on the Nigerian soil a synthetic political uniformity to further administrative and commercial efficiencies. Before then, the country was governed disparately as autonomous protectorates, provinces, colonies and from 1939 as three distinct regions. In legal terms, the Richards constitution collapsed two separate colonial administrative units – the north and the south of Nigeria – into one. At its most formal, it fused two contrasting and soon to be competing social formations, with different political cultures and general outlooks. British colonialism treated the north and the south differently, upholding feudal prestige and religious authority in the north, including toleration of slavery, whilst reshaping the whole basis of traditional governance in the south. This disparity could only lead to a misplaced sense of cultural superiority among the northern elite, as well as a terrible foreboding about its relationship with the polities in the south.[17] In 1966, nearly 20 years after his first warning about the dangers of glossing over the critical challenge of state formation, Awolowo remarked warily that 'the continuance of feudalism in certain parts of the Federation and the real threat of its spread to the other parts'[18] was a key factor in the collapse of the first post-independence republic.

How then is the Nigerian state to be understood against backgrounds of imperial and anti-colonial antinomies? We posit two answers. The first is that one needs to go beyond economism, which, in the words of Nicos Poulantzas, 'considers that other levels of social reality, including the State, are simple epiphenomena reducible to the economic "base"'.[19] The second is to look at the structure of politics and how effective or otherwise this is for responding to issues of national sovereignty, citizenship and development. We argue that as it is presently constituted, politics in Nigeria is driven by the need to contain imperial and anti-colonial antinomies. We further contend that the state is the author of this strategy of containment, which to all intents and purposes amounts to the ethnicisation of the right and left hands of the Nigerian state.

Origins of the Left and Right Hands of the State

The right hand of the state is where the ultimate power of physical coercion resides. This is the military and the network of intelligence, sometimes but not always including the police. The left hand of the state is represented in those areas where a measure of technical and/or professional education is required to operate effectively and analytically. This will include vital areas such as bureaucracy, the judiciary, and the administrative and professional cadres of the broad public service. This is the arm which, through its work output and knowledge, builds and sustains civil society. The university, which we come to later in this chapter, is a highly ambiguous sphere, not quite part of either setup, because in theory, and hopefully in practice, it is expected to retain an autonomy from which it can function as producer of objective knowledge. By the late nineteenth century, an emergent bourgeoisie in the littoral south of Nigeria was displacing the 'traditional elite' and successfully incorporating itself into the imperial economy and colonial bureaucracy.[20] As beneficiaries of mostly missionary-led education, this bourgeoisie was subjectively committed to the ideal of modernity attained through Western education. It also construed an anti-colonial struggle as a battle for the acceleration of modernity.[21] In several ways, this bourgeoisie were the nucleus of what was to become the left hand of the Nigerian state, through their early occupation of positions in the colonial bureaucracy and also through the independent professional practices they were able to establish.[22]

Lord Lugard noted that this group were 'chiefly to be found in West Africa' – an interesting observation given the origins of independence movements in sub-Saharan Africa. For all their prestige, however, this bourgeoisie occupied a liminal position in the unfolding ideology of the state. In relative terms, they were looked upon favourably in the hinterlands; moreover in the eyes of the rural poor they were seen as 'protectors' from the excesses of colonial administration. However, for the colonial establishment, they were 'Europeanised Africans' who 'represented no tribe or community'.[23]

In comparison with the south, elite formation in the north was not so much circumscribed as controlled by the Sokoto Caliphate, which ruled the whole of modern northern Nigeria, apart from Borno and the 'Middle Belt', from 1879 until the British conquest of 1903. The Caliphate was an organised state and, by all accounts, a deeply established feudal society.[24] By this we mean 'a whole social order whose principal feature was the domination of the rest of society, mainly peasants, by a military, landowning aristocracy'.[25] The later incorporation of feudal values into the formation of Nigerian sovereignty was also to be the nucleus of the right hand of the Nigerian state. It is worth stressing that the right hand of the state, in general terms, is not always dominated by feudal values. Republican virtues are more the norm.

Unsurprisingly, the conquering British incorporated the feudal Caliphate state machinery into the administrative system they introduced.[26] Thus the defeated feudal order retained power under colonialism, but with a new, modern aura. The *quid pro quo* in this transaction was that the feudal establishment continued to direct social formation. The result was that many of the major social changes taking place in the south were kept at bay in the north.[27] In 1950, for example, there was not a single secondary school in Kano, which was the most populous city in northern Nigeria. In the whole of the northern region, there was not 'a singled trained medical doctor, a lawyer or even a university graduate in any field' who was of northern origin.[28] If the post-independence choice was between a middleman (comprador) and a bourgeois–nationalist state, the reality of the northern situation was that the former was the only option.

Federal Character

At the beginning of its incursions into governance, the Nigerian military had become a distinct national elite. However, the coups of January and July 1966 exploded the latent asymmetrical relationship between the right and left hands of the state into a full national crisis, reflecting the ethnic disparities described above. Military coups after July 1966 amounted to private struggles among the northern elite, who dominate the country's military, over the instruments of the whole state.[29]

In policy terms, nothing encapsulates the confusion and aberration of military rule better than the constitutional principle of 'federal character' introduced by the military regime of 1975–79. Taking the form of affirmative action, the ostensible aim of this policy was to spread the geographical basis of representation and participation in the state and its statutory institutions. In practice, however, federal character has been a technocratic strategy to displace natural political conflicts,[30] and it goes so far as to prescribe the internal structuring of political parties.[31]

Three observations about federal character illustrate its ongoing centrality to the asymmetrical operations of the right and left hands of the state. First, federal character was institutionalised by the same military regime that normalised the dependency of regional states on the centre – a relationship made more desirable by an abundance of oil revenue in central government coffers. Second, federal character, rather like its manifestation in the structuring of party politics, also interfered with entrepreneurial competition and helped to undermine the position of the pre-independence bourgeoisie.[32] Third, the hierarchy of nearly all the military regimes that pursued federal character was, ironically, dominated by northerners.

Pre-independence southern leaders did not see the military as a necessary component of national development. This was informed by their social-democratic priorities.[33] Unfortunately, this meant that hegemony over the military was largely open to the influences of northern feudal power. In many ways, the power of the right hand of the state, fundamental to the primal articulation of sovereignty exercised against the external world, was instead internalised and turned against the left hand of the Nigerian state. All that remained for the left hand of the state to do in this context was to follow orders. Properly understood, this means that Nigeria's political development in industrial, fiscal, labour, immigration, education and social policy continues to be dominated by feudal attitudes. Consequently, at nearly every level of society, social relations are conceived of as a series of pyramid structures.

THE UNIVERSITIES

The university is an important arena of analysis in the understanding of the Nigerian state. As we suggested earlier, higher education represents, theoretically at least, an arena of autonomy. Objective knowledge produced in this arena is of value to both the left and right hands of the state. The distinctive socio-economics of Nigeria's oil economy and the history of ethnicity and class make the expansion of higher education in postcolonial Nigeria a complex manoeuvre. Until 1975, Nigerian universities had academic freedom, democratic governance and considerable research standing. Under the Murtala/Obasanjo regime (1975–79) this situation changed when the federal government centralised the political control of universities by forming the National Universities Commission (NUC) and established the Joint Admission and Matriculation Board (JAMB). From this period the appointment of vice chancellors became more politicised by the direct intervention of the federal government. Subsequent corruption under military and civilian regimes, Structural Adjustment Programme (SAP) funding cuts, crumbling infrastructure, staff and student strikes, all contributed to the further dismantling of a highly regarded system; but 1975 remains the critical turning point for university autonomy in Nigeria. The breakdown in the secular civic culture of the university can be gleaned from the emergence of religious fundamentalism, whose intimidation inhibited intellectual activity, and also the violent student cults that effectively 'militarised' campuses.[34]

A point of repeated and unresolved confrontation between the Academic Staff Union of Universities (ASUU) and the federal government is the academics' claim that the government has regarded public universities more for their political uses than for their role in a developmental state. The main government solution to the crisis of higher education has, until recently, been the licensing of private universities. However, in 2010, it was announced that six new federal universities were to be built in the six 'geopolitical zones'.[35] This term reflects the underlying propensity of the Nigerian state to promote 'packaged decisions which contain something for each influential group'.[36] Nonetheless the underlying causes of the crisis afflicting the university system remain largely ignored. Added to the critiques from academics about the role of higher education in development is the threat to break up collective bargaining through a two-tiered system split between federal and state public universities. Private universities already prohibit trade unionism on their campuses.

The government's emphasis on expanding higher education through a mixture of private and federal universities threatens to price state-owned universities out of higher education provision.[37] Since private universities were first licensed by the National University Commission (NUC) in 1999, the number of institutions has grown rapidly.[38] There are currently 41 private universities out of a total of 92, and their 'entrepreneurial ethos' now also pervades public universities in general. Professor Julius Okojie, executive secretary of the NUC, maintains that, despite the emergence of different types of university and different funding sources, national standards are being sustained and all universities share a 'level playing field' of regulation.[39] However, Okojie's claims meet with a good deal of criticism from academic staff and from some vice principals.

The NUC aims to foster an 'enabling environment' for investors in universities, by providing the infrastructure and general services, such as information and communications technology, that will attract the higher fees from students and research income from business now increasingly sought by universities.[40] However, by outlawing union activities, private universities are also a disabling environment in which academic freedom and freedom of association are curtailed. Indeed, Okojie regards ASUU as an aberration in the internal governance of universities; he thinks academic staff issues should be negotiated through a professional association, and not through what he refers to as 'a mainstream labour union'.[41] This attitude implies an official disavowal of the Unesco principles of freedom of association and it means that the playing field of regulation is anything but level.

Nigeria's current higher education policy is directed, like that of many other nations, towards creating an 'enabling environment' for the marketisation of teaching and research. Envisaged on this commercialised horizon are potential financial gains through the development of commercially valuable patents[42] and increased direct revenue to universities through higher student fees. However, running against the grain of commercialisation is the residual sensibility in academia that national development may not be synonymous with what are seen as the 'one size fits all' policies of International Financial Institutions.

The NUC's 'enabling environment' for income generation is consistent with World Bank projects, such as 'Step Two', the assisted programme to develop science and technology in senior secondary and tertiary education.[43] This programme seeks to build an entrepreneurial curriculum geared towards the creation of patents and 'spin-off' businesses. The new entrepreneurial curriculum exemplifies an employer-led approach that redefines both the critical terms of research and teaching to respond more directly to business requirements and the needs of employers as 'the end users of graduates'.[44] University business objectives and potential partnerships with international companies are supposedly enhanced by the World Bank scheme. However, working conditions for staff and new graduates are subject to the disciplining of academic labour, which is a necessary part of the business-led ethos of the World Bank.[45]

In addition to the values and funding priorities of the World Bank programme, labour discipline in the university is reinforced by the increasing precarity of employment. The rolling back of the state, which began under structural adjustment policies in the 1980s, has resulted in a shortage of graduate jobs. This was quantified in a 2004 survey which found that just 10 per cent of the 100,000 students graduating each year worked in a 'graduate post', while 90 per cent had to 'create jobs for themselves' as entrepreneurs, or take deskilled work as 'adaptable' employees in jobs unrelated to their qualifications.[46] Nevertheless, as critical thought is diminished in academia, it would appear that graduates are more easily reconciled to getting by in self-employment, which means that a devalued graduate workforce now adds to an already highly entrepreneurial economy. Against the charge that Nigeria already has too many entrepreneurs, which in itself reflects underdevelopment,[47] the policy logic of the knowledge economy upheld by the World Bank and implemented by the NUC implies the upgrading and modernisation of an entrepreneurial culture. The NUCs adaptation to the logic of entrepreneurial knowledge economy, alongside Nigeria's wholesale neglect of more fundamental educational needs, from primary school upwards, suggests a misplaced instrumentalisation of the intellect.

Obstacles to the Entrepreneurial Knowledge Economy

Nigeria's policy of creating an 'enabling environment' in which a 'knowledge economy' might develop faces three main obstacles. These are endemic corruption, the limits of investment capital and, perhaps most fatally of all, the lack of worldliness of private universities set up as gated communities. These obstacles are so fundamental as to suggest that the policies geared towards a knowledge economy in Nigeria are misconceived in the first place.

First, the building of six new federal universities presents typical opportunities for the corrupt distribution of government contracts, many of which may never be fulfilled. The patrimonialism associated with the distribution of oil-based revenues is already evident in the decision to locate one of the new federal campuses in President Goodluck Jonathan's village in Bayelsa state. This is surely a sign of politicisation of public enterprise and the endemic corruption that goes along with this process.[48]

However, the real shortage of investment capital, which is the second obstacle for Nigeria's 'knowledge economy', is a sign of a lack of realism on the part of Nigeria's ruling elite. Despite the founding of private universities by wealthy members of the political class, including the former president, Olusegun Obasanjo (Bells University of Technology), his deputy, Atiku Abubakar (American University in Nigeria), and the former military ruler Ibrahim Babangida (Ibrahim Badamasi Babangida University), there is still a shortage of investment capital for university expansion.[49] The plan at Bells University to attract 95 per cent of funding from external sources, and the lack of any external investment to date,[50] suggests that the shortage of international investment capital presents a serious impediment to the growth of a knowledge economy.[51]

The recent interest of private investors in universities, since the return of elected government in 1999, is often seen to be driven by the desire to convert illegitimate wealth into legitimate political and social capital. Such precarious capital investment can only sustain short-termism in research. Significant scientific and social research requires more secure, long-term sources of funding. However, regardless of the limits of internal investment, whatever entrepreneurially driven venture capital Nigerian institutions can source is subject to the same impetus that propels 'capital flight'. Therefore, Nigeria has no way to guarantee a return on the state's share of investment in the knowledge economy.

The third obstacle to the success of knowledge economy projects is the limited intellectual and social scope of the private universities, which in many respects are gated communities. The privileging of religious affiliation in private faith universities, the outlawing of normal political participation on private campuses, and the notion of 'guided freedom'[52] in place of academic freedom, means that for at least one potential NGO employer these universities are 'producing morons and training robots'.[53] There is a real sense that private universities are not concerned with matters of national development. However, those private universities that are affiliated to overseas institutions, like the American University Nigeria, in Yola, do at least sustain a broad university curriculum. As we now go on to examine, the contradictory impulses in the development of the university system point to an underlying contest between the values informing a comprador state, and those of a bourgeois–nationalist one.

KNOWLEDGE AND LABOUR

It has been argued in some academic circles that the future of African development lies in transition from conventional democracy to technocracy, where 'the role of the expert will be recognised and appreciated'.[54] This idea takes after the systems theory in the United States, which evolved into a theory of crisis management, the operations of which have been called 'technocorporatism' (Fischer 1990). Centred on a politics of expertise, this 'apolitical politics' appears to be a mobile and repeatable strategy that allows for states to be rolled back at the same time as the mechanisms of neoliberal governmentality are rolled out.[55] Although neoliberal economic doctrines may be under more suspicion after a major financial collapse, the architecture of neoliberal governmentality, which includes a plethora of NGOs (non-governmental organisations), GONGOs (government organised non-governmental organisations) and BONGOs (bank organised non-governmental organisations), looks more ideologically resilient.[56]

Technocorporatism poses key dilemmas for the Nigerian labour movement. Among these, the uncertainty about forms of organisation, the role of leadership and the supposed invulnerability of the ruling class stand out. These dilemmas can be captured from three moments during a protest against fuel price deregulation in Abuja on 29 October 2009. The protest was organised by the

Labour Civil Society Coalition (LASCO), the Nigeria Labour Congress (NLC) and the Trade Union Congress (TUC) of Nigeria.[57]

Crammed into the back of a taxi on the way to the march, Owei Lakemfa, an NLC official, spoke critically about NGOs and suggested lightly that United Action for Democracy (UAD), part of LASCO, was just another NGO. Sitting next to him the UAD leader, Abiodun Aremu, looked shocked. He replied 'How can I be in an NGO? I've always been against them!' The moment ended in shrugs and uncertain smiles. Later, as the march went on its way to the National Assembly Complex, moving along Abuja's wide avenues and passing state buildings and company offices, demonstrators chanted *ole! ole! ole!* (thieves! thieves! thieves!) at a largely invisible opposition. If there was an imaginary dock, the accused parties were not in it and security guards and police looked on only at the accusers. Then, as the demonstration neared the House of Representatives, some marchers spotted a senator's limousine stuck in a traffic jam and broke away to surround the vehicle, chanting and shouting questions at the politician who remained invisible behind tinted glass. A moment of peaceful but uncomfortably real confrontation ended quickly when stewards reined in the stray protestors. Once the rally convened in front of the House of Representatives the vocabulary of the protest shifted as leaders made their final speeches, two of the speakers addressing themselves to 'honourable members of the House of Representatives'. From the crowd, cries of derision rose against this unwarranted deference in the face of a discredited political elite. The whole event was brought to an end with an attempt to sing the national anthem. The crowd booed instead.

Labour Power and Rights

How are these snapshot moments mentioned above significant in the story of the Nigerian labour movement? The first is suggestive of the confusion over what constitutes an NGO, and particularly the character of pro-labour civil society organisations set up in the 1990s. Secondly, the taunts directed at a power elite, out of sight and quite probably beyond earshot, point to the difficulty of identifying and targeting the Nigerian ruling class. Thirdly, the sycophancy of labour leaders fits with the resigned perspective of those African analysts, such as Chabal and Daloz (1999), who suppose that class is still not a meaningful enough social identity in the patrimonial context of a country like Nigeria.[58]

Needless to say, the attitude expressed by the mass of demonstrators mentioned above does not fit comfortably with the analysis of a polity entirely given over to neo-feudal relations. Moreover, from the point of view of writers closer to international labour movement issues than Chabal and Daloz, the interesting thing about Nigerian labour history is the extent to which trade unionists have circumvented government manipulations and legal restrictions intended to deliver an ideologically docile workforce into a corporatist system.[59] Indeed, some Nigerian trade unionists have shown great courage in this respect. On further examination, we see that it is not so much corrupt patrimonial tendencies that are disarming the labour movement, but a neoliberal and profoundly technocratic form of governmentality. In Nigerian labour circles this phenomenon, ostensibly intended to strengthen civil society and conquer corruption, is known as NGOism.

To examine the paradox of policies which are intended to strengthen civil society but which weaken the labour movement, we would emphasise the importance of distinguishing the 'right to have rights' from positive liberties and substantive rights.[60] In arguing against a socialist determinism, which effectively robbed workers of their civil rights in so many historic instances, Rhoda Howard (1988) draws some of these distinctions in rights discourse to argue for the importance of labour power in winning and protecting substantive human rights. Moreover, in Howard's eyes independent labour movements form a crucial barrier to the recurrence of bureaucratically founded class systems dressed up in the language of socialism or communism.

Workshops held in Nigeria in 1995 by the Committee for the Defence of Human Rights (CDHR), sponsored by the Friedrich Ebert Foundation, were a watershed in the development of the sort of pro-labour politics envisaged by Howard. However, the analytical discussions that supported a broad civil society agenda also emphasised how the ruling class had succeeded in shielding itself from conventional labour action. In a privatised society, almost devoid of public goods and basic services, where water and electricity are usually sourced from private boreholes and generators, activist intellectuals like Abayomi Ferreira argued persuasively that the neocolonial setting required 'new strategies for the mobilisation of the socially disadvantaged'.[61] Yet, from the perspective of veteran oil workers' leaders like Frank Kokori and Elijah Okougbo, or younger leaders like Peter Esele, it is not the isolation of the ruling class – in essence a gated community – which really counts, but a lack of strategic leadership and the erosion of conventional solidarity between unions.[62]

Until recently the oil workers' unions, NUPENG and PEGASSAN, held the NLC in distrust.[63] Indeed, the criticism coming from oil workers' leaders pointing to the erosion of solidarity ought to be taken seriously. In 1994 Kokori led the unions in an anti-dictatorship pro-democracy strike, for which he was held in jail for four years without trial. NUPENG and PEGASSAN also represent labour's strongest foothold in the private sector, and oil workers' leaders are quite unashamed of the political capital their unions derive from the potential to take control of Nigeria's fundamental means of production. Leaders of these unions are well aware of their ability to cut off Abuja (surely the home territory of the ruling class) from essential supplies and services. Echoing the sentiments of rank and file protestors, Kokori sees no need to ingratiate himself with the political class.[64] Studies of political economy in Africa from the 1980s increasingly detached class analysis from the means of production; and discussions of 'new strategies' amongst Nigerian activists echo this drift away from an analytical emphasis upon labour within the broad political economy of oil and gas.[65]

Here we return to Owei Lakemfa's criticism of NGOs. Lakemfa argues that 'NGOism' is the biggest problem for the Nigerian labour movement, a view informed by his experience as treasurer of CDHR in the early 1990s. The problems of pro-labour civil-society organisations, which set out to avoid becoming part of the NGO plutocracy in Nigeria, are encapsulated by a pivotal struggle over the control of CDHR. Lakemfa points out that graduates emerging from the universities in the 1980s with an understanding of colonialism and neocolonialism increasingly found that by modifying anti-imperialist thinking they could find a relatively comfortable niche working for foreign-funded NGOs. Controversially, in the early 1990s CDHR turned to the National Endowment for Democracy (NED) in the United States for funding. Lakemfa recalls how the CDHR, a voluntary organisation of the Nigerian left, was overtaken by opportunism as a war broke out over control of CDHR's newly found resources. This led to a fragmentation shaped by ethno-national vigilante politics. From the military annulment of the election of 12 June 1993, the Oodua People's Congress (OPC) portrayed Nigeria's historic situation through the lens of Yoruba ethno-nationalism. The CDHR is based in Lagos, the commercial hub of Nigeria and a predominantly Yoruba city. The chaos caused by the contest over CDHR supports the argument that although foreign aid is never enough to solve the problems it aims to address, a little donor money can still do a lot of damage.[66]

It would be easy to show the troubles of CDHR in the 1990s as another example of prebendalism and grievance turned into greed. But a closer look at the faction fighting inside the OPC and the pro-poor aspects of their ideology reveals how ethno-nationalism is also fractured by class. The thorn in the side of the OPC's founder, the medical doctor and businessman Frederik Fasehun, is Gani Adams. In one of his more defensive rebukes, Adams said:

> This Fasehun who is calling me an illiterate went through free education. If I had the chance of free education, you know what I could have been now? I could be a PhD in political science, but I came from very poor family.[67]

While Adams's remarks here recall the education policies of Obafemi Awolowo in the south-west of Nigeria and expose the internal class divisions of OPC today, his sentiments might as well be directed against the character of Nigeria's left-leaning civil society as a whole, dominated as it is by university graduates and professionals of all kinds.

For many years the academic staff union was regarded as the epicentre of labour politics in Nigeria, where the leaders of the labour movement and the left, almost without exception, are the beneficiaries of higher education.[68] If the core of pro-labour politics is not a national bourgeoisie, its expression of the national interest is perhaps the closest thing Nigeria has to one. However, this elite is poorly positioned to lead a labour movement. For example, the fragility of the academic staff union and their actions is a point of difference within the wider labour movement. Oil workers' leaders see a lack of strategy and meaningful solidarity in the new civil-society strategies coming from the left-wing intelligentsia. This shift towards a broad civil-society coalition echoes Rhoda Howard's proposed linkage between labour power and human rights. However, despite their vocabulary, it is clear that pro-labour organisations have not strengthened trade union rights in Nigeria. Rather, LASCO has helped to spread liberal-rights discourses more than it has articulated a politics based on substantive rights, as someone following Howard's arguments would have hoped. This is unfortunate, and it reflects labour's vulnerability to NGOism and bourgeois technocratic politics more generally. But the theoretical retreat from class analysis, whereby the ruling class came to be seen as beyond the reach of workers' power, is a more surprising turn. As the left moved further away from analysis related to the means of production, it left a gap which, rather predictably, was filled by disenfranchised youths' direct assaults on the oil business in Niger Delta. This opened up a lucrative but murky political field.[69]

CONCLUSION

David Lewis (2010) has argued that NGOs and associated development discourses create the sense of 'a perpetual present' which strengthens weak ideas.[70] The concept of the 'failed state' should be seen as one of these ahistorical ideas, not least because it sets off misleading discussions in international relations.

In 2009 a former US ambassador to Nigeria, Princeton N. Lyman, attempted to call the country's elites to account for their failure to translate a national imagination into a political reality. In Lyman's view the Nigerian nation state was in danger of becoming irrelevant to US energy interests, as oil and gas from countries such as Brazil and Angola could provide more stable sources of energy. In this scenario, 'Nigeria's greatest strategic importance would be that it can fail'.[71] Playing producing nations against one another may give some comfort to US listeners, but the potential impact of a Nigerian collapse also poses the grave risks amply acknowledged by Lyman. According to him, even more important than Nigeria's corruption is the inability of its elite to articulate the national interest.

As we have shown, in Nigeria, the national interest is fractured by a class struggle over the meaning of Nigerian sovereignty. Moreover, it is impossible to address these faultlines without discussing the relationship between capitalism – particularly of the comprador variety – and feudalism. This is a matter consistently avoided by diplomats and NGOs, who are dependent on the good will of ruling elites. One of the most problematic aspects of US leadership in world affairs is its own exceptional history in this respect. As Hans Gerth and C. Wright Mills noted in their analysis of 'master trends', published in 1953, there was no feudal age in the United States, and therefore the economic ascendancy of the middle classes was largely uncompromised.[72] It was not until the Great Depression, and then only quite briefly, that the American middle classes saw merit in class consciousness of any kind.

Less clear, at least in the account given by Gerth and Mills, are the ways in which United States imperialism is coloured by an exceptional history that undoubtedly gave rise to a certain national egoism. This means, for example, that someone like Lyman compares Nigeria's entrepreneurial and political capacities unfavourably to those of China. It should be remembered that China freed itself from feudalism in the most painful of ways and that labour power is almost nullified by official communist policies now turned to providing for capitalism. But the expression of Pax Americana follows the logic of Pax Britannica (as is often the case), recasting the feudal ethos as a geopolitical instrument. This does not mean of course that feudalism would otherwise stagnate. Rather, feudal relations are rearticulated by capital, as can be seen in the 'guided freedom' on private university campuses, or in the plethora of NGOs which the labour movement regards as dignifying plutocracy. Perhaps even more problematic, since it also permeates unions and pro-labour civil-society organisations, is the neo-feudal ethos, in which social relations are conceived much more widely as a series of pyramid structures.

NOTES

1. See Bach 2006.
2. See Chabal and Daloz 1999, p.xviii.
3. See Lee 2006, pp.303–30.
4. Reported in the *New York Times*, 29 September 2000, 'THE MARKETS: COMMODITIES; OPEC's Unity Is Undercut by the Saudis' by Larry Rother, www.nytimes.com/2000/09/29/business/the-markets-commodities-opec-s-unity-is-undercut-by-the-saudis.html?pagewanted=1, accessed January 2010.
5. Reported by Associated Press (15 March 2009), at www.msnbc.msn.com/id/29706228/, accessed January 2010. Saudi Arabia, Venezuela and Nigeria are the top three OPEC suppliers to the United States. Venezuela, under the leadership of Hugo Chávez, has been the maverick producer, selling oil at a discount to cement political alliances, especially in Latin America.
6. In June 2002, a report by the Trade and Community Sub-committee of Nigeria's Federal House Petroleum Resources Committee stated that communities in the Delta were 'exploited, misused, abused, polluted, underdeveloped, and almost completely dead; like a cherry fruit sucked and discarded'. The phrase 'a death economy' is used to sum this up in Turner and Brownhill 2004, p.70.
7. De Oliveira 2007, p.52.
8. Terje Tvedt argues that the impact of NGOs on state–society relationships is 'a political innovation of world historical dimensions' which ought to be examined dispassionately. As Paul Opoku-Mensah points out in the same volume, 'a lack of realism and self reflexivity' bedevils the field of NGO research and undermines its legitimacy. See Opoku-Mensah, Lewis and Tvedt 2007, pp.9–55.
9. See Bourdieu 1998.
10. We concur here with writers such as Joshua B. Forrest, who argues that 'collusion between Western Capital and the African state is not a one-way relationship'. Moreover, the state is an 'institutional composite of elites who hold national political power in order to advance their self-defined organisational, political and economic interests'. See Forrest 2004, p.97.
11. See Dean 1994, p.156.

12. An example of the problem here is the contest between the nascent technocracy and the comprador class, extensively discussed by Terisa Turner. See Nore and Turner 1980, pp.199–223.
13. Awolowo 1947, p.30.
14. Bottomore 1964, p.105.
15. Awolowo 1947, p.48.
16. This statement is often used by critics of Awolowo to label him a Yoruba nationalist, which is to say that he wanted to preserve Yoruba hegemony. However, Awolowo's critical position on feudalism shows that this would be to underestimate his commitment to true Nigerian independence.
17. Although excluded from the north of Nigeria, thanks to colonial agreements, an important consideration here is the missionary view at the time, that Christianity would unify Africans. See 'Political Activity in British West Africa, 1900–1940', in Ajayi and Crowder 1974, pp.575–6. With a comparable religious fervour, the conference of northern chiefs in 1942 responded to a letter from the West African Students' Union in London in which the authors pleaded for North-South co-operation on development and anti-colonial struggle: 'Holding this country together is not possible except by means of the religion of the Prophet ... If they want political unity let them follow our religion.' See Awolowo 1947, p.51.
18. Awolowo 1966, p.17.
19. See 'The Problem of the Capitalist State', in Blackburn 1972, p.239.
20. For a good description of this process, see Brandler 1993.
21. See J.F.A. Ajayi, and M. Crowder, 'West Africa 1919–1939: The Colonial Situation', in Ajayi and Crowder 1974, pp 514–41; and O. Aluko, 'Politics of Decolonisation in British West Africa, 1945–1960', ibid., pp.622–63.
22. This is well illustrated by the history of Herbert Macaulay, an engineer and town planner, former colonial civil servant who founded the first political party in Nigeria, NNDP, in 1923.
23. See Lugard 1923, p.80.
24. See R. Adeleye, 'The Sokoto Caliphate in the Nineteenth Century', in Ajayi and Crowder 1974, pp.57–92.
25. See Hilton 1976.
26. The maintenance of law and order was effectively conceded to the feudal authorities. The emirs and chiefs were allowed to run the local (native authority) police, the local (Alkali) courts and the local prisons. These three instruments of oppression were bizarrely retained even after independence in 1960 and were only removed after the first military coup of January 1966. See Abba 2000, p.x.
27. This is illustrated by the history of Northern Elements Progressive Union, NEPU, whose impact as a radical political party was felt more seriously in the north, where its leaders were routinely harassed and jailed by officials using the instruments of native administration, which were controlled by the emirs and village chiefs. Ibid.
28. Ibid., p.xi.
29. Frynas 2000, p.42.
30. See Turner 1980.
31. See Bach 2006, pp.63–96.
32. See Turner 1980.
33. From authors' interview with Chief Anthony Enahoro, 1998.
34. Asobie 1999, p.32.

35. Under President Abacha's regime (1993–98), Nigeria was divided into six geopolitical zones. The zones have now become commonly used terms to describe the different areas of Nigeria. The six zones are; South-West, South-East, South-South, North-West, North-East and North-Central.
36. From Turner 1980, p.213.
37. This is tied to the political economy of the Nigerian federal system, in which states are almost totally dependent on the federal revenue.
38. Hall 2010, p.49.
39. From authors' interview with Professor Julius Okojie, CEO of National Universities Commission, Abuja, 2009.
40. Ibid.
41. Ibid.
42. Authors' interview with Dr Akim Adeoye, Director of Academic Planning, Bells University of Technology, Ota State, 2009.
43. Authors' interview with officials from the World Bank Step Two Assisted Programme, Abuja, 2009.
44. Ibid.
45. World Bank projects in Nigeria are outlined at http://web.worldbank.org/WBSITE/EXTERNAL/COUNTRIES/AFRICAEXT/NIGERIAEXTN/0,,menuP K:368902~pagePK:141159~piPK:141110~theSitePK:368896,00.html, accessed January 2011.
46. Authors' interview with Professor Chinedu Mafiana, National Universities Commission, Abuja, 2009.
47. Global Entrepreneurship Monitor, 'Danish National Executive Report – 2000', www.ebst.dk/publikationer/rapporter/gem/kap5.html, accessed November 2010.
48. Ifedayo Adebayo, 'Jonathan's Village Gets Federal Varsity', 25 November 2010, accessed December 2009, Nigeriavillagesquare.com/forum/main-square/59112-jonathan-s-village-gets-federal-varsity.html, accessed December 2009.
49. Bells University is part of the Bells Educational Services, Obasanjo Holdings.
50. Authors' interview with Dr Akim Adeoye, director of academic planning, Bells University of Technology, Ota State, 2009.
51. The income of profitable private universities in the United States depends upon various avenues of public funding, and is also sustained by the very different position of the US in the world economy. Even in other advanced countries, the knowledge economy is vulnerable to the financialisation of public goods. For example, in 2010 Apollo Group, the owners of BBP University College in the United Kingdom, withdrew £106m of their investment in the university in response to market pressures.
52. From authors' interviews with Professor Isaac Adeyemi, vice chancellor of Bells University of Technology, Ota State, 2009.
53. From authors' interview with Olasupo Ojo, president of Committee for the Defence of Human Rights (CDHR), Lagos, 2009.
54. See Owakah and Aswani 2009, pp.87–99.
55. See Ferguson and Gupta 2002, pp.981–1002.
56. Aradhana Sharma offers the vivid example of a network of Indian GONGOs devoted to women's empowerment which fired its women workers who were struggling for unionisation. See Sharma 2006.

57. Top of the agenda was the threatened deregulation of fuel prices; but the rally was also demanding a review of the minimum wage and full implementation of the Justice Uwais Electoral Reform Committee report.
58. From a Weberian standpoint in political analysis, Chabal and Daloz see the African state as 'not just weak but essentially vacuous'. In the Nigerian context we would agree with these authors that the state is not sufficiently autonomous from the particularities of society. However, as we have demonstrated here, we disagree with their conclusion that 'it is difficult to establish, other than in ideological terms, whether there are in Africa identifiable social classes with discrete and coherent political ambitions'. See Chabal and Daloz 1999, pp.1–5.
59. See, for example, N. Van Hear, 'Recession Retrenchment and Military Rule: Nigerian Labour in the 1980s', in Southhall 1988, pp.144–59.
60. See Howard 1988.
61. See Ferriera's 'Strategies for Mobilising the Socially Disadvantaged', in Olorode et al. 1997, pp.94–109.
62. From authors' interviews, 2009.
63. From authors' interviews, 2009.
64. From the time before his imprisonment Kokori remembers turning away a presidential jet sent to usher him to negotiations in Abuja. As Kokori sees it, a political oil strike is the closest thing to a national armed struggle. From authors' interviews, 2009.
65. An important example of the Marxian focus on class development in relation to the means of production is Turner 1980.
66. Lakemfa goes further, and argues that donors turn a blind eye to the effects of competition over scarce resources, knowing that many projects are not properly fulfilled and that this flexibility effectively devalues concrete activism and encourages corruption. From authors' interviews, 2009.
67. Quoted in Maier 2002, p.241.
68. The current president of CDHR, Olasupo Ojo, remarks that for many years the Academic Staff Union of Universities (ASUU) was the 'theoretical storehouse' of the Nigerian left. The Babangida regime forced the disaffiliation of ASUU from the NLC, an act widely regarded as an attempt to sever the head from the body of the labour movement. From authors' interviews, 2009.
69. The full range of actors sowing division and competition between communities in the Niger Delta and exploiting a youth rebellion there is still not entirely clear. However, some of these dangers were noted early on in a CDHR publication; see Raji, Ayodele and Akinsola 2000, pp.172–3. What can be seen clearly now is that a political commerce, between militants, local authorities, oil companies and the political elite, has thrived on the basis of reaching the lowest common denominator with each transaction. Important to consider here is the development of 'partnership development' examined by Zalik, A. (2004), pp.401–24.
70. See Lewis 2010.
71. See 'Former US Ambassador Princeton N. Lyman Speaks at Achebe Colloquium', www.youtube.com/watch?v=NqMXoA1jfDs, accessed December 2010.
72. See Gerth and Mills 1953.

REFERENCES

Abba, A. (2000) *The Politics of Principle in Nigeria: The Example of the NEPU* (Zaria: CEDDERT).

Ajayi, J.F.A. and Crowder, M. (1974) *History of West Africa*, vol.2 (London: Longman).

Asobie, A. (1999) 'Military Rule, Militarism and Violence in Nigerian Tertiary Institutions', in J. Ogunye, S. Jegede and E. Akinsola (eds) *Citadels of Violence* (Lagos: Committee for the Defence of Human Rights).

Awolowo, O. (1947) *Path to Nigerian Freedom* (London: Faber and Faber).

——— (1966) *Thoughts on Nigerian Constitution* (Ibadan: Oxford University Press).

Bach, D. (2006) 'Inching Towards a Country Without a State', in C. Clapham, J. Herbst and G. Mills (eds) *Big African States: Angola, DRC, Ethiopia, Nigeria, South Africa, Sudan* (Johannesburg: Witwatersrand University Press).

Blackburn, R. (1972) *Ideology in Social Science* (UK: Fontana/Collins).

Bottomore, T. (1964) *Elites and Society* (Harmondsworth: Penguin Books).

Bourdieu, P. (1998) *Acts of Resistance: Against the New Myths of Our Time* (London: Polity Press).

Brandler, J.L. (1993) *Out of Nigeria* (London and New York: Radcliffe Press).

Chabal, P. and Daloz, J.-P. (1999) *Africa Works: Disorder as Political Instrument* (Indiana and Oxford: International African Institute/James Currey/Indiana University Press).

Chomsky, N. (2006) *Failed States: The Abuse of Power and the Assault on Democracy* (London: Hamish Hamilton).

Dean, M. (1994) *Critical and Effective Histories: Foucault's Methods and Historical Sociology* (London: Routledge).

Ferguson, J. and Gupta, A. (2002) 'Spatializing States: Toward an Ethnography of Neoliberal Governmentality', *American Ethnologist*, 29(4).

Fischer, F. (1990) *Technocracy and the Politics of Expertise* (London: Sage).

Forrest, J.B. (2004) 'The Contemporary African State: A "Ruling Class"?', in G. Mohan and T. Zack-Williams (eds) *The Politics of Transition in Africa: State, Democracy and Economic Development* (Trenton N.J. and Asmara, Eritrea: Africa World Press/Oxford: James Currey).

Frynas, J.G. (2000) *Oil in Nigeria* (Hamburg and London: LIT Verlag).

Gerth, H. and Mills, C.W. (1953) *Character and Social Structure: The Psychology of Social Institutions* (New York: Harcourt, Brace and Co.).

Hall, P. (2010) 'Privatisation and the Transformation of Higher Education in Nigeria since 1986: An Analysis of Global Inequalities', in T. Claes and D. Preston (eds) *Frontiers of Higher Education* (Amsterdam: Rodopi).

Hancock, G. (1989) *The Lords of Poverty: The Power, Prestige, and Corruption of the International Aid Business* (New York: Atlantic Monthly Press).

Hilton, R. (1976) 'Introduction', in P. Sweezy, M. Dobb, et al. (eds) *The Transition from Feudalism to Capitalism* (London and New York: Verso).

Howard, R. (1988) 'Third World Trade Unions as Agencies of Human Rights: The Case of Commonwealth Africa', in R. Southall (ed.) *Trade Unions and the New Industrialisation of the Third World* (London: Zed Books).

Lee, M.C. (2006) 'The 21st Century Scramble for Africa', *Journal of Contemporary African Studies*, 24(3).

Lewis, D. (2010) 'The Strength of Weak Ideas? Human Security, Policy History, and Climate Change in Bangladesh', in J.-A. McNeish and J.H. Sande Lie (eds) *Security and Development* (New York and Oxford: Berghahn Books).

Lugard, F. (1923) *The Dual Mandate in British Tropical Africa*, 5th edn (London: Frank Cass).

Maier, K. (2002) *This House Has Fallen: Nigeria in Crisis* (Boulder, Colo.: Westview Press).

Nore, P. and Turner, T. (1980) (eds) *Oil and Class Struggle* (London: Zed Books).

Oliveira, R. de (2007) *Oil Politics and the Gulf of Guinea* (London: Hurst and Co.).

Olorode, T., Raji, W., Ogunye, J. and Jegede, S. (eds) (1997) *Nigeria: Non-Governmental Organisations and Democracy* (Lagos: CDHR).

Opoku-Mensah, P., Lewis, D. and Tvedt, T. (eds) (2007) *Reconceptualising NGOs and Their Roles in Development: NGOs, Civil Society and the International Aid System* (Aalborg: Aalborg University Press).

Owakah, F. and Aswani, R. (2009) 'Technocracy and Democracy: The Challenges to Development in Africa', *Thought and Practice: A Journal of the Philosophical Association of Kenya*, 1(1).

Raji, W., Ayodele, A. and Akinsola, E. (2000) (eds) *Boiling Point: A CDHR Publication on the Crisis in the Oil-Producing Communities* (Lagos: CDHR) .

Sharma, A. (2006) 'Crossbreeding Institutions, Breeding Struggle: Women's Employment, Neoliberal Governmentality, and State (Re)Formation in India' (Middletown, Conn.: Social Sciences Division II Faculty Publications, Wesleyan University).

Turner, T. (1980) 'Nigeria: Imperialism, Oil Technology and the Comprador State', in Nore and Turner 1980.

—— and Brownhill, L.S. (2004) 'Why Women are at War with Chevron: Nigerian Subsistence Struggles Against the International Oil Industry', *Journal of Asian and African Studies*, 39(1–2).

Zalik, A. (2004) 'The Niger Delta: "Petro Violence" and "Partnership Development"' *Review of African Political Economy*, Vol. 31, No. 101 (London: Taylor and Francis).

11
The Race to the Bottom and the Demise of the Landlord: The Struggle over Petroleum Revenues Historically and Comparatively

Anna Zalik

The 2010 British Petroleum blowout in the Gulf of Mexico prompted a flurry of mainstream media attention to the US oil and gas industry. Of note was the extraordinary coverage in the spill's aftermath to crony corruption and regulatory gaps in the US Minerals Management Service. The *New York Times* reported that the Deepwater Horizon rig flew the flag of the Marshall Islands so that its proprietor, Transocean, could avoid paying US taxes.[1]

This move by Transocean, so as to circumvent oil and gas revenue allocation to a national jurisdiction, is not atypical among private operators. While international analysts of energy security have made much of the importance of national oil companies' possession of oil and gas reserves since 9/11 (largely from OPEC states), in many sites actual production is operated and managed – and thus access to information concerning volume and profit is controlled – by private operators. The US Gulf of Mexico shares certain basic fiscal attributes with other major international exporters, in that offshore leases are under national government proprietorship. Accordingly, both rents and a portion of profit are, formally, to be paid to the government. The extent to which this payment is substantive, however, or negated by subsidies, is – as in many oil-producing regions – a topic of controversy. The Transocean example is instructive. Indeed, given the token media and legislative scrutiny such actions by private operators receive in the global North – here the United States, it is unsurprising that global South oil exporters choose to (re)assert territorial ownership over hydrocarbon resources; equally unsurprising is that those resident populations marginalized from corporate profits and negatively affected by extraction would call for greater allocations from industry.

Only a few months before the BP blowout, in February 2010, the US National Petrochemical and Refiners Association (NPRA) had launched a legal suit against the California state government. Their suit protested against the state's recent 'low-carbon fuel standard' (LCFS), one seeking to ban tar sands fuels from the California market.[2] Including both BP and Shell among its membership, the NPRA suit alleged that the LCFS puts 'undue and unconstitutional burdens on interstate commerce'.[3] But concurrently, two popular US retailers, Bed Bath and Beyond, and Whole Foods, announced that they would no longer employ fuel from the Canadian tar sands in their operations. The environmental NGO lobbying the retailers, Forest Ethics, has targeted Fortune 500 companies with ties to the tar sands.[4] Headlined in the *Financial Times* as 'Suppliers of oil sands fuel shunned', this initiative followed the failure at Copenhagen to deliver binding commitments on carbon reductions. At first glance it appeared that consumer retail capital, prompted by Forest Ethics, had reacted negatively to the energy industry and their lobbyists.[5] The *Financial Times* described the retailers' decision as 'underlin[ing] how industry is moving to fill the void left by inaction at Copenhagen and the failure of the US Congress to limit carbon emissions'. Within days, however, the retailers had weakened their position, confronted by the painful reality that their suppliers at all levels were probably purchasing fuel from the tar sands. A number of the companies that signed on to the ban indicate that they are seeking to avoid vendors who purchase fuel that has been sourced from the area. That said, the North American economy is far too interwoven, and oil industry supply far too complex, for an easy boycott of tar sands fuel (Altvater 2010).

This Forest Ethics campaign forms part of a broader set of trends over the past decade. A range of corporate watchdog organisations has increasingly monitored the relationship between the oil industry and state institutions in various northern and southern countries.[6] Among these, liberal programmes such as the Extractive Industry Transparency Initiative (EITI) have sought greater access to information and accountability in oil operations, focusing on the activities of so-called 'host states', largely oil exporters in the (global) south, as a means of addressing inefficiencies and corruption associated with the attributes of the 'resource curse'. A set of trends toward information availability and other such initiatives is heralded by industry insiders as movement into a period of perfect transparency.[7] Such industry pronouncements of growing transparency, however, seem one-sided. In the case of the EITI, the activities of home states and private firms are not subject to the same scrutiny as the southern exporters; and northern exporters, such as Canada, are not economically pressured to the same degree to join this initiative. Additionally, because the organisational relations between private firms and states are frequently concealed, and access to records blocked by proprietary information clauses, scholars meet roadblocks in trying to analyse the political sociology and political economy of the industry. In various sites of formal nationalisation of the oil and gas industry, in fact, private firms still largely control data and information on operations, thus limiting open discussion on questions of safety, ecology and production figures. Recognising this discrepancy between claims to greater transparency and inequities or non-substantive access to data by civil society and scholars, it is pressing to examine how fiscal regimes around hydrocarbon revenues, and transparency and responsibility on the regulation of hydrocarbon extraction, are interconnected in practice (Bridge and Wood 2005; Zalik 2009, 2010).

Demands such as those by the EITI for host government transparency are clearly embedded in global geopolitics. The policies of Hugo Chávez and the position of the current Venezuela government towards foreign firms, in effect raising 'land rent' through royalty increases, reflect the growing geopolitical prominence of tensions over fiscal regimes under late twentieth- and early twenty-first-century capitalism. Analysts on the right of the political spectrum have honed in on Chávez's nationalist anti-market 'authoritarianism' and blamed it for stripping private multinationals of their rights to extractive profits. On the left, Chávez's moves are portrayed as a victory of the people over capital, seeking the socialisation of oil profits and weakening the role of transnationals in shaping the energy future of Venezuela generally, and that of the Americas more broadly.[8] As described by Tom O'Donnell,[9] ExxonMobils's ability to take Venezuela to arbitration over increased royalties resulted partially from the Petroleos de Venezuela (PdVSA) externally oriented, neoliberal policies of the pre-Chávez 1990s (the *apertura*, or opening), through which global trade agreements like the WTO's GATT and Washington Consensus-oriented policies came to trump state levies on oil revenues. Venezuela's moves for a larger percentage from the heavy crude projects in the Orinoco region, in contrast, exemplify what Chávez has termed 'nationalisation without expropriation'.[10]

To explore the link between proprietorial regimes and social demands for access to revenues, the analysis in this chapter employs Bernard Mommer's (2002) theorisation of the 'landlord state'. Mommer[11] provides an analysis in part informed by Venezuela's significant role in the key global cartel of southern exporters, OPEC, that turned 50 in 2010. OPEC's founding expressed a territorial sovereignty movement of southern oil exporters seeking to ensure a price regime in their interests. Employing Mommer's theorisation, this chapter embeds the notion of the 'landlord' in a number of conflicts over oil industry fiscal and ecological regimes and contemporary demands for revenue transparency. Thinking through Mommer's discussion of the landlord and land rent, I argue that in privately dominated sites of oil extraction, an ideology of either frontier or neoliberal capitalism indicates how liberal private-property ideologies and some particularistic demands for petroleum-revenue may weaken the developmental potential of the proprietorial landlord. That is, individual or small-group allocations are compatible with an increasingly neoliberalised, private regime of resource extraction that squares well with private capital. Consequently a fragmented landlord claim, including demands for resource sovereignty at the local and or individual level that do not articulate with other demands, may obstruct collective claims for progressive resource redistribution.

In this chapter, disputes over revenues in the Canadian, Nigerian and Mexican cases help to demonstrate the importance of popular assertion of rents to constituting and contesting energy and industrial 'security', and suggest how conflicts over collective ownership/sovereignty claims have been central to organising more or less redistributive corporate forms.[12] Thus the chapter explores controversies over the control of oil industry revenues, as expressed by agrarian residents, aboriginal/indigenous nationalities, organised labour and insurgent groups in these three extractive sites. Nigeria, Canada and Mexico are highlighted in the analysis as strategically significant, but developmentally divergent, oil exporters. Domestic politics in the first two have been marked by the rise of regional/ territorial separatist movements over the past 50 years. Given these social dynamics in Nigeria and Canada and their corresponding fiscal regimes, in which private operators are dominant, they exhibit socio-political dynamics in marked contrast to those of Mexico. Mexico, a southern exporter external to OPEC, presents a historically exceptional case. Mexico's expropriation of foreign private subsidiaries in 1938, notably those of US and UK firms: La Huasteca (a Mexican firm purchased by Standard Oil) and El Aguila (a subsidiary of Shell), broke new ground historically. Although in decline by the 1930s, Mexico played a significant role in defining global (largely northern) oil markets in the early twentieth century, and its nationalisation had clear anti-imperialist implications (Meyer 1972; Knight 1994). As described by Yergin:

> To the Americans, important interests and rights, including those of private property, were being attacked, and contracts and bargains were being broken. When Washington looked south toward Mexico, it saw instability, insecurity, banditry, anarchy, and a dangerous threat to the flow of strategic resources, and welching on contracts. But when Mexico looked toward Washington and the American oil companies, it saw foreign exploitation, humiliation, the violation of sovereignty, and the enormous weight, pressure and power of 'Yankee imperialism'.[13]

Drawing on Mommer's analysis, the chapter suggests how Nigeria, Canada and Mexico emerge differently from international and domestic social struggles seeking 'land rent' from state and private capital. The three cases point to what are typically understood as negative 'rentierist' attributes, i.e. the states are dominated by extractive revenues, with rents frequently being associated with corruption, elite accumulation and opportunism.[14] By conducting comparative, relational and multi-scalar research, it is possible to illustrate the geopolitical and social variations that have shaped state fiscal regimes and the varied outcomes that such regimes can produce. In this way we can see how proprietorial norms may in fact occur even where a liberal capitalist approach to frontier property is ideologically dominant, as in Alaska. The chapter thus demonstrates that proprietorial regimes that are dominated by a frontierist ethic involve pitfalls for those who are seeking either radical reform or redistribution. Indeed, I argue that they create a kind of 'race to the bottom' in socio-ecological regulation. It is also demonstrated that this largely arises from an individualist or atomised approach to negotiations with capital, considered typical of the western frontier imaginary.[15] That is, a liberally inflected proprietorial regime may in fact deepen alienation – ideologically and culturally – of residents from the land (as a means of production), while cementing a direct interest and identification with the interests of extractive, rather than productive,[16] uses of territory.

THE NIGERIAN AND CANADIAN FRONTIERS

The Nigerian and Canadian cases arguably exemplify typical attributes associated with land tenure relations in so-called 'frontier' zones of settlement. In these settings relations typified by rugged individualism dominate and human settlements have been forced to struggle for control over increasingly valuable territory and trade routes. The Niger Delta region, while central to the European transatlantic slave trade, was constructed as a frontier zone in the colonial conceptualisation of Africa. This was later reproduced in the relations of this geographically complex and difficult-to-navigate riverine area.[17] In this geography, the land-based, spatially expansive kingdoms to the north and west of Nigeria have tended to dominate the federal centre and were able to express their dominance. The complex cultural geography of the nations of the Delta region, with a range of language groups, shaped a more divided landscape when the time came to 'settle' with European encroachers and to establish the basis for colonial indirect rule at the clan level.[18] In the Canadian north, the constitution of a 'staples' economy based on resource extraction (Innis, cited in Watkins 1984) and a particular set of frontier relations in a less densely populated landscape, also shaped colonial indirect rule, crystallised in treaty negotiations. The role of the provincial, as opposed to the federal government, as key representative of the crown in control over subsoil revenues, and their negotiation and regulation, also distinguishes the Canadian context from the Mexican or Nigerian – making it in some ways akin to that unique setting in the United States, Alaska, to be discussed further below.

The ongoing fragmentation of claims against the state in these sites – whether among farmers, ethnic–territorial groups or indigenous nations – was further heightened as a result of the deepening of liberal–individualist social values under neoliberalism.[19] Indeed, in both Nigeria and Canada, economically insecure farmers and residents who self-identify as oilfield 'landlords' have demanded better terms from energy companies. Securing these terms, however, remains a significant challenge. In the Canadian context, for instance, see the work of CAEPLA (the Canadian Association of Energy and Pipeline Landowner Associations). For Nigeria, see proposals for a fund similar to the Alaska oil fund, the Niger Delta Fund. Both

CAEPLA and the Niger Delta Fund call for revenue allocations to individuals based on property and residence rights. In the context of the Niger Delta, persistent inequality and insufficient redistribution to local residents has buttressed armed insurgency and contributed to the rise to power of the region while also compromising social regulation.[20] The central state's response, in part associated with the rise to political prominence of the historically excluded Niger Delta region in the national government, includes a new petroleum reform bill seeking to raise royalties and indigenous participation in the Nigerian oil industry. In both the Canadian and Nigerian settings, accordingly, calls for localised resource sovereignty have tended to dominate the political discourse. This in turn has been shaped by state and industry strategy to divide regionally displaced and marginalised groups who reside next to oil installations. Indeed, the assertion of collective, state, sub-state and provincial power to extract rent from profit-making corporations – what we can call the demands of a 'landlord state' – have frequently been overshadowed by such atomistic trends. Yet these fragmentary trends have been countered by solidarity actions in varied forms, as in the work of Defenders of the Land – in which environmental NGOs and First Nations demand a halt on extractive development in the tar sands and other western Canadian energy fields. Resource development has certainly been influenced by socio-ecological demands in the Canadian North and in Nigeria, including through formal policy channels, illustrating the weight of such territorial claims.[21]

In 2007/8 a coalition in the province of Alberta[22] employed slogans such as 'Thinking like an owner' and 'Selling the family silver' to demand greater royalty revenues from private industry in the tar sands. Its key objective was to demonstrate to the residents of the province the extent to which corporate petroleum interests are robbing inhabitants of rightful income, through a sweetheart royalty and tax scheme intended to encourage 'risky' investment in this now very lucrative resource frontier. Such demands came from varying ends of the political spectrum, and the Alberta government temporarily raised these royalties.[23] Quite arguably a petro-province, Alberta has one of the longest histories of conservatively dominated provincial governments under Western democratic categorisation. It also has a long history of alienation from the federal centre – expressed in regional separatism, in particular with regard to its oil resources and the extent to which they have been used by central Canada. In the 1970s, Alberta's premier, Peter Lougheed, famously spurned the National Energy Plan of the then prime minister, Pierre Elliot Trudeau, stating in response to a national move to take further control over the province's energy resources, 'Let them [central Canadian provinces] freeze in the dark'. It is unsurprising, then, that increased Alberta royalties gave way to a fuelled fear of capital flight, in the wake of the financial crisis. Responding to these fears, the Alberta government in early 2010 reversed the new royalty measures in response to pressure from private operators, including the key industry pressure group the Canadian Association of Petroleum Producers (CAPP).

It is notable that in this period, also, a Calgary-based law firm published an article arguing that foreign corporations might be able to employ NAFTA Chapter 11[24] to demand compensation from the provincial government for royalty increases.[25] The royalty reversal, described as a provincial 'fiscal competitiveness' policy, was praised by CAPP, who called for the Alberta government to take the 'further step' of *regulatory* competitiveness (CAPP 2010) – that is, the streamlining of environmental and other approval processes. In the context of regulatory capture by industry, this move underlined Alberta's petro-state characteristics,[26] including the interpenetration of provincial government and industry executives.

In Nigeria, insurgent groups have leveraged the discourse of 'resource control' to demand employment opportunities for disaffected youth marginalised from the oil wealth extracted from their land. Youth movements, at one time associated with the Ijaw Youth Council, emerged to lead the Deltan struggle following the death of Ken Saro-Wiwa. These groups have become increasingly radicalised since 2002, with some sections affiliating themselves with the guerrilla struggle. At times overlapping with the greater claims of youth on a long-standing trade in contraband oil (a trade at one time firmly controlled by certain military elites), the Niger Delta People's Volunteer Force, and later the Movement for the Emancipation of the Niger Delta (MEND), have demonstrated considerable capacity to destabilise the global oil industry in the region. Youth leaders from the Delta have even called for the partial legalisation of their siphoning off and sale of (contraband) oil.

Arguably the presence of armed insurgents does not substantively damage corporate interests. Indeed, the impressive returns associated with rising oil prices due to violence, and the profitable financial risk industry that insures this risky *yet lucrative* extraction in 'insecure regions',[27] have shaped their functionality to capital. Nevertheless, their presence has opened an unexpected and growing space for

Niger Deltan civic leaders in national politicscs. Indeed, the ability of these youth to disrupt industrial profits for transnational private operators has contributed to the political fortunes of the current president, Goodluck Jonathan. As a Niger Deltan 'son of the soil', Jonathan has served as a mediating force between the militant groups and power-holders from the north and west of the country, thereby facilitating his campaign for the vice presidency and his constitutional claim on the presidency following the death of Yar'Adua in 2010. This has resulted in more substantive returns to the Deltan states, in part through the promotion of key leaders to the federal centre. Under the Yar'Adua and Jonathan administrations, a sweeping bill to reform the petroleum industry has led to protest and threats of withdrawal by key transnational operators.

MEXICO'S NATIONALISED EXTRACTIVE SPACE

The Canadian and Nigerian regionalist contexts differ markedly from the explicitly popular labour–agrarian alliance that was central to the legacy of the Mexican revolution.[28] In Mexico, the corporatist state has employed payments and resource benefits to agrarian organisations and individuals as a means to secure political support. Such state agrarian–industrial corporatism characterised the petroleum-producing south-east as well as various rural areas during the extended political rule of the PRI (Institutional Revolutionary Party) in the twentieth century (Meyer and Morales 1990; Brown and Knight 1992). Thus alongside legal suits against Pemex for environmental damage resulting from pollution, a so-called 'claims industry' exists in Mexico's petroleum producing region. This is typical of many extractive zones facing socio-ecological impacts – including Canada and Nigeria. PEMEX's compensation to affected agrarian producers (farmers, fishermen) in the extractive region of the Gulf of Mexico demonstrates the competing forces of contestation, response and consent in the countryside (Bozada Robles 1999; Uribe Iniesta 2005). Mexican state corporatism, responding to social claims through the provision of (limited) resources, also has its corollary in access to the parastatal firm. For both its workers and those who study it, PEMEX is a considerably more penetrable institution than the transnational firms, which closely guard their data. (Proprietary information is, globally, frequently protected in exploration and production contracts involving private firms.) With creeping denationalisation and privatisation, however, the loci of such demands are being transferred to private contractors.

The most recent production agreements call for foreign or private firms contracted by PEMEX to dedicate 1.5 per cent of their budget to 'social work'[29] of some kind. This reduces PEMEX (and thus the state's role) as a community arbiter, and legally restricts and deflects demands for local, public redistribution of revenues and social compensation to private firms and individuals.

Nevertheless, despite these contemporary shifts, and in contrast to Nigerian and Canadian settings of de facto privately controlled industry (even if in the Nigerian case the state holds a de jure majority stake in oil extraction projects),[30] the Mexican oil industry's unique history expresses how nationalisation may be rooted in labour struggles, animated by anti-imperialist ideology yet undergirded by pacts with national capital. Initially the Mexican nationalisation aimed in part to restrict export of national resources and promote energy 'sovereignty', in order to ensure a decent price, and internal distribution, at home.

In the 1930s President Lazaro Cardenas sought to fully implement key elements of Mexico's revolutionary constitutional reform of 1917 – among these was included Article 27, calling for national energy sovereignty. As an act of expropriation preceding the Second World War, Mexico's 1938 nationalisation was considerably more radical than the later OPEC nationalisations (discussed in more detail below), due to its direct expulsion of foreign capital. Following the actual expropriation of US and British firms, PEMEX was driven by domestic demands to place limits on the export of oil for some years. Concurrent with this process, Mexico's global significance as a supplier declined due to its efforts to develop its national infrastructure and economy as well as to the effects of the Second World War and the hostile embargo put in place by the United States and Britain as a result of the expropriation of their firms' assets. The nationalisation process has also been described as a key moment in President Cardenas's government's pursuit of autonomy from capital in the reformist–revolutionary era of the 1930s.[31] However, the need for economic support of national capital to finance the expropriation of foreign firms may have resulted, inadvertently, in compromising governmental autonomy from capital.

It was only after the oil boom of the 1970s, and the development of Mexican offshore reserves for export, that export revenues came to serve as a key source of government finance. Today, despite the aforementioned increasing privatisation (and creeping dena-tionalisation) through so-called 'multiple service contracts', as well as new risk contracts with foreign firms in the offshore marine zone, the role of PEMEX remains both symbolically and practically distinctive. Expropriation remains a lynchpin of anti-imperialist nationalism, despite the Salinas era advent of neoliberalism in the 1980s. Thus, reforms and 'modernisation' of PEMEX have been a central focus of national policy debate and public struggle for the last two decades (Shields 2003, 2006). The weight of oil sovereignty remains politically salient. Neoliberal and rightist governments have cautiously altered the oil industry context, as in Calderon's 2008 National Action Party (PAN) energy and oil sector reform. This reform was accepted by some segments of the nationalist left only after considerable public debate. In March 2011 the Mexican daily *La Jornada* once again highlighted how the current petroleum regime favours transnationals by exporting crude oil to private refineries in the United States and later reimporting it at much higher prices – a point made by critics of the creeping denationalisation of PEMEX for many years. In that article, Shell, due to its refining operations in Texas, is identified as a key corporate beneficiary.[32]

The Mexican nationalist attachment to a sovereign oil industry, which has both popular and populist dimensions, shares key attributes with historic and contemporary Latin American movements of the political left, as in Venezuela. The historical symbolism of the landlord state as an emancipator also remains clearly prominent in Latin America. In contrast to the Canadian and Nigerian cases, and most explicitly evident today in Bolivia, Venezuela and Ecuador (see chapters by McNeish; Wanderley, Mokrani and Guimarães; and Strønen), claims for resource control based on anti-imperialist sovereignty movements have fostered support for proprietorial fiscal regimes that challenge liberal approaches to property rights. In those countries, explicitly agrarian–indigenous coalitions have managed to win control of the state and have altered in radical ways, albeit to varying degrees, the proprietorial regime surrounding hydrocarbon extraction. While not ideologically unproblematic in their tendency towards reification of state–society relations, these movements do reflect collective responses to colonial dispossession from the land across the region.

In the following section, I discuss the notion of land rent and 'landlord' status and its relationship to Mommer's critiques of free-market policies that emerged in the 1980s and 1990s. I furthermore refer to arguments made by anthropologists and historians of the Americas concerning the relationship between nationalisation, natural-resource conservation/extraction and state–subject formation.

THE NATURE OF THE LANDLORD: PROPRIETORIAL REGIMES UNDER STATE AND 'COMMUNITY'

Bernard Mommer (2002) describes the salience of land rent to understanding the formation of modern oil exporters and the formation of OPEC. In contrast to the Mexican case, the nationalisations undergirding the formation of the OPEC cartel did not involve wholesale expropriation of foreign firms. Scholars have pointed out how OPEC's existence ultimately served transnational operators as well as parastatals, since its quotas have supported the higher oil prices necessary to maintain profit margins under capitalist competition. Thus, OPEC's demand for and constitution of fiscal regimes ensuring a minimum 'land rent' did not involve the wholesale control over extraction called for by the oil workers union (STPRM) in Mexico, the clarion call of PEMEX's popular support and an important pillar in the PRI corporatist state apparatus. Nevertheless, the OPEC states share certain national-sovereignty attributes with Mexico. That is, its creation was also a reflection of the postcolonial southern oil exporters (such as Mexico) which sought to leverage territorial power over their resources from northern imperial firms. But in the Mexican context the role of the workers in the oil industry was a crucial factor in nationalisation (despite historiographical debate).

In his work on the revenue policy guiding private oil-company production and profits in key producing and consuming regions, Mommer distinguishes between *proprietorial* and *liberal* fiscal regimes. In countries that adopt liberal rather than proprietorial regimes, private oil companies benefit and oil production is facilitated in the present – as opposed to retaining oil reserves for later production, as in a proprietorial regime. In analysing these variations, Mommer offers a historically detailed theorisation of the role of land rent in state development, and the salience of property rights regimes to state returns from extracted resources. His work underlines, among other points, that the United Kingdom adopted an increasingly liberal approach to oil industry revenues, so as to incentivise production by private firms. As a result, Britain claimed a relatively small amount of royalties from North Sea riches. As Mommer highlights, inasmuch as this approach makes Britain less of an 'oil state', given that its GDP is thus less dependent on oil revenues, its position sets an example for the other key Western oil importers unified under the International Energy Agency (which acts as a counterweight to OPEC). This example-setting aims to ensure both a more favourable international price regime and profits for Western (private) firms. Not only were proprietorial royalty measures more or less eliminated, but, under Thatcher in 1983 and later Labour governments, corporate taxes were further reduced to some of the lowest rates in the world. While this example to other importing nations to maintain a friendly regime for operators was defended on the basis of maintaining lower oil prices for consumers, oil consumption in Britain has in reality been very heavily taxed at the pump. Thus, Mommer underlines, media and public attention have been focused on the disputes between truck drivers, cabbies and the government over consumption-end taxes, with minimal attention being paid to the windfall profits allowed to the transnationals – who pay corporate tax, but avoid the land rent that the OPEC member states demand.

In contrast, Mommer explains, Alaska has manifest a highly proprietorial regime. This is in part the result of the private mineral rights that have historically accrued to the individual landowners. According to Mommer, this creates a strong public attitude among Alaskans that they are the rightful 'owners' of the resource – ironically in a form 'more deeply rooted' than in Venezuela. However, and crucial to the analysis here, the Alaskan regime emerges from a frontierist ethic, as well as in the US context of surface-owner subsoil rights. This dynamic *privileges individual claims* on territory and, considering Alaska's sparse population, makes the benefits from oil, as in the key Persian Gulf states, a significant income boost to the individual. So, whilst production takes place on public land, Mommer suggests that the relationship between the state and the oil industry in Alaska must be seen in light of the unique history of private mineral property in the United States. Under these historical conditions, the proprietorial model at work in Alaska supports, somewhat peculiarly, an ideology associated with private-property rights and a liberal capitalist framework. While now under state jurisdiction, the ideology in part emerged from the private tenure predominant in the US context, known as the 'Law or Rule of Capture', in which on adjacent privately held plots the person who extracts the resource first, owns it.[33] The Alaska setting avoids the inefficient elements of this model, which lead to overuse of machinery in a competitive context, but sustains the individualised approach to oil-rent distribution.

Of course, the proprietorial regime among OPEC states differs markedly. Within the historical anthropology of Venezuela, Fernando Coronil, an anthropologist of Venezuela's relationship with the oil resource influenced by Mommer's work, encapsulates the demand for 'land rent' amongst the southern oil exporters in OPEC as a central moment in Third World anti-imperialism preceding the debt crisis. Coronil (1997) stresses that prior to the 'oil shocks' and corresponding assertion of OPEC as a key player in the oil market, the market price (of oil) determined land rent, but in the post Oil-Shock period, land rent came to determine market price.[34] As Coronil explains, summarising a history that is described in an entrepreneurial fashion in Yergin's *The Prize*,[35] the increase in oil prices during the shocks was not the result of a shortage. 'It was rather the outcome of a long historical process by which OPEC nations, acting as landowners, developed the means to extract a rent on the basis of their ownership of the oil fields – an absolute rent – in addition to the differential rents they had collected in the past. In 1973[36] a set of converging political and economic conditions helped establish their collective ability to restrict the world supply of oil. With this power, OPEC felt entitled to set the market price for oil, thus freeing the level of rent from the previous constraint of the market price. Now rent (absolute and differential) would in its own right determine the market price for oil.'[37]

Coronil demonstrates the salience of land rent to the formation of OPEC and thus to the formation of the Venezuelan petro-state. He goes on to suggest that Marxian theory has neglected the salience of ground rent, land as a natural resource, a question examined in more detail in the accounts of ecological Marxists, for instance John Bellamy Foster and Jason W. Moore (2000). But Coronil's view serves as a strategic intervention in some Marxist theory in a form similar to Mommer's in neoclassical theory. Mommer, for example, indicates that the neoliberal, Washington consensus, via which ground rent is minimised in favour of the broader benefits (a sort of trickle down), arising from oil industry assumption of financial risks, in fact encourages lack of conservation of the resource and the kinds of tragic 'common property' problems identified by liberal theorists of land tenure.[38] Coronil, relatedly, points to the need for greater attention to the role of natural-resource endowments in shaping social claims on accumulated capital.

CONTESTED OILFIELDS

A more nuanced application of the notion of 'landlord' status, drawing on both Coronil and Mommer, requires us to understand the historical emergence of social claims on petroleum revenues by populations most affected by the erosion of agrarian society and ecology characteristic of the oil industry.[39] Here, the Nigerian, Canadian and Mexican cases offer examples of how claims of landlord status have been made by affected residents and workers, or those excluded from extractive revenues. Varying claims of ownership are thus central to claims for resource sovereignty.

For both Mommer, and Coronil, land rent is a historically constituted means of making claims on industrial petroleum revenues. In the case of the oil industry, it has historically been the private firm which first held the sizeable, accumulated capital necessary to undertake petroleum exploration and production. In the case of Mexico, this was expropriated from those firms in the 1930s, in a historical period when the physical human labour needed to maintain the industry was proportionally more dominant – and thus held more socio-political power. Crucially, Mommer emphasises how land rent is a significant element in efficient resource use by either private or public owners, thus challenging neoclassical economists to note the contradictions inherent in their own favoured policies.

Alberta's brief lifting of royalties in 2008 could be described as having raised the rent on the oil companies who hold leases. Its quick retraction following industry pressure is clearly the dominant trend guiding disputes over Alberta provincial oil revenues since the oil boom of the 1970s. Historically, the province has expressed separatist currents within Canada, seeking greater control over its oil wealth from the federal government in Ottawa – a claim that resonates with Nigerian claims of regional sovereignty against the 'federal centre' in the capital Abuja. Canadian contemporary social mobilisation around oil industry revenues, as in Nigeria, has thus been predominantly embedded in regional, ethnic and indigenous identity movements which make claims on the space from which oil is extracted. In its most autonomous form, this ownership structure would apply to data currently heavily guarded by private firms. Socio-ecological regulation would thus be facilitated.

Chávez's current policies operate as a partial reversal of the earlier neoliberal *apertura* through which a pre-Chávez generation of PdVSA managers had built alliances with, and increased the participation of foreign, private capital in Venezuelan oil fields. The Venezuelan disputes over the oil industry in the past decade, while the result of a historically constituted set of struggles between various social sectors constitutive of that nation state, is of considerable import to contemporary debates over natural-resource policy, with obvious reverberations beyond Venezuelan borders, particularly in the global South. It points at the way in which revenue distribution formulas and notions of ownership over the subsoil have been historically constituted alongside national movements for popular sovereignty over natural resources, with aftershocks in global oil markets.

This discussion, like the regulatory dilemmas exposed by the Deepwater Horizon accident, sheds light on the dynamics critiqued by popular movements, liberal environmental organisations and corporate monitoring groups, as well as some Latin American governments, concerning fiscal revenue and ecological reporting by the oil industry. While industry representatives may argue that the global economy is entering a period of unprecedented transparency, non-insiders to industry face major challenges in accessing information on industrial revenues, corporate strategy and production data. Thus, a regulatory 'race to the bottom' is facilitated.

NOTES

1. D. Kocieniewski, 'As Oil Industry Fights a Tax, It Reaps Subsidies', *New York Times*, 3 July 2010. See also Freudenburg and Gramling 2011.
2. T. Macalister, 'Oil Giants Demand Open Market for World's Dirtiest Fuel: Oil Groups Mount Legal Challenge to California's Tar Sands Ban', *Guardian*, 15 February 2010.
3. As stated by the NPRA:

   The California LCFS is unlawful for a number of reasons, including the fact that it violates the Commerce Clause of the United States Constitution by imposing undue and unconstitutional burdens on interstate commerce. California's LCFS also would have little or no impact on GHG emissions nationwide and would harm our nation's energy security by discouraging the use of Canadian crude oil – our nation's largest source of crude – and ethanol produced in the American Midwest.

4. While ForestEthics continues to encourage major corporations to distance themselves from tar sands fuel, the dynamics on the oil/gas supply chain complicate this attempt. Canada's *National Post* continued attacking ForestEthics on this score into the fall of 2010. Its work has provoked criticism among the environmental justice community for advancing a green capitalist approach to containing further development of the tar sands. For background on the debate about tar sands development in Canada, see Chastko 2004 and Harrison 2005.
5. S. McNulty, 'Suppliers of Oil Sands Fuel Shunned', *Financial Times*, 10 February 2010.
6. See for instance the work of the international southern network Oilwatch, the previously active Project Underground, the work of Global Exchange, Platform London, The Price of Oil, Sustainable Energy, and Environment Network at

the Institute for Policy Studies as well as organisations working on related environmental or climate justice questions.
7. De Kuijper 2009.
8. For details, see stories in *Financial Times*, 8 and 9 February, 5 and 6 March 2008.
9. See O'Donnell's work at http://www-personal.umich.edu/~twod/.
10. Cited from O'Donnell, personal communication, 10 February 2008.
11. Once a scholar at the Oxford Institute for Energy Studies and director of Petroleos de Venezuela (PdVSA) as well as deputy minister for hydrocarbons, energy and petroleum. See also Harvey 2006 and Smith 2007.
12. Soederberg 2010.
13. Yergin 1992, p.232.
14. Humphreys, Sachs and Stigliz 2008; Karl 1997.
15. Vitalis 2009; Mitchell 2009; Redclift 2006; Blomley 2003; Blomley and Pratt 2001; Peluso and Watts 2001.
16. Orthodox Marxist accounts would not necessarily distinguish between these uses. The point here is to incorporate the insights of ecological Marxist accounts as well as spatial accounts of dispossession, recognising that a 'fossil capitalism' precludes other forms of industrial development in key extractive sites.
17. Alagoa 1970; Watts 1999; Zalik 2004.
18. Ekeh 1975; Mamdani 1996; Okonta and Douglas 2001.
19. Mommer 2001.
20. Watts 2004; Peterside and Zalik 2008.
21. Sabin 1995; Okonta 2008.
22. Including the liberal environmental think tank the Pembina Institute and the Parkland Institute at the University of Alberta.
23. Gibson 2007.
24. For the controversy over NAFTA Chapter 11 and state regulatory autonomy and protections, see Clapp and Dauvergne 2005.
25. R. Boychuck, 'Searching for a Reason for the Tories' Royalty Cuts', *Edmonton Journal*, 3 April 2010; Roth 2009; C. Tait, 'Lower Oil Prices Won't Stop Alberta Royalty Hike', *Edmonton Journal*, 16 October 2008.
26. Carter and Zalik, forthcoming.
27. Not to mention the fact that they also deliver private security services to industry.
28. Santiago 2006.
29. Author's interviews in southern Veracruz state, 2011. Note, these are very new developments and are likely to meet significant social challenges in the region.
30. See Zalik 2008 for how the operations of the Nigerian and Mexican extractive regimes, one transnational and the other parastatal, shaped divergent claims for resource sovereignty.
31. Hamilton 1982.
32. See the work of the Comité Nacional de Estudios de la Energía, Mexico.
33. Daintith 2010.
34. This followed from Perez Alfonso's attempt to negotiate a quota guarantee of imports to the United States, without interference of the private oil companies – such as that of the Texas Railroad Commission, which sought to control output and control prices; see Yergin 1992, pp.249 and 512–13.
35. Yergin's narrative supports this, but pays greater attention to the difficulties suffered by the oil companies in a context of increased production leading up

to the 1960 creation of OPEC. In this period market prices were lower than the posted prices paid to the governments, due to the fact that 'more oil was in search of markets than there were markets for oil' – forcing oil companies to take less in pay than the amount they guaranteed to the government in the 1950s (a situation reversed with the creation of OPEC). Oil companies responded by dropping the posted price – which led to considerable annoyance in the producing countries. In this sense, OPEC as a cartel serves as a means of regulating common property over usage of land, on the part of southern oil-exporting states as protectors of national/collective property.

36. The first two shocks led to price rises: first during the Arab Oil Embargo of 1973/4, and second during the Iranian revolution and subsequent hostage crisis, 1978–81. The third was associated with the plummet in prices arising from recession in the 1980s and Saudi Arabia's loss of markets.

37. Coronil 1997, p.360.

38. A view that is critiqued by various political economists for not attending sufficiently to issues of power and distribution.

39. In a recent paper I describe how industry currently addresses the contradictions arising from over-extraction through liquefied natural gas transfers from Nigeria and Mexico.

REFERENCES

Alagoa, E.J. (1970) 'Long Distance Trade and States in the Niger Delta', *Journal of African History*, 11(3): 319–29.

Altvater, E. (2010) 'The Social and Natural Environment of Fossil Capitalism', in L. Panitch and C. Leys (eds) *Coming to Terms with Nature: Socialist Register 2007* (New York: Monthly Review Press).

Blomley, N. (2003) 'Law, Property, and the Geography of Violence: The Frontier, the Survey, and the Grid', *Annals of the Association of American Geographers*, 93(1): 121–41.

—— and Pratt, G. (2001) 'Canada and the Political Geographies of Rights', *Canadian Geographer*, 45(1): 151–66.

Bozada Robles, L. (1999) *El subdesarrollo pesquero y acuícola del estado de tabasco* (Villahermosa: Asociation Ecological Santo Tomas).

Bridge, G. and Wood, A. (2005) 'Geographies of Knowledge, Practices of Globalization: Learning from the Oil Exploration and Production Industry', *Area*, 32(2): 199–208.

Brown, J. and Knight, A. (1992). *The Mexican Petroleum Industry in the Twentieth Century* (Austin: University of Texas Press).

Carter, A. and Zalik, A. (forthcoming) 'Fossil Capitalism and the Rentier State: Towards a Political Ecology of Alberta's Oil Economy, in L. Adkin and B. Miller (eds) *Petro-Politics in Alberta*.

Chastko, P.A. (2004) *Developing Alberta's Oil Sands: From Karl Clark to Kyoto* (Calgary: University of Calgary Press).

Clapp, J. and Dauvergne, P. (2005) *Paths to a Green World: The Political Economy of the Global Environment* (Cambridge, Mass.: MIT Press).

Coronil, F. (1997) *The Magical State: Nature, Money and Modernity in Venezuela* (Chicago: University of Chicago Press).

Daintith, T. (2010) 'The Rule of Capture: The Least Worst Property Rule for Oil and Gas', in A. McHarg, B. Barton, A. Bradbrook and L. Godden (eds) *Property and the Law in Energy and Natural Resources* (Oxford Scholarship Online).

Ekeh, P. (1975) 'Colonialism and the Two Publics in Africa: A Theoretical Statement', *Comparative Studies in Society and History*, 17: 91–112.

Freudenburg, W. and Gramling, R. (2011) *Blowout in the Gulf: The BP Oil Disaster and the Future of Energy in America* (Cambridge, Mass.: MIT Press).

Gibson, D. (2007) *The Spoils of the Boom: Incomes, Poverty and Profits in Alberta* (Edmonton: Parkland Institute).

Hamilton, N. (1982) *The Limits of State Autonomy: Post-Revolutionary Mexico* (Princeton, N.J.: Princeton University Press).

Harrison, T. (ed.) (2005) *The Return of the Trojan Horse: Alberta and the New World (Dis)Order* (Montreal: Black Rose Books).

Harvey, D. (2006) [1982] *The Limits of Capital* (New York: Verso).

Humphreys, M., Sachs, J. and Stiglitz, J. (2007) *Escaping the Resource Curse* (New York: Columbia University Press).

Karl, T.L. (1997) *The Paradox of Plenty: Oil Booms and Petro-States* (Berkeley: University of California Press).

Knight, A. (1994) 'Peasants into Patriots: Thoughts on the Making of the Mexican Nation', *Mexican Studies*, 10(1): 135–61.

Kuijper, M. de (2009) *Profit Power Economics: A New Competitive Strategy for Creating Sustainable Wealth* (Oxford: Oxford University Press).

Mamdani, M. (1996) *Citizen and Subject: Contemporary Africa and the Legacy of Late Colonialism* (Princeton: Princeton University Press).

Meyer, L. (1972) *Mexico and the United States in the Oil Controversy 1917–42* (Austin: University of Texas Press/El Colegio de Mexico).

—— and Morales, I. (1990) *Petróleo y nación: la política petrolera en México, 1900–1987* (México D.F.: Colegio de México).

Mitchell, T. (2009) 'Carbon Democracy', *Economy and Society*, 38(3): 399–432.

Mommer, B. (2001) 'Fiscal Regimes and Oil Revenues in the UK, Alaska and Venezuela', Oxford Institute of Energy Studies.

—— (2002) *Global Oil and the Nation State* (Oxford: Oxford University Press).

Moore, J.W. (2000) 'Environmental Crises and the Metabolic Rift in World-Historical Perspective', *Organization and Environment*, 13(2): 123–57.

Okonta, I. (2008). *When Citizens Revolt: Nigerian Elites, Big Oil and the Ogoni Struggle for Self-Determination* (Trenton, N.J.: Africa World Press).

—— and Oronto, D. (2001) *Where Vultures Feast: Shell, Human Rights and Oil in the Niger Delta* (San Francisco: Sierra Club Books).

Peluso N. and Watts, M. (eds) (2001) *Violent Environments* (Ithaca, N.Y.: Cornell University Press).

Peterside, S. and Zalik, A. (2008) 'The Commodification of Violence in the Niger Delta', in L. Panitch and C. Leys (eds) *Violence Today: Socialist Register 2009* (New York: Monthly Review Press).

Redclift, M.R. (2006) *Frontiers: History of Civil Society and Nature* (Cambridge, Mass.: MIT Press).

Roth, B. (2009). 'NAFTA, Alberta Oil Sands Royalties, and Change: Yes We Can?' *Alberta Law Review*, 46(2): 335.

Sabin, P. (1995) 'Voices from the Hydrocarbon Frontier: Canada's Mackenzie Valley Pipeline Inquiry (1974–1977)', *Environmental History Review*, 19(1): 17–48.

Santiago, M. (2006) *The Ecology of Oil: Environment, Labor and the Mexican Revolution 1900–1938* (Cambridge: Cambridge University Press).

Shields, D. (2003) *Pemex: un futuro incierto* (México D.F.: Editorial Planeta Mexicana).

—— (2006) *Pemex: la reforma petrolera* (México D.F.: Editorial Planeta Mexicana).

Smith, N. (2007) 'Nature as Accumulation Strategy', *Socialist Register*, 43:16–36.

Soederberg, S. (2010) *Corporate Power and Ownership in Contemporary Capitalism: The Politics of Resistance and Domination* (London: Routledge).

Vitalis, R. (2009) *America's Kindgom: Mythmaking on the Saudi Oil Frontier* (New York: Verso).

Watkins, M.H. (1984) 'The Staple Approach', in W.T. Easterbrook and M.H. Watkins (eds) *Approaches to Canadian Economic History* (Ottawa: Carleton University Press).

Watts, M. (1999) 'Collective Wish Images: Geographical Imaginaries and the Crisis of National Development', in D. Massey, J. Allen and P. Sarre (eds) *Human Geography Today* (Massachusetts: Polity Press).

—— (2004) 'Resource Curse? Governmentality, Oil and Power in the Niger Delta, Nigeria', *Geopolitics*, 9(1): 50–80.

Yergin, D. (1992) *The Prize: The Epic Quest for Oil, Money and Power* (New York: Free Press Mexico).

Zalik, A. (2004) 'The Niger Delta: Petro-Violence and Partnership Development', *Review of African Political Economy*, 31(101): 401–24.

—— (2008) 'Oil Sovereignties: Ecology and Nationality in the Nigerian Delta and the Mexican Gulf', in K. Omeje (ed.) *The Rentier Space: Extractive Economies and Conflicts in the Global South* (London: Ashgate).

—— (2009) 'Zones of Exclusion: Offshore Extraction, the Contestation of Space and Physical Displacement in the Nigerian Delta and the Mexican Gulf', *Antipode*, 41(3): 557–82.

—— (2010) 'Oil Futures: Shell's Scenarios and the Social Constitution of the Global Oil Market', *Geoforum*, 41(4): 553–64.

12
Law's Role in the Tension Between Security and Sovereignty in the Field of Energy Resources

John Paterson

It is a truism that oil and gas are strategic resources of unparalleled significance. At the beginning of the second decade of the twenty-first century oil and gas still occupy a special position in global markets and international relations. They appear set to do so for the foreseeable future,[1] even as commodities such as rare earth metals take on a new relevance because of their importance to new technologies and because of their precise distribution in particular parts of the world,[2] and even as previous concerns with energy shortages are compounded by fears over climate change.[3] As a result, countries which discover that they possess hydrocarbon resources look forward not only to the benefits that these can bring in terms of income and employment, but also to the stronger bargaining position they can offer when it comes to dealing with neighbours.

The possession of hydrocarbon resources thus has a number of important consequences for *sovereignty*, i.e. for 'the legitimate exercise of power and legal authority over territory by a state'.[4] On the one hand, states have been at pains to establish and defend their sovereignty over oil and gas within their territories or under their continental shelves. This is usually in interplay with commercial actors they engage with in relation to exploration, development and production activities,[5] but also as against neighbouring states, when the resources lie across international boundaries.[6] On the other hand, states have utilised their possession of such resources as a political lever in their relations on the international stage.[7]

The global concern with *energy security* is thus intimately bound up with the question of sovereignty. A consumer nation is, for example, concerned to ensure reliable access to energy to meet current and likely future fuel needs at a reasonable cost, and is thus also concerned to ensure that arrangements for supply are robust and enforceable. Insofar as significant proportions of the world's supply of oil and gas are in the hands of state companies rather than purely commercial organisations,[8] a crucial factor in this calculus is the political risk that decisions to honour or renege on obligations will be taken on grounds that are not commercial in nature, but influenced by considerations of sovereignty. A producer nation, on the other hand, is concerned to ensure reliable access to investment and to markets, and is thus also concerned to ensure that, for example, the ability to obtain capital and technology are not compromised by international sanctions imposed because of other aspects of its domestic or foreign policies, or that investors do not hold it to ransom over taxation on the basis that other options are open to them globally.[9]

In short, the possession or the lack of resources can have a significant impact on the ability of a state to exercise its sovereignty – and not always only in the most obvious ways. In all of these circumstances, producers and consumers make efforts to achieve certainty in their dealings with each other and with commercial actors. Similarly, commercial actors seek to achieve certainty in their dealings with states. The way in which this certainty is supposed to be achieved in most cases involves a legal instrument of one form or another: for example, an international treaty between states or a contract between a state and a commercial entity.[10]

The question arises, therefore, as to whether legal obligations entered into by a state with a view to offering certainty to other states or to commercial actors in relation to resources are sufficient to prevent the further exercise of sovereignty, which has the effect of negating the first. In other words, is the longed-for certainty that treaties and contracts are supposed to bring to the domain of energy security more a pious hope than achievable reality?

This chapter seeks to emphasise this issue. It does so by tracing the evolution of law's role in energy security through a series of domestic and international legal instruments, each of which is at once an expression of sovereignty and an effort to constrain the future exercise of sovereignty. The picture it presents is necessarily partial and fragmented given the scale and scope of the area it is concerned with. Its aim, however, is to indicate to readers who are not lawyers what it is that law can bring to the energy security table, and to indicate that it may be asking too much of law to achieve the objectives set for it. The chapter also highlights how even legally sanctioned exercises of sovereignty can often have unforeseen and wholly unwanted consequences, many of which paradoxically take the form of expressions of sovereignty via law.

The chapter begins by considering the United States Mandatory Oil Import Quota Program, before moving on to the Statute of the Organisation of Petroleum Exporting Countries and the Agreement on the International Energy Program. As well as demonstrating some of the many and varied ways in which sovereignty can be expressed through law in the field of energy security and also its inherent tensions and limitations (can one expression of sovereignty ever rule out a later contradictory one?), these examples have been chosen because of the intimate connections that exist between them. Different as each one is in form and substance, the IEP Agreement exists as a direct result of the OPEC Statute, which in turn exists as a consequence of the Mandatory Oil Import Quota Program. Conclusions are then drawn in relation to the question of whether the legal expression of sovereignty in the realm of energy security is ever likely to be successful, or whether it inevitably provokes unintended consequences, leading possibly to the more socially and historically complex articulations of sovereignty examined in previous chapters.

THE US MANDATORY OIL IMPORT QUOTA PROGRAM

Despite a keenness to promote international trade and open markets, the United States has not been immune to the concern that when it comes to strategically important commodities markets it may have to give way to straightforward state intervention. In the years following the Second World War the United States moved quickly from being a net exporter of oil to being a net importer. Insofar as the foreign oil was both readily available and cheaper to produce than the domestic, there were concerns that the growing domestic demand would be met principally from imports and that the incentives for ongoing domestic exploration and production would be reduced. According to free-market ideals, any question about where the oil is produced should be a matter of indifference, as the market will ensure, firstly, the efficient allocation of capital and technology to those places where it can be found and produced most cheaply and secondly, the ready supply of oil to those places where the demand is greatest. In the context of a strategically important resource, vital for the military–industrial growth that was a feature of the cold war, this free-market calculus was, however, by no means regarded as sufficient. Lacking incentives for ongoing investment in exploration and production, the domestic industry might decline relative to the foreign, leaving the United States dangerously exposed in the event of any reduction in supply in time of war. In short, the supply of oil to meet demand could not be left to the simple operation of the market, as the risks were simply too great.

The roots of the approach that developed during the 1950s may be found at the end of the Second World War when the Petroleum Industry War Council resolved that for reasons of national security 'it should be the policy of [the United States] to so restrict amounts of imported oil so that such quantities will not disturb or depress the producing end of the domestic petroleum industry'.[11] The same approach was endorsed by a Senate Committee in the aftermath of the war, which offered a stark choice between, on one hand, hoping that imports would not be cut off in time of war and, on the other, taking steps to ensure adequate domestic supplies, not least by way of incentives for investment in exploration both onshore and offshore.[12] Despite this consensus between the industry and the Senate Committee, a variety of alternatives for achieving the objective of domestic energy security were offered over the next few years. Perhaps defying expectations, the Department of Defense was an apparent enthusiast for meeting the growing demand essentially from imports. Noting that the 'trend of demand as against availability has become such that ... we must adopt an active policy of favoring sizable importations of oil', it is clear that the Secretary of Defense at the time, James Forrestal, was sceptical of the ability of domestic supply to meet likely future needs.[13] In laying down principles for a national oil policy, the successor to the Petroleum Industry War Council, the National Petroleum Council, more predictably focused on 'a healthy domestic oil industry', stating that '[c]ontinuing supply to meet our national oil needs depends primarily on availability from domestic sources'.[14] A few years later, in 1952, however, the Presidential Materials Policy Committee was clearly of a similar mind to the Secretary of Defense in 1948 when it expressed doubt about the sufficiency of domestic supplies, but differed to the extent that it sought to respond to this observation by calling for the 'expansion of *both* domestic reserves *and* reserves in other producing Western Hemisphere countries'.[15]

The key step, however, was taken by President Eisenhower, when he established the Advisory Committee on Energy Supplies and Resources Policy in 1954. Reporting in 1955, this committee at one level looked to be in favour of a similarly balanced approach to that of the Presidential Materials Policy Committee, when it concluded that in the complex domain of energy security 'both domestic production and imports have important parts to play; neither should be sacrificed to the other'. Nevertheless, it was concerned that unless an appropriate balance was struck between the two 'the domestic fuels situation could be so impaired as to endanger the orderly industrial growth which assures the military and civilian supplies and reserves that are necessary to the national defense'. The precise mechanism of this impairment of the domestic dimension was expressed to be 'an inadequate incentive for exploration and the discovery of new sources of supply'.[16] This report proved to be crucial insofar as for the first time action followed in the wake of the expression of concern about the balance between domestic and imported supplies.

The initial action taken, however, did not have legal force. The president set up the Voluntary Oil Import Program in July 1957, which simply asked oil companies to restrict their imports of oil voluntarily.[17] Insofar as this was essentially asking those companies to reduce their profit margins by forcing them to prioritise the sale of more expensive domestic production over cheaper foreign production,[18] it is not surprising that many companies simply ignored the request. It appears that those least likely to comply were those who had begun foreign operations after 1948, before which time most foreign production by US companies was in the hands of five corporations, namely Exxon, Gulf, Mobil, Standard Oil and Texaco.[19] An adjustment to the Voluntary Oil Import Program on the basis of the recommendations of a Special Committee to Investigate Crude Oil Imports had the perverse effect of disadvantaging precisely the companies most willing to comply with the initial version of the scheme, while those least likely to comply with the initial version proved similarly unwilling to comply with the second.[20]

In the light of this failure of a voluntary approach to the restriction of oil imports (which with the benefit of hindsight appears in any event to have been remarkably optimistic), the Special Committee to Investigate Crude Oil Imports recommended a mandatory system. This was introduced by a presidential proclamation in March 1959 and fixed the national import quota at 12.2 per cent of domestic production.[21] The details of the Mandatory Oil Import Quota Program are complex, but even a brief overview provides an insight into the extent to which its operation constituted a significant intervention by the state in the functioning of the market for crude oil. Thus, for example, in order to avoid a situation in which long-established companies suddenly experienced a dramatic reduction in the amount of oil allocated to them, a historical minimum of 80 per cent of their allocation under the previous system was introduced. In addition to the historical minimum quota, however, there was also a sliding scale which ensured that smaller companies would receive a proportionally larger allocation. While this dual approach sought to achieve a balance between the interests of the different companies affected, it was also necessary to make adjustments on the basis of the differing needs of refiners in coastal areas of the country, which were most likely to utilise imported oil, and those in the interior, which might use none at all. Exchanges of quotas were accordingly permitted. Beyond the borders of the United States, there was also the question of whether imported oil from Canada and Mexico could realistically be regarded in the same category as oil shipped from, say, the Middle East in terms of security of supply in time of war. Thus an exemption for overland supplies was permitted – with Canada and Mexico being the only possible beneficiaries. At the same time, a yet further adjustment to the quotas allocated to refineries had to be made to ensure that cheaper Canadian oil did not flood the domestic market.[22]

What this brief review of a little-discussed state intervention in the oil market from over half a century ago reveals is the extent to which energy security and the possession or otherwise of hydrocarbon resources can impact on a country's behaviour and on its exercise of sovereignty in particular. There can be no more fervent supporter of the free market than the United States. Nonetheless, faced with overriding considerations of national security in the context of the cold war and with the unwillingness of oil companies to cooperate voluntarily, it had no hesitation in exercising sovereignty in such a way that it limited the ability both of commercial actors to trade freely and efficiently and of other states to take advantage of the capital and expertise of US companies and to export their products to a market where there was a demonstrably growing demand.[23] It is also significant that when a voluntary approach to the problem failed, the solution was the imposition of legally enforceable obligations. In other words, the achievement of security with respect to the supply of hydrocarbon resources was pursued through the exercise of sovereignty expressed through law. The fact that such actions could produce unintended side effects was, of course, already recognised in the efforts to account for the interests of commercial actors as well as the position of neighbouring countries in the detailed implementation of the mandatory programme. But these fairly obvious unintended consequences pale into insignificance compared with what happened next.

THE ORGANISATION OF PETROLEUM EXPORTING COUNTRIES

In any discussion of energy security and the way in which producer nations exercise their sovereignty to take advantage of their possession of hydrocarbon resources, the Organisation of Petroleum Exporting Countries (OPEC) is practically always the centre of attention. The popular picture is of a cartel-like organisation established with the explicit aim of raising oil prices and with the capacity to use disruptions to the supply of oil as a political lever. The truth of the matter is somewhat different. Most accounts of the founding of OPEC point to the problems facing producer nations by the end of the 1950s as a result of the domination of the industry by the so-called 'seven sisters', the five major US oil companies together with BP and Shell. The ability of these companies to set prices at low levels detrimental to the interests of the producer nations is seen as prompting the latter to join forces to counterbalance the influence of the commercial actors.[24] While this is undoubtedly part of the story, it also needs to be recognised that the interests of the founder members of OPEC (Iran, Iraq, Kuwait, Saudi Arabia and Venezuela) had all been directly affected by the US Government's Mandatory Oil Import Quota Program discussed above. As a consequence, it has been pointed out that President Eisenhower's efforts in this way 'to improve energy security may have inadvertently played a role in creating the organisation that later posed the central threat to energy security'.[25] However, even if a causal link can be established between the implementation of the Mandatory Oil Import Quota Program and the establishment of OPEC, the implication that the latter poses an inevitable threat to energy security also needs to be qualified.

In even the more serious media, it is hard to find in the coverage of OPEC any that refers to the organisation's foundational legal document: the OPEC Statute of 1961. This has been amended over the years, but it is instructive to look at the detail of the organisation's objectives and the obligations that the members have signed up to. In this regard, Article 2 is particularly important. This indicates that OPEC's key aim is 'the coordination and unification of the petroleum policies' of its members, as well as establishing the best way to protect their individual and collective interests.[26] So far, this is entirely consistent with the popular image of the self-serving cartel, but what follows immediately afterwards is at best more ambiguous. Article 2 continues that OPEC 'shall devise ways and means of ensuring the stabilisation of prices in international oil markets with a view to eliminating harmful and unnecessary fluctuations'.[27] This can be read as code for price fixing in favour of the producer, or perhaps at best as an indication of an unwillingness to allow market forces to operate, but it has to be conceded that it can also be read as entirely consistent with the interests of consumers, who benefit from stable prices which allow clarity in the planning of budgets, whether household or commercial. It is in any case clear from the discussion in the foregoing section that not even the United States is in a strong position to criticise others in relation to intervention to prevent the operation of the market when it comes to a strategically important commodity like oil. Article 2 concludes with a similarly ambiguous provision to the effect that

> [d]ue regard shall be given at all times to the interests of the producing nations and to the necessity of securing a steady income to the producing countries; an efficient, economic and regular supply of petroleum to consuming nations; and a fair return on their capital to those investing in the petroleum industry.[28]

The first part of this element of Article 2 is clearly focused on the members of OPEC, but read as a whole this could equally be presented as a statement of what should be expected from a properly functioning free market in crude oil. In other words, read as a whole, it turns out that OPEC is concerned with ensuring a balance among the interests of all of those involved in the oil supply chain, from the point of investment in exploration and production through to the end consumer and including an appropriate return to the state whose natural resources are involved.

All of this said, however, the question of sovereignty over hydrocarbon resources as opposed to the operation of the market quickly came to dominate OPEC's thinking. In 1968, the organisation adopted a Declaratory Statement of Petroleum Policy in Member Countries, which 'emphasised the inalienable right of all countries to exercise permanent sovereignty over their natural resources in the interest of their national development'.[29] The message here for international oil companies operating in OPEC member countries was clear: such states reserved the right to nationalise their oil industries. This once again ran counter to the presumptions of the market, but was in all respects in accordance with the general attitude of developing countries, who at that time were eager for clarity with respect to sovereignty over their natural resources. While OPEC resolved this issue by means of a simple declaration, the United Nations pondered the matter over a longer period. A Commission on Permanent Sovereignty over Natural Resources was set up in 1958.[30] A subsequent resolution in 1962[31] endorsed the conclusions of the commission, but did not provide the required clarity on the meaning of permanent sovereignty. More than that, the text of the resolution appeared to shift the matter of nationalisation out of the realm of domestic law and into that of international law, raising concerns among developing countries that the longed for permanent sovereignty would be attenuated by undue consideration of the interests of commercial actors based in developed nations.[32] Such concerns led in due course to the landmark developments of 1974: the Declaration[33] and Programme of Action on the Establishment of a New International Economic Order[34] and the Charter of Economic Rights and Duties of States.[35] The last of these resolved the issue of sovereignty in unequivocal terms insofar as it provided, inter alia, that '[e]very state has and shall freely exercise full permanent sovereignty ... over all its wealth, natural resources and economic activities'.[36] It also made clear that in its dealings with transnational corporations a state had the right to regulate them in accordance with 'its economic and social policies'.[37] Furthermore, a state was also explicitly able to 'nationalise, expropriate or transfer ownership of foreign property' – albeit on payment of compensation – and in the event of a dispute to have that settled in its own courts according to domestic law, unless the parties had agreed otherwise.[38] OPEC's declaration in 1968 may have raised eyebrows and ruffled transnational corporate feathers, but by 1974 it was clear that it was in very good company indeed.

Also by 1974, of course, consumer nations had something else to complain about in regard to OPEC. By then, it (or, more accurately, the Organisation of Arab Petroleum Exporting Countries or the Arab members of OPEC) had famously imposed an embargo on the United States and certain other countries in retaliation for their support for Israel in the Arab–Israel War of 1973, the action which appears to colour the popular perception of the organisation more than any other. Arguments continue as to whether it was the embargo itself that led to the emotive pictures of long queues for gasoline, or the 5 per cent production cuts which the countries involved also imposed, or indeed the excessive purchases of oil on global markets by the United States and other consumer governments. In any event, in much the same way that the efforts of the United States to exercise sovereignty in relation to energy security in the form of the Mandatory Oil Import Quota Program produced unintended consequences with the formation of OPEC, so it was the case that the exercise of sovereignty by the organisation's key members, in the form of the embargo and production cuts, led to consequences that were not foreseen.

The essential utilisation of oil supplies as a tool of foreign policy by certain OPEC members is hard to square with the objectives of the organisation set out in Article 2 of the founding statute, unless one interprets key terms in an extremely loose way. It is not at all clear that this action, which caused the first oil shock in the shape of the significant increase in prices experienced in 1973, advances any of the Article 2 objectives in terms of market stability or security of supply to consumers. Indeed, it would only be by means of the most tortured logic that one could escape the conclusion that the embargo was anything other than a complete rejection of the organisation's stated aims. But it is equally clear that, given the firmly held (and internationally supported) views with respect to permanent sovereignty over natural resources, it is not only contracts with international oil companies that could be disregarded (or at best renegotiated) in the furtherance of national interests, but international agreements as well. In other words, the clear terms of Article 2 of the statute – and thus of the legal obligations which the member countries had taken on – exercised no pull over those who had decided that foreign policy considerations supervened in the context of the conflict in 1973. Strikingly, no sanctions from within OPEC were imposed on those members who had been involved in the embargo and production cuts, as there are no provisions within the statute that would allow member countries to be disciplined in any event. The fact that the action was led by Saudi Arabia, by far the strongest member of the organisation, also serves to explain the quiescence.

The idea that there might have been some internal penalty or sanction for the apparent breach of the statute that the embargo constituted might appear fanciful, if not indeed bizarre. But this observation, if nothing else, serves to highlight a crucial feature of this international agreement: member countries sign up to a series of obligations, but it is not at all clear what the remedy would be should they fail to meet them. And by any measure the embargo and production cut can be said to have radically altered OPEC's standing – so much so, indeed, that despite the undoubted impact on supplies and, in due course, on economic growth in the United States and in the West generally, the whole project has been described as a failure. Among the arguments adduced to support this conclusion is the fact that by linking supply to foreign policy the member countries involved in the action called into question the reliability of the organisation as a supplier. The balanced, apparently market-friendly, terms of Article 2 rang rather hollow in the years following 1973. It can be argued that the expansion of non-OPEC (and especially non-Middle Eastern) supply during those years (along with attendant technological and market innovations) is directly attributable to this fact.[39]

Among the unintended consequences of the embargo and production cuts, one of the most striking from the point of view of the concerns of this chapter was the behaviour of the Organisation for Economic Cooperation and Development (OECD).

THE INTERNATIONAL ENERGY PROGRAM

The OECD was established in 1961 with the core concern of advancing economic development with a view to preserving individual liberty and improving well-being.[40] This was to be achieved by way of cooperation and consultation among the member countries, recognising the extent to which their economies were intertwined. The key means of implementing this cooperation and of achieving those objectives was to be 'the further expansion of world trade' on the basis that it 'is one of the most important factors favouring the economic development of countries and the improvement of international economic relations'.[41] Among the obligations to which the member countries agreed was to 'pursue their efforts to reduce or abolish obstacles to the exchange of goods and services and current payments and maintain and extend the liberalisation of capital movements'.[42] The organisation was and is accordingly focused on free trade and the liberalisation of global markets. Accordingly, the action of certain OPEC members in 1973 in imposing an embargo and cutting production as a political gesture was entirely at odds with the ethos of the OECD. It also indicated to consumer nations just how vulnerable they were to supply cuts from what now appeared to be an unreliable source. This was the context in which the OECD members came together to form the Agreement on the International Energy Program (IEP), which also established the International Energy Agency (IEA).[43]

Immediately evident from the preamble to the IEP agreement is the absence of any explicit reference to the OECD's core concern with free trade. Instead there is reference to the need 'to take common effective measures to meet oil supply emergencies by developing emergency self-sufficiency in oil supplies, restraining demand and allocating available oil among [participating countries] on an equitable basis' and to the need 'to reduce ... dependence on imported oil'. Behind all of this is the recognition that governments have a 'special responsibility ... for energy supply'. That said, however, the overarching concern with the operation of the market is still implicit insofar as the preamble also indicates that outside of emergency situations the participating countries are keen to foster cooperation between producer and consumer nations and to establish 'a comprehensive international information system'.

The precise means by which the IEP seeks to achieve its objectives are the following. Firstly, in order to achieve self-sufficiency in the event of an emergency, each participating country is required to hold stock equivalent to 90 days' of net oil imports.[44] Secondly, as part of the response to an emergency, each participating country must be ready to implement a programme of demand restraint 'enabling it to reduce its rate of final consumption' by an agreed amount.[45] Thirdly, measures are put in place for the allocation of oil as between participating countries in the event of an emergency[46] with allocation calculations taking account of any non-compliance by a participating country.[47] The mechanisms which would see the emergency provisions activated and deactivated are contained in Chapter IV of the agreement.

These interventions are clearly at odds with the idea that the market is best placed to respond to increases in demand in one place and surpluses in another, but they are justified in essence on the basis that they only apply when the market has failed for one reason or another. Nevertheless, it is significant that the cooperation required by the IEP from commercial actors has led to fears of antitrust violations or anti-competitive behaviour sufficient to require specific exemptions under US and EU law.[48] It is also noteworthy that the IEP is at pains to ensure that its operation does not unduly interfere with the resumption of normal market operations. Thus, for example, oil is to be allocated at a price based on the 'price conditions prevailing for comparable commercial transactions'.[49] Similarly, it is expressly stated that '[i]t is not an objective of the [IEP] to seek to increase, in an emergency, the share of world oil supply' that the participating countries received 'under normal market conditions' and that '[h]istorical oil trade patterns should be preserved as far as is reasonable'.[50] It should also be acknowledged that while the provisions of the agreement relating to an information system on the international oil market are 'designed to ensure the efficient operation' of the emergency measures, they also provide reliable information to the buyers and sellers at other times, thus contributing to the desire of the OECD (which, of course, is also shared by OPEC) for stable markets.[51] Finally, the agreement includes provisions reminding participating countries of the need to promote good relations between consumer and producer nations and in particular of the need to seek 'opportunities and means of encouraging stable international trade in oil and promoting secure oil supplies on reasonable and equitable terms'.[52]

The emergency provisions of the IEP have never been activated. The second oil shock of 1979/80 associated with supply cuts caused by the Iranian Revolution followed by the commencement of the Iran–Iraq war required the close attention of the IEA, and both Sweden and Turkey came close to the threshold that would have required specific action, but the group as a whole did not face cuts at the appropriate level. The political action of the participating countries in encouraging a collective reduction in demand (though weak compared to a legally binding action), coupled with the willingness of participating countries to allow the individual drawdown of stock, permitted the crisis to be managed without activation of the emergency procedures.[53]

Lessons were nevertheless learned from this experience and it was acknowledged that binding coordinated action would be appropriate also in circumstances short of a supply cut at the level required under the IEP. Thus, in 1984, the Governing Board of the IEA adopted the Decision on Stocks and Supply Disruptions, which established a lighter-touch response mechanism, designated the Co-ordinated Emergency Response Measures system (CERM).[54] While reiterating the importance of demand restraint, the focus of the CERM is on rapid stock drawdown as a means of calming markets in the event of supply cuts. This approach has been activated on two occasions, the first at the start of the first Gulf War in 1991 and the second in the aftermath of the hurricanes which disrupted production in the Gulf of Mexico in 2005.[55] It could thus be inferred that the IEA has never been quick to activate even the lighter-touch mechanism, preferring where possible (and certainly in any case short of war or unprecedented natural disaster) to allow the market to function. That said, however, the market now operates in the knowledge of the presence of the backstop of the very significant strategic reserves built up under the IEP and CERM, which significantly alter the landscape compared to 1973. In other words, the countries of the world most committed to the notion of the market as the most efficient mechanism for the allocation of resources have had to take action in the form of stockpiling, which in any other setting would be seen as potentially destructive of the market. They furthermore require cooperation from oil companies, which in turn requires specific exemptions from the antitrust law that exists to ensure the operation of competitive markets. All of these extraordinary actions are required precisely because of the ability of other countries to breach legal obligations and to exercise sovereignty in relation to the supply of hydrocarbon resources.

CONCLUSIONS: BY WAY OF THE ENERGY CHARTER TREATY

What lessons, if any, may be drawn from this consideration of the sequence of domestic and international legal instruments running from the American Oil Import Quota Program of the 1950s through to the establishment and operation of the International Energy Program? At one level, it could be suggested that as long as these instruments (both in their substance and in their operation) are focused on the ideal, but not the operation, of the free market, then there is relatively little contention. Article 2 of the OPEC Statute and the IEP's CERM interventions may be cited in support of that proposition. However, in marked contrast, as soon as these instruments (whether in their substance or in their operation) run counter to the functioning of the market – i.e. come to be seen as opportunities for the expression of sovereignty for political ends – problems arise. The Mandatory Oil Import Quota Program and the Arab embargo of 1973 may be cited in support of this proposition.

Can it therefore be concluded that the lesson for both producer and consumer nations is that the apparently shared objective of stable markets will only be achieved insofar as legal expressions of sovereignty in relation to hydrocarbon resources remain focused on that ideal and are not diverted by protectionist or foreign policy concerns? The Energy Charter Treaty (ECT),[56] whilst beyond the scope of this chapter, would seem to suggest that such a simplistic conclusion cannot be drawn. A creation of the immediate aftermath of the end of the cold war, the ECT is the most ambitious international legal instrument in the realm of energy security insofar as it attempts to put in place market conditions across much of

Eurasia in relation to investment, transport and trade in oil and gas. Signed up to with alacrity both by former Soviet nations hungry for investment in production, development and pipelines and by consumer nations keen to reduce further their dependence on the Middle East, the project nevertheless experienced tensions from the outset as especially Russia and the EU differed over key issues, not least the terms of a draft transit protocol to stiffen the provisions relating to this matter in the treaty.[57] These tensions were manifest especially in the failure of Russia to ratify the treaty and then its decision to terminate its provisional application of the treaty in 2009.[58] Examination of the points of contention between the EU and Russia reveal in essence very different ideas about the role that the market should play in achieving the objective of energy security, with Russia apparently unwilling to accept the notion of competition and thus the threat to the dominant position of its quasi-state companies.[59] In the end, it appears that the constraints on its ability to exercise sovereignty in relation to its energy resources persuaded Russia that it should no longer subject itself to those restrictions. The fact that the treaty extends protection to investors for 20 years beyond any termination of provisional application may mean that Russia's efforts to escape prove futile.[60] Foreign shareholders in the Yukos company whose assets were seized by Russia to cover alleged tax avoidance have taken the matter to the Permanent Court of Arbitration in the Hague. That tribunal has already confirmed, against Russia's objections, that it has jurisdiction and that Russia's obligations in relation to then existing investments do indeed persist for 20 years beyond the termination of provisional application.[61] The tribunal's findings on the merits of the case are awaited, but if they are in favour of the shareholders then there will be a potential liability to the Russian government of $100 billion. Insofar as such an award would have been made by an international tribunal, but enforcement would have to be in Russia, there is a question as to the likely attitude of the Russian courts. And here of course once again we see the potential for the rule of law to find itself prey to the supervening sovereign interests of the state. A solution exists in the shape of the New York Convention on the Recognition and Enforcement of Foreign Arbitral Awards of 1958, which would allow the successful shareholders to seek enforcement in contracting states where they have located commercial assets of the Russian state. Whatever the legality of any such move, there is once again clear potential for a political clash on the basis that Russian sovereignty is apparently challenged.[62]

There are, then, no easy answers to the question of whether the longed-for certainty that treaties and contracts are supposed to bring to the domain of energy security is more of a pious hope than an achievable reality. There are, it seems, only further questions. As this chapter has demonstrated, it is difficult to achieve such certainty when the object of the contract or treaty is strategically important hydrocarbon resources. The fact that the very legal act by which a state purports to bind itself in its relations with other states or with commercial actors is itself an expression of sovereignty indicates the difficulty in persuading a state that a further legal act negating or at least qualifying the first is thereby ruled out: there is indeed a powerful argument that the very idea is a logical impossibility. In other words, are there any circumstances in which the apparently binding legal obligations entered into by a state (whether in the context of a treaty or a contract) can really be regarded unequivocally as such, insofar as any obligation if genuinely binding would constitute a constraint on a state to exercise sovereignty in future – something which the very notion of sovereignty appears to rule out? In such circumstances, the fact that states and commercial actors continue to have recourse to treaties and contracts appears to suggest the triumph of hope over experience. And yet it is precisely because the stakes are so high when it comes to sovereignty over oil and gas resources that law is both indispensable and yet on occasion apparently powerless.

Where does this leave the whole question of energy security, which, as the foregoing discussion has demonstrated, remains a key priority for producer and consumer nations alike? Does the analysis in this chapter reveal that there is an inescapable tension between sovereignty and security which not even law in the form of binding obligations is able to resolve? It seems clear that despite the ideal (even the ideology) of the market which underpins so much of international discourse about energy security, what ultimately matters is the way in which market participants, state and commercial, actually behave.

Most significant, perhaps, is the recognition that state actors remain not just important, but key to the operation of markets. It is easy to characterise states as being in thrall to markets, but the extent to which markets depend upon states should not be underestimated. Thus, as the various instruments considered above reveal, when it comes to the functioning of global energy markets the divergence between theory and practice, between the ideal and the actual, has produced a succession of legal efforts at the international level aimed at either modifying the behaviour in particular of state actors or compensating for it. And despite the desire in each case to make things better, it could certainly be concluded on the evidence that in many instances these legal efforts actually went some way towards making them worse.

Such an assessment would, however, fail to recognise the magnitude of the task that is set for law in the context of the tension between security and sovereignty in the domain of energy. On the one hand, there is perhaps a naivety on the part of states when it comes to their ability to intervene in markets in ways that will produce predictable effects. On the other, there is perhaps a failure on the part of commercial actors to understand the extent to which markets are complex social phenomena as opposed to purely economic mechanisms and thus to understand the limits to what state actors are willing to tolerate in terms of the working out of pure competitive operations.

If there is a lesson to be drawn from this analysis, then, it is surely that of recognising the limitations of what may be possible within the confines of the economic, political and legal models currently prevailing. Whether current travails in international markets (as well as global politics) indicate that a deep change is at hand of the sort that would see some fundamental readjustment of these models is another question, but one that surely points in the direction of fruitful further analysis. Without making any predictions, it is at least possible to suggest that there may at least be indications of some sort of epochal shift. In this regard, the work of Karl Polanyi has received renewed attention in recent years as observers of first economic and now political upheaval speculate as to whether the 'great transformation' he foresaw in the closing days of the Second World War may now be at hand.[63]

Polanyi was mainly concerned in 1944 with the shift from a position in which the market is peripheral to social relations to one in which it becomes central. He was seeking to account in particular for the emergence of the European liberal state in the nineteenth century and to work through its ongoing evolution. Thus, by the time he was writing, he was also concerned to account for the rise of fascism, which he characterised as a second great transformation associated with the end game of the market's dominance of society. For Polanyi, the ascendancy of markets, beginning especially in the nineteenth century, was linked in no small measure to industriali-sation and the development of complex machines. The need for significant capital to build such machines meant that investments would only be made if their profitable operation was assured.[64] As a consequence, everything required for such profitable operation became a factor of production – including energy. This is what Polanyi referred to as the emergence of the fictitious commodities of land, labour and money, that is, things which came to be traded even though they did not fit the usual category of things produced with a view to trade. With the commoditisation of both humankind and nature in the service of industrialisation, it is not difficult to see the logic of Polanyi's argument that, all else equal, there is nothing to stop this dynamic ending in their destruction.

All else is not equal, however, as far as Polanyi is concerned, because he is convinced that society will always in the end resist the relentless advance of the market in order to avoid ultimate destruction.[65] It is clear, however, that the defeat of fascism was not the precursor to the sort of rebalancing of society and markets that Polanyi had in mind. Indeed, the years after the war have seen the exponential growth of global markets and there are strong suggestions that financial markets in particular have become dangerously decoupled from the real economy.[66] In such a context, the recent financial crisis together with political upheavals in the Middle East and North Africa are certainly suggestive developments for those who are keen to see a Polanyian retreat of markets in favour of society. But is this the only possible direction of travel? Might it not be suggested, for example, that increased democracy in producer nations (and OPEC members) such as Libya could actually strengthen the role of markets in the domain of energy? Even if the state in such circumstances were to seek to retain a greater measure of control, is it not the case that the experience of OPEC discussed above exposes the paradox inherent in attempting to protect fictitious commodities against the depredations of the unconstrained market?

The working out of this conundrum will require more than a purely legal analysis. While law is the means by which states seek to exert control over sovereign interests as against the market, the motivations are political and economic. Further investigation accordingly needs to be multidisciplinary. But it also needs to be clear on what would appear to be the desirable balance between market and society. In this respect, Polanyi's perspective was never *anti*-market, but rather only concerned that markets should serve society and not the other way round. The scale of the challenge, however, should not be underestimated. As the experience of both producer and consumer nations discussed above amply reveals, both the sovereign interests of other states and the dynamic of the market are significant obstacles in the way of the achievement of what might be a broadly acceptable balance between society and economy at the domestic level. Equally, the prospects for international cooperation are by no means all positive.

In this last regard, developments at the time of writing in relation both to OPEC and the IEA provide a useful focus for the conclusion to this chapter. In the run-up to the 159th meeting of the OPEC Conference on 8 June 2011, which took place against a backdrop of sustained supply cuts from Libya and a generally fragile world economy, especially in the developed consumer nations, Saudi Arabia had already signalled its intentions by increasing production unilaterally.[67] Then, in his opening address, the president of the conference acknowledged the pressures on consumer nations of the high oil price and also the contribution to this situation of the lack of spare downstream capacity. However, he also called for the consumer nations to play their part in minimising the impact of high prices by taking action to curb speculation, especially on futures markets.[68] Internal tensions within OPEC, however, ensured that the conference closed without any agreement on revised quotas. Given that Saudi Arabia described the 159th meeting as 'one of the worst ... we have ever had' and went on to continue its increase in production,[69] the IEA's extraordinary intervention only a few days later in announcing the release of two million barrels per day from emergency stockpiles for the next month sends a confusing signal.[70] Only the third intervention under the CERM, and the first outside of a war or natural disaster situation, it must be wondered whether this will be read by OPEC as the sort of intervention to curb speculation that it had in mind or rather as an unwelcome and even threatening exercise of sovereign power by consumer nations to adjust supply in a way that has heretofore been the preserve of the producers' grouping.

In other words, is there evidence here of, if not coordinated then at least coherent action by producers and consumers to mitigate the damaging effects of markets on society – and thus of a development that might be in line with the most optimistic Polanyian reading? Or is this only yet another event in the sequence of action and reaction between the producer and consumer blocs that ultimately encourages the most pessimistic Polanyian interpretation – namely of the relentless working out of the destructive effects of markets in spite (and even because) of the exercise of sovereign power by states by means of legal instruments designed to protect and guarantee those self-same societies? And even if one accepts the most optimistic reading, does this in turn signal a new coherence between consumer nations and only *certain* members of OPEC (such as Saudia Arabia and Qatar), thus opening up the prospect of a damaging and perhaps fatal split with the more hawkish (such as Iran and Venezuela)? If the last of these alternatives comes to pass, then the sequence of action and reaction traced in this chapter could take a quite dramatic turn with the emergence of a new set of international agreements reflecting new global alignments that move beyond the consumer/producer dichotomy – and perhaps even beyond the current form of the Energy Charter Treaty. Were that indeed to be the case, then the tension between security and sovereignty in the field of energy resources and law's role within it would take on a quite different appearance – and might indeed justifiably be described as a 'great transformation'.

NOTES

1. Note the extent to which the growth in demand from emerging economies such as India and China has attracted international attention and also prompted these countries to establish strategic oil reserves. For details of India's strategic reserve, see www.isprlindia.com/ (last accessed 26 June 2011) and for China's, see Neely 2007, p.1.
2. See Humphries 2010, pp.1–9.
3. This is a key point in the argument advanced by Giddens 2009.
4. See Webb 2009, p.471.
5. See White 1975, pp.542ff.
6. See Igiehon 2006, pp.208ff.
7. See Shihata 1974, pp.591ff.
8. Some estimates suggest that as much as 90 per cent of global oil reserves are in the hands of state oil companies. See, for example, 'Really Big Oil', *Economist*, 10 August 2006.
9. See Taverne 2000, pp.87–98.
10. See Maier 2010, pp.95ff.
11. Petroleum Industry War Council, 'Resolution', 24 October 1945. Reproduced in Fulda and Schwartz 1970, p.315.
12. Special Committee Investigating Petroleum Resources, Senate Report no.9, 79th Congress, 31 January 1947. Reproduced in Fulda and Schwartz 1970, p.316.
13. Hearings on Petroleum for National Defense before the Special Committee on Petroleum of the House Committee on Armed Services, 80th Congress, 2nd session, 133, quoted in Maynard 1969, p.151.
14. National Petroleum Council, 'Resolution', 13 January 1949. Reproduced in Fulda and Schwartz 1970, p.315.
15. Kohn 1970, p.89 (emphasis added).
16. Advisory Committee on Energy Supplies and Resources Policy, 26 February 1955. Reproduced in Fulda and Schwartz 1970, p.317.
17. Kohn 1970, p.90.

18. For an indication of the difference in production levels and costs at this time between average US wells and average foreign wells, see Maynard 1969, p.154.

19. James 1972, p.374.

20. Ibid., p.375.

21. Presidential Proclamation 3279, 24 Fed. Reg. 1781 (1958) 19 U.S.C. § 1352(a).

22. For an excellent overview of the mandatory program, see James 1972, pp.377–84. For an in-depth analysis, see Dam 1971.

23. It is important to note that there were plenty of objections to the idea of import quotas, based precisely on arguments that these offended free-market principles. For a review, see Maynard 1969, pp.154–7.

24. See Cuervo 2008, p.464.

25. Bialos 1990, p.245.

26. OPEC Statute (as amended to 2008), art.2(A).

27. Ibid., art.2(B).

28. Ibid., art.2(C).

29. OPEC, 'Brief History', www.opec.org/opec_web/en/about_us/24.htm (last accessed 26 June 2011).

30. United Nations General Assembly Resolution 1314 (XIII), 12 December 1958, 'Recommendations Concerning International Respect for the Rights of Peoples and Nations to Self-Determination'.

31. United Nations General Assembly Resolution 1803 (XVII), 14 December 1962, 'Permanent Sovereignty over Natural Resources'.

32. Taverne 2000, p.54.

33. United Nations General Assembly Resolution 3201 (S-VI), 14 May 1974.

34. United Nations General Assembly Resolution 3202 (S-VI), 14 May 1974.

35. United Nations General Assembly Resolution 3281 (XXIX), 12 December 1974.

36. Ibid., art.2(a).

37. Ibid., art.2(b).

38. Ibid., art.2(c).

39. For a convenient review of these arguments, see Copaken 2003.

40. Convention on the Organisation for Economic Co-operation and Development, Paris, 14 December 1960.

41. OECD Convention, 'Preamble'.

42. Ibid., art.2(d).

43. See also Scott 1994a, pp.27–58.

44. IEP Agreement, art.2.

45. Ibid., art.3 and ch.IV.

46. Ibid., ch.III.

47. See Redgwell 2004, p.30.

48. For a discussion, see Scott 1994b, pp.107–9.

49. IEP Agreement, art.10.

50. Ibid., art.11.

51. Ibid., ch.V.

52. Ibid., art.47.

53. See Scott 1994b, pp.114–20.

54. Decision IEA/GB(84)27, 11 July 1984.

55. See IEA 2011, p.11.

56. The Energy Charter Treaty (Annex 1 to the Final Act of the European Energy Charter Conference), 17 December 1994. For details and background, see Energy Charter Secretariat 2004.

57. Draft Final Act of the Energy Charter Conference with respect to the Energy Charter Protocol on Transit, 31 October 2003.

58. Russia informed the Depository (Portugal) on 20 August 2009 of its intention not to become a Contracting Party to the ECT. As a consequence of the terms of Article 45(3) (a) of the ECT, its provisional application of the treaty terminated on the expiration of 60 days from that notification, i.e. 18 October 2009. For details, see www.encharter.org/index.php?id=414 (last accessed 26 June 2011). See further Szlagowski 2010.

59. For a discussion, see Doeh, Nappert and Popov 2006 and Hober and Nappert 2007.

60. ECT art.45(3)(b).

61. In the matter of arbitration before a tribunal constituted in accordance with Article 26 of the Energy Charter Treaty and the UNCITRAL Arbitration Rules 1976 between Hulley Enterprises Limited (Cyprus) and the Russian Federation, Interim award on jurisdiction and admissibility, 30 November 2009, PCA Case no.AA 226.

62. For a discussion, see Riley 2010.

63. See Polanyi 2001. For an indication of recent interest in Polanyi's work, see Hann and Hart 2009.

64. Polanyi 2001, pp.42ff.

65. Ibid., pp.71ff.

66. See Menkhoff and Tolksdorf 2001.

67. See Blass and Blair 2011.

68. See the speech by HE Mohammad Aliabadi, acting minister of petroleum of the Islamic Republic of Iran and president of the conference, available online at www.opec.org/opec_web/en/2071.htm (last accessed 26 June 2011).

69. See Blair 2011.

70. For details, see www.iea.org/press/pressdetail.asp?PRESS_REL_ID=418 (last accessed 26 June 2011).

REFERENCES

Bialos, J.P. (1990) 'Oil Imports and National Security: The Legal and Policy Framework for Ensuring United States Access to Strategic Resources', *University of Pennsylvania Journal of International Business Law*, 11(2): 235.

Blair, D. (2011) 'Oil leaps as OPEC descends into acrimony', *Financial Times*, 8 June.

Blass, J. and Blair, D. (2011) 'Saudis raise oil production to curb prices', *Financial Times*, 6 June.

Copaken, R. (2003) 'The Arab Oil Weapon of 1973–74 as a Double-Edged Sword: Its Implications for Future Energy Security', Working Paper, University of Durham, Centre for Middle Eastern and Islamic Studies.

Cuervo, L.E. (2008) 'OPEC From Myth to Reality', *Houston Journal of International Law*, 30(2): 433.

Dam, K. (1971) 'Implementation of Import Quotas: The Case of Oil', *Journal of Law and Economics*, 14:1.

Doeh, D.S., Nappert, S. and Popov, A. (2006) 'Russia and the Energy Charter Treaty: Common Interests or Irreconcilable Differences?', *International Energy Law and Taxation Review*, 2006, 7:189–91.

Energy Charter Secretariat (2004) *The Energy Charter Treaty and Related Documents: A Legal Framework for International Energy Cooperation* (Brussels: Energy Charter Secretariat).

Fulda, C.H. and Schwartz W.F. (1970) *Regulation of International Trade and Investment* (Mineola, N.Y.: Foundation Press).

Giddens, A. (2009) *The Politics of Climate Change* (Cambridge: Polity Press).

Hann, C. and Hart, K. (eds) (2009) *Market and Society:* The Great Transformation *Today* (Cambridge: Cambridge University Press).

Hober, K. and Nappert, S. (2007) 'Provisional Application and the Energy Charter Treaty: The Russian Doll Provision', *International Arbitration Law Review*, 2007, 10(3): 53–7.

Humphries, M. (2010) 'Rare Earth Elements: The Global Supply Chain', Congressional Research Service, R41347.

IEA (2011) *IEA Response System for Oil Supply Emergencies* (Paris: OECD/IEA).

Igiehon, M.O. (2006) 'Present International Law on Delimitation of the Continental Shelf', *International Energy Law and Taxation Review*, pp.208–15.

James, W.F. III (1972) 'The Mandatory Oil Import Program: A Review of Present Regulations and Proposals for Change in the 1970s', *Texas International Law Journal*, 7(3): 373.

Kohn, V.L. (1970) 'The Oil Import Question: Research, Report, Reaction', *Case Western Journal of International Law*, 88(3): 88.

Maier, B. (2010) 'How Has International Law Dealt with the Tension Between Sovereignty over Natural Resources and Investor Interests in the Energy Sector? Is There a Balance?', *International Energy Law Review*, 4: 95–109.

Maynard, J.N. (1969) 'Oil Import Controls: A Critical Appraisal', *Texas International Law Forum*, 5(1): 150.

Menkhoff, L. and Tolksdorf, N. (2001) *Financial Market Drift: Decoupling of the Financial Sector from the Real Economy?* (Berlin: Springer-Verlag).

Neely, C.J. (2007) 'China's Strategic Petroleum Reserve: A Drop in the Bucket', Federal Reserve Bank of St Louis, Economic Synopses, 2007, no.2.

Polanyi, K. (2001) [1944] *The Great Transformation: The Political and Economic Origins of Our Time* (Boston: Beacon Press).

Redgwell, C. (2004) 'International Energy Security', in B. Barton, C. Redgwell, A. Rønne, and D.N. Zillman (eds), *Energy Security: Managing Risk in a Dynamic Legal and Regulatory Environment* (Oxford University Press).

Riley, A. (2010) 'The EU–Russia Energy Relationship: Will the Yukos Decision Trigger a Fundamental Reassessment in Moscow?', *International Energy Law Review*, 2010, 2: 36–40.

Scott, R. (1994a) *The History of the International Energy Agency 1974–1994, vol.1: Origins and Structure* (Paris: OECD/IEA).

—— (1994b) *The History of the International Energy Agency 1974–1994, vol.2: Major Policies and Actions* (Paris: OECD/IEA).

Shihata, I.F.I. (1974) 'Destination Embargo of Arab Oil: Its Legality under International Law', *American Journal of International Law*, 68: 591.

Szlagowski, P. (2010) 'Review of the "New Legal Framework for Energy Cooperation" and Dispute Resolution Mechanisms in Energy Transit', *International Energy Law Review*, 2010, 5: 147–54.

Taverne, B. (2000) *Petroleum, Industry and Governments: An Introduction to Petroleum Regulation, Economics and Government Policies* (Dordrecht: Kluwer Law International).

Webb, J. (2009) *Dictionary of Law* (London: Penguin).

White, R.C.A. (1975) 'A New International Economic Order', *International and Comparative Law Quarterly*, 24: 542–52.

13
Fossil Knowledge Networks: Industry Strategy, Public Culture and the Challenge for Critical Research

Bret Gustafson[1]

It is 'frightening'. So spoke Steven Leer, the clean-cut CEO of Arch Coal, one of the world's largest coal companies. Arch Coal is headquartered in St Louis, Missouri, home also to Washington University in St Louis, where I teach, and on whose board of trustees Leer also sits. Also a member of one of the university's advisory boards on research, energy, and sustainability, Leer had been invited to speak to an audience of several hundred at a university forum on 'America's Energy Future'.[2] Leer's message was simple. Coal is cheap and abundant, and we are competing with China for access to resources. American coal is the future. Against alternatives, coal was cheap. 'I'm a capitalist,' he said, 'and I believe in the free markets.' Despite his assurance that coal had a 'voice in the Senate', he dismissed the promise of renewables and then attacked the threat of new regulation of carbon emissions. Ultimately, what Leer thought was 'frightening' about America's energy future was not global warming, environmental degradation or even the poor air quality of St Louis, which leads the nation in asthma.[3] Rather, Mr Leer was referring to the 'frightening' scenario that the United States Environmental Protection Agency (EPA) might evade corporate lobbyists in Congress and act on its own to curb carbon emissions under the Clean Air Act.

What was remarkable was that a position in defence of the carbon emissions status quo could be voiced within the prestigious halls of Washington University, which prides itself on the rhetoric of greenness and sustainability and on its initiatives in public health.[4] Yet the fossil men speaking as collaborators of the university continued expounding their fossil knowledge. Following Mr Leer, one Mr Frederick Palmer, with hair like Mark Twain and a gravelly, twangy voice, spoke as vice president of government relations of Peabody Energy. Peabody, the world's largest private coal company, is also headquartered in St Louis. Its CEO also sits on the university's board of trustees.

Palmer treated the audience to a rousing story about how 'near zero emissions' from coal burning would be achieved soon with carbon capture and sequestration. With bar graphs representing 'coal' in the colour green, he preached that we will no longer talk of clean coal but of 'green coal' – the 'world's future fuel'. He led the audience through a vigorous defence of the 'normal people' of the coal industry doing good work providing cheap electricity for the public. Denying any political affiliation, he said, 'Our political party is coal.' To a smattering of applause from, among others, the university scientists and engineers receiving support for 'clean coal' research, he took his seat with other panellists to take questions. A student asked a rather modest question about the other costs of coal, like mountaintop removal. Palmer dismissed the question as a false issue, saying mountaintop removal provided little to the overall production of coal. Sitting beside him, the representative of St Louis's regional electricity company, Ameren UE, also dependent on coal-burning (and whose company is also represented on the university board of trustees), spoke too. He argued that coal had contributed greatly to the socio-economic benefit of local communities. A young lady in front of me squirmed and turned in her seat, whispering, 'What about poverty in the Appalachians?' Palmer then returned to the microphone to dismiss another question about Europe's success with cap-and-trade. 'Europe?' he sneered. 'There is nothing about Europe that we should emulate.' This was curious, given that an earlier presentation by the university's chancellor had spoken glowingly of how efficient Europe was with its energy. In fact, Palmer explained, we should emulate China, a model of growth, a country 'run by engineers, not by lawyers'. Here he gestured towards the panel of distinguished notables, university professors, scientists, and administrators sitting before him, 'like our own Chancellor Wrighton [a chemist]'.

At the event just described – a conclave in which the 'experts' were distinguished university scientists and these industry leaders – 'America's energy future' seemed to reside in a curious set of contradictions: science and anti-science, fossil power and democratic retreat, and a free-market ideology bolstered by generous government subsidies. Put another way, the university was positioning itself – in the name of science – alongside industries which spoke of merging corporate and public interests through the language of price and national security. At the same time, this expert knowledge promoted transfer of control over public goods (air, knowledge, democracy) to private hands. Dirty air, ideologised science and police states were not frightening scenarios for these fossil men. The university, as suggested by Stefan Collini, describing how universities are redirecting their research toward corporate contracts and interests, was 'supping with the devil'. Here they did so with a very short spoon.[5] Meanwhile, the university charges ahead with its work on 'clean' coal, public health, and 'sustainability'. For its part, two months after the forum, based on its claims that the science of global warming was spurious, Peabody joined nine other energy countries in a collective industry attack on the EPA's power to regulate air pollution.[6]

In this chapter I offer observations on characteristics of fossil knowledge – representations of truth, sentiment and experience produced by, or in relation to, the oil, gas and coal industries. I draw primarily on the perspective of the United States, drawing on observations of the public politics of oil knowledge as expressed in advertising and popular culture, regional 'regimes' of fossil power, think-tank production, and the implications of corporate support of university research. My objective here – based on my concerns about global warming and the anti-democratic agenda of the American fossil industries – is to consider where and how scholars in relatively marginal fields like anthropology might best engage and critique hegemonic models of fossil knowledge production and diffusion. To this end, I suggest that the broadly networked character of fossil knowledge – which articulates private sentiments, public culture, and the institutionalised hypocrisy of science and anti-science – is an ideological project sustained through diverse, multi-scalar interventions into public life.

I understand knowledge here, with a nod to Latour (1993, 2007), as a networked phenomenon which traverses and mobilises different nodes of actors, resources and symbolic projects – some more, some less reliant on the discourse of scientific truth. My use of the concept of networks does not, however, share Latour's concern for critiquing scientific practice or positing 'networks' as the privileged metaphor of social organisation. Following Barry (2006), a Latourian formulation does not displace a political–economic understanding of structural power. Clearly, fossil power and knowledge is a manifestation of capitalist power in the United

States. While it uses 'science' selectively, what is merged, purified and performed by fossil knowledge is not 'pure' science, but a culturally mediated public truth about the 'good' of fossil fuels. As evidenced above, and whether cast as science or advertising, fossil knowledge expresses at its core an ideological project. What is at stake is a struggle against the dispossession of public goods by private interests, a struggle being waged with agents who – by virtue of the geological and geopolitical materialities of hydrocarbons – hold an inordinate amount of power to influence, and thus appropriate, public goods, space and desire. To explore fossil knowledge as networked knowledge is to draw attention to political strategies and to better understand connections, nodes, and flows – such as those linking corporations and universities. This requires thinking in a Gramscian way about the complex war of position being waged on the terrain of public culture. In what follows, I juxtapose expressions of fossil knowledge in distinct manifestations – from the culture of automobility to think tanks and universities. I draw attention to the performative and spectacular qualities of fossil knowledge, and to the contradictions of its articulated fabrications, which seek to merge the culturally mediated valuations and transformations of oil – as power, masculinity, security, desire, and technology, to name a few – with regimes of science. Making these processes visible, I suggest, raises questions of theoretical interest, but also sheds light on political strategy. In particular, the very grounded modes through which fossil knowledge comes to ground in regional political assemblages suggest that work aimed at an empirical and ethical critique of nodes and articulations, like that of the university supping with the devil, is of proximate and primary importance.

Fossil knowledge is a spectacular vortex which seeks to entangle itself with public interest and popular desire, and does so through an identifiable assemblage of institutional arrangements, each with inevitable geopolitical dimensions. It is powerful, yet not hegemonic, and is thus in constant ideological struggle, on a war footing, against leakage, spillage, attack, and exposure. Barry (2006), borrowing from Harvey (2003), offers the metaphor of the vortex, because the fossil industries both spew out and obscure or devour 'knowledge'. Using the example of transparency – and following the general argument of this volume – Barry points out that claims to transparency necessarily entail strategies of exuberant knowledge diffusion and performance about what companies supposedly do; but he also suggests a necessary obfuscation. Any cursory contact with fossil self-representations, in newspaper and media advertising for example, shows that fossil industries strive to be visible and audible, spewing forth (mis)representations of the industry in print and Internet imagery. At the same time, industry seeks to blot out other truths about reserves, revenues, bribes, chemical use, security arrangements, fossil impacts, and so forth.[7] In the realm of science, fossil industries invest intensely in 'scientific' research and embrace 'technology' as the solution to the world's ills, while working to mislead the public on climate science or to challenge evidence tied to the violence and socio-environmental impacts of extraction (see the case discussed by Sawyer 2003). This vortex-like production of knowledge draws our attention to a series of contradictions, but should remind us of the inherent weakness of fossil knowledge as a claim to truth, and reveals the inherent defensive nervousness of an industry that faces the inevitable demise of these energy resources.

A second characteristic of fossil knowledge is its spectacular production of imaginaries and desires. This is a characteristic of oil knowledge regimes more broadly, which tend to produce grandiose visible signs of development, power and wealth, despite hollow, narrow-based economies, and fragile social fabrics.[8] The rise of oil architecture in sites like Dubai, Baku, and Houston is one such manifestation of the spectacular. One might find numerous others in the flamboyant projects and tactics of oil states and oilmen, from Rockefeller to the less memorable Glenn McCarthy, immortalised by James Dean in *Giant*. In the realm of knowledge production, the performance of grandeur is tied not only to specific actors or ideological projects (which, as above, seek to make invisible the faultlines like exploitation and natural destruction), but aims at aligning corporate interests with public sentiments and structures of feeling. Of late, these efforts have been tied to the propagation of fear and a discourse of security, the notion of inevitable technological innovation, growth and a maintenance of current patterns of consumption, and the production of gendered and classed consumptive desires. I return to these themes below.

A third characteristic of fossil industries and fossil knowledge is tied to its geopolitical grounding in specific expressions of regionalism and nationalism, despite its trans-territorial operation and global reach. Fossil knowledge may of course be linked to relatively progressive nationalist projects and social agendas, as in such places as Bolivia or Brazil. Yet for the consuming north – and in oil enclaves globally – fossil knowledge produces national and regional space-times of a certain kind. This privileges autonomous regional enclaves, wherein the temporal priorities of free extraction and dependence on coal or oil or gas predominate beyond the consumer into regional, corporate cluster economies.

At this regional scale, fossil industry seeks to capture relevant institutions and symbols, while expelling other kinds of social pressures or obligations.[9] Fossil industries rely on these corporate friendly clusters and enclaves (Houston, St Louis, Bakersfield) where their need to manage trans-local fossil extraction networks seeks political and institutional synergies that allow them to perform narratives of good citizenship while distancing themselves from wider regulatory control. In the case of St Louis, growth elites have of late explicitly embraced the language of corridors, clusters and nodes, an anti-national promotion of uneven development as the core strategy of growth.[10] Tactical alliances between 'regional' interests and fossil interests follow. Positioning itself as a region of 'science', St Louis embraces Monsanto, Boeing, Arch Coal, Peabody and Patriot as anchors in its striving to become a satellite node or 'hub' for trade with China, a fantastical dream that has yet to congeal. Additionally, the city is positioned as a carbon-dependent transit node (river, rail, highway, pipeline) along a carbon corridor linking strip mines in Wyoming and the tar sands of Canada with points south, including the massive refinery just across the river. While global city regions like New York position themselves as financial managerial centres, carbon regions like St Louis offer another 'niche'. Physical and institutional occupation of such regional niches shapes fossil knowledge production intensely, and is key to their recent embrace of regional universities as part of a broader strategy of enclaved self-defence.

The fossil industry – as knowledge and experience producer – works hard to reproduce the very short temporalities linked to individualised concerns with price and the impulses of desire in the US context. In a parallel way, knowledge production at broader regional and national scales that is sympathetic to the fossil industry generally frames its concerns within atemporal, futuristic and dehistoricised narratives about security. The convergence of short-term desire and long-term security displaces other temporal frames and knowledges that might subvert fossil power. As observed by Logan and McNeish (n.d.), the struggle over temporality is ultimately a struggle between the public and the private, and as such is inseparable from projects aimed at making space and scale, the terrains on and across which political struggle unfolds.[11] At the national scale, the battle, as Logan points out, is over the narrative of transition or stasis between forms of energy production and the urgency (or not) of regulation and control. The core ideological stance of the fossil men is to push into the future the question of renewables and to position present government taxation, regulation or control as obstacles to short-term growth and accumulation. National narratives of security and prosperity, to which I return below, characterise these knowledge and time-fabricating priorities.

In the sections below I consider these characteristics through two fields of fossil knowledge, one tied to the cultural production of public sentiment, the other to the academic production of 'social scientific' knowledge.

AUTOMOBILITY AND THE AMBIGUITY OF DESIRE

At the risk of converting a point of national pride (the American car) into a source of national embarrassment, it is useful to consider how deeply imbricated particular forms of fossilised sentiment, desire and experiential knowledge are tied to automobility and the making of personhood in this country.[12] If one asks – as I often do of my middle- to upper-middle-class private university students – what we know about oil, very little substantive empirical knowledge is forthcoming. While some general comments on oil and conflict, the Middle East or Venezuela may bubble up, students have little to say until the conversation turns to the price of gasoline, and from there, to the automobile. Car driving is a nearly ubiquitous experience for this segment of American youth and the wider population. The 'culture of automobility' is the dominant matrix through which hydrocarbon knowledge of some sort is produced and experienced. The geological and geographical sources of oil, modes of extraction, transport and processing, historical connections between the USA and extractive regions and countries, and the linkages between oil and anti-democratic politics at home and abroad, are all opaque at this scale. Clearly, the advertising work of the fossil industry deploys its spectacular vortex here – foregrounding an array of eroticised possibilities tied to oil consumption while creating distance from oil's origins and other manifestations. That 'oil has something to do with' situations and relations with places like Iraq is certainly acknowledged by the informed student–citizen, but little is known about the dynamics of oil and the United States at home or elsewhere. The rare activist or environmentalist provides the exception. For the individual, oil knowledge is about gasoline price knowledge and the deeply emotive characteristics of automobility culture (Sheller 2004) and the 'driver–car' assemblage as a reflection of American personhood (Dant 2004).

Of late, the American love for automobility retains its centrality despite the collapse of Detroit and the Deepwater Horizon oil disaster. Along with the recent public relations onslaught of the American Petroleum Institute (API), the government-backed attempt to revive Detroit converges with a renewed celebration of the car in advertising. It is here that oil, in particular, works to redirect class ideologies and articulated identities into liberatory, usually masculinist and white fantasies of nationalist power. These surround oil-fuelled symbols such as the Dodge Ram, whose recent ad campaign invoked working men and tough trucks, sharing the optimistic message, 'My tank is full.' Despite rising unemployment and the decline in audiences, the nation's most popular spectator sport, NASCAR (National Association for Stock Car Auto Racing), exerts an enthralling power through massive spectacles marked by red, white and blue, flyovers of F-14 fighter jets, heroes, villains, fried chicken, cold beer and the roar of combustion. Admittedly, the roar of 30 stock cars passing close by the fence pushing nearly 200 miles per hour is an unparalleled sensory experience, one deeply imbricated with the production of (largely white, male) working-class culture in much of the country. Another example is the movie *Cars*, which raised to a near religious status icons of the road trip, heroic individualism and sexual conquest – all in a children's movie – while offering a near tear-jerker, which illustrated the 'driver–car' fusion of human bodies and cars in the American psyche. Surrounded by peripheral ethnic others and a dim-witted yet loveable working hick of a tow truck, the race car hero Lightning McQueen and the sexy Porsche, Sally Carrera – whose rear end is even adorned with a tattoo colloquially known as a 'tramp stamp' – bring hetero-normative American sexualities into play with a nostalgic celebration of the road trip westward. Cars traverse a natural landscape with buttes and plateaus shaped like the hoods of 1940s-era Chevrolets. Here again a subtly populist narrative of small-town survival contradicts the movie's embrace of cars, which fuelled patterns of capitalist expansion that undermined these very imaginaries. If pressed, one might conjure up critical traction in the movie as a critique of modernity and capitalist abstraction. Indeed there are throwaway lines against oil conspiracies, the villainy of hostile takeover banks, and the sponsorship of the flamboyant, yet fossilised, dinosaur oil company. Yet the ultimate narrative is one of a love story – with ourselves, with our nation, with consumption and with our cars. The 'our' of course, is the white American. *Cars 2*, out in the Summer of 2011, goes global – with nefarious offshore oil dealings and new Others: Japan, Germany, Italy, Spain, France, the United Kingdom and Brazil. The storyline has the cars racing in a World Grand Prix – backed by a British oil baron, Sir Miles Axelrod, who has used his wealth to invent the alternative green fuel of the future, Allinol. Stay tuned for its twists and turns on global automobility.

What is absent from most everyday fossil-related popular culture and knowledge is any sustained critical narrative against the political–economic relationships between privatised oil-industry power, the nation state and individualised citizen–consumers. There is of course a subtly resistant experiential knowledge and intuitive critical morality among the public that is suspicious of 'Big Oil'. This diffuse public suspicion articulates around contradictory sentiments bridging gasoline prices and a populist distrust of flamboyant oil wealth and power. Big Oil as a cultural phrase thus has a negative valence. Yet the contradictions make this a shallow moral reserve of critique, based as it is on a kind of moral economy – as long as prices are low or reasonable, the wealth and power of Big Oil is not questioned. Note for instance that the TV series *Dallas*, which ran from 1978 to 1991, and in which J.R. Ewing, an oilman, was the villain, emerged in the wake of the oil crisis. An earlier series, *The Beverly Hillbillies*, among others, romanticised the possibility that we all might become Big Oil. The spectre of Big Oil arises in times of high prices or perceived oil-industry malfeasance, but otherwise lies dormant, because of its dependence on the subjectivity of the consumer–citizen. The fossil industry understands this moral economy well. Recent ad campaigns by Chevron in fact try to resignify Big Oil and embrace the ambiguous label, proclaiming that Big Oil helps the [little] 'people' and 'small business'. Similarly, the API's recent media strategy includes mockumentary video that reports how ordinary people, retirees and shareholders in fact own and benefit from Big Oil.[13]

In a somewhat more politicised vein that transcends price–consumer moralities, popular culture productions like the movies *Syriana* and *There Will Be Blood*, among others, do restage the trope of Big Oil as evil. Yet most such movies suffer the narrativising work of Hollywood which transforms structural violences into morality tales. *Syriana* leaves viewers with a sense of individual disempowerment against the military–oil–intelligence regime. *There Will Be Blood* demotes Sinclair Lewis's impassioned socialist tract,

Oil, into a tale of moral degradation.[14] Whether seen through cars or *Cars*, popular fossil knowledge and culture revolve around individual subjectivities, desires, agencies and moralities linked primarily to the position of consumer–citizen. Outside of activist arenas, there is little diffuse evidence of a critical popular cultural knowledge that critiques the wider structural and political workings of fossil power.[15] While this may seem obvious to some readers, it is radically divergent from the very different histories of popular knowledge and oil in sites like Bolivia, Venezuela and Brazil. In such places, popular knowledge articulates a quite different set of relationships between sentiment, subjectivity and oil from the position of nationalist and citizen narratives constructed around anti-imperialist sentiments and the critique of inequality and exploitation (Gledhill 2011). As I discuss further below, the fossil industry is also hard at work fomenting a particular kind of nationalism that is precisely *not* like these popular Latin American forms.

THINK, TANKS

At a very different scale, the labour of professional knowledge producers in think tanks is also deeply imbricated in the making of public fossil knowledge. These include institutions like the Brookings Institution (e.g. Pascual and Elkind 2010), the Council on Foreign Relations (e.g. 2006); the CATO Institute, and perhaps most prominently, CERA (Cambridge Energy Research Associates). The latter, associated with the author of *Prize*, Daniel Yergin, has positioned itself as the leading global purveyor of fossil fuel knowledge, a commodity that can be bought and sold by those engaged in the workings of the industry. CERA's work echoes the generally Whiggish treatment of oil narrated by Yergin, producing knowledge that furthers the priorities of access and extraction that has long characterised American dependency on foreign oil. Agencies like the Brookings Institution, while offering some critical assessments of oil dependence, are also concerned with particularly 'national' priorities like 'energy security' (advised, in fact, by Daniel Yergin). Merging security concerns tied to geopolitics, economics and the environment, such efforts orient research guided by the paradigm of 'energy security'. By this is meant the 'access to secure, adequate, reliable, and affordable energy supplies'. As such, security discourse mobilises a concern to produce macroeconomic knowledge about price shocks and the management of risk, as well as geopolitical knowledge related to national security and concerned with the fact that oil and gas are 'concentrated in unstable regions'.[16] The concern with energy security is linked closely to a paradoxical convergence of market liberalisation (which brings with it 'commodity price risk') and the resurgence of national oil companies (and questions of security of 'access'). The issues of access to reserves and the regulation of flows, or 'networks', of fossil commodities are of crucial importance to the fossil-dependent industries and the fossil industry itself. Research with these ends tends to predominate in the world of 'think-tankery'.

For its part, the American Petroleum Institute also works to produce knowledge in the form of business consulting and research. These efforts complement the production of ads on television, radio, and in print that seek to shape public 'knowledge' of the industry. These 'studies' are carried out by Beltway consulting firms or friendly academics, and are *timed* for release in relation to key debates, such as that over offshore drilling (e.g. Vidas and Hugman 2008), debates over taxation (Wood Mackenzie Energy Consulting 2010), or the putative contributions of the industry to jobs in the midst of the economic crisis (Price, Waterhouse and Coopers 2009). The API also projects itself as having a role in educating the public, with dedicated interactive websites to test your knowledge and to teach you about oil, such as the mock college course, 'Oil and Gas 101' (API 2011a). The API maintains a network of websites, each named differently yet all in some ways subsumed under the API umbrella. These offer 'knowledge' on oil and gas, the 'building blocks' of society, defend the industry against critical documentaries such as *Gasland*, and attack social and natural scientists who produce critical knowledge as questionable academics.[17] The industry's own 'academic' efforts circulate as press releases to industry media and the popular press (Porter 2011; Legere 2011). The API also mobilises imaginary popular 'movements' of people through its Internet sites. These 'movements' conjure up the image of a mass national public whose interests are defended by the industry. These fictive movements speak of a security-oriented populist vision of 'we the people' joined together in an 'energy nation' of 'energy citizens'[18] working hard against taxes, regulation and government intervention, and for 'American' energy, revenue and jobs. All of these sites rely heavily on video and YouTube pages that purport to share the voices of hard-working Americans. 'Energy Citizens' has 10,000 Facebook fans. The pages here are distinctly red, white and blue, with energy – and the private fossil industry – portrayed as defending 'our way of life'. This attempt to popularise Big Oil

– against the image of the white male oilman as the prototypical corporate executive, the 'villain' of popular media – has also led to an API effort to represent itself through women. Although it sounds like the title of a calendar of spurious prurience, the API's 'Women of Oil and Gas' is a series of YouTube videos of testimonials by female industry executives (Energy Tomorrow 2011). These women recently travelled to Washington to testify about oil's commitment to the American family, thus seeking to domesticate oil through patriarchal ideologies that position women as nurturers rather than violent conquerors. The group also included a few women of colour, ostensibly a bid to diversify what has long been a deeply racist corporate project (API 2011b).[19] Clearly, the industry, with a deep and intimate understanding of the American audience, is on a war footing and wages its struggle over truth at multiple scales and on multiple fronts.

UNIVERSITY CAPTURE

The industry has also expanded its efforts in recent years to embed itself within a range of university research centres that have emerged to address questions of energy. Most of these are linked to the hard sciences. Many are financed directly by fossil capital. At my own university, the giant coal companies (including Arch Coal, whose CEO opened this chapter, and Peabody Energy) collaborated in promoting research on 'clean coal'. Small groups of students have mobilised to contest this fusion of scientific work with corporate branding. Yet the university defends its work as part of the pursuit of sustainability (through carbon sequestration) and its wider support of a pro-growth 'clustered' regionalism that seeks to articulate with the perceived hegemony of China in the arena of coal, carbon sequestration and future markets. These efforts are necessary, participants suggest, given that China will continue consuming coal (as will we), and that we must find solutions to coal emissions in the near term. As a result, we both compete and collude with China in the search for workable carbon sequestration technologies. Again, inevitability, both a particular temporality and national security pervade these ways of talking about and making knowledge. These discourses in defence of 'science' ignore wider political agendas (such as the industry attack on the EPA) and more obvious deep contradiction with public health issues regionally. My own university's emphasis on sustainability is rife with other such contradictions, and, as with other university–industry collaborations, the relationship is tightly managed as part of the public 'branding' of the university.

As these 'energy institutes' proliferate geographically, they reaffirm the spatial and geopolitical materialities and particularities of fossil fuels as embedded in distinct places, institutions and actors, as described above. This sets up region-specific regimes of knowledge production where fossil capital attempts to capture universities – as it also seeks to capture and redefine energy cities and regions – while proclaiming a distinct kind of loyalty to place and people (or portions thereof). Aberdeen's own embrace of the label 'World Energy City' – along with others in the World Energy Cities Partnership – goes along with the broader tactics of uneven neoliberal development and sets the stage for attempts by industry to capture, sequester and reorient university labour as well as other region-specific cultural and political processes and spaces.[20] Congruent with a wider turn toward the discourse of regional 'autonomy' here and elsewhere in the world, this model of corporate–scientific regionalism mirrors the uneven development of neoliberalism and capital flows by creating a network of knowledge nodes globally, nodes that are geographically and politically linked to specific places and institutions (regions and universities) (Gustafson 2006, 2009). The logic of the university–industry nexus suggests in part that industries maintain an interest in outsourcing their own research and development to relatively cheaper scientific labour. In addition, in the case of publicly questioned sunset industries like oil and coal, industries seek to use the veneer of university and scientific prestige to polish their reputations through the language of scientific validation. However, within university settings there is a clear bias toward the hard sciences. In intellectual milieu marked by commercialisation, the marginalisation of the social sciences and humanities, and hard (but unprofitable) disciplinary boundaries, tend to mean that the social sciences in general, and more particularly any sense of critical social research, have little relevance. This nexus of fossil industry and university 'science' has little room for critical social science.[21]

Yet there is social science carried out under industry sponsorship at other such energy institutes. A survey of the scholarship of these university think tanks, for instance the list of publications generated by the Baker Institute at Rice University and the Oxford Energy Institute over the past few years, reveals a central concern with the paradigms of 'security' and price 'risk' and the management of both. Albeit a limited sample, out of 82 research publications generated by Rice and Oxford's respective energy institutes, 43 focused on market concerns (supply, pricing, regulation), 16 were on geopolitical disputes, 15 directly invoked the theme of security, five were on renewable energy, and three on resource management.[22] As above, this reflects an intellectual and ideological orientation toward market liberalisation, in which academic labour is aligned with corporate sponsors' interests. The geopolitical positioning of this intellectual work is at once regional, national and transnational, but firmly aligned with the interests of the consuming north. This may seem obvious and unremarkable to those engaged in this work, yet there are clear epistemological and ideological implications for knowledge production. Consider, for instance, how such a research institute or think tank might craft their research priorities were they writing from the stance of the global south, or more precisely, an oil-dependent nation of the global south – or better yet, from the perspective of social movements affected by oil regimes in the south. Even when delving into issues like poverty – as did one of scores of articles published by the Baker Institute – the approach highlights energy access as the key to poverty reduction, as might be expected.[23] A testament again to the geographic and geopolitical specificity of these research ventures themselves, Oxford's publications included 20 on Europe and associated regions, with particular concern for gas supplies to Europe, while Rice, based in Houston, had no publications on the European situation, but focused more broadly on extractive regions (Latin America, Canada, the Caspian, and the Middle East) linked directly to US foreign policy and corporate concerns with access. Clearly the fixation on security as an epistemological anchor is productive in multiple ways, addressing issues of supply and access that worry companies, but also working discursively to frame academic and public conversations in a defensive stance. As the anthropologist Daniel Goldstein suggests, 'a public that is highly fearful of perceived external threats may be more likely to authorize extraordinary state [or corporate] powers in exchange for a greater sense of personal or collective security'.[24]

As related by Fernandes (2011), and reviewed by Agpak (2011), the 'embeddedness' of the oil industry in the academy of the consuming global north parallels the academy's rapid militarisation, commercialisation and securitisation. Fernandes (cited in Agpak 2011), writes of the (now) scandalous embrace of Qaddafi by the London School of Economics – a relationship in which oil was transformed into academic credentials, with connections to BP's interests in Libya. Agpak notes that a BP executive sat on LSE's board at the time. Among scores of other such examples, as this book went to press, news accounts emerged of the oil-rich Koch Brothers and their virtual purchase of the economics department at Florida State University, where they will have a say in the hiring of economists who promote free enterprise and critique regulation.[25] Even without such public scandal, the shifts reflected in these university–industry relations highlight deeper challenges to the autonomy of universities – both public and private, and to knowledge production more generally as a public good threatened by dispossession (Washburn 2010; Simms 2003). In the US context, Washburn, working from the relatively progressive think tank, the Center for American Progress, reported on the ten largest of 55 research agreements signed between universities and energy companies identified in 2007 and 2008. The top ten were all associated with Big Oil, with funding ranging into the hundreds of millions of dollars, most of it aimed at research tied to the putative pursuit of alternative energy technologies, most of it in biofuels. What was most significant, the report argues, based on the analysis of contractual agreements, was the overall trend toward cession of intellectual authority from the university to the corporations. In nine of the ten cases, public universities ceded majority control to the companies over the boards that oversaw these research activities, ceded control over open publication rights and information sharing, and weakened the peer review system as it pertained to overseeing grants that emerge out of this relationship. The implications are that academic integrity yields to corporate commercial concerns, and university labour is skewed against public funding that might influence other types of research, whether in the social sciences or in the hard sciences, aimed at post-fossil energy. As with public schools, the reorientation of public universities toward private interests, while touted as 'public–private' partnership, suggests a privatisation effect through accumulation by dispossession. Such corporate strategies appropriate the value and legitimacy of public institutions and knowledge workers. It is of little consequence that, as Washburn points out, these investments are relatively small compared to oil industry revenues.[26] It suggests merely that knowledge production is cheap for Big Oil, and is significant as theatrical spectacle, perhaps even more so than as economic functionality. Moreover, such arrangements – as with the touting of the region of science or the energy city – tend to exert a hegemonic urge to control the wider 'academic culture' and its ideological underpinnings, exercising the vortex effect by absorbing universities into the language of entrepreneurialism while devaluing knowledge pursuits that have little market or 'branding' value.

REFLECTIONS

Barry (2006) suggests that what is at stake is not a reification of the networked quality of oil knowledge, nor, following Huber (2009), a reification of all-powerful 'oil'. Rather, what is of concern is how the very specific agents and relations tied to oil regimes articulate (or oppose) relationships between 'scientific and technical expertise and political action' which may 'demand new ways of thinking about politics'.[27] It would seem then that the task of critical social scientists, anthropologists and their colleagues in related fields is not only to inquire into the local impacts of hydrocarbon regimes, nor to theorise the transformative work of oil regimes in processes of value transformation and circulation. Rather, taking a cue from investigative journalists, it seems that anthropologists might turn their rhetoric of 'public engagement' toward attention to the vertical and horizontal workings of fossil knowledge networks. Against the tendency of traditional anthropological research to focus on the individual, culture, and moralities of consumption (Wilk 2009), such ethnographic work might try to describe and critique – through traces I have tried to sketch here – the practices and relationships through which fossil knowledge captures, articulates and contains critical ways of knowing. The multiple nodes of connection and articulation between public and popular experience – as described through our embodied car-selves and the everyday of consumption – and the work of institutionalised knowledge production, set out a range of scales and nodes for engaging in critical knowledge work. Thinking in a Gramscian way, through wars of position, requires understanding critique not as a singular dialectic but as a multidimensional cultural struggle over truth. The API certainly has captured this understanding, and uses it to great advantage. Critical scholars should work to position themselves to critique and dismantle the nodes of these fossil knowledge network articulations at different scales.

CODA

Oil has a right to be heard. And aid to higher education is a responsible approach, however much one may quail at the assumption that the search for knowledge should ultimately reveal private enterprise as the highest creation of man and however much one may deplore the support of education in so rich a society by the back door of corporate generosity. But when viewed in the context of the full range of oil's courtship of the American people, from broad advertising to political persuasion, this concern for education emerges as one more tactic for dealing with public reactions, for reinforcing public acceptance of private power and privilege. (Robert Engler, *The Politics of Oil*)[28]

Robert Engler's 1961 study – a manifesto of sorts – reveals that much of what I have presented here is not new, but reflects a longer history of the joint ascendance of oil power and American power in the post-Second World War era. Engler detailed how the API had since its founding in 1919 maintained a singular strategy that worked to confuse the public interest with the interest of privately held oil giants – as it still does today. In the 1930s, the API targeted 'New Dealers' and progressives, but in the 1940s it rolled out the idea that 'petroleum is progressive' against regulation and in defence of the idea that supply and demand were behind price. The chairman of the board of Standard Oil, Frank Abrams, gave the first speech announcing the need for business to stake its place in higher education in 1947. In the 1950s, the API's 'Oil Information Committee' sought to merge oil interests, national interests and security interests, while intensifying efforts to cultivate and shape the work of prestigious university researchers. By 1955, oilman K.S. Adams, of Phillips Petroleum, was speaking at Drury College in Springfield, Missouri against the perceived threat of nationalism. As if speaking against the bogeyman of socialism today, he argued that 'only when the entire field of production is privately owned and operated will the spirit of man be free'.[29] The oilmen targeted public education as well, seeking to shape curricula and promote oil interests in schools, a precursor of intervention into public goods which has shifted today to the oil-funded onslaught on public education and public-sector unions.[30] Along the way, the fusion of oil with the mythic aesthetic of the wealthy oilman preached to the American everyman that 'you may be next', fuelling, as it does today, the notion of a nation of consumer citizens who enjoy the benefits of oil, and who might, like Jed Clampett in *The Beverly Hillbillies*, strike it rich at any time.

Engler finished his book in 1959, the year of the Cuban Revolution. While we witness the apparent decline of oil power and American empire, it is clear that the aggressive attempt by the fossil industry to capture public interest, sentiment and goods – and in many ways, the state itself – is intensifying in a new cold war of sorts. In this new context, Engler's message is still useful. He argued that oil had so permeated American society that it was able to obscure the 'full nature and impact of the private government of oil', a reality that came into direct conflict with the ideals aimed at 'creating the proper climate for a responsible and democratic society'.[31] He called for a rethinking of the preponderant 'national concern with production, efficiency, and pecuniary incentives' and questioned the 'concentrated international government of oil'.[32] As if he were writing today, he also detailed how in the name of 'national interest' and 'national security' (along with freedom and enterprise) the oil industry had captured law, governmental apparatuses and public opinion while reaping benefits and privileges unavailable to other industries.[33] Particularly prescient, albeit unconsciously so, Engler wrote of the contradiction between private power and public purposes as a growing threat to democracy:

> The nation has been living on the fat of its heritage and wealth that has allowed an unparalleled margin for error and waste. Moral smugness has fostered an attitude of superiority and fear, rather than understanding toward the multiple revolutions convulsing much of the world. This insensitivity places the United States on the brink of war wherever people are on the march against want and tyranny. At home ignorance and mass absorption in personal advancement have resulted in complacency toward fundamental antidemocratic developments.[34]

Engler died in 2007; but were he able to sit in our university auditorium to hear coal-man Palmer wax poetic on how nice 'America's energy future' would be with a China-like state led by scientists and businessmen, and to hear the applause of university officials, he could not put it better than he did in those lines from 1959.

NOTES

1. I thank John-Andrew McNeish and Owen Logan for the invitation to participate in the 'Flammable Societies' project, and for the critical suggestions and insights by them and others that led to the ideas formulated here. Owen Logan provided sources that allowed me to draw crucial conceptual connections. Conversations with Nicole Fabricant, Glenn Stone, Lia Haro and with the participants in the Flammable Societies Conference held in Bolivia in 2009 also contributed to this chapter. Its shortcomings are mine alone.
2. These statements were taken down by me as field notes at the event, on 2 November 2009.

3. St Louis led the nation in asthma in 2009, was second in 2010, and dropped to sixth in 2011. St Louis is a region characterised by urban sprawl and high commuter rates and an economy heavily dependent on its role as a crossroads in rail, interstate, river and air transport and warehousing, and is surrounded by coal-fired power plants, manufacturing and hospital centres – large emitters – and a large oil refinery. Rankings from the Asthma and Allergy Foundation of America (www.aafa.org).
4. See www.wustl.edu/initiatives/sustain/.
5. See Collini 2011.
6. Based on the now debunked claim that the East Anglia emails undermined climate science, in February 2010 Peabody and nine other energy companies submitted petitions questioning the EPA's endangerment finding of December 2009 on the risks posed by key greenhouse gases to health and future generations; see EPA 2011 and Peabody Energy 2011. Peabody's petition was signed by Frederick Palmer, among others. The climate-science denial website Science and Public Policy (www.scienceandpublicpolicy.org) published and circulated the petitions of Peabody and other energy companies, all of which were denied by the EPA in 2010. On Science and Public Policy's site, one finds links to several books for sale, among them *The Many Benefits of Atmospheric CO_2 Enrichment*, which according to the site was co-authored by Peabody's former director of environmental science Craig Idso. Idso, who, like Palmer, hails from Arizona, also runs the Center for the Study of Carbon Dioxide and Global Change (www.co2science.org/). This centre was funded at one time by ExxonMobil, and allegedly funded by Western Fuels, where Palmer was previously president; see Greenpeace 2003 and exxonsecrets.org 2011. Without the need to speculate on circumstantial connections, Palmer's own view of science parallels these climate-science deniers. The association between these companies and Washington University is paradoxical, given that the university positions itself as a bastion of science (though it receives support from Peabody Energy for its 'clean coal' research). In an interview with PBS (2000), Palmer said,

> Well, one thing we will keep doing is, we will keep funding scientific research to try and help answer the question: Are we going to have an apocalypse or not? So far, everything we see is extremely reassuring in terms of not only are we not going to have an apocalypse, but things are going to be better on earth because we're putting more CO_2 in the air.

7. Consider for instance, the recent onslaught of advertising waged by the American Petroleum Institute (API), in juxtaposition with the energetic refusal by companies involved in 'fracking' (hydraulic fracturing) of 'tight' or 'shale' gas to disclose the chemicals used in the process.
8. Apter 2005 examines oil, spectacle and the production of race and nation in Nigeria; Coronil 1997 examines the spectacle of oil power in Venezuela. On narrow-based economies and spectacles of power in Bolivia, see Gustafson 2006.
9. See Zalik 2009 on oil techniques for containing and expelling 'social' connections to place. On autonomy as a priority of capital in general, see Comaroff and Comaroff 2001; on oil enclaves, Ferguson 2005 and Reyna 2007.
10. See the 'one region' campaign of the St Louis Regional Chamber and Growth Association, which promotes St Louis as 'perfectly centered, remarkably

connected' (www.stlrcga.org). As with clean coal, the regional chamber's initiatives, such as the 'St Louis Climate Prosperity Project', suggest deep contradictions and a rather cynical embrace of climate talk given the 'carbon lock-in' (Unruh 2000) that characterises the regional economy more broadly.

11. On the centrality of temporality as it relates to the cultural and political making of natural 'resources', see also Ferry and Limbert 2008.

12. See Margonelli 2007 for a popular treatment of American gasoline consumption. Urry (2004) and others in *Theory, Culture and Society*, vol.21 (4/5) address systems of 'automobility' more widely. Huber 2009 approaches gasoline through the lens of use value. As with my argument here, Huber highlights how the cultural meanings of gasoline consumption – or in my framing, a mode of experiential knowledge articulated with the tactical knowledge-making efforts of the fossil industry – undermine critical political action aimed at transforming the broader structures of fossil power.

13. See www.chevron.com/media/ads/printweagreesmallbusiness.pdf, and API's 'Do You Own an Oil Company?' at www.api.org/aboutapi/ads/upload/Do_You_Own_2011H.wmv.

14. Sinclair's book was a blistering condemnation of oil as it was linked to a politics of dispossession, political corruption and the exploitation of labour. On *There Will Be Blood*, see Klawans 2008.

15. Benson and Hirsch 2010 argue that capitalism, through its tactical manipulation of science and doubt, pursues self-defence through the active production of political 'resignation'. The argument, which addresses long-standing strategies of corporate crisis management, has some utility for thinking about oil knowledge in cases of industrial impact, litigation and scientific dispute. Yet fossil knowledge is not only, or even necessarily, a unilinear battle over science and public truth, but is a networked and multi-scalar phenomenon of cultural production, social relations and geographically uneven political economies that works in a more diffuse way than dyadic public–corporate conflicts or even 'science wars' suggest.

16. Bordoff, Deshpande and Noel 2010, p.214.

17. Most recently, this was reflected in the API defence of 'fracking' used in 'tight' shale gas fields. A research note by Cornell University scientists (Howarth, Santoro and Ingraffea 2011) had drawn attention to the dangers posed by fracking – research attacked by API via www.energyindepth.org and other outlets.

18. See www.energycitizens.org and www.energynation.org.

19. The articulations between American ideological and structural racism and the oil industry are beyond the scope of this work, but on America's plantation-style occupation of Saudi Arabia, see Vitalis 2009.

20. Based on unpublished summaries of conferences and exchanges with the University of Aberdeen. Thanks to Owen Logan for these documents. See also www.energycities.org/; and on university capture, Simms 2003 and Agpak 2011.

21. As full disclosure, I received a grant from Washington University's I-CARES (International Center for Advanced Renewable Energy and Sustainability) to carry out pilot ethnographic research on the gas pipeline running between Bolivia and Brazil. I do not know the direct source of university funding to this centre, which totals $55 million, of which a small portion, some $500,000 each year, funds research projects by faculty, mostly in the physical and biological sciences. Grants range from $5000 to $50,000. I received $7000. I thank and

acknowledge I-CARES for this support, which facilitated acquisition of some of the insights reported here. See http://icares.wustl.edu/.

22. Thanks to Nicole Solawetz for tabulating these publications, drawn from each institute's respective website.

23. Clearly a concern for fuel poverty is a central component of any critical or justice-oriented approach to hydrocarbon issues. However, as with coal company deployment of rhetoric about electricity consumption as a measure of well-being, there are clear differences in the ways that discourses on fuel poverty are articulated in relationship to wider views of the industry–state nexus, whether these relate to the promotion of liberalisation (Baker Institute Energy Forum 2009) or the critique of liberalisation and privatisation's effects (Foster 2007).

24. Goldstein 2010, p.127.

25. Hundley 2011.

26. Washburn 2010, p.8.

27. Barry 2006, p.244.

28. Engler 1961, p.472.

29. Cited in ibid., p.466.

30. Ibid., pp.428–45

31. Ibid., p.482.

32. Ibid., p.497.

33. Ibid., p.9.

34. Ibid., p.485.

REFERENCES

Agpak, K. (2011) 'Academic Capture', *Variant*, 4.

API (2011a) 'Oil and Gas 101', American Petroleum Institute, http://energytomorrow. org/issues/oil-and-gas-101/, accessed 14 April 2011.

—— (2011b) 'The Women of Oil and Natural Gas', American Petroleum Institute, www.youtube.com/watch?v=b2ge3dFTTOQ, accessed 19 September 2011.

Apter, A. (2005) *The Pan-African Nation: Oil and the Spectacle of Culture in Nigeria* (Chicago: University of Chicago Press).

Baker Institute Energy Forum (2009) 'Energy, Poverty, and Society', www.rice.edu/ energy/research/poverty&energy/index.html, accessed 11 February 2010.

Barry, A. (2006) 'Technological Zones', *European Journal of Social Theory*, 9.

Benson, P. and Hirsch, S. (2010) 'Capitalism and the Politics of Resignation', *Current Anthropology*, 51(4).

Bordoff, J., Deshpande, M. and Noel, P. (2010) 'Understanding the Interaction Between Energy Security and Climate Change Policy', in Pascual and Elkind 2010.

Collini, S. (2011) 'The University Funding System Is Set Up to Invite Supper with the Devil', *Guardian*, 4 March, www.guardian.co.uk/commentisfree/2011/mar/04/ university-funding-lse-libya-legitmacy-source?INTCMP=SRCH, accessed 15 April 2011.

Comaroff, J. and Comaroff, J. (2001) 'Millenial Capitalism: First Thoughts on a Second Coming', in J. Comaroff and J. Comaroff (eds) *Millenial Capitalism and the Culture of Neoliberalism* (Durham, N.C.: Duke University Press).

Coronil, F. (1997) *The Magical State: Nature, Money, and Modernity in Venezuela* (Chicago: University of Chicago Press).

Council on Foreign Relations (2006) 'National Security Consequences of U.S. Oil Dependency', Council on Foreign Relations Publication no.0876093659, October.

Dant, T. (2004) 'The Driver–Car', *Theory, Culture and Society*, 21(4/5).

Energy Tomorrow (2011) 'The Women of Oil and Natural Gas Talk to Congress', www.EnergyTomorrow.org, available at www.youtube.com/watch?v=PM5BBW1JF0c, accessed 14 April 2011.

Engler, R. (1961) *The Politics of Oil: Private Power and Democratic Directions* (Chicago: University of Chicago Press).

EPA (2011) 'Endangerment and Cause or Contribute Findings for Greenhouse Gases under Section 202(a) of the Clean Air Act', United States Environmental Protection Agency, http://epa.gov/climatechange/endangerment.html, accessed 19 April 2011.

exxonsecrets.org (2011) 'Factsheet: Center for the Study of Carbon Dioxide and Global Change, Center for the Study of Carbon Dioxide and Climate Change', www.exxonsecrets.org/html/orgfactsheet.php?id=24#src3, accessed 19 April 2011.

Ferguson, J. (2005) 'Seeing Like an Oil Company: Space, Security and Global Capital in Neoliberal Africa', *American Anthropologist*, 107.

Fernandes, D. (2011) *Embedded Experts, Commercialisation, Securitisation, and Militarisation of the UK Academy* (Stockholm: Apec Press).

Ferry, E. and Limbert, M. (eds) (2008) *Timely Assets: The Politics of Resources and Their Temporalities* (Santa Fe, N.M.: SAR Press).

Foster, J. (2007) 'Cold Death by Neoliberalism: The Political Economy of Fuel Poverty', *Variant*, 28.

Gledhill, J. (2011) 'The Persistent Imaginary of "the People's Oil": Nationalism, Globalisation and the Possibility of Another Country in Brazil, Mexico and Venezuela', in A. Behrends, S.P. Reyna and G. Schlee (eds) *Crude Domination: An Anthropology of Oil* (London: Bergahn Books).

Goldstein, D. (2010) 'Security and the Culture Expert: Dilemmas of an Engaged Anthropology', *Political and Legal Anthropology Review*, 33(S1).

Greenpeace (2003) 'Investigations (ExxonMobil document on Public Information and Policy Research)'. http://research.greenpeaceusa.org/?a=view&d=4389. Accessed April 19, 2011.

Gustafson, B. (2006) 'Spectacles of Autonomy and Crisis: Or, What Bulls and Beauty Queens have to do With Regionalism in Eastern Bolivia', *Journal of Latin American and Caribbean Anthropology*, 11 (2).

—— (2009) 'Manipulating Cartographies: Plurinationalism, Autonomy, and Indigenous Resurgence in Bolivia', in *Anthropological Quarterly*, 82(4).

Harvey, D. (2003) *The New Imperialism* (Oxford: Oxford University Press).

Howarth, R.W., Santoro, R. and Ingraffea, A. (2011) 'Methane and the Greenhouse-Gas Footprint of Natural Gas from Shale Formations' in *Climatic Change Letters*, DOI: 10.1007/s10584-011-0061-5.

Huber, M. (2009) 'The Use of Gasoline: Value, Oil, and the "American Way of Life"', *Antipode*, 41(3).

Hundley, Kris (2011) 'Billionaire's Role in Hiring Decisions at State University Raises Questions', *St Petersburg Times*, May 9.

Klawans, S. (2008) 'A Hard Man', *The Nation*, 28 January.

Latour, B. (1993) *We Have Never Been Modern* (Cambridge: Harvard University Press).

——— (2007) *Reassembling the Social: An Introduction to Actor-Network Theory* (Oxford: Oxford University Press).

Legere, L. (2011) 'Fracking Study Reviewers Represent Academia: No Industry Employees', *Times–Tribune* (Scranton, Pa.), www.rigzone.com/news/article. asp?a_id=103229, 19 January.

Logan, O. and McNeish, J.-A. (n.d.) 'The Politics of Energy Transition and Public and Private Temporality', unpublished notes.

Margonelli, L. (2007) *Oil on the Brain: Petroleum's Long Strange Trip to Your Tank* (New York: Doubleday).

Pascual, C. and Elkind, J. (eds) *Energy Security: Economics, Politics, Strategies, and Implications* (Washington, D.C.: Brookings Institution Press).

PBS (2000) 'Interview: Fred Palmer', Nova Online, *What's Up With the Weather*, www.pbs.org/wgbh/warming/debate/palmer.html, accessed 19 April 2011.

Peabody Energy (2011) 'Endangerment and Cause or Contribute Findings for Greenhouse Gases under Section 202(a) of the Clean Air Act: Petition for Reconsideration by Peabody Energy Company', http://scienceandpublicpolicy. org/images/stories/papers/reprint/no_legal_option.pdf, accessed 19 April 2011.

Porter, Reid (2011) 'API Responds to Bunk Study on Natural Gas', American Petroleum Institute, www.api.org/Newsroom/natural-gas-study.cfm, accessed 14 April 2011.

Price, Waterhouse and Coopers (2009) 'The Economic Impacts of the Oil and Natural Gas Industry on the US Economy: Employment, Labor Income, and Value Added', prepared for the American Petroleum Institute, www.api.org/Newsroom/upload/ Industry_Economic_Contributions_Report.pdf, accessed 13 May 2010.

Reyna, S. (2007) 'Waiting: The Sorcery of Modernity, Transnational Corporations, Oil and Terrorism in Chad', *Sociologus*, 26.

Sawyer, S. (2003) 'Subterranean Techniques: Corporate Environmentalism, Oil Operations, and Social Injustice in the Ecuadorian Rain Forest', in C. Slater (ed) *In Search of the Rain Forest* (Durham, N.C.: Duke University Press).

Sheller, M. (2004) 'Automotive Emotions: Feeling the Car', *Theory, Culture and Society*, 21(4/5).

Simms, A. (2003) 'Degrees of Capture: Universities, the Oil Industry and Climate Change', New Economics Foundation and Corporate Watch, www. platformlondon.org/carbonweb/documents/DegreesofCapture.pdf, accessed 26 April 2011.

Unruh, G.C. (2000) 'Understanding Carbon Lock-In', *Energy Policy*, 28.

Urry, J. (2004) 'The System of Automobility', *Theory, Culture and Society*, 21(4/5).

Vidas, H. and Hugman, B. (2008) 'Strengthening our Economy: The Untapped US Oil and Gas Resources', ICF International/American Petroleum Institute, 28 December.

Vitalis, R. (2009) *America's Kingdom: Mythmaking on the Saudi Oil Frontier* (London: Verso).

Washburn, J. (2010) *Big Oil Goes to College: An Analysis of 10 Research Collaboration Contracts Between Leading Energy Companies and Major US Universities* (Washington, D.C.: Center for American Progress), www.american-progress.org/issues/2010/10/big_oil.html, accessed 14 January 2011.

Wilk, R. (2009) 'Consuming Ourselves to Death: The Anthropology of Consumer Culture and Climate Change', in S. Crate and M. Nuttall (eds) *Anthropology and Climate Change: From Encounters to Actions* (Walnut Creek, Calif.: Left Coast Press).

Wood Mackenzie Energy Consulting (2010) 'Energy Policy at a Crossroads: An Assessment of the Impacts of Increased Access Versus Higher Taxes on US Oil and Natural Gas Production, Government Revenue, and Employment', www.api.org/policy/tax/recentstudiesandresearch/upload/SOAE_Wood_Mackenzie_ Access_vs_Taxes.pdf, accessed 14 January 2011.

Zalik, A. (2009) 'Zones of Exclusion: Offshore Extraction, the Contestation of Space and Physical Displacement in the Nigerian Delta and the Mexican Gulf', *Antipode*, 41.

14
Conclusion: All Other Things Do *Not* Remain Equal

John-Andrew McNeish and Owen Logan

> Why can't we simply finish with oil? The world today is completely reliant on oil. This reliance will not become any less with time as the world's population increases and more people at the same time are brought out of poverty. On the other hand, if we continue to use oil as we do today, the escape of carbon dioxide and climate change will make the world impossible to live in. This is the dilemma that both challenges and inspires us. (Award-winning Statoil advertisement, Aftenposten, 23 May 2011)

CRUDE SOCIO-ECONOMICS

It may be an inescapable fact that humanity is currently reliant on oil, but as we have argued in this book there are options for its governance. This may be stating the obvious, given the details of the cases studied in this volume and the contrasts between them. However, as the text of the full-page advertisement[1] printed in all of Norway's leading newspapers in May 2011 might suggest (through what it omits to say as much as through what it does say), the general recognition of these options remains largely tacit. It is not that there is no recognition that fundamental changes in the global energy economy are likely to occur; but for the time being at least, its driving factors are beyond our collective control. In these final pages we try to redress the balance between the spoken and the unspoken, highlighting some of the critical uses of this book as we go along. A closer examination of the Statoil advertisement will be our vehicle for collecting together these concluding points.

Reading between the lines, and thinking about the wider context in which this advertisement has been produced, makes it obvious that Statoil is well aware of and concerned with the possible power and influence of public opinion. Why else mount such an expensive and notably text-laden advertising campaign? Society, it would appear, still has a key role in determining through vote and

Hvorfor kan vi ikke bare slutte med olje?

Verden er i dag helt avhengig av olje. Behovet blir heller ikke mindre etter hvert som jordens befolkning øker og stadig flere mennesker samtidig bringes ut av fattigdom. På den andre side. Fortsetter vi å bruke olje som i dag, kan CO_2-utslipp og klimaendringer gjøre kloden ulevelig for oss. Dette er et dilemma som både utfordrer og inspirerer oss.

På den ene side. På den andre side. Mer energi. Mindre CO_2. Dette er dilemmaet verden i dag står overfor, som preger samfunnsdebatten, og som også vi som jobber i Statoil tar på alvor og bruker evner, krefter og penger på å finne løsninger på.

Men det vil ta tid. Olje dekker i dag nesten 35 prosent av verdens energibehov. Hver eneste dag trenger vi ca. 80 millioner oljetønner for å lage strøm, produsere mat, bygge byer, frakte varer og mennesker – og til å utvinne metallet og mineralene vi trenger for å produsere alle vindmøllene, solpanelene, vannkraftturbinene og høyspentmastene som må til for å stoppe klimaendringene.

Omtrent to millioner av disse daglige oljetønnene kommer fra norsk sokkel. Det gir Norge et ansvar for verdens energiforsyning, og skaper store verdier for landet vårt og for det samfunnet de fleste nordmenn ønsker å bygge og leve i.

Samtidig har vi som olje- og gasselskap et ansvar for å løse den delen av energidilemmaet vi kan påvirke.

Som å redusere CO_2-utslippet fra produksjonen vår og øke utnyttelsen av eksisterende funn. Vi bruker også kunnskapen vår til utvikling av fornybar energi. Ta for eksempel vindkraftsatsingen vår. Havvindparken vi nå bygger utenfor England og den flytende vindmøllen som testes utenfor Karmøy, er direkte resultater av hva vi har lært i Nordsjøen. I en framtid hvor utvikling av slik fornybar energi blir lønnsom, kan dette bli en av løsningene som kan stoppe klimaendringene.

Men på veien dit trenger verden hvert fat vi kan finne og få opp fra sokkelen vår. I mange tiår til. For alternativene er ikke et skal-skal ikke, eller et enteneller. Det er et både-og.

Vil du vite mer, og har meninger om energiutfordringene vi og samfunnet står overfor? Delta i #energidebatten på goodideas.statoil.com eller på twitter. Tidene har aldri vært bedre for gode ideer.

consumption the direction and outcome of energy policy. Indeed, oil companies such as Statoil, and the governments with whom they have to deal and negotiate, make considerable investments in order to win over and secure public consent so that their operations can continue to expand. In saying this, however, certain differences must be acknowledged. Winning consent in Norway has taken place by peaceful means, although not without socio-political struggle.

In other contexts, such as Russia or Nigeria, less democratic and more brutal techniques for winning acceptance have often been set in action. Nevertheless, as we have seen, especially in Parts 1 and 2 of this book, various historic balances of power and social contracts play an important role in both delimiting and unlimiting the exploitation of natural resources. And in Part 3, on governmentality, we have found that the operation of a free market is widely seen as anything but neutral in this context; rather, the energy marketplace is infused with political, strategic and ideological implications that also play out as dilemmas over the extent of sovereignty and the scope of law. Despite the emphasis on technocratic solutions in formal policy and policy prescriptions, society clearly matters, and greatly so. While the politics of oil and gas may be one area in which the terrain of socio-economics is regularly mentioned, or at least implied, it is usually traversed only in part. Therefore, the interconnected problems surrounding the (fictional) commodifica-tion of land/nature, labour and money (recalling the works of Karl Polanyi and others referred to in the introduction) have tended to disappear from view. With that shift of perspective, what would otherwise be an inevitably sceptical discussion about the spread of capitalism turns into a rather more optimistic one about resource extraction – not politics – producing public wealth and well-being. Nevertheless, it is the character of politics that socio-economics ought to examine.

Without mentioning a word of it, Statoil's advertisement plays on a socio-economic memory, absent from official histories and recent policy documents. Nevertheless the key contribution played by the public, and especially labour unions, through their protagonism for domestic investments and work security in establishing the basis of the national oil and gas industry, is remembered by many Norwegians. This may also be gleaned from the efforts to promote social-movement trade unionism in campaigning for the welfare state in Norway.[2] As we have seen in previous chapters, attempts to articulate the public interest involve varied institutional and constitutional mechanisms and politicised social identities. These stem from a consciousness of class, ethnicity and gender. Looking beyond the North Sea, the struggle over resources and public utility may appear to be highly unpredictable from a Western perspective. We have argued that this is largely a result of a lack of recognition of contested and overlapping sovereignties. We think it is vital to acknowledge the multifaceted nature of sovereignty, which, it may be added, is not easily converted to the cause of consumer sovereignty. Nor is the problem of sovereignty confined to relatively young postcolonial nations. Sovereignty issues come to the fore in older former imperial nations too. Indeed, as we discussed in our introduction, a key issue is just how broadly one might wish to define imperialism and empire today. Does empire still have an inside and outside?

We have not sought to decide this issue, but the extent of the debate about the functioning of latter-day imperialism, especially at the level of finance capitalism, and our empirical evidence of the rehearsal of historic grievances in this context of 'liquid modernity',[3] give us ample reason to fundamentally question the scientific plausibility of applying *ceteris paribus* to social contexts. This means that a limited set of rational predetermined variables are applied, while other factors are levelled out and excluded from analysis. This results in a set of standard technical prescriptions for dealing with resource-based conflict and oil and gas management. The cases included in this volume, and the depth of detail observed in each, demonstrate that it is precisely because of social complexity that all other things do *not* remain equal. Laboratory conditions cannot be applied to society and politics. The idea of *ceteris paribus* in this context can therefore be regarded as an ordering device, used only to circumvent the historical messiness of comparative politics. As such, the resource-curse thesis increasingly looks like academic voodoo rather than an accurate description of experiences on the ground. While it is true that we can find wars and violence at different levels, sporadic violence and militant contestation – often exposing the internal faultlines of sovereignty – are more the norm. Indeed, evidence of this is even plainly stated in the 2011 World Development Report.[4]

The political issues of resource sovereignty, collective consumption and governmentality discussed in previous chapters have shown some of the ways in which the social is connected to the economic, although, in keeping with liberal market ideology, the economy remains discursively disconnected from society. Indeed, perhaps more than ever before in the history of capitalism, the operations of the market are presented as an anonymous force functioning above and beyond any one society or any power elite. On the basis of this near-religious faith, the market is widely posited as the most objective and efficient means of assessing value and distributing resources. Whatever credibility this idea has owes a great deal to the utopian belief that information technology is capable of making the global free market into a new force for consumer-led democracy and that state sovereignty is outmoded. It is evident, however, that oil and gas, in common with other territorial resources, are only partly integrated into this sort of market rationalism and are sites upon which struggles take place to reassert or protect sovereignty. We must stress that these struggles are complex. They take place at different levels and vastly different purposes and intentions are captured within them, although the articulation of some kind of social contract is their common outcome and frequently this depends on public goods and collective consumption. In this process, modernity and tradition, territory and ethnicity, may be problematically fused together, partly through the linkages (as we have seen in cross section) of community politics, state power and the flows of capital and resources.

KNOWLEDGE AND IDEOLOGY

Another interesting thing about the Statoil advertisement is that market rationalism is seen from a temporal point of view. In the words of the publicity, it is 'the dilemma that both challenges and inspires us'. The advertisement makes a series of claims, central among which is that the world as we know it is reliant on oil. While it is recognised that green technologies and alternative energy sources have to be developed (in which Statoil proudly states it is now investing), we are also reminded that oil currently provides nearly 35 per cent of the world's energy requirements. The small text following the headlines of the advertisement states that:

> Every day we need c.80 million barrels of oil to produce electricity, produce food, build cities, transport goods and people – and to refine the metal and minerals we need to produce all the windmills, solar cells, hydropower turbines and electricity masts needed to stop climate change ... Around 2 million of these daily barrels of oil come from the Norwegian oil fields. This gives Norway responsibility for the world's energy supply, and creates wealth for our society and for the society most Norwegians want to build and live in.

This is an obvious appeal to the Norwegian public to understand the necessity for Statoil and Norway to continue producing oil at current rates, despite growing environmental concerns. It is an appeal that is also timed in terms of contemporary debates in the country. Statoil, together with its largest shareholder, the Norwegian state, has been the focus of widespread media critique and discussion for its decision to operate in the Alberta oil sands of Canada.[5] Similarly, as we have seen, an argument has raged recently about the government's decision to explore the previously proposed world heritage zone[6] of the Lofoten Vesterålen area for possible oil and gas deposits. Effective campaigns, also referring to the Deepwater Horizon incident, have been run by environmental organisations and have garnered widespread public support to oppose these two initiatives.[7] Parallel to these two environmental scandals there has been considerable discussion in Norway about the growth of the Norwegian International Pension Fund. Questions are being asked about investments overseas and about the current government's refusal to draw on the fund to make necessary investments in national infrastructure and basic services.[8] Considerable media coverage has also been given to signs that North Sea oil production may be reaching its peak,[9] despite the recent discovery of new giant fields.[10] All of this has had an effect on public opinion, and more specifically has affected Statoil's performance in the international financial markets.

In the interests of development and security then, it would appear that a campaign is needed to win back hearts and minds. This is something reminiscent of other parts of international security discourse, which have sought a 'comprehensive approach' that joins security to development.[11] Indeed, as Norwegian bombs fall on Libya, thanks to international agreements on the 'right to protect' (R2P), it is worth noting that Norway is currently earning 220 billion kroner (US$40 billion) extra per day as a result of the effect that the Libyan crisis is having on international oil prices.[12] In this context it is easy to see how a comprehensive securitisation discourse can pay off and help to smooth over ethical issues which have arisen as a result of Norway's oil business increasingly being conducted overseas. Thus, media spin is glossing over the obvious ethical cracks that are created in continuing the Norwegian oil 'fairy tale' overseas.

The claim that the functioning of the world economy is reliant on oil is based on solid scientific findings. Indeed there is evidence to suggest that there are no quick technical alternatives to this situation. However, as was argued in Chapter 13, there is evidence of a vortex in which a set of selected facts may beguile and mislead us into thinking that all that can be done is being done and that the wealth and technical expertise amassed through the exploitation of oil will form a bridge to a post-hydrocarbon energy framework.

As the advertisement implies, oil production is not only essential to the world as we know it but it is also central to what comes next. Norway, however, is not only reliant on oil and gas production to meet domestic energy needs. Ninety-nine per cent of its electricity (one of the highest rates in the world, as a result of its northerly climate) is in fact derived from hydropower. It is also worth remembering that the development of the hydropower industry in Norway was closely related to the national oil industry; the latter industry laid the foundations necessary for developing the concessionary system on which hydropower control and profits have been secured.

Alternative energy technologies, whilst needing further development and investment, are not then something new or only for the future. Notwithstanding the influence and obvious importance of corporate actors such as Statoil, the crucial factor to bear in mind here is the potential role of states in facilitating the decentralisation and decommodification of energy production. On this count, important changes have taken place in Norway that obscure the facts of the case. The arrival of economic liberalism in the 1990s resulted, as Ryggvik (2010) describes, in the freeing-up of controls over commodity markets and in creeping privatisation. Previous logics of moderate growth were replaced by logics of accelerated extraction and exponential growth. In the oil sector this led to a new bonanza of activity and a relaxing of concessionary controls that allowed Statoil to expand and many other private actors to join the field. There has been a series of hiccups. Burgeoning financial markets led to over-speculation in the real estate markets, resulting in the 1998 economic downturn, but, with the exception of successfully avoiding a new financial crisis by way of the creation of the Oil Fund, the logic of market liberalisation has persisted. Privatisation has also taken place in the hydroelectricity sector. Over the course of the 1990s a series of moves was made to liberalise both the production and transport of hydropower, including the linkage of the national grid with neighbouring countries. The result of this connection has been the development of an international market for Norwegian hydropower. However, while this has been profitable for the Norwegian state and various private interests, the public experience of these changes has been of inflated electricity costs at home, and the closure of local industries whose survival was dependent on the previously low power costs.[13] Statoil is of course not responsible for these changes. However, its advertisement does misdirect us from the facts about what really keeps the lights on in Norway.

The advertisement also claims to know what kind of society most Norwegians want to live in, glossing over the fact that there is no real agreement on this matter.[14] As the other chapters in this book have highlighted, there are severe internal disagreements about the value, ownership and management of oil and gas resources in all the societies in which we have worked. Norway may stand out as a country which has been successful in balancing economic interests with social needs; but this can only be said in relative terms, and even this may be slipping away. At risk of repetition, this is a political issue that ought not to be reconceived as the result of a curse. Recognising its history of social contestation, involvement in imperial capitalist projects, and current public doubts and debates about resource sovereignty, Norway belongs neatly amongst other flammable societies. Undoubtedly, oil has had an impact on Norway's internal social order and political thinking. In a recent book by Simon Sætre (2009), the author describes how he 'travelled through the world's richest countries to find out what money does to us'. In his conclusion Sætre reflects on how Norway's social divisions (class and ethnic) and social psyche (seen in attitudes about leisure, dependency and protectionism) increasingly resemble other 'especially oil-rich states'. In Sætre's opinion, claims to being anything else 'are steeped in national chauvinism ... and follow the route of exceptionalism – the thought that our land is something unique, leading Norwegians to claim themselves to be a *humanitarian superpower* or the *exceptional country* [*annerledesland*]'.[15]

As we have seen from all the cases covered in this book, the materiality of oil has an intimate, although not inevitable, connection with changing social mores, as it does with ideological contest. Another finding that is necessary to stress here is the importance of historical processes and change with regard to the analysis of oil- and gas-dependent societies. It is simply not enough to evaluate the quality of governance in these societies on the basis of quantitative snapshots, or as neatly distinct subjects of study. Our emphasis on an extended case-study methodology draws attention to both temporal and spatial interconnections. As a result, the approach supported here concurrently draws attention to phenomenology and the structures of international political economy. It also explicitly recognises the operation of ideologies as mechanisms not only determining oil and gas governance, but directing and limiting the knowledge on which judgments are made, both within and beyond state bureaucracies. In short, 'oil-knowledge regimes' ought to be taken seriously and not be regarded, too simplistically, as the flow of propaganda from highly visible oil companies. Ultimately, what is at issue is capitalist-led growth, as may be gleaned from reading between the lines of the Statoil publicity. It is not that there is no recognition of technical solutions in this type of corporate pronouncement, or that fundamental changes are not envisaged; it is that the practical and political issues are effectively put off until a later date. It is implied that at some point in the future the market will have solved the technical problems in accordance with future regimes of cost-effectiveness. Consequently, wind turbines appear in the advertisement as a symbolic graphic device, as if seen on a distant horizon. And as the advert states:

> In a future where the development of such renewable energy can be profitable, this can be the solution that can stop climate change. But on our way there the world needs every barrel that we can get up from our oilfields. For many years to come. Because the alternative is not only a choice of will or will not, or either or. It is that we can have both [både og].

What can be seen in the above remarks about profitability is a widespread rationalisation of technical progress, whereby humanity waits not so much for technological solutions, but for money to speak. Arguably, this is a cornerstone of the structural privatisation of time. Just as the Canadian tar sands were envisaged in the early 1980s as a resource that would eventually become 'economic' with rising crude oil prices, so too are the alternatives to fossil fuels largely kept on the economic back burner. We need not rehearse the possible social and environmental costs of this deferral to capital, or the arguments for the precautionary principle when it comes to climate change. The main point to stress here is the difficulty of conceiving public temporality in the face of an ideological timescale calibrated by capitalist-led growth. If public temporality can be exemplified, say in earlier Norwegian policies geared towards a moderate pace of production, it is worth questioning whether the private values driving capitalist growth are as deeply rooted as they now appear to be. In his examination of the 'moral' emphasis in US politics, Alan Sokal (2010) shows the somewhat hidden extent of concern about greed and materialism, which is strongly criticised right across the political spectrum. Sokal argues that pro-rich politics in the United States have in fact been aided considerably by a left-leaning politics that pays scant regard to political virtue, and is not really interested in the depth of human beings' moral consciousness – the concerns of which have all too easily been hijacked by the political right.[16] To some extent this may be an international phenomenon, and in this regard much more work ought to be done about the public-relations industry and the adoption of Freudian ideas in order to 'engineer consent' through the manipulation of fears and desires.[17]

There is considerable evidence in various countries of the erosion of public deliberation and democratic contest. This is a race to the bottom in 'morality', which means that many people may judge capitalism by impoverished ethical standards – not wishing to apply different rules to corporate power than they would to individuals. Indeed this corrosive trend can be seen in the Statoil advert too: it blithely assumes that all of Norway wants to continue down the path of oil production under the same economic model, where all that counts is profitability and economic growth. As it suggests, in time 'we can have our cake and eat it'.[18] However, the extent of the advertising campaign suggests that Statoil is not entirely confident in its own arguments. There are many people in the country who actively seek to diverge from the train of thought and value which the advertisement pushes. Despite Norway's outward appearance of homogeneity, the pressures of globalisation[19] mean that the country is just as divided as many of its European neighbours over what socio-economic values the state ought to promote: cooperation or competition?

The answer to this dilemma in many countries, not just in Europe, has been political corporatism, or a 'friendly fascism' that offers to reconcile cooperation with competition under the banner of national entrepreneurialism. Typically, in this neoliberal vision, the nation is compared to a corporate entity (for example, 'UK PLC') regardless of the important legal, financial and social differences between states and limited-liability businesses. However, the promise of delivering public well-being through the pursuit of profit and consumer sovereignty has grown out of all proportion to the actual functions of the global market governed according to neoliberal dogma. As Pierre Bourdieu (1998) concluded, following an exploration of its claims, neoliberalism is a political programme disguised as science to increase the economic power of the few. The Norwegian Oil for Development Programme claims to offer a definitive answer to 'good governance' on the basis of technocratic expertise. However, as Audun Solli argues, 'oil for development brings the state back in to development discourse but it does so by keeping politics out'.[20] Therefore, far from countering neoliberal doctrines which curtail the role of the state, oil for development may compound the problems of the lack of democratic deliberation and accountability seen in various countries today. Statoil appears to follow suit by insinuating that it knows what Norwegians want, and this is more of the same liberal, market model. In contrast to this hollow confidence, a key conclusion of this book is that such presumption is highly misguided.

VALUE, GROWTH AND GOVERNANCE

In this book we have drawn on earlier anthropological work that discusses how different cultures define the world in different ways. In particular we have drawn on work that questions rational-actor theories by showing how cultural values complicate accepted ideas about the development subject as *homo economicus*. Elements of these analyses provide a portal to reorient political economy towards a global socio-economics of resource governance in a way that opens up the possibility of better defining the social nature of commodities without losing sight of the violent interplay of positions and structures at work in global capitalism.

In the introduction, we stressed the need to return to the ethical reasoning of classical political economy so as to re-examine theories of value and capital, recognising the need for a variety of different social vernaculars and means of expression. The chapters of the book also acknowledge such differences. In conclusion, we think it important to reflect further on theories of value, seeing that these can provide a necessary antidote to the liberal idealisation of the market seen in the Statoil advertisement. Such a focus on value also makes evident when and where the mechanisms that are integral to a corporate engineering of consent come into play. Value is an undeniable factor of corporate policy making on the basis of focus groups and lifestyle categories. Here 'it's not that the people are in charge but that the people's desires are in charge', as a US witness to the corporate psycho-political project puts it.[21] As we have seen above, environmental issues are not excluded from the capitalist calculus, but by a marketing sleight of hand become entirely framed by free-market ideology. By putting theories of value back into the equation, insight is given to the political process here. Theories of value also provide an opening to issues that have not been covered in this book, and which call for further research and study (such as pollution and the human costs of environmental contamination).

Revisiting over a century of anthropological thought, David Graeber (2001, 2005) has highlighted anew the contrasting logic between Marx's labour theory of value and the claims of objectivity inherent in the liberal theories. In doing so Graeber makes a fruitful comparison between Marx's acceptance of the human imagination in determining the interaction between self-making and economic value, and the similar emphasis on creativity in the work of the early sociologist and ethnographer, Marcel Mauss. As a socialist writing in critical response to the consequences of the rational orientation of the Bolshevik revolution, Mauss (2000) argued that new thought needed to be given to economic alternatives to the market. He critiqued the 'rational' assumptions of economic science, which determined that what drives human beings is their desire to maximise their pleasures, comforts and material possessions (their utility), and that all significant human interactions can be registered in these terms. Ironically, it was the partial recognition of a more psychologically complex socio-economic reality that prompted the public relations industry in the twentieth century to colonise and manipulate desires with the intention of making representative democracy synonymous with the idealisation of the free market. At the same time, anthropologists were discovering societies in which economic life was based on utterly different principles, and most objects moved back and forth as gifts – and almost everything we would call 'economic' behaviour was based on a show of generosity and a refusal to calculate exactly who had given what to whom.

Such 'gift economies' could on occasion become highly competitive, but when they did it was in exactly the opposite way from basic capitalist logic. Instead of vying to see who could accumulate the most, the winners were the ones who managed to give away the most. Even when objects of great value changed hands, what really mattered was the relations between the people; exchange is about creating friendships, or working out rivalries, or obligations, and only incidentally about moving around valuable goods. Indeed, similar traits can be seen at work in capitalist plutocracy. What non-Western ethnographic examples demonstrated was that dominant European theories of value accumulation were far from universal. Moreover, highlighting common European practice, and the attractiveness of socialist ideas in a European context, Mauss questioned whether, despite first appearances, 'gift giving' was really something that belonged only to the past or to non-European societies. Indeed, he questioned whether there was not something universal about the morality of gift and exchange, since these values could be found within European societies. And in this sense, of course, the anthropology of far-flung places has often been an attempt to reflect critically on aspects of one's own society.

By setting Marx and Mauss together, Graeber argues that there are indications of what could be the basis for an anthropological theory of value. It may go without saying that we think this offers an important perspective, although we would stress there is nothing particularly novel about it. As Karl Polanyi remarked in his 1944 book *The Great Transformation*, 'the outstanding discovery of recent historical and anthropological research is that man's economy, as a rule, is submerged in his social relationships'.[22] In recognition of this basic nexus, Graeber extends Marxian and Maussian ideas into each other, arguing that the ultimate stakes of politics or social order is the struggle, not to appropriate value, but to establish what value is. Drawing on further ethnographic examples, Graeber (2005) also shows that the construction of meaning involves imagining totalities (systems of meaning). Even if this project can never be completely translated into reality, it recognises that in any real social situation, there are likely to be any number of imaginary totalities at play, organised around different conceptions of value. These conceptions 'may be fragmentary, ephemeral, or they can just exist as dreamy projects or half-realised ones, defiantly proclaimed by cultists or revolutionaries'.[23]

Whilst most historical change is not as self-conscious as Marxist thought might argue, in times of crisis this can change; therefore a social order can be seen primarily as an arena in which certain types of value can be produced and realised. They can be defended on the basis of the social order, or alternatively they can be challenged by those who reject certain values or who wish to call an entire value system into question. According to Graeber, this analysis has political utility in so far as the ultimate freedom is not the freedom to create or accumulate value, but the freedom to decide (collectively or individually) what it is that makes life worth living. Moments of crisis are also moments of possibility. Of course such an anthropological analysis of value can seem distant from oil and gas, but it is relevant in thinking about the choices made in its governance and production. For example, regardless of the longstanding Arab efforts within OPEC to keep the price of oil low by keeping production high, oil, as R.T. Naylor writes, is

a modern version of the Holy Sepulchre to be wrested from the Saracen hordes ... [S]ince oil in the Middle East costs so little to pull out of the ground ... its price ought to be low. This is like arguing that a piece of machinery should be valued according to the cost of the labour necessary to pick it up and cart it out of the factory door.[24]

Such an ideological rationale requires a level of consent in producing nations that is unlikely to be forthcoming given the growing inequities of the global free market. Indeed a strong comparison can be drawn between the obvious tensions about natural-resource production today and the municipal efforts during the industrial revolution in Britain, examined by Polanyi (1944), to protect natural resources and labour from total commodification. The difference – which recalls our title again because it is such an inflammatory one – is that where there was room for municipal experimentation and divergence from the liberal market in Britain's national context, in the interests of social stability or cohesion, any real experimentation in the contemporary international context has become more or less synonymous with unforgivable political deviancy. Threats of assassination, invasion or 'regime change' coming from outside producing nations give great support to already powerful free-market interests within them; but in light of the invasion of Iraq it is easy to see the sort of hubris that can underpin these liberal allegiances.

Once again, these insights call into question the ideas expressed in Statoil's advertisement, and the assumptions which orient various actors towards 'supply-side governmentality'. This is the label we have applied to a dominant, but far from uncontested, mentality in which development issues are caught up in the trickle-down economics of oil supply rather than the conservation and gradual use of these resources. Therefore, in many instances a free-market calculus is brought to bear on the very problems that have resulted from the adoption of a free-market ideal, and with it an unreasonable belief in the market's capacity to deliver equilibrium. Yet by revealing again the social nature of material cultures, writers such as Pieterse (1998) and McMichael (2010) indicate a more acute understanding of markets and development, in which development is not only anchored in liberal institutions and structures, but also in the lives of its subjects. This work draws attention to how subjects of development receive, legitimise or contest development; and this is indispensable to an understanding of how development is accomplished, the terms through which it is challenged, and how new possibilities are reformulated. Contrary to Statoil's claims then, the path of development is not necessarily anchored to existing models for growth. As we have argued, resource governance is highly political and there are many more options than might first meet the eye. However, since the Club of Rome's 1972 publication of *The Limits to Growth*, and the United Nations Conference on the Human Environment, held in the same year, it has been clear that the depletion of resources and market-led growth is a political issue divided by technocratic and political reasoning. In this context too, technocratic idealism has sought to overcome the messy politics of sovereignty and the contested terms of citizenship with promises of systematised equilibrium.[25] Coming at no political cost to capitalism (and with the attractive prospect of bringing about cybernetic regimes of accumulation), such technocratic idealism attempts to supersede some of the key debates about development. Predictably such approaches search for an improved social engineering, or 'social system design', not an improved social discussion of value.[26]

As a recent book, *Prosperity Without Growth*,[27] makes clear from the wide range of supporting references mentioned in its opening pages, radical changes to the existing model of growth are beginning to pick up credibility amongst people at the centre of the political spectrum. The reasoning of this book by Tim Jackson connects to the recent international economic crisis, and he makes a direct and very necessary link between environmental technology and society, and criticises 'the folly of separating economy from society and environment'.[28] Jackson aims for a more comprehensive 'Global Green New Deal' than has so far been discussed. However, more practical thinking needs to be applied to this. What is striking about mainstream discussions of these 'hot' issues, which, by their nature, involve a discussion of capitalism's failures, is how the system is portrayed in potentially benign terms. This overlooks, for example, the bitter strife and the necessity of the radical political virtues which accompanied the original New Deal in the United States. So although it is recognised that entirely new models of investment are required to support sustainable development and public well-being, how such a system is to be wrenched from the hands of capital is left out of the picture. This looks like radical social change without tears, an illusion which carries its own dangers. There is also a parting relevance here for the conclusion of this book, because contrary to the dominant logics of capital, other values do exist and some of these offer realistic alternatives for oil and gas governance as well as other natural resources. There is then a better message than the one contained in the advertisement we started with. Business does not have to continue as usual, nor can it. The tensions between the politics of resource sovereignty and those of free-market ideology are too great.

NOTES

1. The first of a series of advertisements published on a weekly basis in the main Norwegian newspapers and linked to the Statoil website: www.goodideas.statoil.com.
2. See articles on the campaign for the welfare state by A. Wahl (2007), also available online, http://solidaritymagazine.org/backissues/Issue%2020.pdf.
3. See Bauman 2000.
4. http://wdr2011.worldbank.org/.
5. www.aftenposten.no/nyheter/uriks/wikileaks/article3959336.ece.
6. http://whc.unesco.org/en/tentativelists/1751/.
7. http://folkeaksjonen.no/.
8. http://michael-hudson.com/2011/03/norway%E2%80%99s-oil-fund-is-it-realizing-its-full-potential/.
9. www.aftenposten.no/okonomi/innland/article4115006.ece.
10. www.aftenposten.no/okonomi/innland/article4245586.ece.
11. See McNeish and Sand Lie 2010.
12. www.aftenposten.no/okonomi/innland/article4041344.ece.
13. www.klassekampen.no/57814/article/item/null.
14. Sadly, recent acts of domestic terrorism in Norway have underlined this fact, gruesomely.
15. See Sætre 2009, p.244.
16. See Sokal 2010, pp.416ff.
17. This is the subject of Adam Curtis's 2009 BBC documentary series 'The Century of the Self'.
18. I.e. as suggested by the Norwegian phrase '*både og*' used in the ad.
19. These pressures, seen in new waves of economic migration and the issues of political refugees and 'social dumping' combine with traditions of free thought, which include a growing academic reference to alternative schools of ecological thought.
20. Solli 2011, p.81.
21. From 'The Century of the Self' (see n.17).
22. Polanyi 1944, p.39.
23. Graeber 2005, p.58.
24. See Naylor 1990, p.21.
25. This owes a great deal to the ideas of Jay Forrester, the founder of System Dynamics.
26. See J.W. Forrester, *Designing the Future*, 1998, www.clexchange.org/ftp/documents/whyk12sd/Y_1999-03DesigningTheFuture.pdf, last accessed June 2011.
27. Jackson 2009a.
28. Jackson 2009b, p.83.

REFERENCES

Bauman, Z. (2000) *Liquid Modernity* (Cambridge: Polity Press).

Bourdieu, P. (1998) *Practical Reason: On the Theory of Action* (Stanford, Calif.: Stanford University Press).

Graeber, D. (2001) *Towards an Anthropological Theory of Value* (London and New York: Palgrave Macmillan).

—— (2005) 'Value as the Importance of Action', *The Commoner*, 10 (Spring–Summer), available online at www.commoner.org.uk/the_commoner_10.pdf.

Jackson, T. (2009a) *Prosperity Without Growth: Economics for a Finite Planet* (London: Earthscan).

—— (2009b) *Prosperity Without Growth? The Transition to a Sustainable Economy* (London: Sustainable Development Commission), available online at www.sd-commission.org.uk/data/files/publications/prosperity_without_growth_report.pdf.

Mauss, M. (2000) [1950] *The Gift: The Form and Reason for Exchange in Archaic Societies* (New York and London: W.W. Norton).

McNeish J.-A. and Sand Lie, J. (2010) *Security and Development*, Critical Interventions in Anthropology Series (Oxford: Berghahn Books).

Naylor, R.T. (1990) *Bankers, Bagmen and Bandits: Business and Politics in the Age of Greed* (Montreal and New York: Black Rose Books).

Pieterse, J.N. (1998) 'My Paradigm or Yours? Alternative Development, Post-Development, and Reflexive Development', *Development and Change*, 29: 343–73.

Polanyi, K. (1944) *The Great Transformation: The political and Economic Origins of Our Time* (Boston: Beacon Press).

Ryggvik, H. (2010) *The Norwegian Oil Experience: A Toolbox for Managing Resources?* (Oslo: University of Oslo, Centre for Technology, Innovation and Culture).

Solli, A. (2011) 'From Good Governance to Development? A Critical Perspective on the Case of Norway's Oil for Development', *Forum for Development Studies*, 38(1): 65–85.

Sætre, S. (2009) *Petromania: En reise gjennom verdens rikeste oljeland for å finne ut hva pengene gjør med oss* (Oslo: J.M. Stenersens Forlag).

Sokal, A. (2010) *Beyond The Hoax: Science, Philosophy and Culture* (Oxford: Oxford University Press).

Wahl, A. (2007) 'The Norwegian Method' (parts 1 and 2), *Solidarity*, 20 and 21.

Contributors

Terry Brotherstone is honorary research fellow in history at the University of Aberdeen, where he lectured from 1968 to 2008. His publications include essays and edited or co-edited books on Scottish history from the 1320 Declaration of Arbroath to the North Sea oil industry, labour history, gender history, oral history and Marxist theory. They include *Covenant, Charter and Party: Traditions of Revolt and Protest in Scottish History* (Aberdeen: AUP, 1989), *The Trotsky Reappraisal* (Edinburgh: EUP, 1992), *History, Economic History and the Future of Marxism* (London: Porcupine Press, 1996), *The City and its Worlds: Aspects of Aberdeen's History Since 1792* (Glasgow: Cruithne Press, 1996), *Gendering Scottish History: An International Approach* (Glasgow: Cruithne Press, 1999), *These Fissured Isles: Ireland, Scotland and British History, 1798–1848* (Edinburgh: John Donald, 2005). He is director of the 'Lives in the Oil Industry' oral history project.

Andrew Cumbers is a reader at the Department of Geographical and Earth Sciences at the University of Glasgow. His research studies the problem of uneven development in capitalist societies, and reflects an interest in the problems facing the United Kingdom's old industrial cities and regions, particularly the consequences of economic restructuring and the changing nature of work and employment. In recent years he has continued to work on economic restructuring issues but has also become increasingly interested in exploring economic and political alternatives to neoliberal globalisation. This has involved joint work with Paul Routledge on global justice networks and his own work on trade union renewal and responses to transnational corporate restructuring. His publications include many internationally published articles, book chapters and anthologies, including the co-editorship of *The Entangled Geographies of Global Justice Network* (Manchester University Press). His new book *Reclaiming Public Ownership: Making Space for Economic Democracy* (Zed Books) will be published in early 2012.

Femi Folorunso is an arts development officer at Creative Scotland where he works on equality policies. He received his Ph.D. at Edinburgh University, where he researched Scottish drama in relation to the nation's political history and identities. He worked as a journalist in Nigeria for twelve years, where he held key editorial positions at the *Nigerian Tribune*, Nigeria's oldest surviving private newspaper. On leaving journalism, he lectured in drama and cultural studies at universities in Nigeria and in the United Kingdom. He holds an honorary research post at the Obafemi Awolowo University, Ile-Ife, Nigeria. His scholarly publications include chapters in *A Black British Canon*, ed. Gail Low and Marion Wayne-Davies (Palgrave 2006) and *Scottish Theatre Since the Seventies*, ed. Randal Stevenson and Gavin Wallace (Edinburgh University Press, 1996). His current research interests are in cultural policy and political economy in the United Kingdom and Nigeria, both as cases of a broader international neoliberal reconstruction of citizenship.

Alice Guimarães is a sociologist and researcher working at the Centre for Postgraduate Study of the Environment and Development (CIDES) at the Universidad Mayor de San Andres in La Paz, Bolivia. She has several years of experience conducting research on the informal economy in Bolivia and she is part of the research group at CIDES working on the social politics of the oil and gas industry.

Bret Gustafson is associate professor of anthropology at Washington University, St Louis, Missouri. He has a Ph.D. from the University of Harvard and is a fluent speaker of Guarani; he has previously carried out research and collaborative work on Guarani language education with the Assembly of the Guarani People of Bolivia. He has helped produce texts for local usage in both Guarani and Spanish and is completing a book on indigenous movements and education reform in Bolivia. Through this work he has also developed further research work on processes of political change in Bolivia, including several articles in international journals and NACLA. In recent years he has also moved into research studying the politics of resources and the anthropology of oil. This work has developed into a project, Flashpoints of Sovereignty: The Ethnography of Gas, Inequality, and Territoriality in Bolivia, and a master's course on Oil and Conflict at Washington University.

Philippa Hall is senior lecturer in sociology at the University of Central Lancashire, Preston, United Kingdom. Her current research interest is in the analysis of discourses of entrepreneurship and employability within higher education policy in Nigeria and the United Kingdom. Her recent book chapter, in *Frontiers of Higher Education* (Rodopi, 2010), examined the history of publicly funded education in Nigeria and considered the impact of the growth of the private university since 2000. She has also written on the history of the press in Nigeria; her article in the *Journal of African Media Studies* (2009) examined the private print and online press as mediators of state and capital in colonial and postcolonial Nigeria.

Heidi Kjærnet is a research fellow at the Energy Programme at the Norwegian Institute of International Affairs (NUPI) and a Ph.D. candidate at the University of Tromsø. Her thesis, with the working title 'Petroleum, Politics and Power: The Cases of Azerbaijan, Kazakhstan and Turkmenistan', analyses the interaction between the three states' national oil companies and their government owners. She recently co-edited with Indra Øverland the book 'Caspian Energy Politics: Azerbaijan, Kazakhstan and Turkmenistan' (Routledge, 2009).

Hilde Kutschera is a researcher at the Norwegian Institute of International Affairs (NUPI). She has previously studied sociology at St Petersburg State University and Bielefeld University.

Owen Logan is a photographer and a research fellow at the University of Aberdeen, where he worked closely with the 'Lives in the Oil Industry' oral history project. He is a contributing editor to *Variant* magazine, which covers 'cross-currents in culture'. His work as a photographer has been widely exhibited and his images are in several public collections, including the Scottish Parliament. Some of his photographic projects are examined in scholarly publications, including *Raw Histories: Photographs, Anthropology and Museums* by Elizabeth Edwards (Berg, 2001), *Scottish Photography: A History* by Tom Normand (Luath, 2008) and *Living in a Globalised World* (Open University, 2006).

John-Andrew McNeish is a senior researcher at Chr. Michelsens Institute (CMI) and associate professor at Noragric Institute of International Environment and Development Studies at the Norwegian University of Life Sciences. His previous publications critically focus on questions of rights, participation, resources and development in the context of Latin America. He is the project leader of the Flammable Societies project and its successor, 'Contested Powers: Towards a Political Anthropology of Energy in Latin America'.

Leila Mokrani is an economist and researcher working at the Centre for Postgraduate Study of the Environment and Development (CIDES) at the Universidad Mayor de San Andres in La Paz, Bolivia. She has several years of experience working with the oil industry and now forms part of the research group at CIDES working on the social politics of the oil and gas industries.

Indra Øverland is head of the Energy Programme at the Norwegian Institute of International Affairs (NUPI) and associate professor at the University of Tromsø. He did his Ph.D. at the Scott Polar Research Institute of the University of Cambridge. His current areas of research include post-Soviet energy politics, reduction of energy subsidies, pipeline conflicts and the politics of LNG. Recent publications include *Caspian Energy Politics: Azerbaijan, Kazakhstan and Turkmenistan* (co-edited, Routledge, 2010) and *Russian Renewable Energy* (co-authored, Ashgate, 2009).

John Paterson is professor of law and co-director of the Centre for Energy Law at the University of Aberdeen. He is co-editor of *Oil and Gas Law: Current Practice and Emerging Trends*, now in its second edition, and of *Oil and Gas Law in Kazakhstan: National and International Perspectives*. He has written extensively on the regulation of safety in the oil and gas industries and has acted as consultant to the OECD Nuclear Energy Agency.

Iselin Åsedotter Strønen is a researcher at Chr. Michelsens Institute and a Ph.D. candidate at the Department of Anthropology, University of Bergen in Norway. Her research is funded by the Norwegian Research Council under the auspices of the Flammable Societies project. Strønen's field research is being carried out in a poor neighbourhood of Caracas and studies the creation and function of social programmes set up by the Chávez government and funded by the national oil company. Strønen has master's degrees in journalism and anthropology and has previously made a visual documentary characterising the process of political and social change under the Chávez administration.

Fernanda Wanderley is a sociologist and senior lecturer at the Centre for Postgraduate Study of the Environment and Development (CIDES) at the Universidad Mayor de San Andres in La Paz, Bolivia. She has had a long career as a development practitioner for the UNDP and as an academic working on different questions of political economy and gender. She is now the leader of a research group based at CIDES working on the social politics of oil and gas management in Bolivia. She has published widely in both national and international journals. Her recent work includes a chapter in Crabtree and Whitehead (eds) *Unresolved Tensions: Bolivia Past and Present* (University of Pittsburgh Press).

Anna Zalik is an associate professor at the Faculty of Environmental Studies at York University in Canada. Her research employs political economy and comparative colonial/postcolonial analysis to examine how corporate aid shapes socio-environmental regulation in extractive sites. She has conducted extensive field research concerning oil industry–social practice in Mexico and Nigeria, with newer work in Canada. Prior to joining York, she was a Ciriacy Wantrup postdoctoral fellow in natural resources and political economy at the University of California at Berkeley. Her recent publications include 'Protest as Violence in Oilfields' in Feldman, Geisler and Menon, *Accumulating Insecurity* (University of Georgia Press, 2011); 'Oil Futures: Shell's Scenarios and the Social Constitution of the Global Oil Market', in *Geoforum* (2010) and 'Zones of Exclusion: Offshore Extraction, the Contestation of Space and Physical Displacement in the Nigerian Delta and the Mexican Gulf', in *Antipode* (2009).

Index

Compiled by Sue Carlton

Page numbers in **bold** refer to photograph captions